.remote.

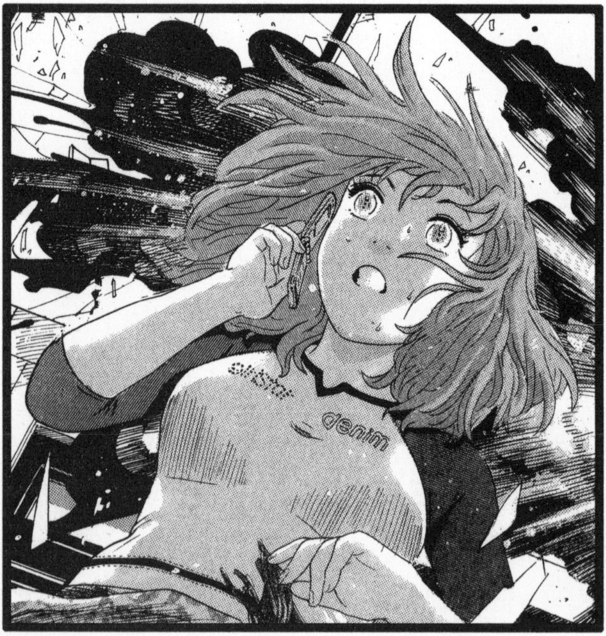
denim

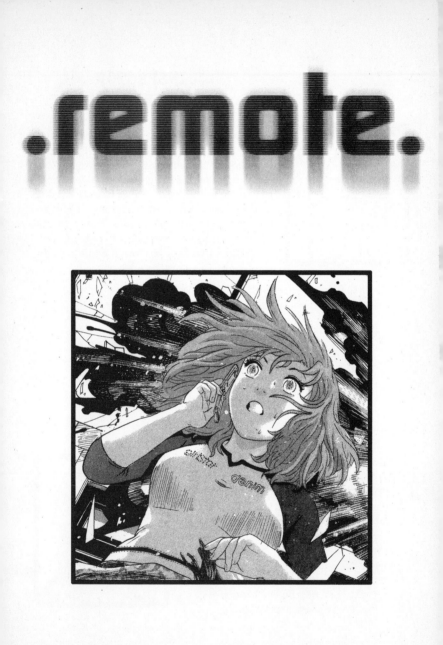

INSPECTOR
KOZABURO HIMURO

Kozaburo Himuro is the reclusive head of Special Unit A (aka the Crypt). From within his secluded headquarters, Himuro uses his genius intellect and understanding of the criminal mind to help solve the most heinous and bizarre cases. Due to mysterious events in his past, he is incapable of leaving the Crypt to face the world and his own personal demons.

DETECTIVE
KURUMI AYAKI

As Inspector Himuro's eyes and ears outside the Crypt, Kurumi Ayaki helps investigate the gruesome crimes assigned to Special Unit A. Although completely out of her element, Ayaki's heart and determination help compensate for her lack of practical experience. It is Ayaki's emotional tenacity combined with Himuro's cold logic that may be the team's greatest asset.

Previously in
REMOTE...

When financial problems force former meter-maid Kurumi Ayaki to take a new assignment, she finds herself partnered with Inspector Himuro, the enigmatic head of the Unsolved Crime Division's special unit. Operating from deep within his office, known only as "The Crypt," Himuro's amazing intellect solves the most diabolical of crimes "remotely," while his partner does the legwork on the street. Unfortunately, Himuro never keeps a partner for long—for reasons the inexperienced Ayaki soon learns.

Her first case: the Serial Killer Circus Murders. Seemingly random victims are piling up all around Tokyo. Their only connection—a killer clown, chanting a children's nursery rhyme. Now it's up to Himuro and Ayaki to stop his insane laughter, but it may all be too much for our young heroine, who's beginning to wonder if any paycheck could be worth this kind of danger...

Remote Vol. 2

written by Seimaru Amagi
illustrated by Tetsuya Koshiba

Translation - Haruko Furukawa
English Adaptation - Steve Buccellato
Associate Editor - Troy Lewter
Retouch and Lettering - Kristina Kovacs
Production Artist - Haruko Furukawa and Yoohae Yang
Graphic Designer - James Dashiell
Cover Artist - Raymond Makowski

Editor - Bryce P. Coleman
Digital Imaging Manager - Chris Buford
Pre-Press Manager - Antonio DePietro
Production Managers - Jennifer Miller and Mutsumi Miyazaki
Art Director - Matt Alford
Managing Editor - Jill Freshney
VP of Production - Ron Klamert
President and C.O.O. - John Parker
Publisher and C.E.O. - Stuart Levy

A  Manga

TOKYOPOP Inc.
5900 Wilshire Blvd. Suite 2000
Los Angeles, CA 90036

E-mail: info@TOKYOPOP.com
Come visit us online at www.TOKYOPOP.com

ISBN: 1-59182-741-8

First TOKYOPOP printing: August 2004
10 9 8 7 6 5 4 3 2 1
Printed in the USA

VOLUME 2
WRITER — SEIMARU AMAGI
ARTIST — TETSUYA KOSHIBA

HAMBURG // LONDON // LOS ANGELES // TOKYO

.remote.

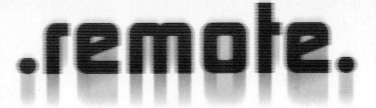

VOL. 2

CONTENTS:

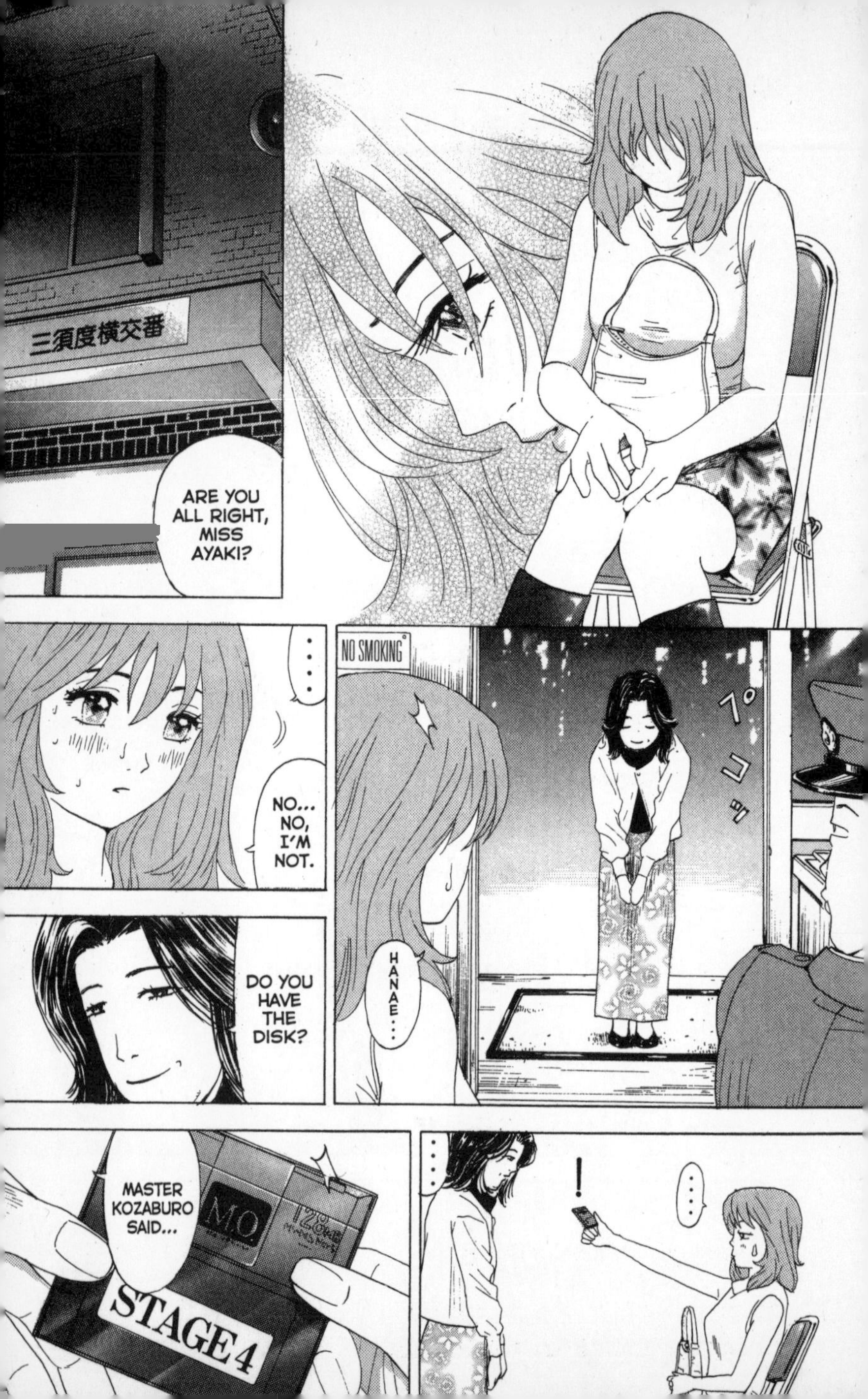
三須度横交番
ARE YOU ALL RIGHT, MISS AYAKI?
ペコッ
NO SMOKING
HANAE...
....
NO... NO, I'M NOT.
DO YOU HAVE THE DISK?
....
!
....
MASTER KOZABURO SAID...
M.O.
STAGE 4

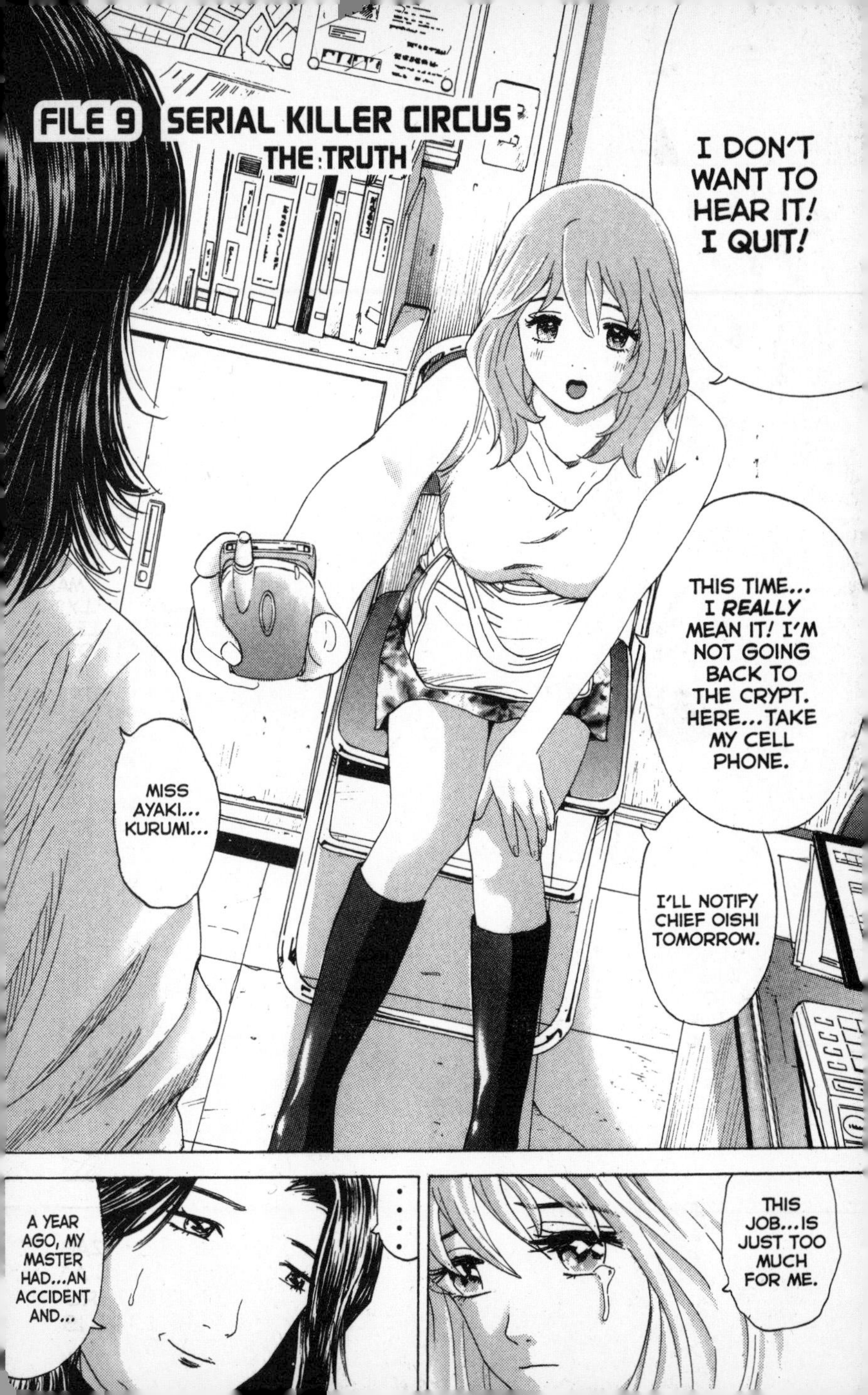
FILE 9 SERIAL KILLER CIRCUS
THE TRUTH
I DON'T WANT TO HEAR IT! I QUIT!
THIS TIME... I *REALLY* MEAN IT! I'M NOT GOING BACK TO THE CRYPT. HERE...TAKE MY CELL PHONE.
I'LL NOTIFY CHIEF OISHI TOMORROW.
MISS AYAKI... KURUMI...
THIS JOB...IS JUST TOO MUCH FOR ME.
A YEAR AGO, MY MASTER HAD...AN ACCIDENT AND...

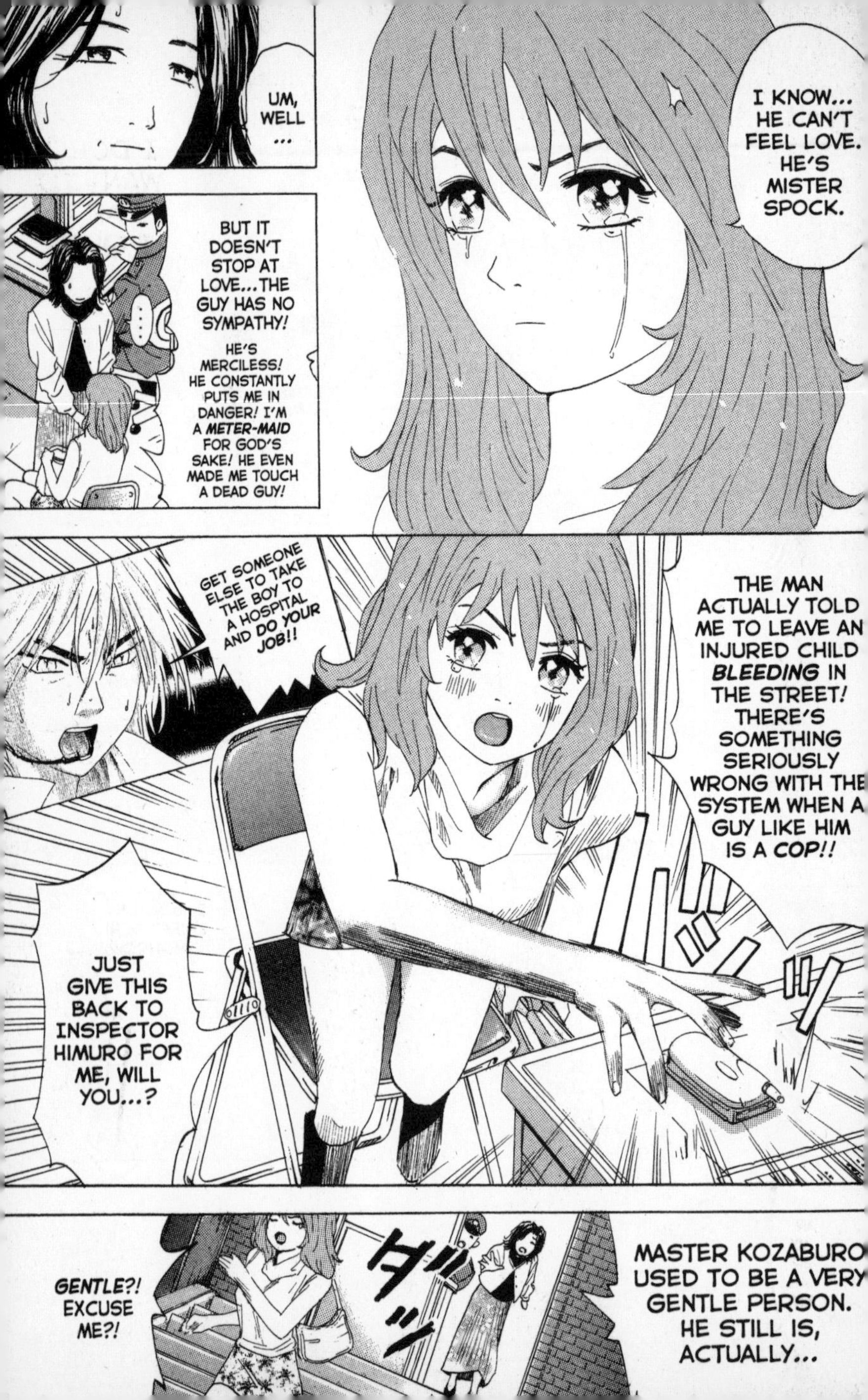
I KNOW... HE CAN'T FEEL LOVE. HE'S MISTER SPOCK.
UM, WELL ...
BUT IT DOESN'T STOP AT LOVE... THE GUY HAS NO SYMPATHY!
HE'S MERCILESS! HE CONSTANTLY PUTS ME IN DANGER! I'M A *METER-MAID* FOR GOD'S SAKE! HE EVEN MADE ME TOUCH A DEAD GUY!
THE MAN ACTUALLY TOLD ME TO LEAVE AN INJURED CHILD *BLEEDING* IN THE STREET! THERE'S SOMETHING SERIOUSLY WRONG WITH THE SYSTEM WHEN A GUY LIKE HIM IS A *COP!!*
GET SOMEONE ELSE TO TAKE THE BOY TO A HOSPITAL AND *DO YOUR JOB!!*
JUST GIVE THIS BACK TO INSPECTOR HIMURO FOR ME, WILL YOU...?
MASTER KOZABURO USED TO BE A VERY GENTLE PERSON. HE STILL IS, ACTUALLY...
GENTLE?! EXCUSE ME?!

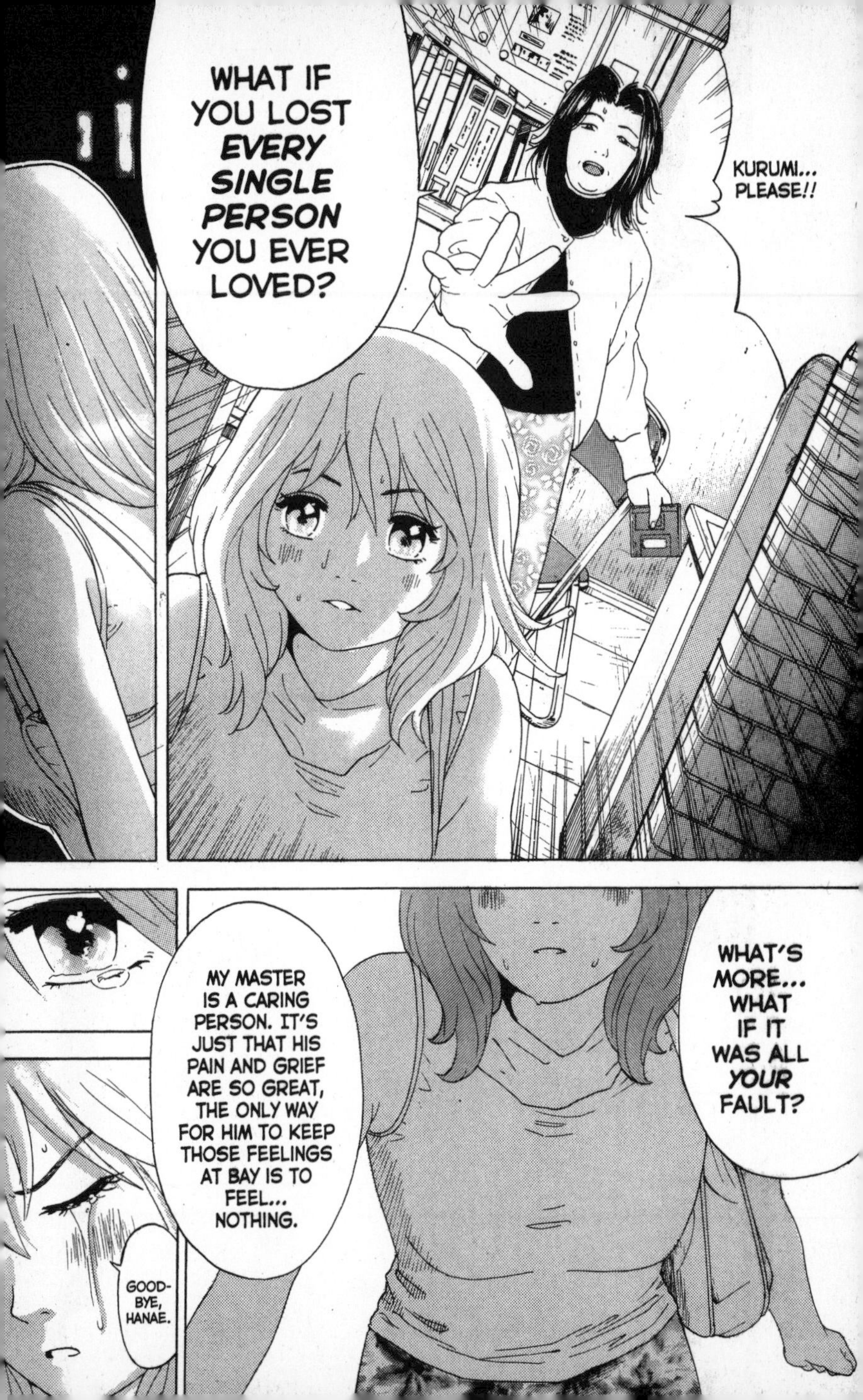
WHAT IF YOU LOST *EVERY SINGLE PERSON* YOU EVER LOVED?
KURUMI... PLEASE!!
WHAT'S MORE... WHAT IF IT WAS ALL *YOUR* FAULT?
MY MASTER IS A CARING PERSON. IT'S JUST THAT HIS PAIN AND GRIEF ARE SO GREAT, THE ONLY WAY FOR HIM TO KEEP THOSE FEELINGS AT BAY IS TO FEEL... NOTHING.
GOOD-BYE, HANAE.

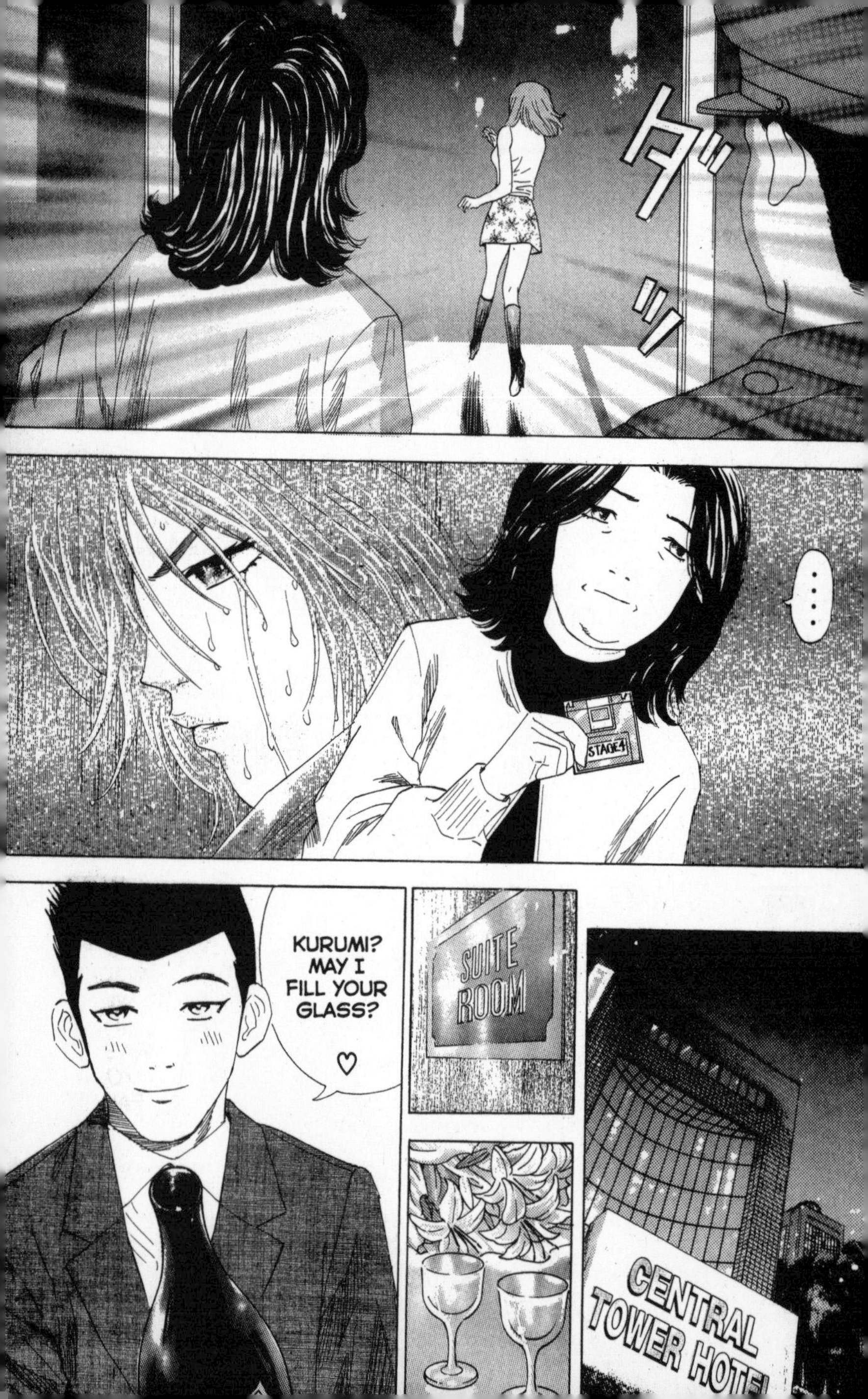
ダッ
……
STAGE4
CENTRAL TOWER HOTE
SUITE ROOM
KURUMI? MAY I FILL YOUR GLASS? ♡

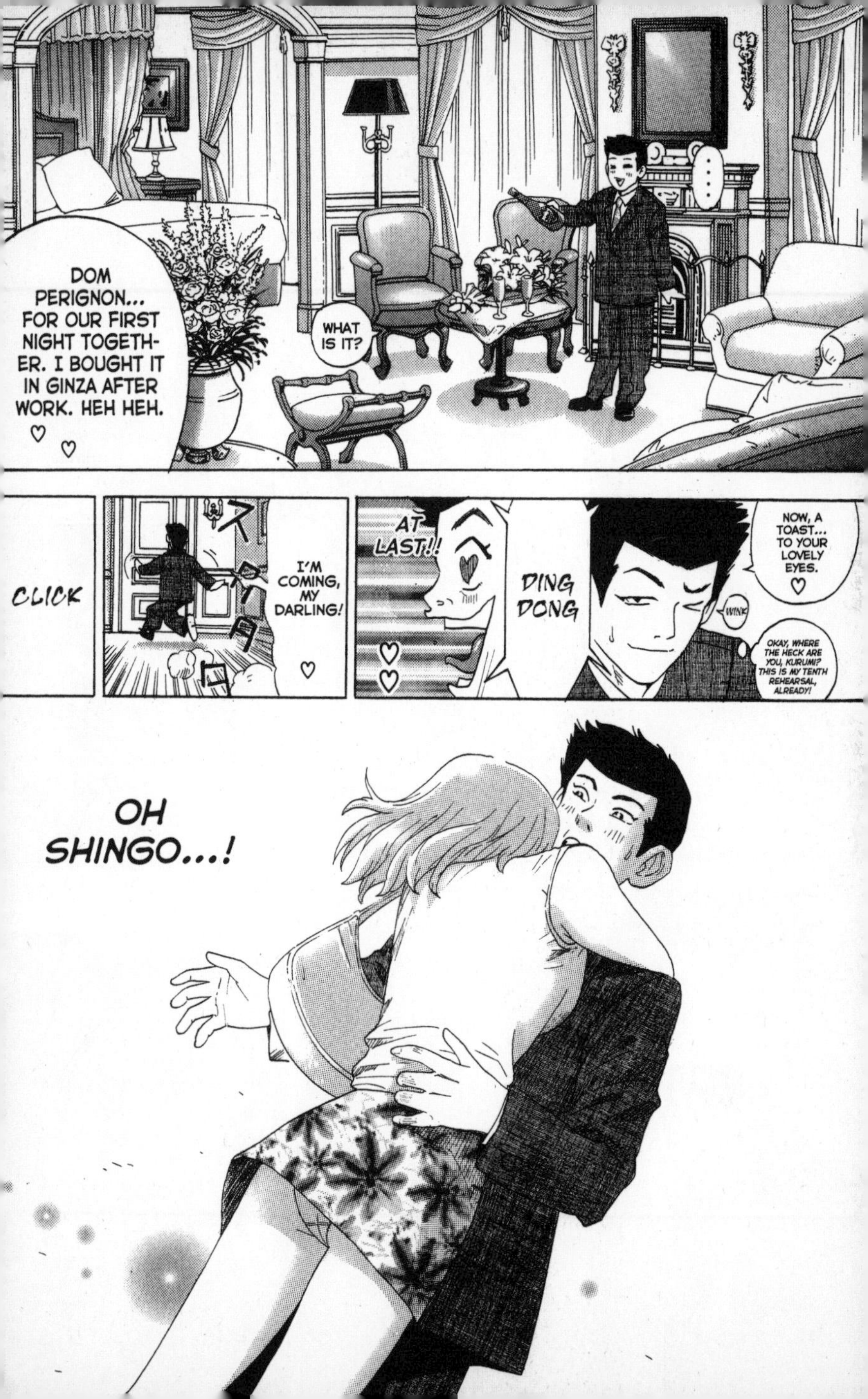
....
WHAT IS IT?
DOM PERIGNON... FOR OUR FIRST NIGHT TOGETH-ER. I BOUGHT IT IN GINZA AFTER WORK. HEH HEH. ♡ ♡
NOW, A TOAST... TO YOUR LOVELY EYES. ♡
WINK
OKAY, WHERE THE HECK ARE YOU, KURUMI? THIS IS MY TENTH REHEARSAL, ALREADY!
DING DONG
AT LAST!!
I'M COMING, MY DARLING! ♡
CLICK
OH SHINGO...!

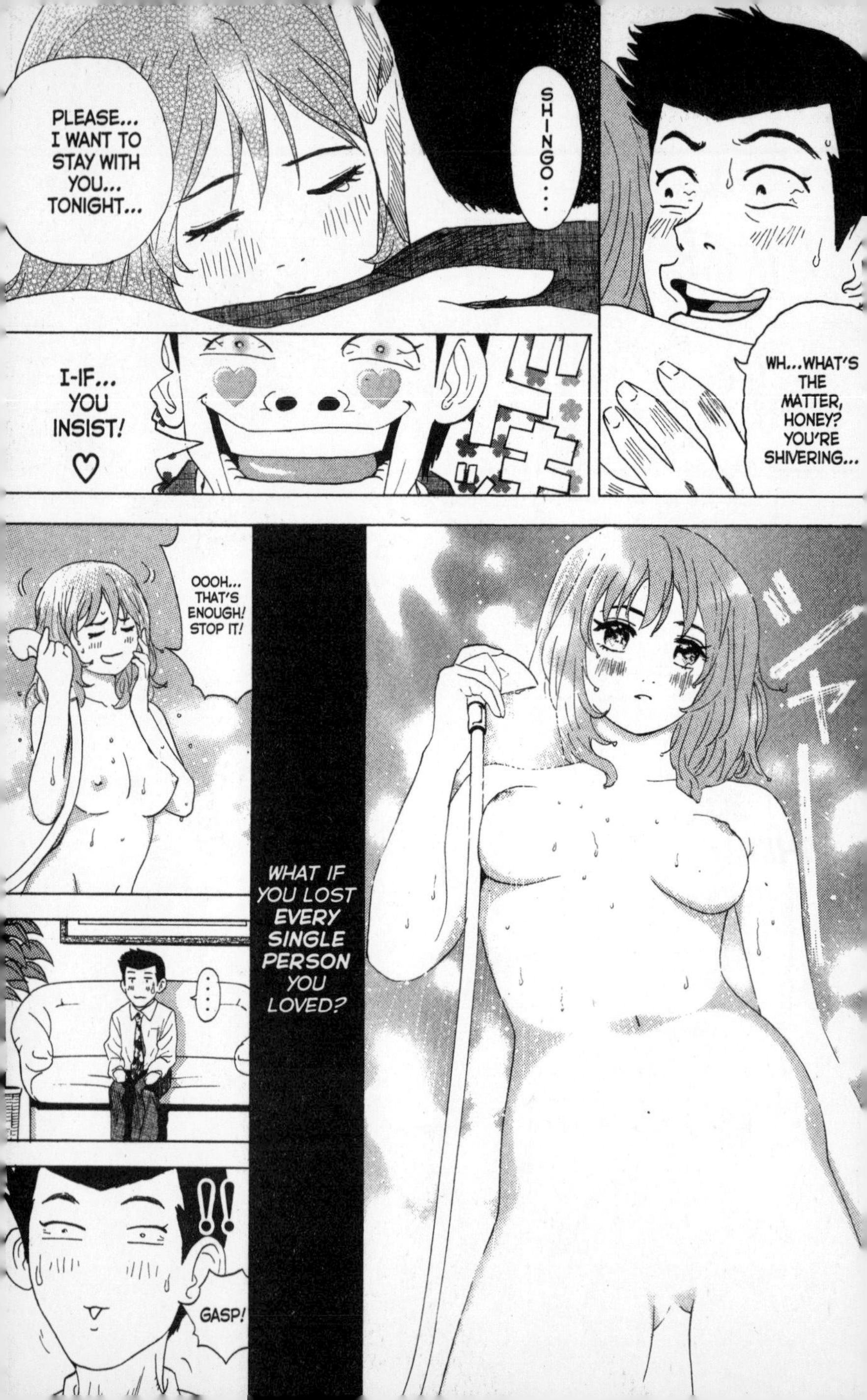
WH...WHAT'S THE MATTER, HONEY? YOU'RE SHIVERING...
SHINGO...
PLEASE... I WANT TO STAY WITH YOU... TONIGHT...
I-IF... YOU INSIST! ♡
WHAT IF YOU LOST EVERY SINGLE PERSON YOU LOVED?
OOOH... THAT'S ENOUGH! STOP IT!
...
!!
GASP!

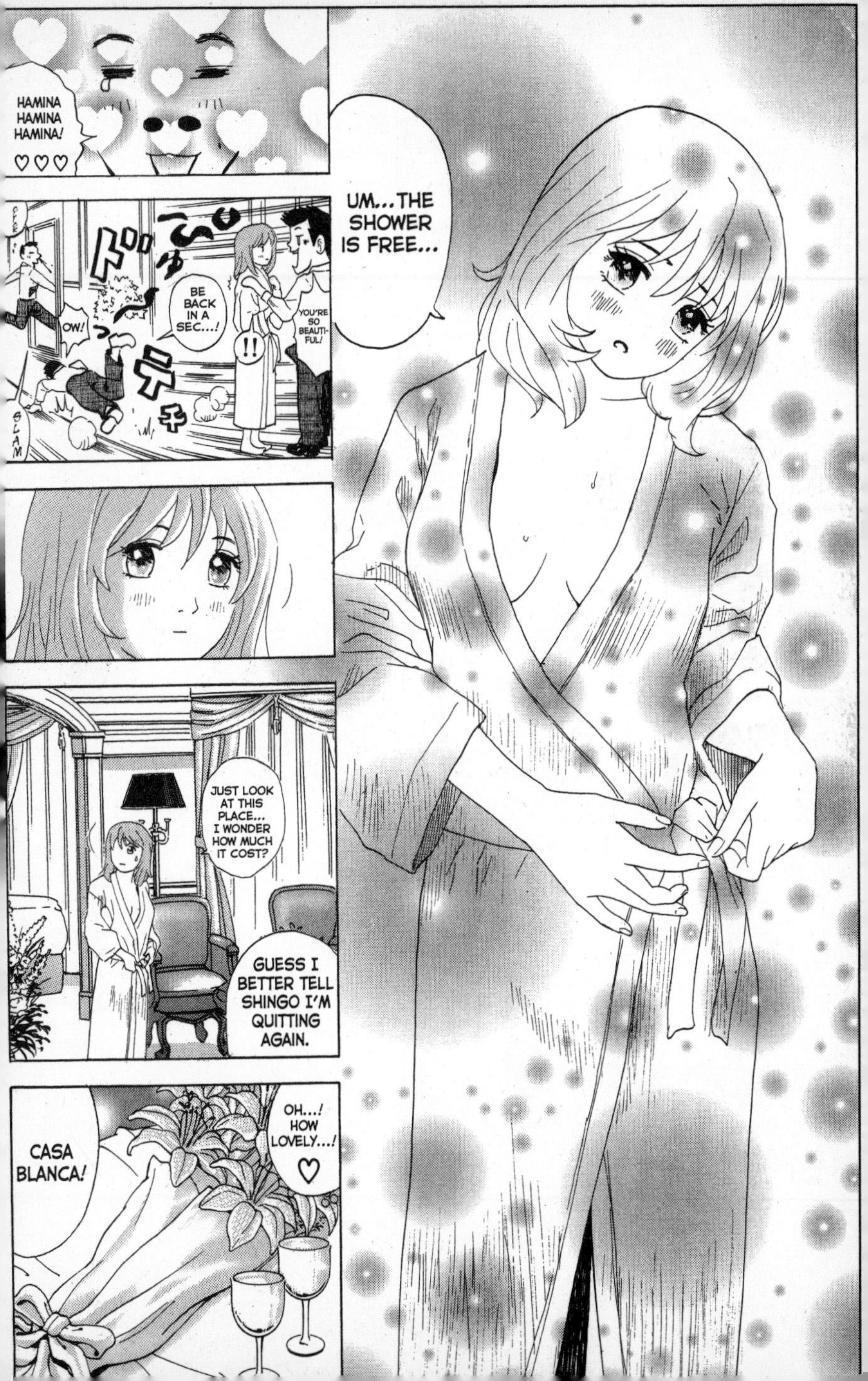
UM...THE SHOWER IS FREE...
HAMINA HAMINA HAMINA! ♡♡♡
YOU'RE SO BEAUTIFUL!
!!
BE BACK IN A SEC...!
OW!
SLAM
JUST LOOK AT THIS PLACE... I WONDER HOW MUCH IT COST?
GUESS I BETTER TELL SHINGO I'M QUITTING AGAIN.
OH...! HOW LOVELY...! ♡
CASA BLANCA!

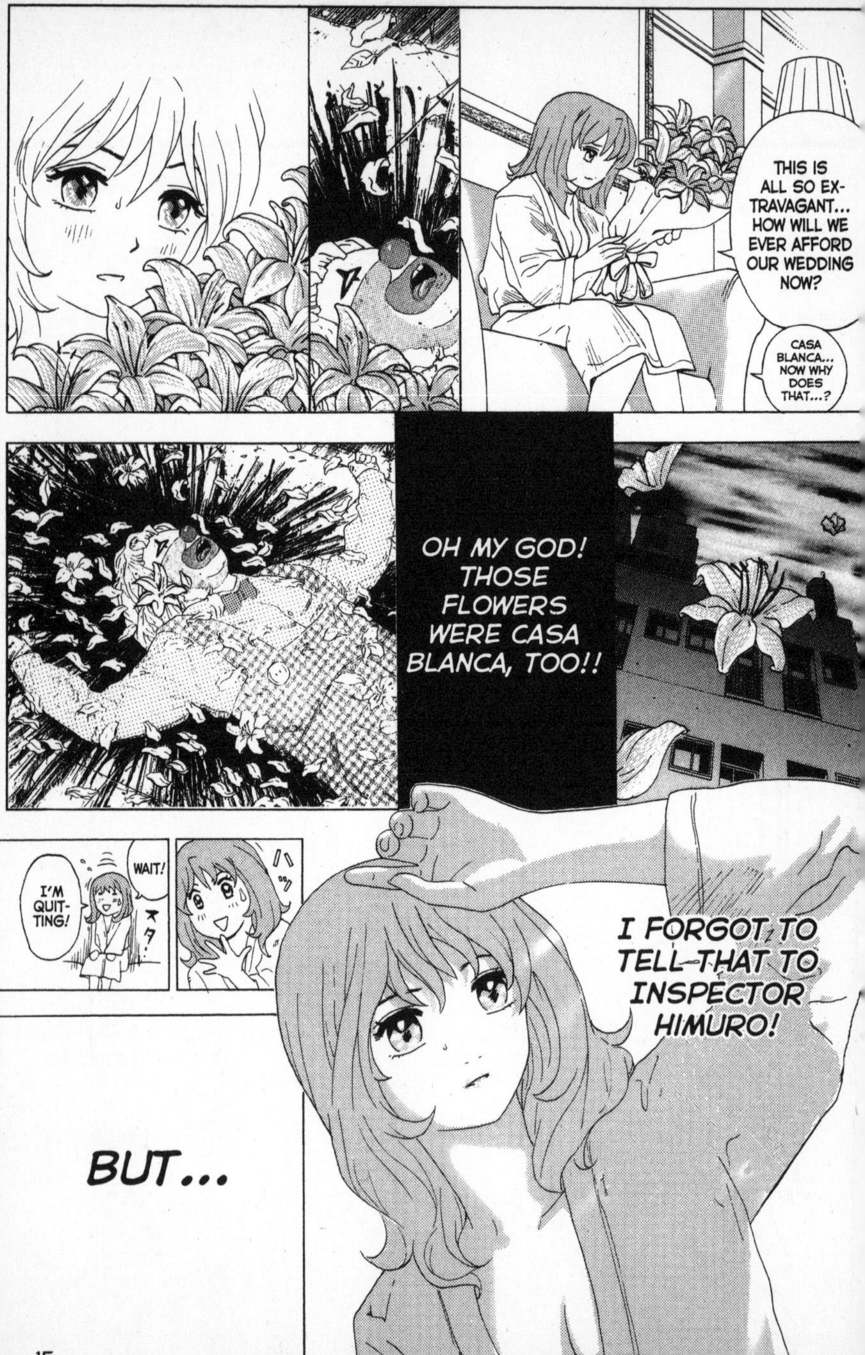
THIS IS ALL SO EX-TRAVAGANT... HOW WILL WE EVER AFFORD OUR WEDDING NOW?
CASA BLANCA... NOW WHY DOES THAT...?
OH MY GOD! THOSE FLOWERS WERE CASA BLANCA, TOO!!
I FORGOT TO TELL THAT TO INSPECTOR HIMURO!
WAIT!
I'M QUIT-TING!
BUT...

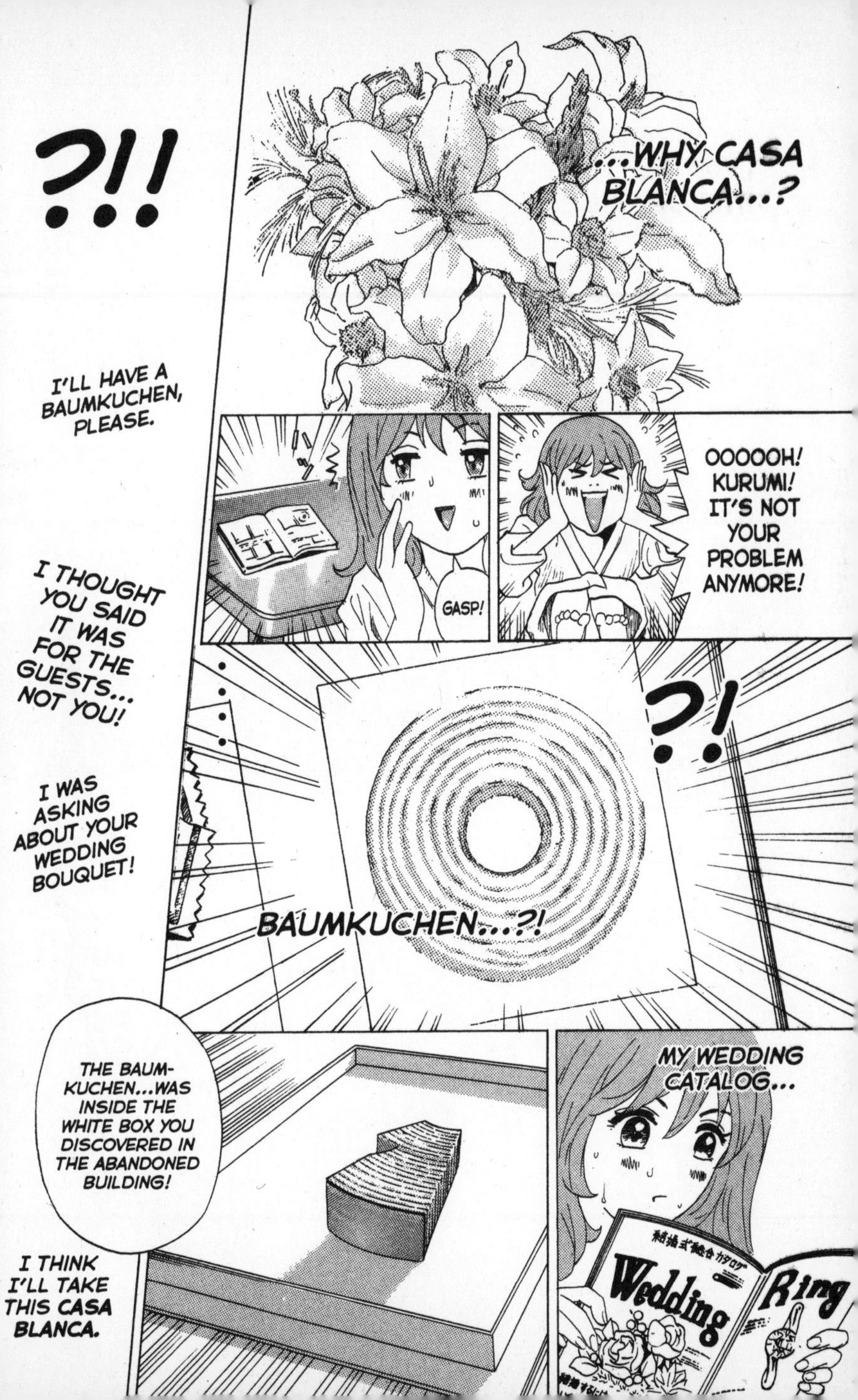
...WHY CASA BLANCA...?
OOOOOH! KURUMI! IT'S NOT YOUR PROBLEM ANYMORE!
GASP!
?!
BAUMKUCHEN...?!
MY WEDDING CATALOG...
結婚式総合カタログ
Wedding Ring
THE BAUM-KUCHEN...WAS INSIDE THE WHITE BOX YOU DISCOVERED IN THE ABANDONED BUILDING!
?!!
I'LL HAVE A BAUMKUCHEN, PLEASE.
I THOUGHT YOU SAID IT WAS FOR THE GUESTS... NOT YOU!
I WAS ASKING ABOUT YOUR WEDDING BOUQUET!
I THINK I'LL TAKE THIS CASA BLANCA.

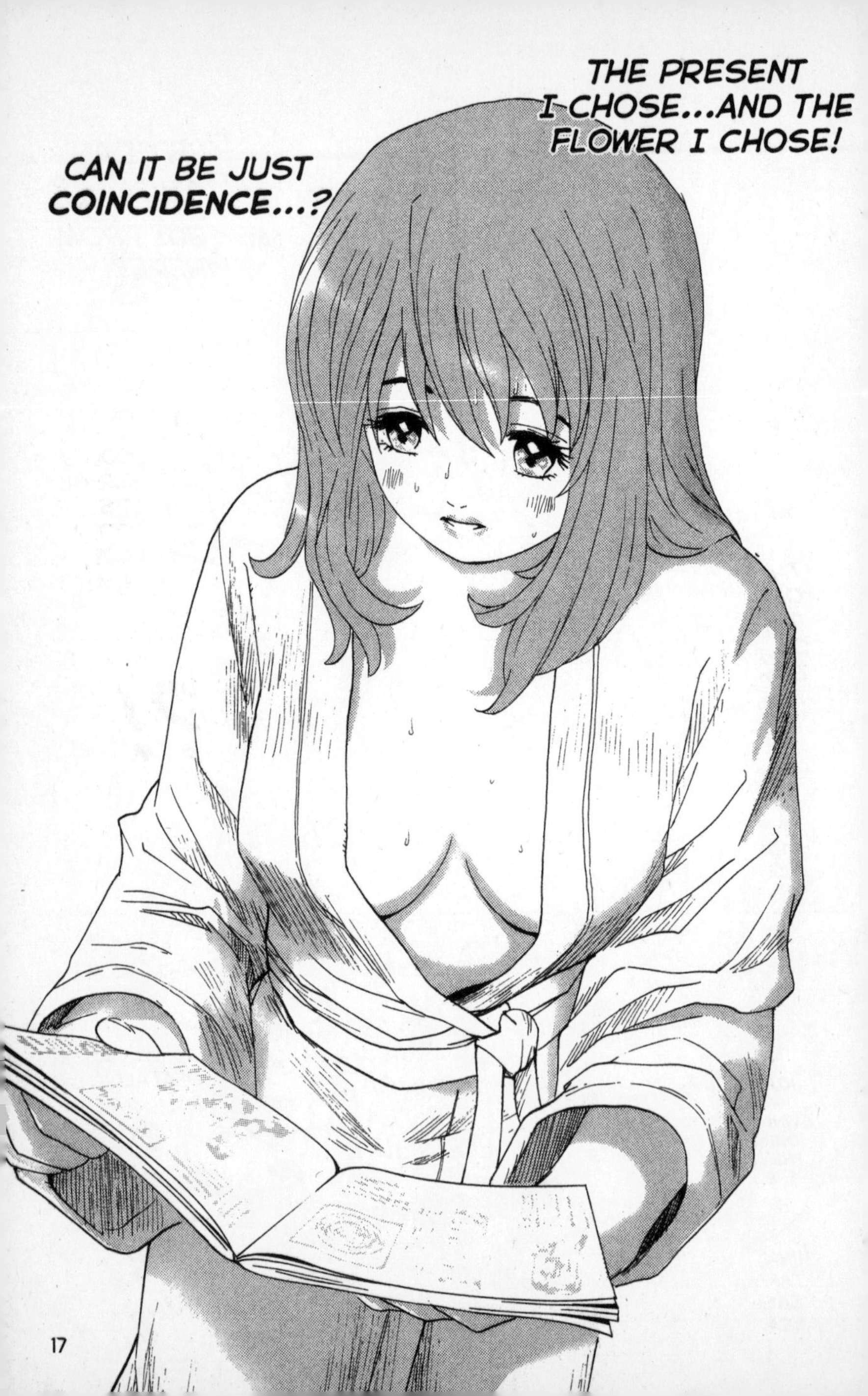
THE PRESENT I CHOSE...AND THE FLOWER I CHOSE!
CAN IT BE JUST COINCIDENCE...?

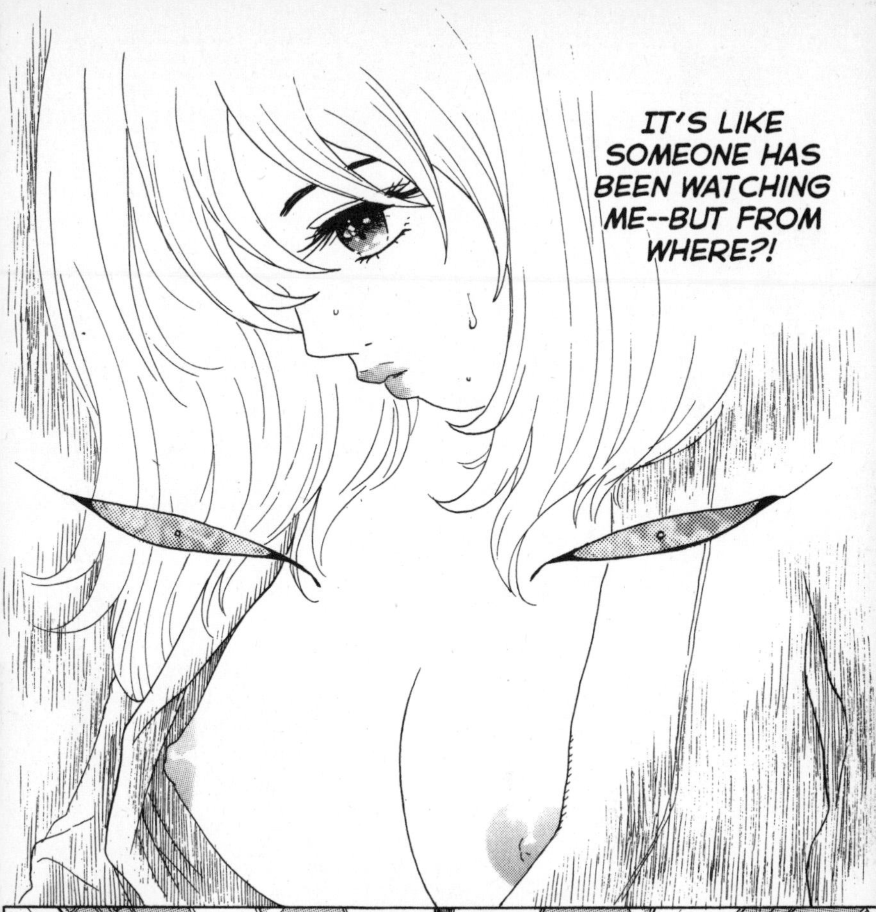
IT'S LIKE SOMEONE HAS BEEN WATCHING ME--BUT FROM WHERE?!
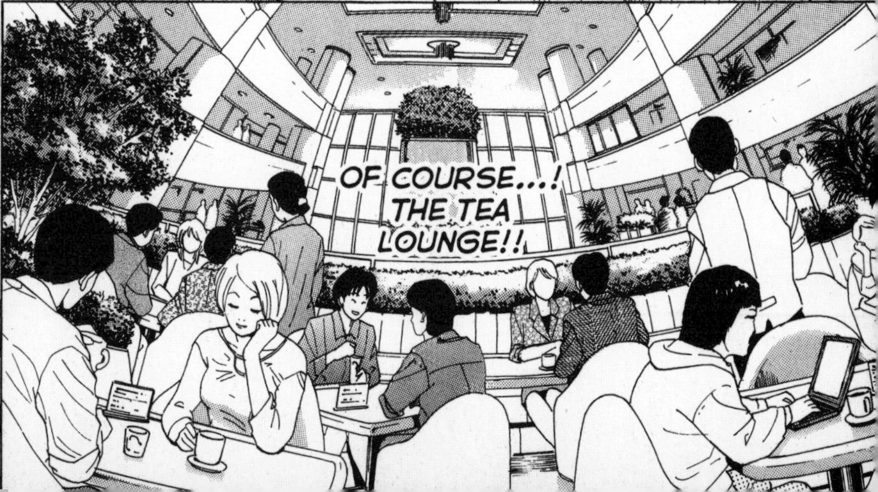
OF COURSE...! THE TEA LOUNGE!!

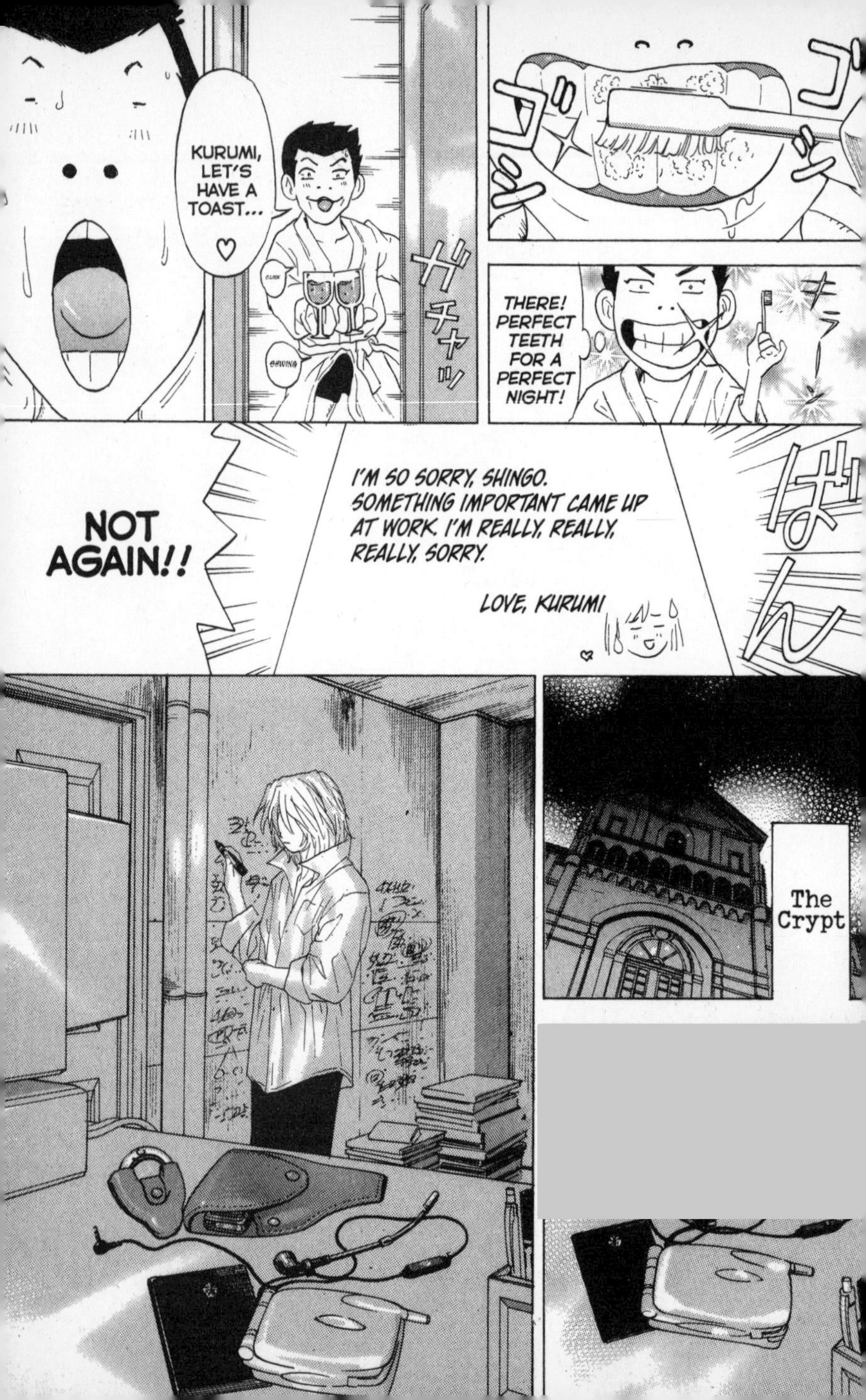
THERE! PERFECT TEETH FOR A PERFECT NIGHT!
キラーン
KURUMI, LET'S HAVE A TOAST... ♡
CLINK
SHWING
ガチャッ
ばん
I'M SO SORRY, SHINGO. SOMETHING IMPORTANT CAME UP AT WORK. I'M REALLY, REALLY, REALLY, SORRY.
LOVE, KURUMI
NOT AGAIN!!
The Crypt

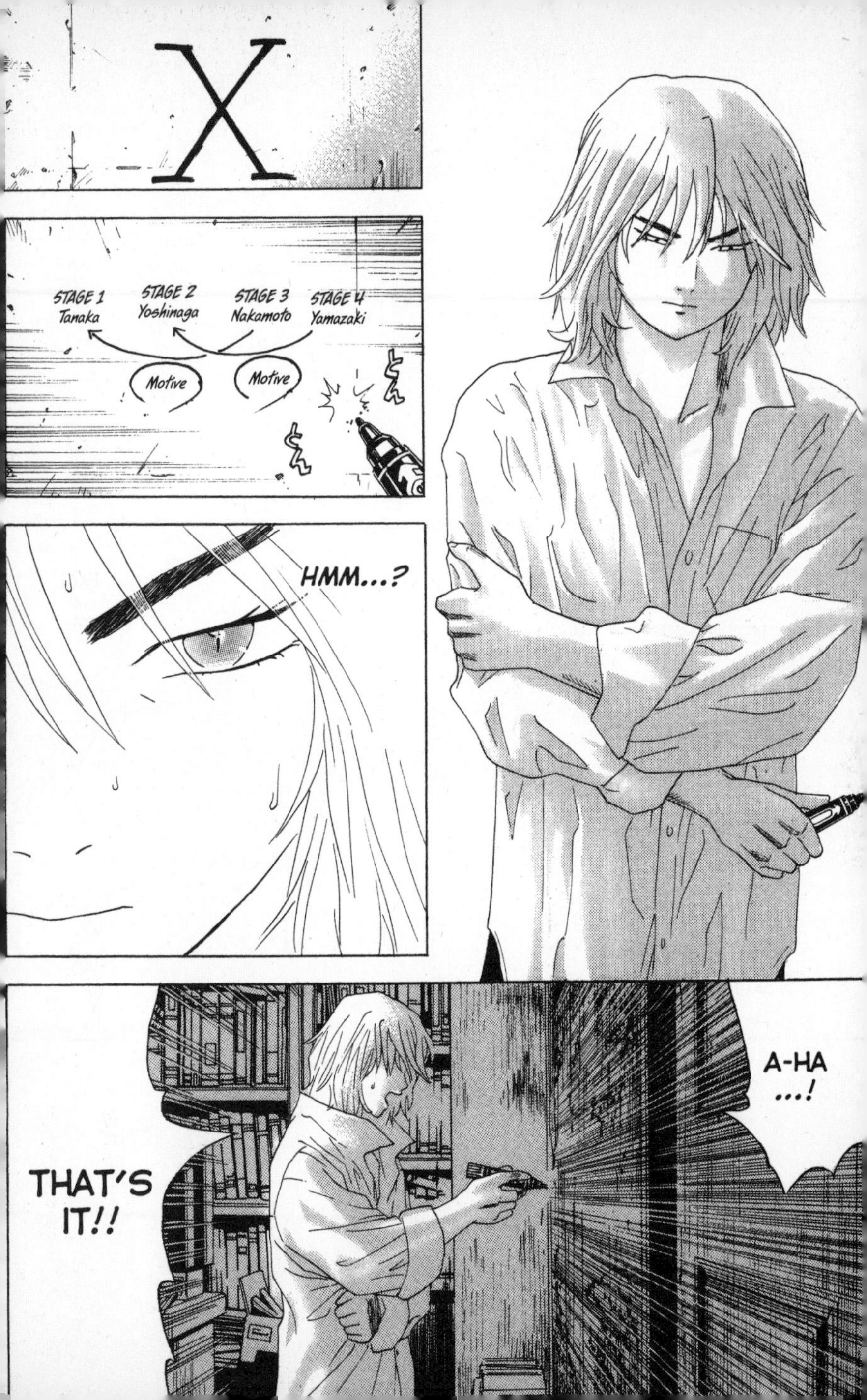
X
STAGE 1
Tanaka
STAGE 2
Yoshinaga
STAGE 3
Nakamoto
STAGE 4
Yamazaki
Motive
Motive
HMM...?
A-HA ...!
THAT'S IT!!

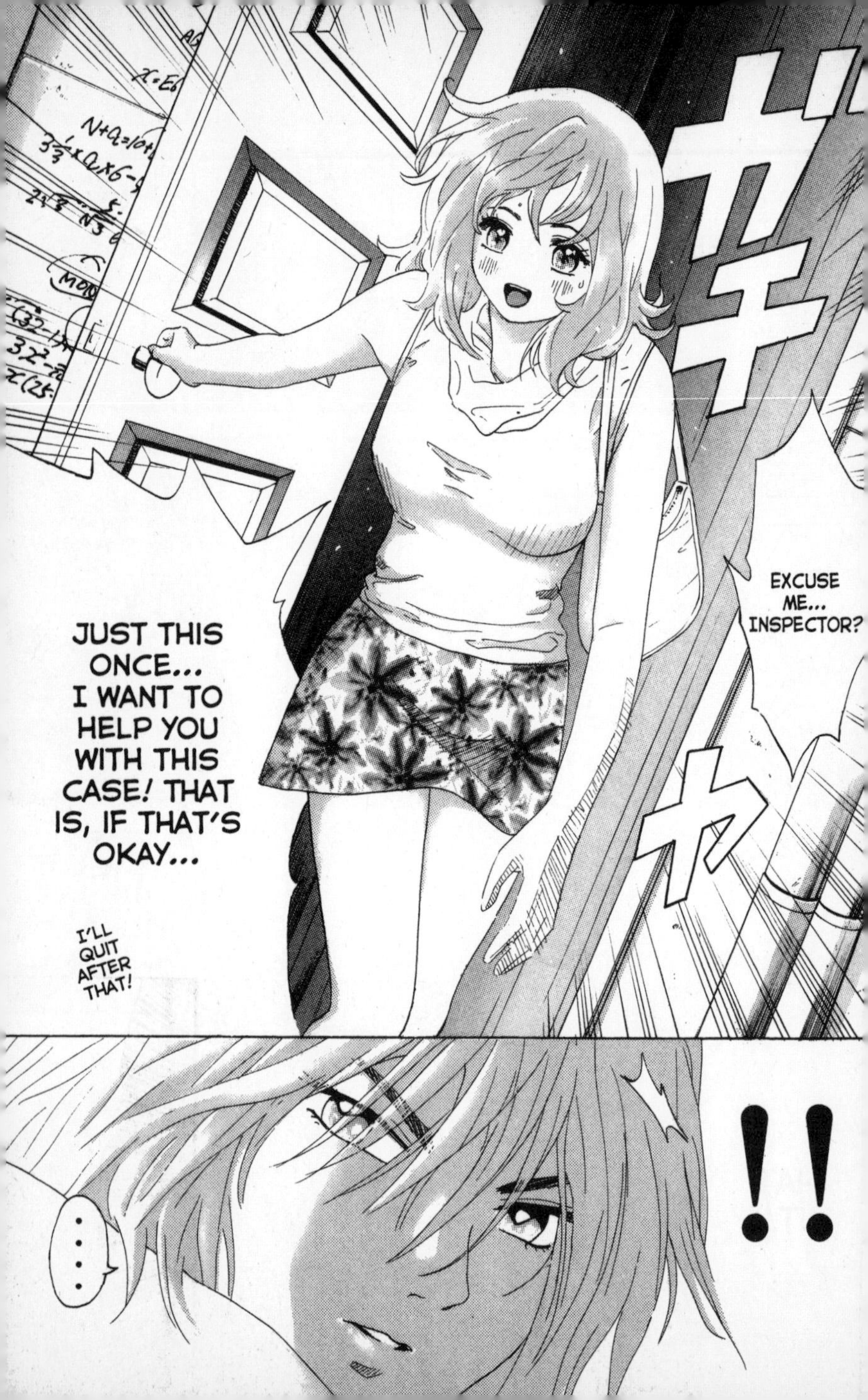
EXCUSE ME... INSPECTOR?
JUST THIS ONCE... I WANT TO HELP YOU WITH THIS CASE! THAT IS, IF THAT'S OKAY...
I'LL QUIT AFTER THAT!
!!
...

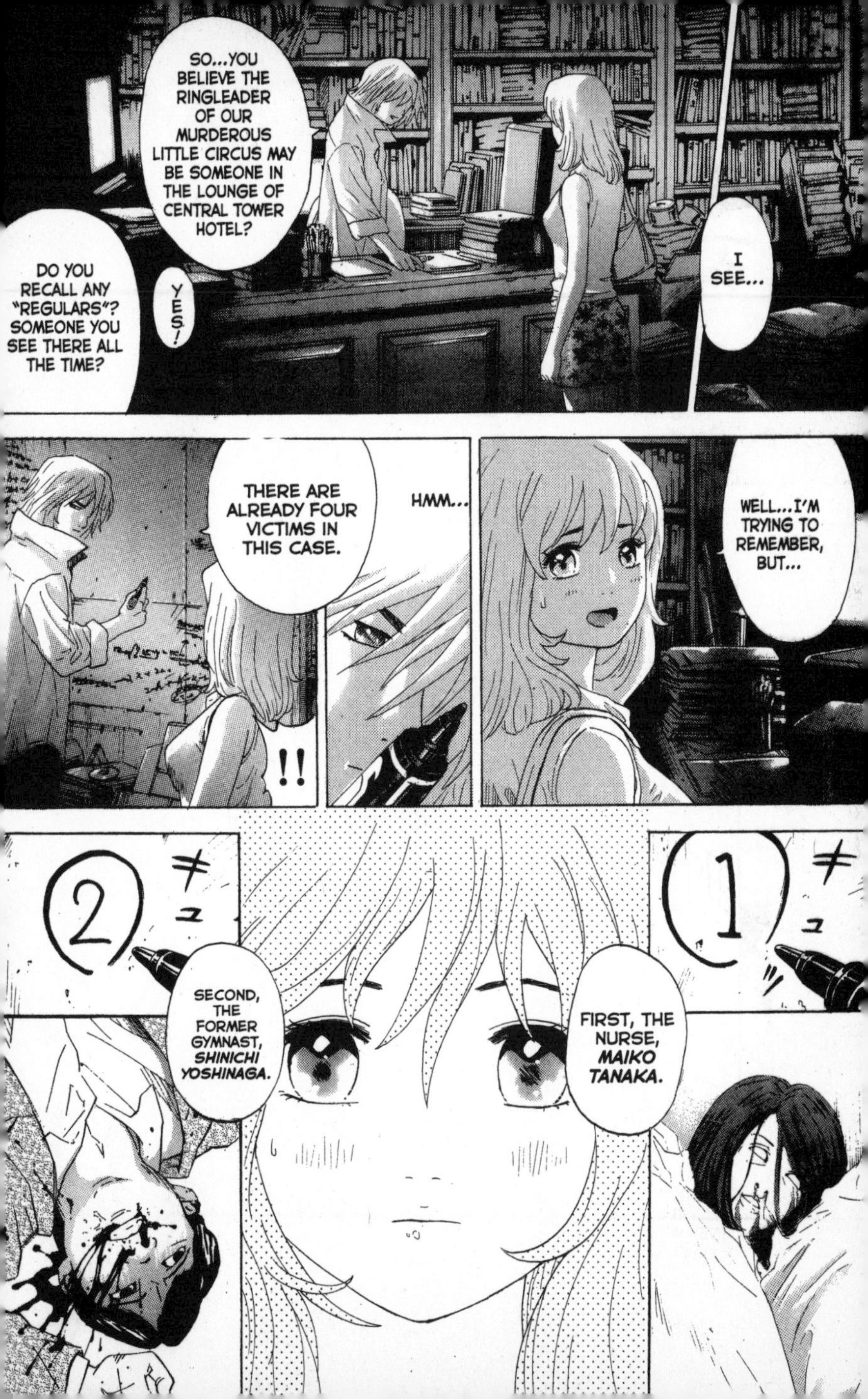
SO...YOU BELIEVE THE RINGLEADER OF OUR MURDEROUS LITTLE CIRCUS MAY BE SOMEONE IN THE LOUNGE OF CENTRAL TOWER HOTEL?
YES!
I SEE...
DO YOU RECALL ANY "REGULARS"? SOMEONE YOU SEE THERE ALL THE TIME?
WELL...I'M TRYING TO REMEMBER, BUT...
HMM...
THERE ARE ALREADY FOUR VICTIMS IN THIS CASE.
!!
1
キュ
FIRST, THE NURSE, *MAIKO TANAKA.*
2
キュ
SECOND, THE FORMER GYMNAST, *SHINICHI YOSHINAGA.*

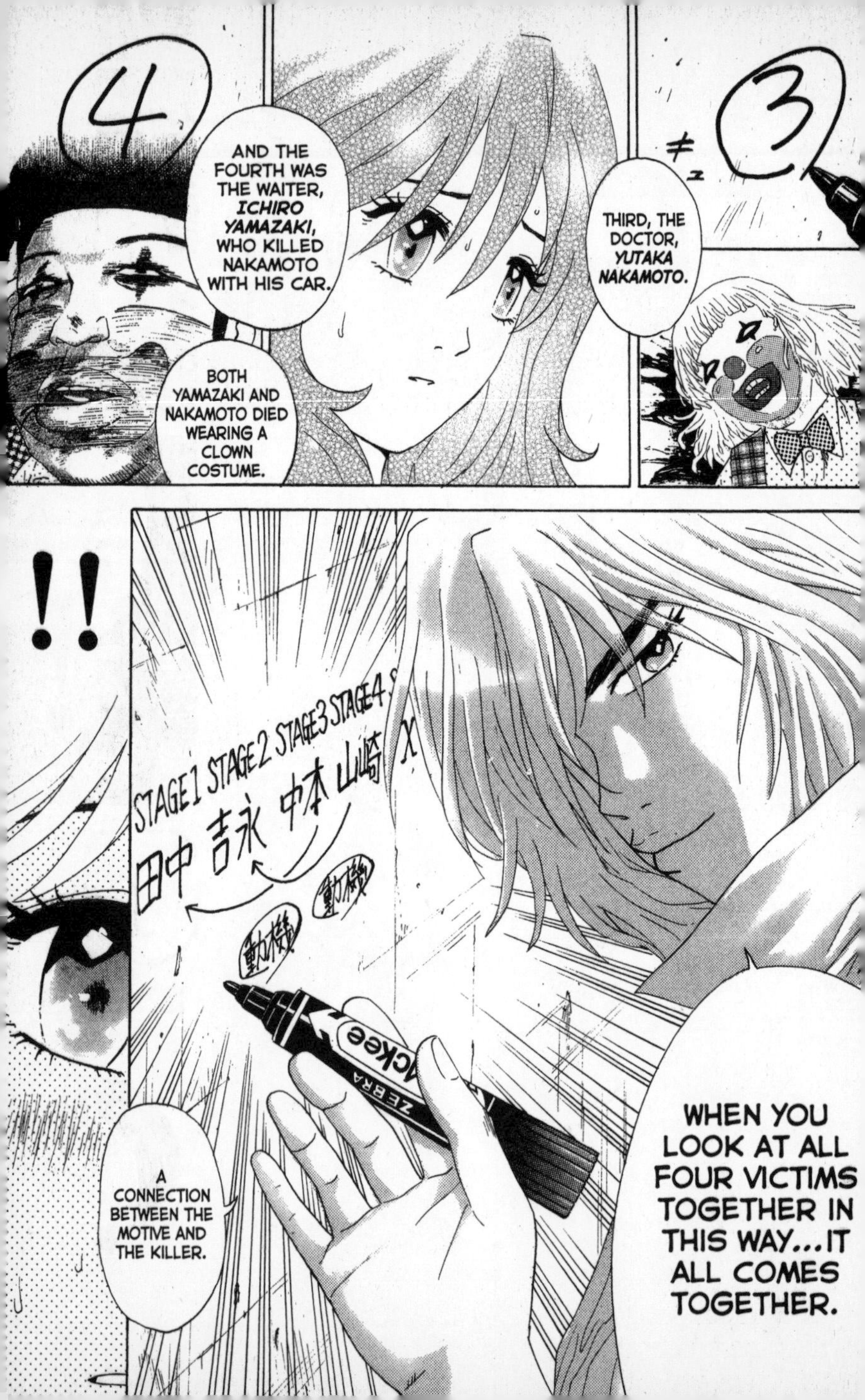
3
キュ
THIRD, THE DOCTOR, YUTAKA NAKAMOTO.
4
AND THE FOURTH WAS THE WAITER, ICHIRO YAMAZAKI, WHO KILLED NAKAMOTO WITH HIS CAR.
BOTH YAMAZAKI AND NAKAMOTO DIED WEARING A CLOWN COSTUME.
STAGE1 STAGE2 STAGE3 STAGE4
田中 吉永 中本 山崎 X
動機
動機
WHEN YOU LOOK AT ALL FOUR VICTIMS TOGETHER IN THIS WAY...IT ALL COMES TOGETHER.
A CONNECTION BETWEEN THE MOTIVE AND THE KILLER.
!!

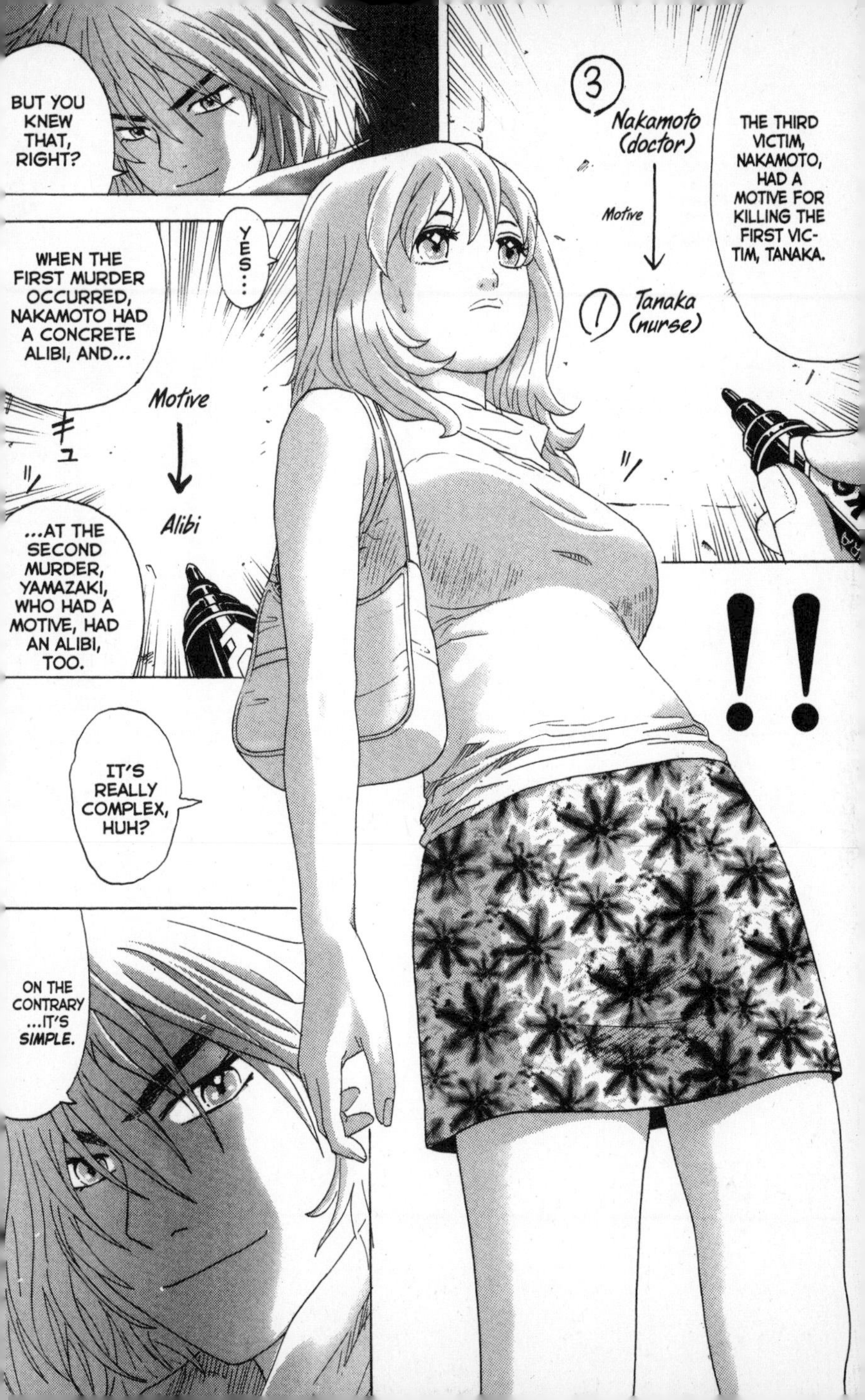

THE THIRD VICTIM, NAKAMOTO, HAD A MOTIVE FOR KILLING THE FIRST VICTIM, TANAKA.
③ Nakamoto (doctor)
Motive
① Tanaka (nurse)
BUT YOU KNEW THAT, RIGHT?
!!
YES...
WHEN THE FIRST MURDER OCCURRED, NAKAMOTO HAD A CONCRETE ALIBI, AND...
キュ
Motive
Alibi
...AT THE SECOND MURDER, YAMAZAKI, WHO HAD A MOTIVE, HAD AN ALIBI, TOO.
IT'S REALLY COMPLEX, HUH?
ON THE CONTRARY ...IT'S *SIMPLE.*

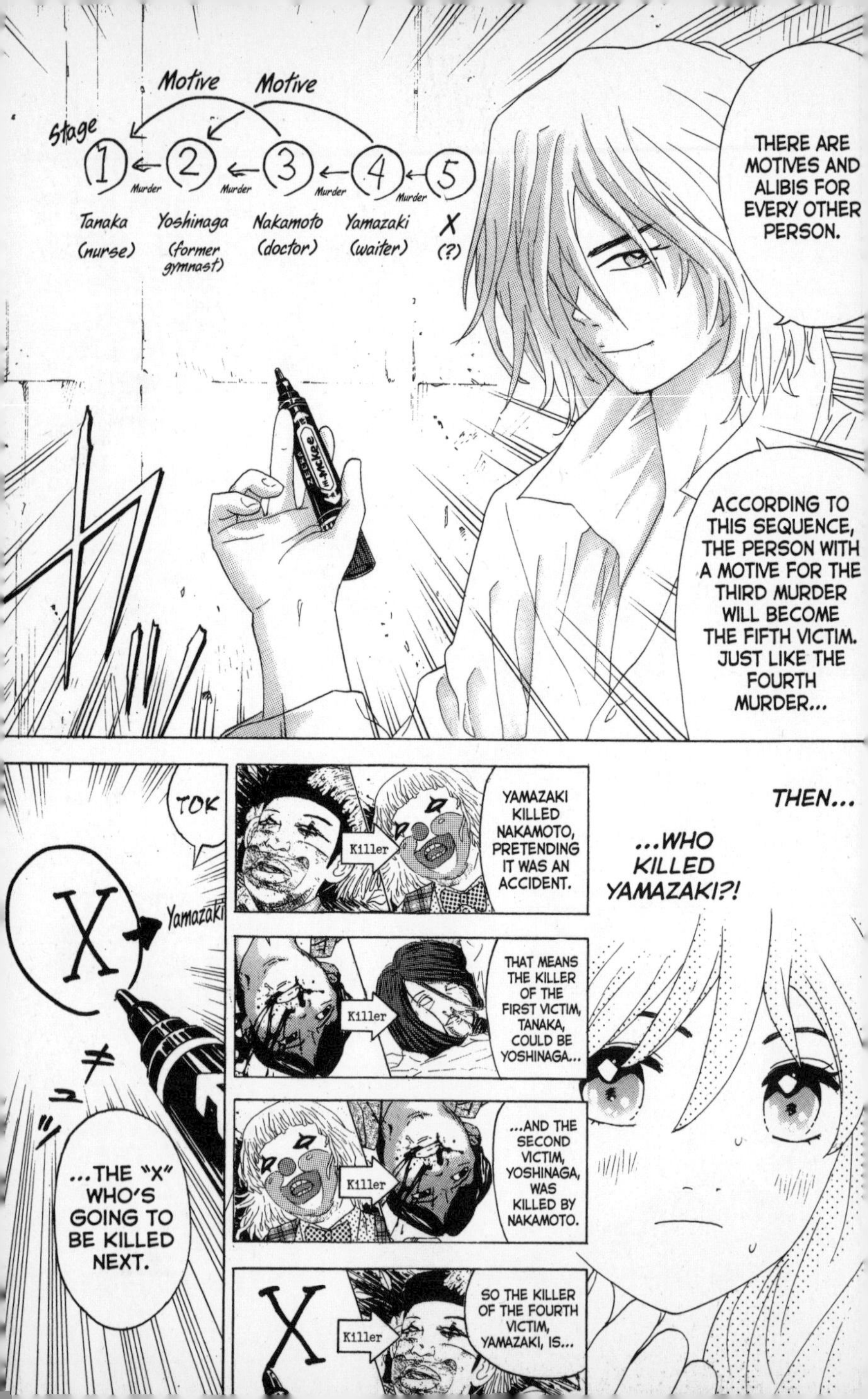
THERE ARE MOTIVES AND ALIBIS FOR EVERY OTHER PERSON.
ACCORDING TO THIS SEQUENCE, THE PERSON WITH A MOTIVE FOR THE THIRD MURDER WILL BECOME THE FIFTH VICTIM. JUST LIKE THE FOURTH MURDER...
Motive
Motive
Stage
1 ← 2 ← 3 ← 4 ← 5
Murder
Murder
Murder
Murder
Tanaka (nurse)
Yoshinaga (former gymnast)
Nakamoto (doctor)
Yamazaki (waiter)
X (?)
THEN...
...WHO KILLED YAMAZAKI?!
Killer
YAMAZAKI KILLED NAKAMOTO, PRETENDING IT WAS AN ACCIDENT.
Killer
THAT MEANS THE KILLER OF THE FIRST VICTIM, TANAKA, COULD BE YOSHINAGA...
Killer
...AND THE SECOND VICTIM, YOSHINAGA, WAS KILLED BY NAKAMOTO.
X
Killer
SO THE KILLER OF THE FOURTH VICTIM, YAMAZAKI, IS...
TOK
X
Yamazaki
キュッ
...THE "X" WHO'S GOING TO BE KILLED NEXT.

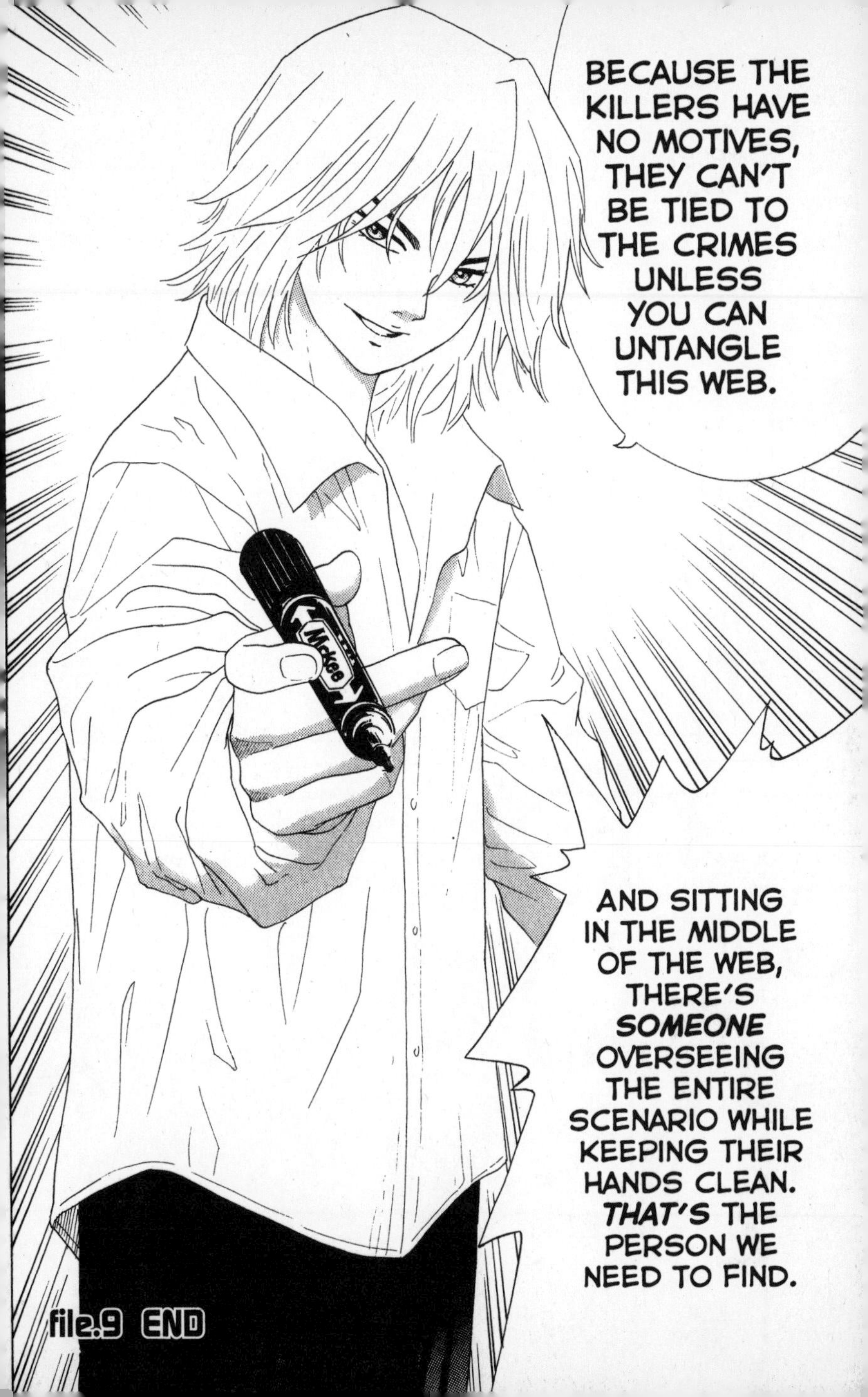
BECAUSE THE KILLERS HAVE NO MOTIVES, THEY CAN'T BE TIED TO THE CRIMES UNLESS YOU CAN UNTANGLE THIS WEB.
AND SITTING IN THE MIDDLE OF THE WEB, THERE'S *SOMEONE* OVERSEEING THE ENTIRE SCENARIO WHILE KEEPING THEIR HANDS CLEAN. *THAT'S* THE PERSON WE NEED TO FIND.
McKee
file.9 END

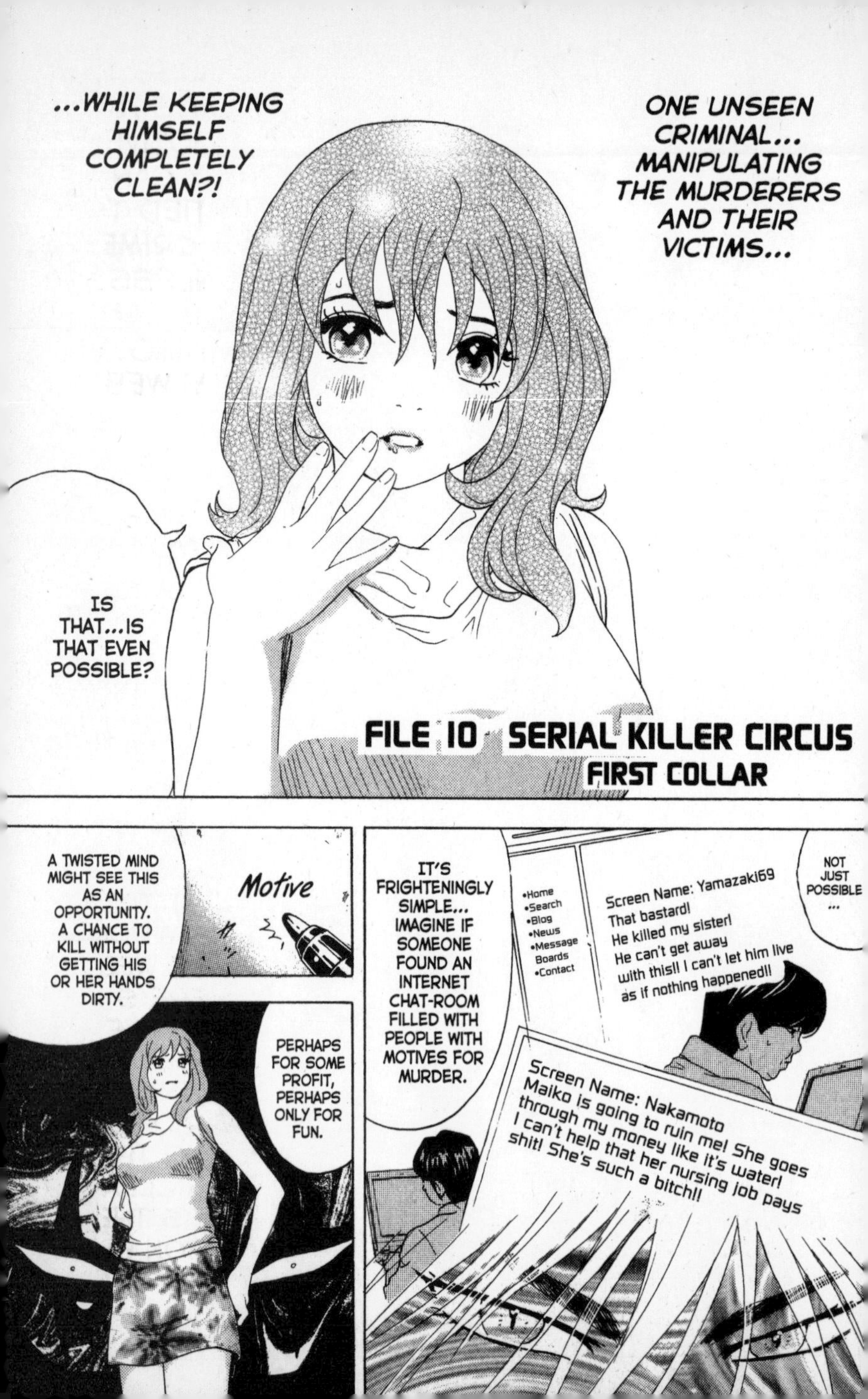
ONE UNSEEN CRIMINAL... MANIPULATING THE MURDERERS AND THEIR VICTIMS...
...WHILE KEEPING HIMSELF COMPLETELY CLEAN?!
IS THAT...IS THAT EVEN POSSIBLE?
FILE 10 SERIAL KILLER CIRCUS
FIRST COLLAR
NOT JUST POSSIBLE...
•Home •Search •Blog •News •Message Boards •Contact
Screen Name: Yamazaki69
That bastard! He killed my sister! He can't get away with this!! I can't let him live as if nothing happened!!
IT'S FRIGHTENINGLY SIMPLE... IMAGINE IF SOMEONE FOUND AN INTERNET CHAT-ROOM FILLED WITH PEOPLE WITH MOTIVES FOR MURDER.
Screen Name: Nakamoto
Maiko is going to ruin me! She goes through my money like it's water! I can't help that her nursing job pays shit! She's such a bitch!!
A TWISTED MIND MIGHT SEE THIS AS AN OPPORTUNITY. A CHANCE TO KILL WITHOUT GETTING HIS OR HER HANDS DIRTY.
Motive
PERHAPS FOR SOME PROFIT, PERHAPS ONLY FOR FUN.

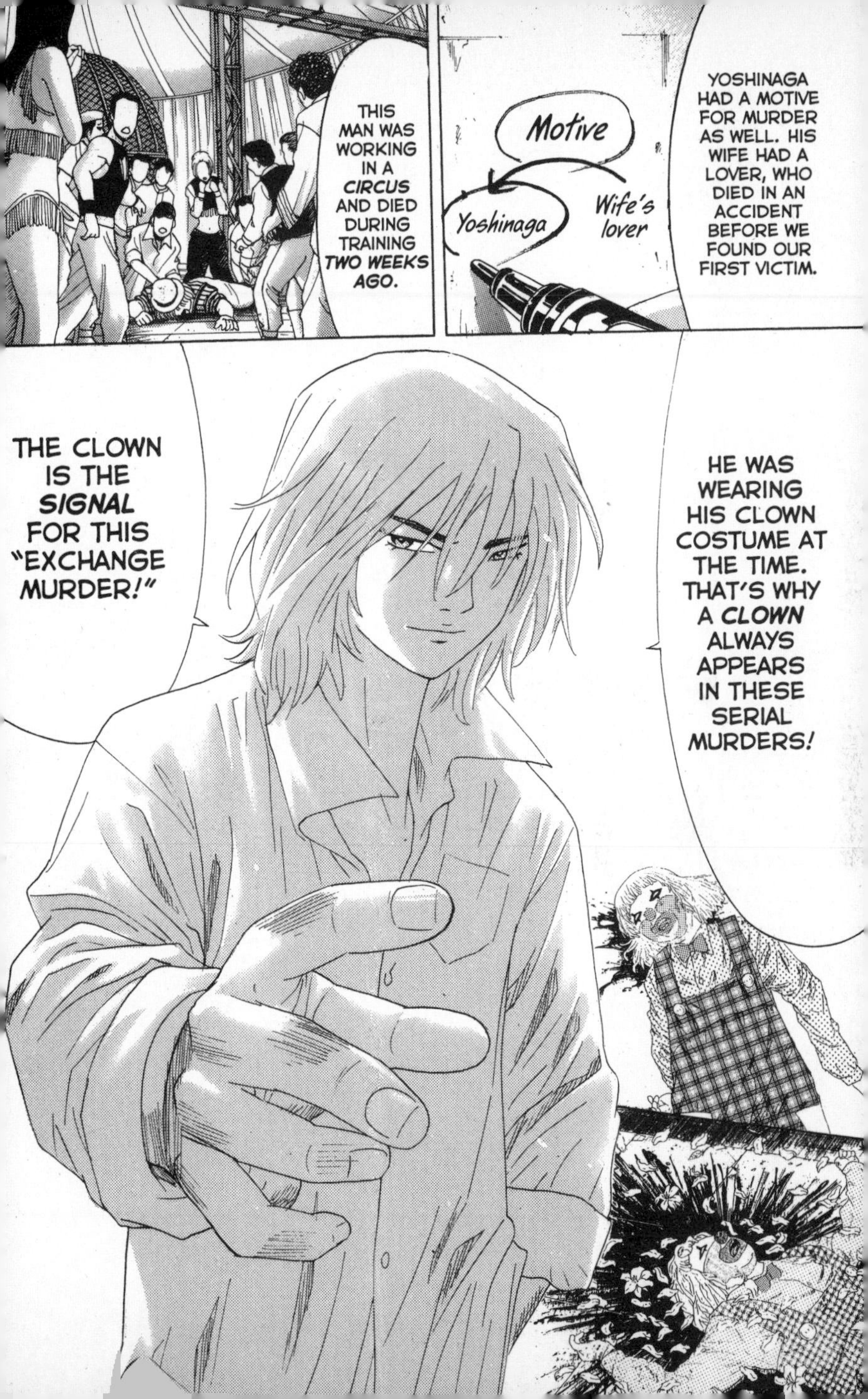
YOSHINAGA HAD A MOTIVE FOR MURDER AS WELL. HIS WIFE HAD A LOVER, WHO DIED IN AN ACCIDENT BEFORE WE FOUND OUR FIRST VICTIM.
Motive
Wife's lover
Yoshinaga
THIS MAN WAS WORKING IN A CIRCUS AND DIED DURING TRAINING TWO WEEKS AGO.
HE WAS WEARING HIS CLOWN COSTUME AT THE TIME. THAT'S WHY A CLOWN ALWAYS APPEARS IN THESE SERIAL MURDERS!
THE CLOWN IS THE SIGNAL FOR THIS "EXCHANGE MURDER!"

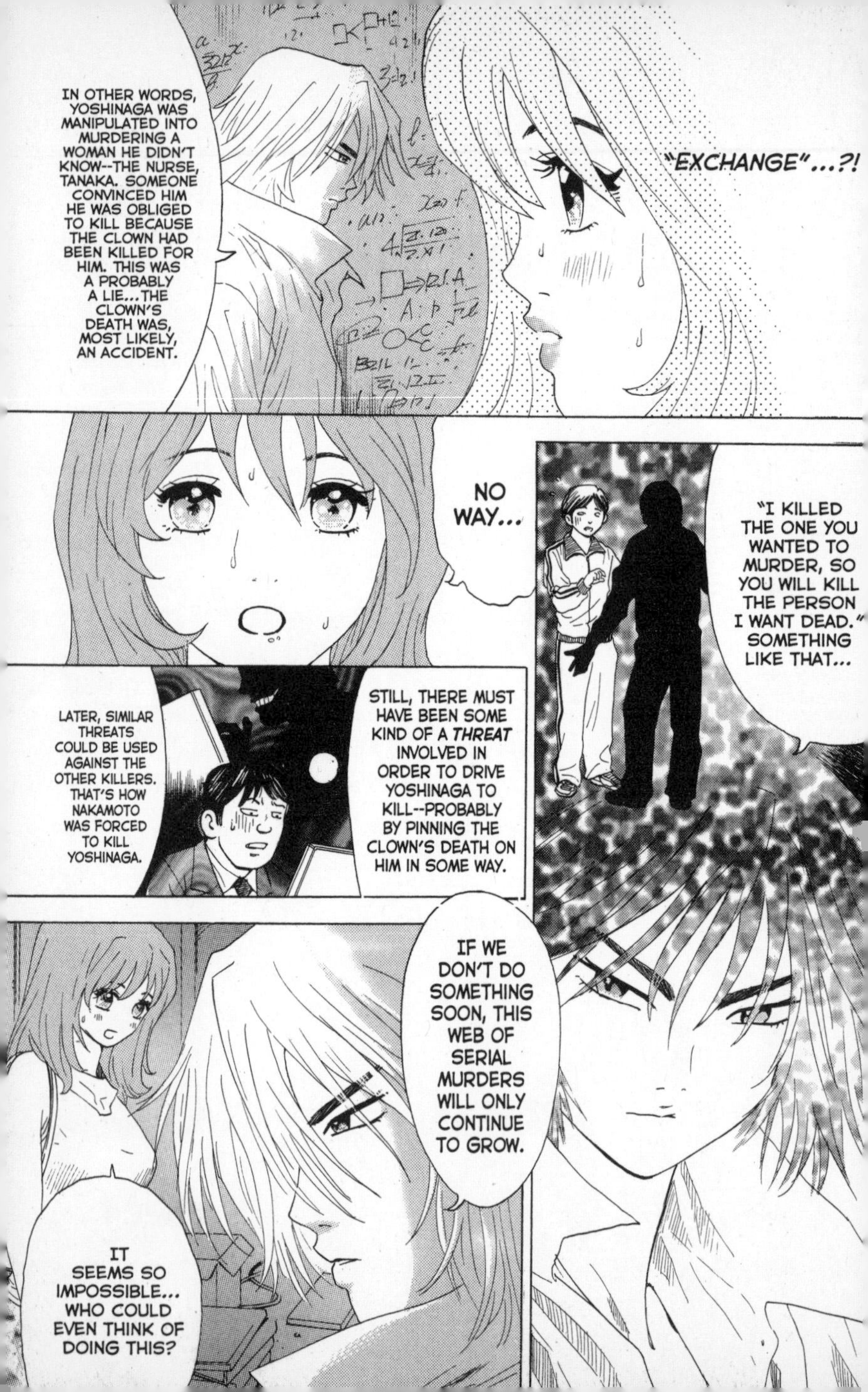
"EXCHANGE"...?!
IN OTHER WORDS, YOSHINAGA WAS MANIPULATED INTO MURDERING A WOMAN HE DIDN'T KNOW--THE NURSE, TANAKA. SOMEONE CONVINCED HIM HE WAS OBLIGED TO KILL BECAUSE THE CLOWN HAD BEEN KILLED FOR HIM. THIS WAS A PROBABLY A LIE...THE CLOWN'S DEATH WAS, MOST LIKELY, AN ACCIDENT.
"I KILLED THE ONE YOU WANTED TO MURDER, SO YOU WILL KILL THE PERSON I WANT DEAD." SOMETHING LIKE THAT...
NO WAY...
STILL, THERE MUST HAVE BEEN SOME KIND OF A *THREAT* INVOLVED IN ORDER TO DRIVE YOSHINAGA TO KILL--PROBABLY BY PINNING THE CLOWN'S DEATH ON HIM IN SOME WAY.
LATER, SIMILAR THREATS COULD BE USED AGAINST THE OTHER KILLERS. THAT'S HOW NAKAMOTO WAS FORCED TO KILL YOSHINAGA.
IF WE DON'T DO SOMETHING SOON, THIS WEB OF SERIAL MURDERS WILL ONLY CONTINUE TO GROW.
IT SEEMS SO IMPOSSIBLE... WHO COULD EVEN THINK OF DOING THIS?

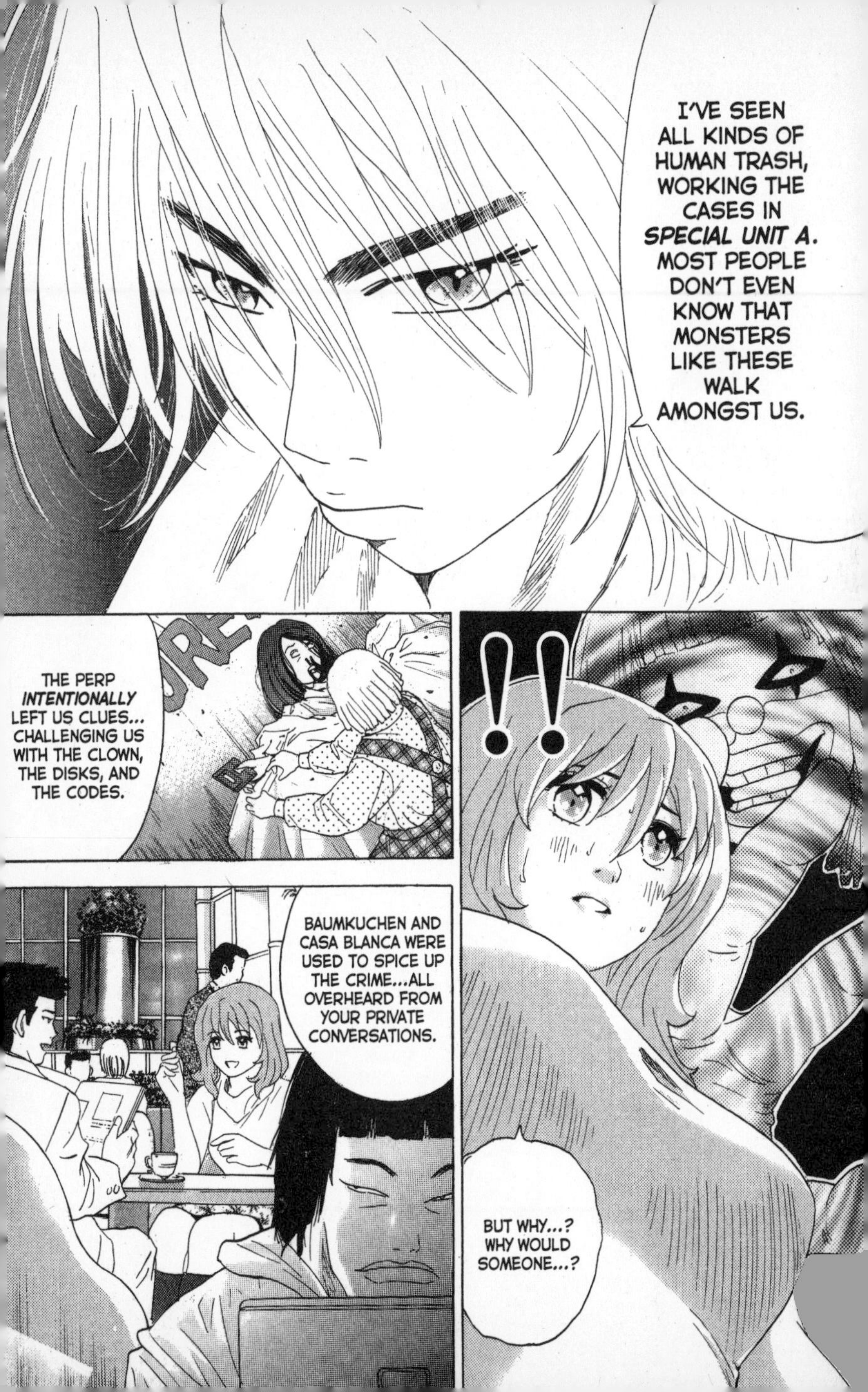
I'VE SEEN ALL KINDS OF HUMAN TRASH, WORKING THE CASES IN *SPECIAL UNIT A*. MOST PEOPLE DON'T EVEN KNOW THAT MONSTERS LIKE THESE WALK AMONGST US.
!!
BUT WHY...? WHY WOULD SOMEONE...?
THE PERP *INTENTIONALLY* LEFT US CLUES... CHALLENGING US WITH THE CLOWN, THE DISKS, AND THE CODES.
BAUMKUCHEN AND CASA BLANCA WERE USED TO SPICE UP THE CRIME...ALL OVERHEARD FROM YOUR PRIVATE CONVERSATIONS.

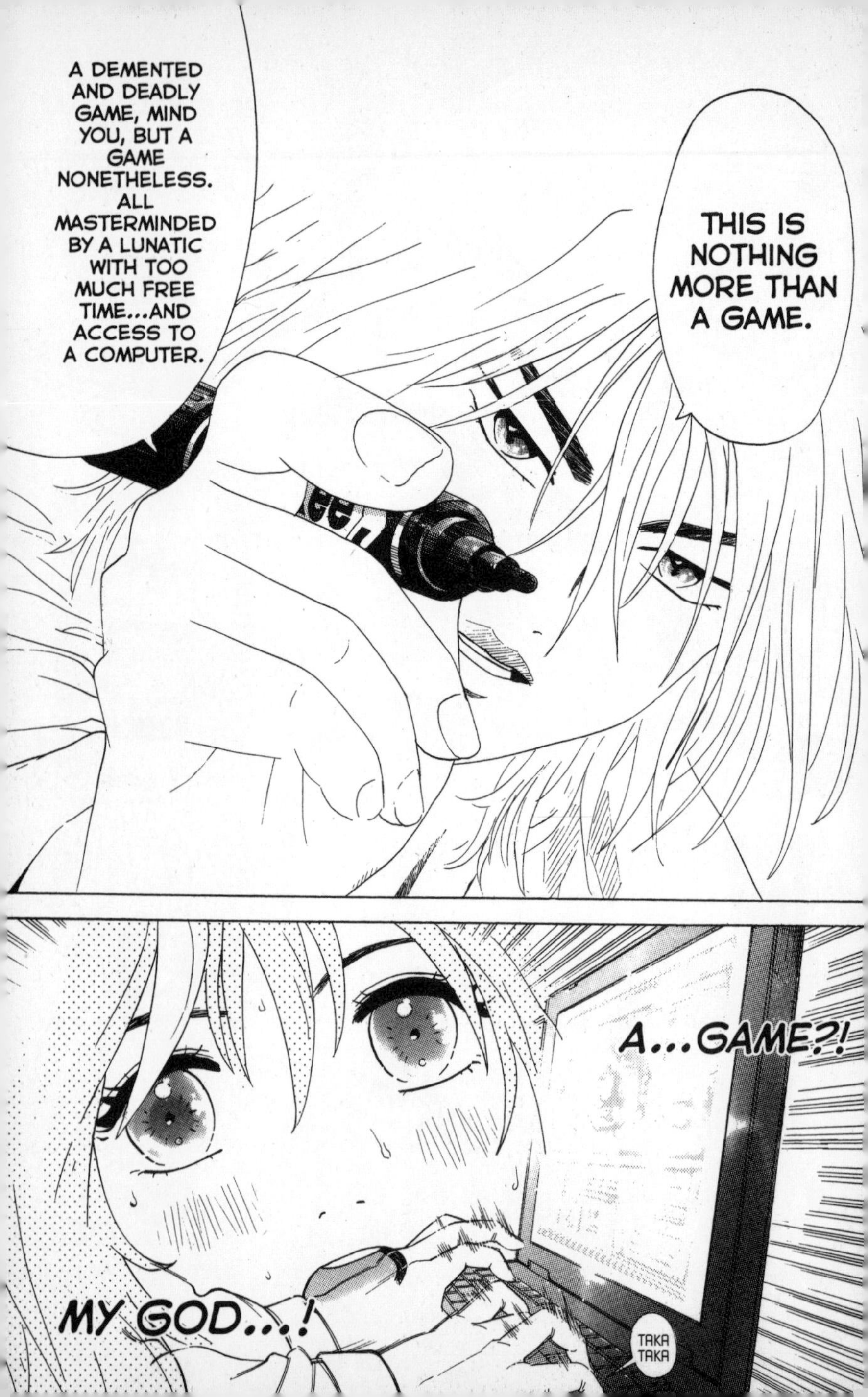
THIS IS NOTHING MORE THAN A GAME.
A DEMENTED AND DEADLY GAME, MIND YOU, BUT A GAME NONETHELESS. ALL MASTERMINDED BY A LUNATIC WITH TOO MUCH FREE TIME...AND ACCESS TO A COMPUTER.
A...GAME?!
TAKA TAKA
MY GOD...!

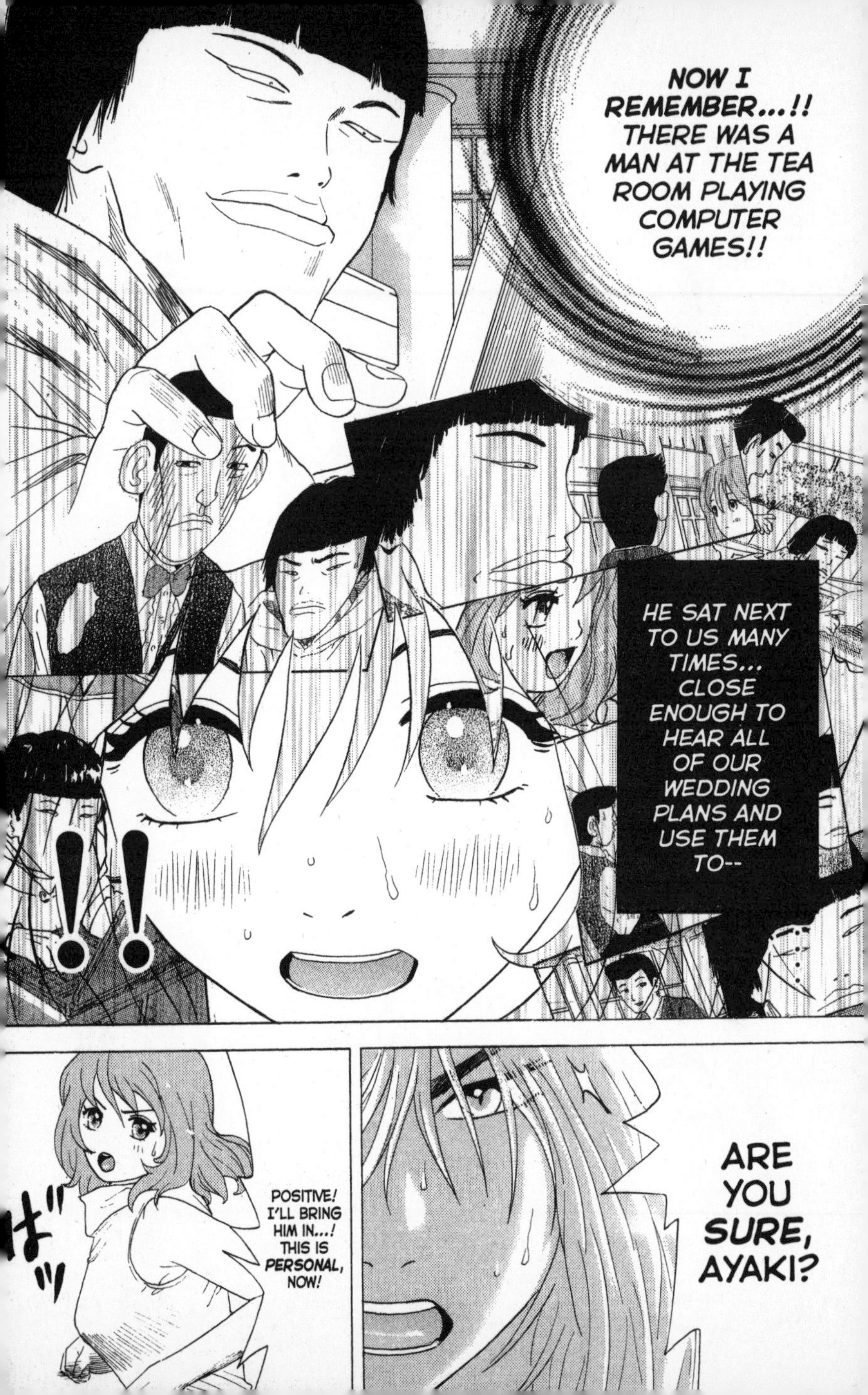
NOW I REMEMBER...!! THERE WAS A MAN AT THE TEA ROOM PLAYING COMPUTER GAMES!!
HE SAT NEXT TO US MANY TIMES... CLOSE ENOUGH TO HEAR ALL OF OUR WEDDING PLANS AND USE THEM TO--
ARE YOU SURE, AYAKI?
POSITIVE! I'LL BRING HIM IN...! THIS IS PERSONAL, NOW!
ばッ

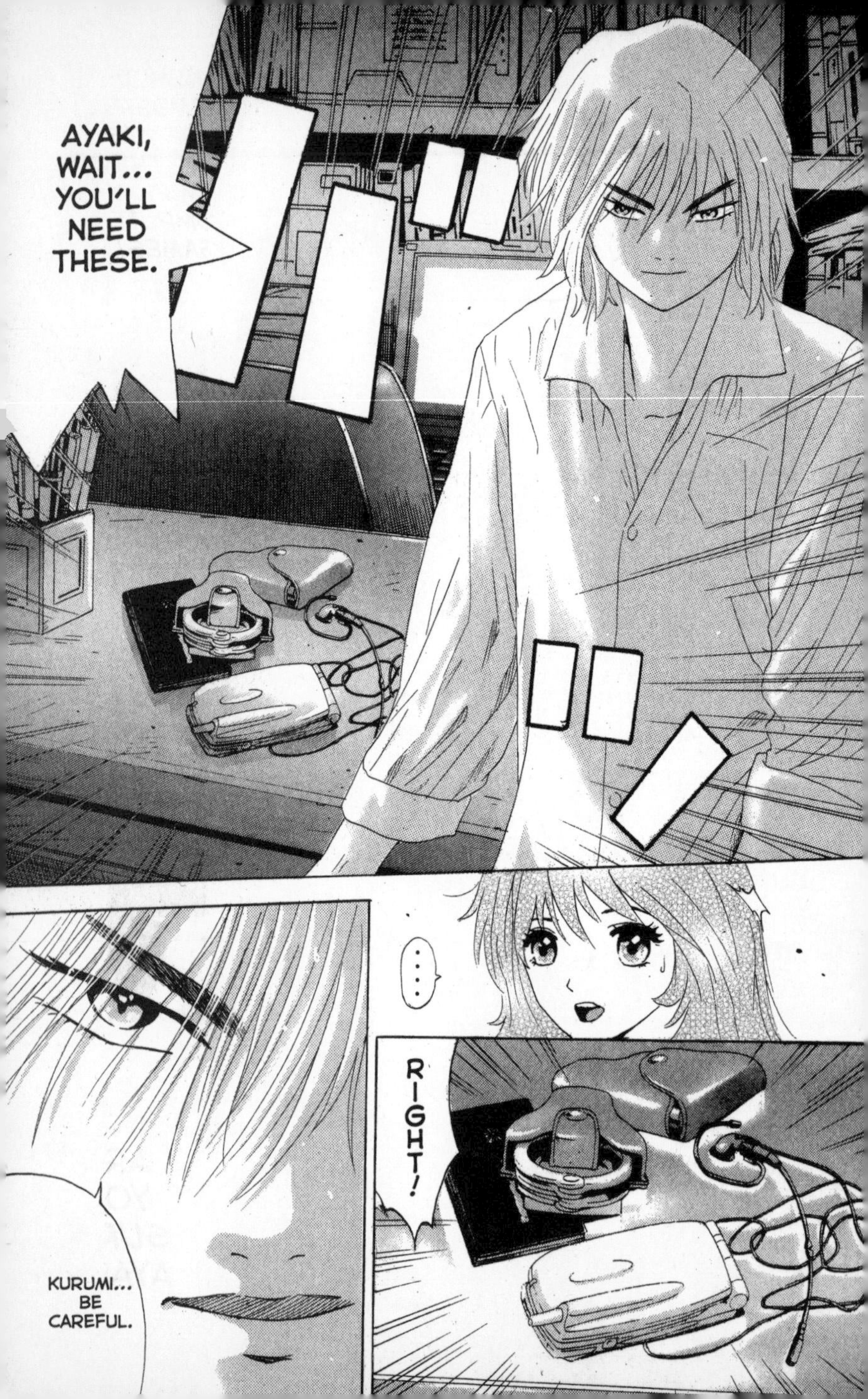
AYAKI, WAIT... YOU'LL NEED THESE.
...
RIGHT!
KURUMI... BE CAREFUL.

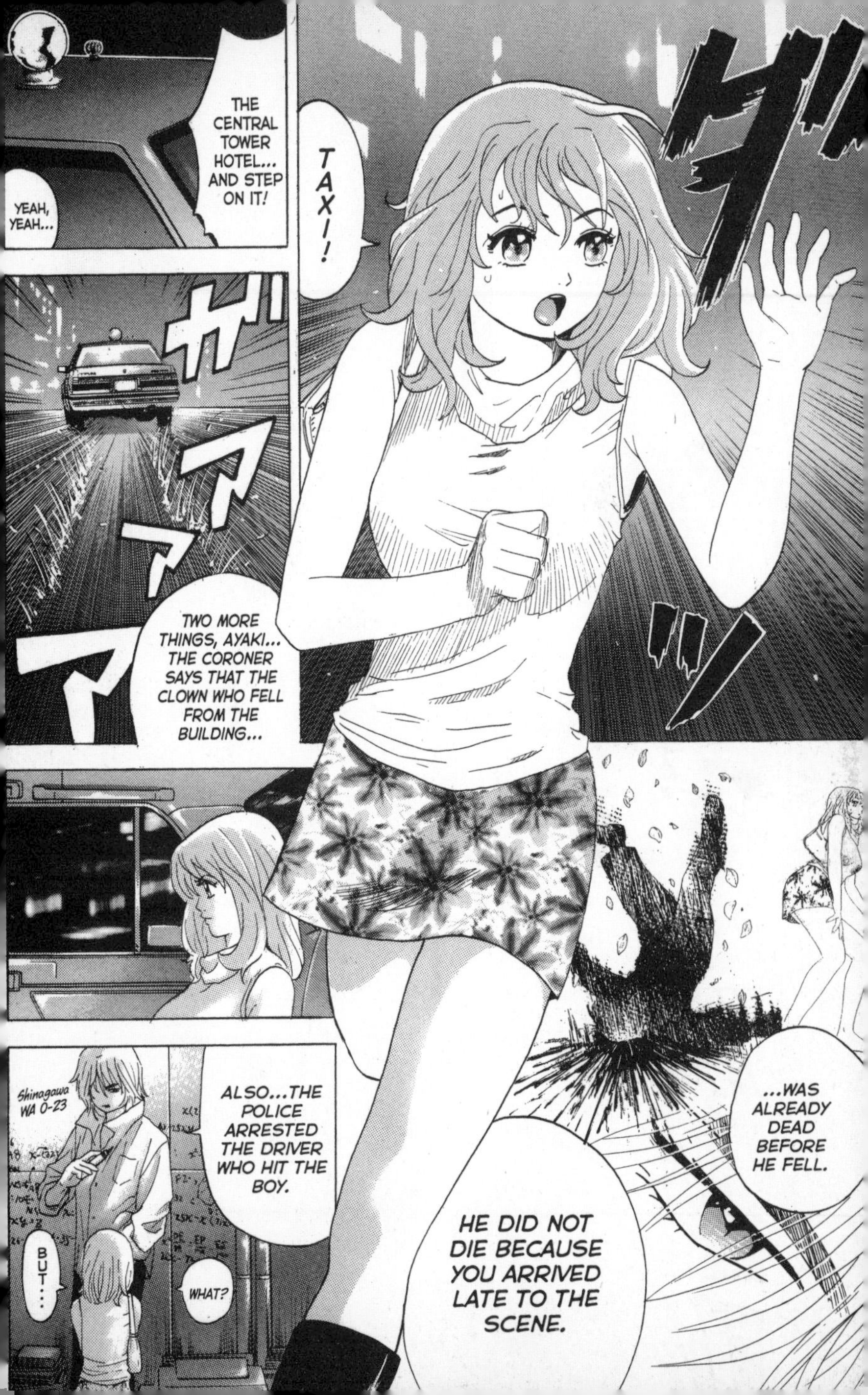
TAXI!!
THE CENTRAL TOWER HOTEL... AND STEP ON IT!
YEAH, YEAH...
TWO MORE THINGS, AYAKI... THE CORONER SAYS THAT THE CLOWN WHO FELL FROM THE BUILDING...
...WAS ALREADY DEAD BEFORE HE FELL.
ALSO...THE POLICE ARRESTED THE DRIVER WHO HIT THE BOY.
HE DID NOT DIE BECAUSE YOU ARRIVED LATE TO THE SCENE.
Shinagawa WA 0-23
BUT...
WHAT?

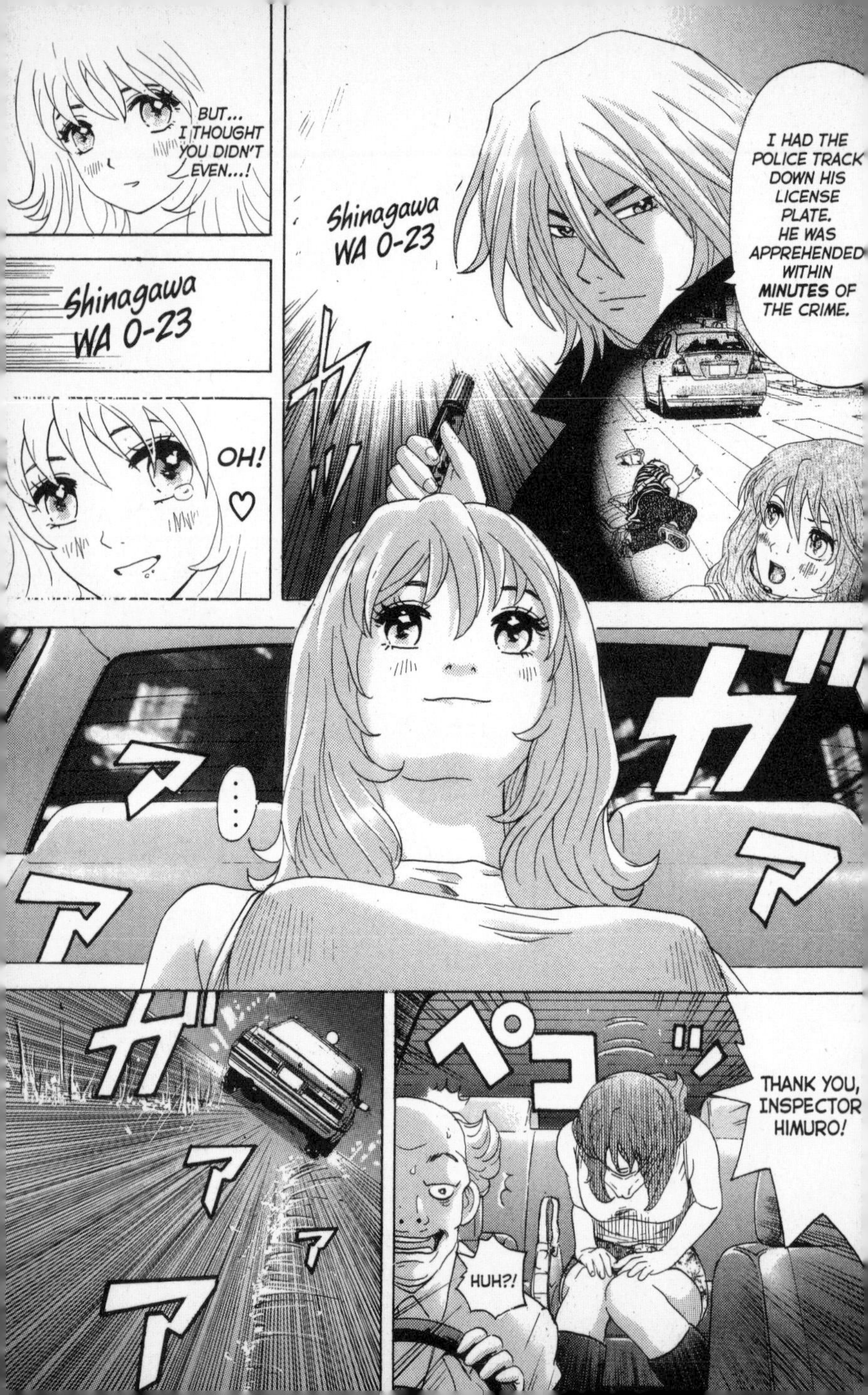
I HAD THE POLICE TRACK DOWN HIS LICENSE PLATE. HE WAS APPREHENDED WITHIN MINUTES OF THE CRIME.
Shinagawa WA 0-23
BUT... I THOUGHT YOU DIDN'T EVEN...!
Shinagawa WA 0-23
OH! ♡
ガァ
ア
...
ア
ペコッ
THANK YOU, INSPECTOR HIMURO!
HUH?!
ガァァァ

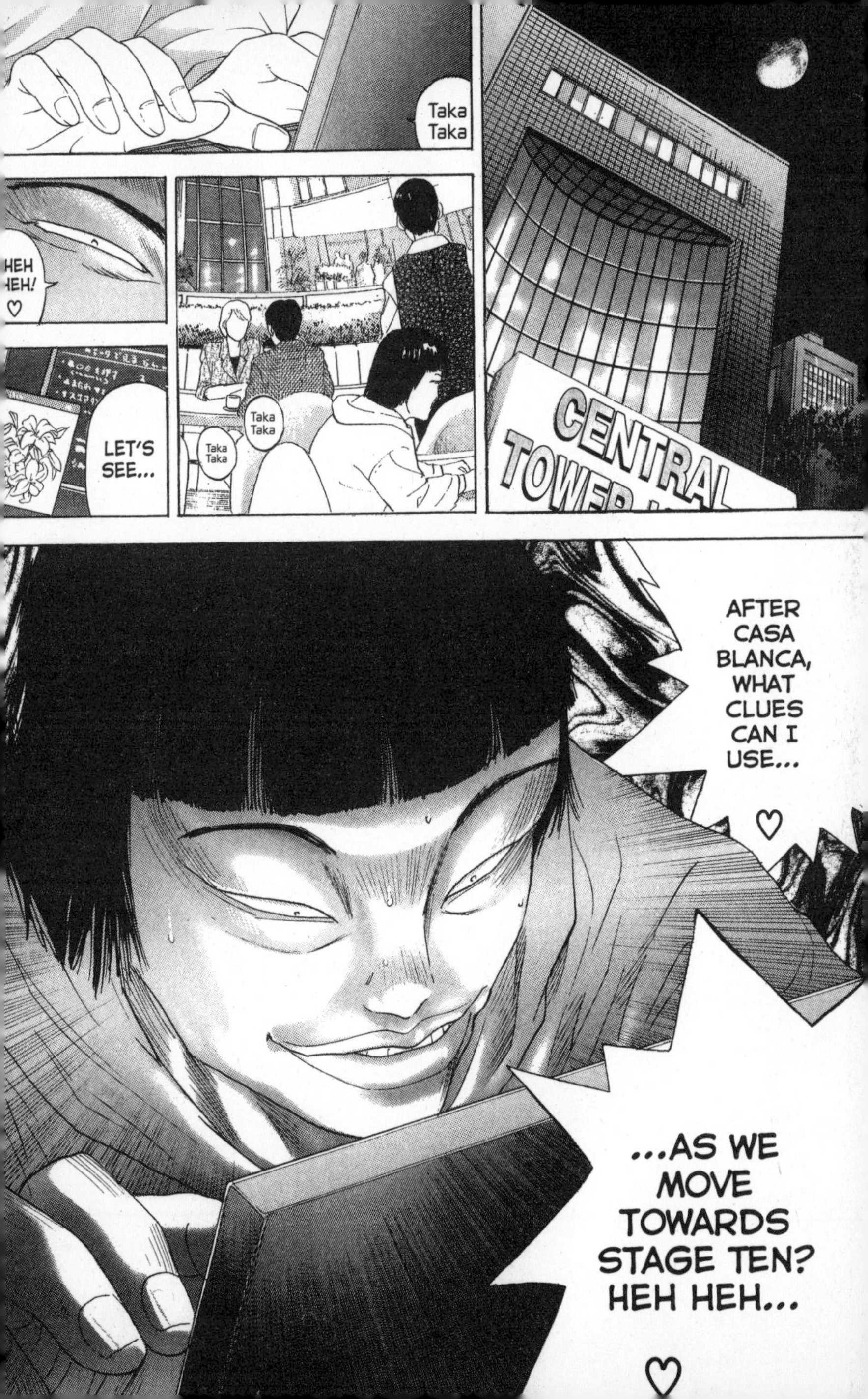
CENTRAL
Taka Taka
Taka Taka
Taka Taka
HEH HEH! ♡
LET'S SEE...
AFTER CASA BLANCA, WHAT CLUES CAN I USE... ♡
...AS WE MOVE TOWARDS STAGE TEN? HEH HEH... ♡

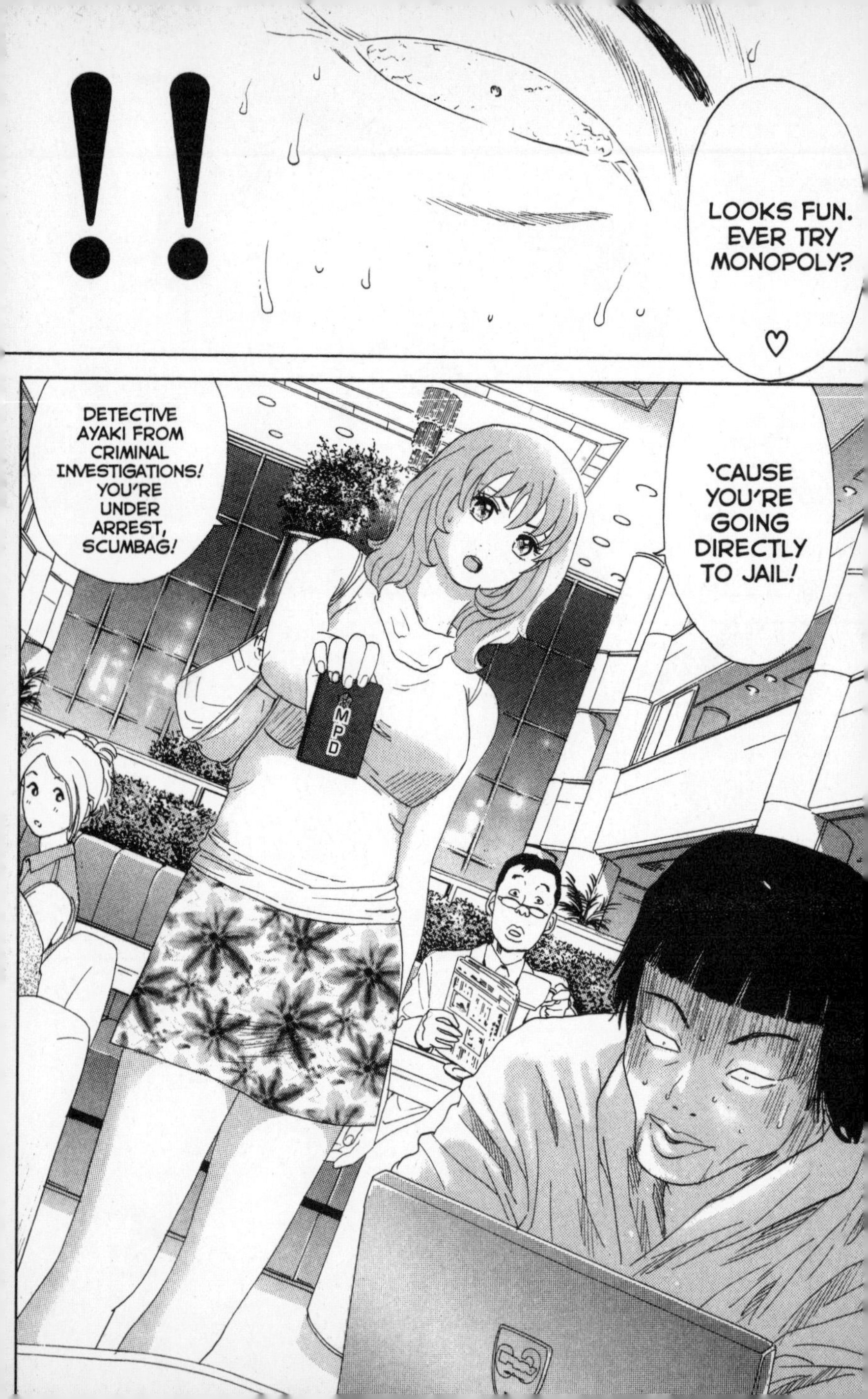
LOOKS FUN. EVER TRY MONOPOLY? ♡
!!
'CAUSE YOU'RE GOING DIRECTLY TO JAIL!
DETECTIVE AYAKI FROM CRIMINAL INVESTIGATIONS! YOU'RE UNDER ARREST, SCUMBAG!
MPD

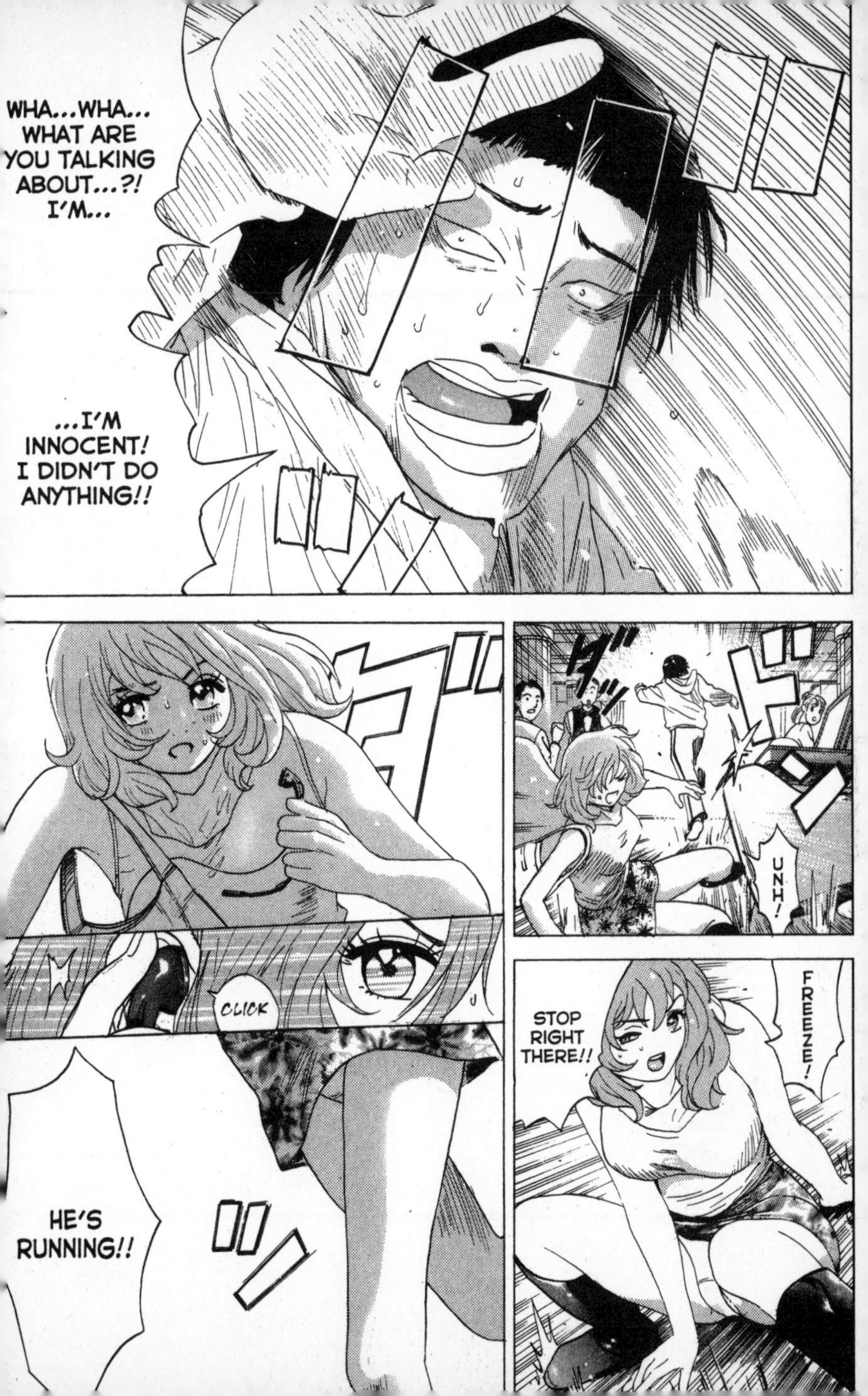
WHA...WHA... WHAT ARE YOU TALKING ABOUT...?! I'M...
...I'M INNOCENT! I DIDN'T DO ANYTHING!!
UNH!
CLICK
FREEZE!
STOP RIGHT THERE!!
HE'S RUNNING!!

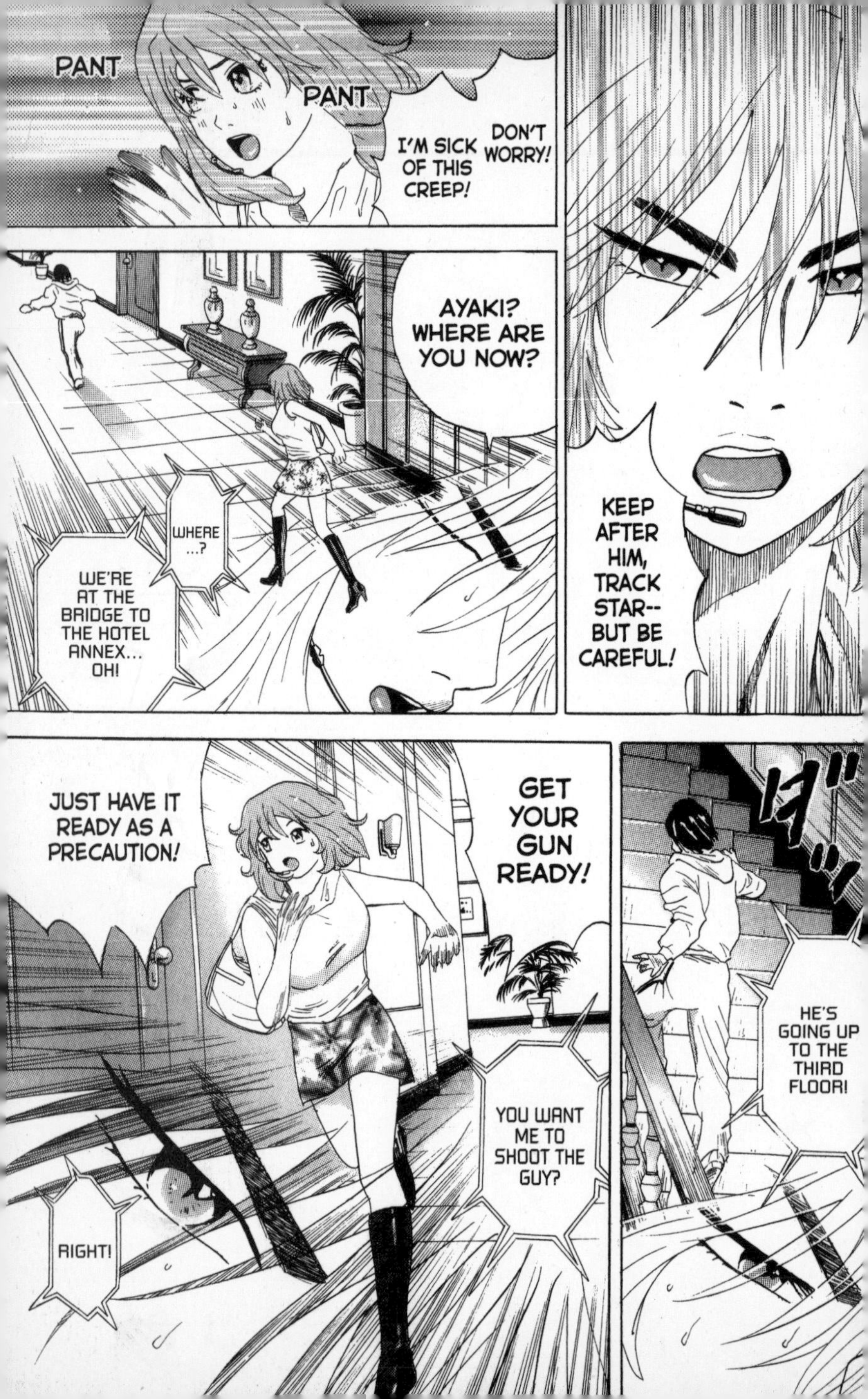
KEEP AFTER HIM, TRACK STAR-- BUT BE CAREFUL!
DON'T WORRY!
I'M SICK OF THIS CREEP!
PANT
PANT
AYAKI? WHERE ARE YOU NOW?
WHERE ...?
WE'RE AT THE BRIDGE TO THE HOTEL ANNEX... OH!
ダッ
HE'S GOING UP TO THE THIRD FLOOR!
GET YOUR GUN READY!
YOU WANT ME TO SHOOT THE GUY?
JUST HAVE IT READY AS A PRECAUTION!
RIGHT!

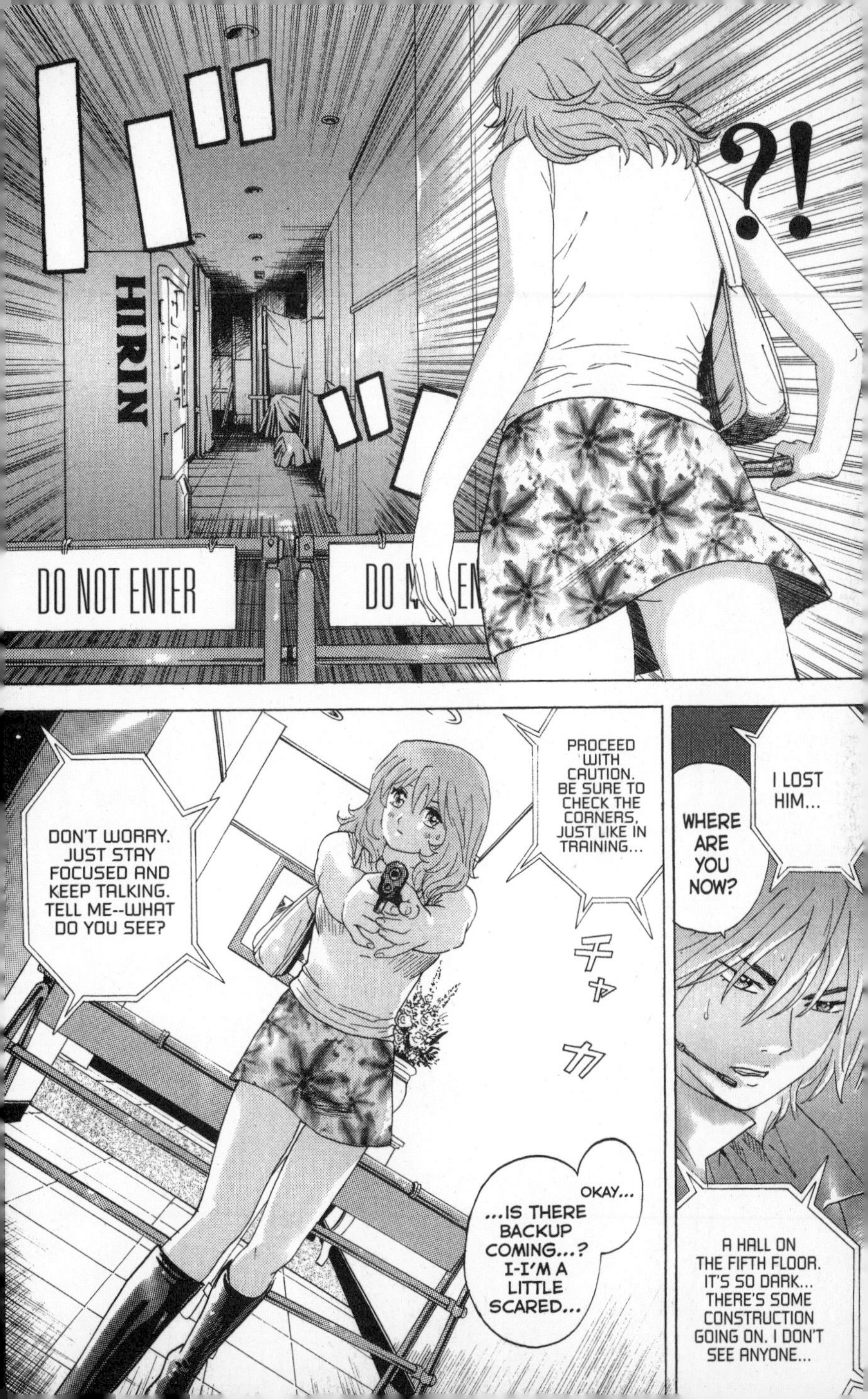
?!
DO NOT ENTER
I LOST HIM...
WHERE ARE YOU NOW?
A HALL ON THE FIFTH FLOOR. IT'S SO DARK... THERE'S SOME CONSTRUCTION GOING ON. I DON'T SEE ANYONE...
PROCEED WITH CAUTION. BE SURE TO CHECK THE CORNERS, JUST LIKE IN TRAINING...
DON'T WORRY. JUST STAY FOCUSED AND KEEP TALKING. TELL ME--WHAT DO YOU SEE?
チャカ
OKAY... ...IS THERE BACKUP COMING...? I-I'M A LITTLE SCARED...

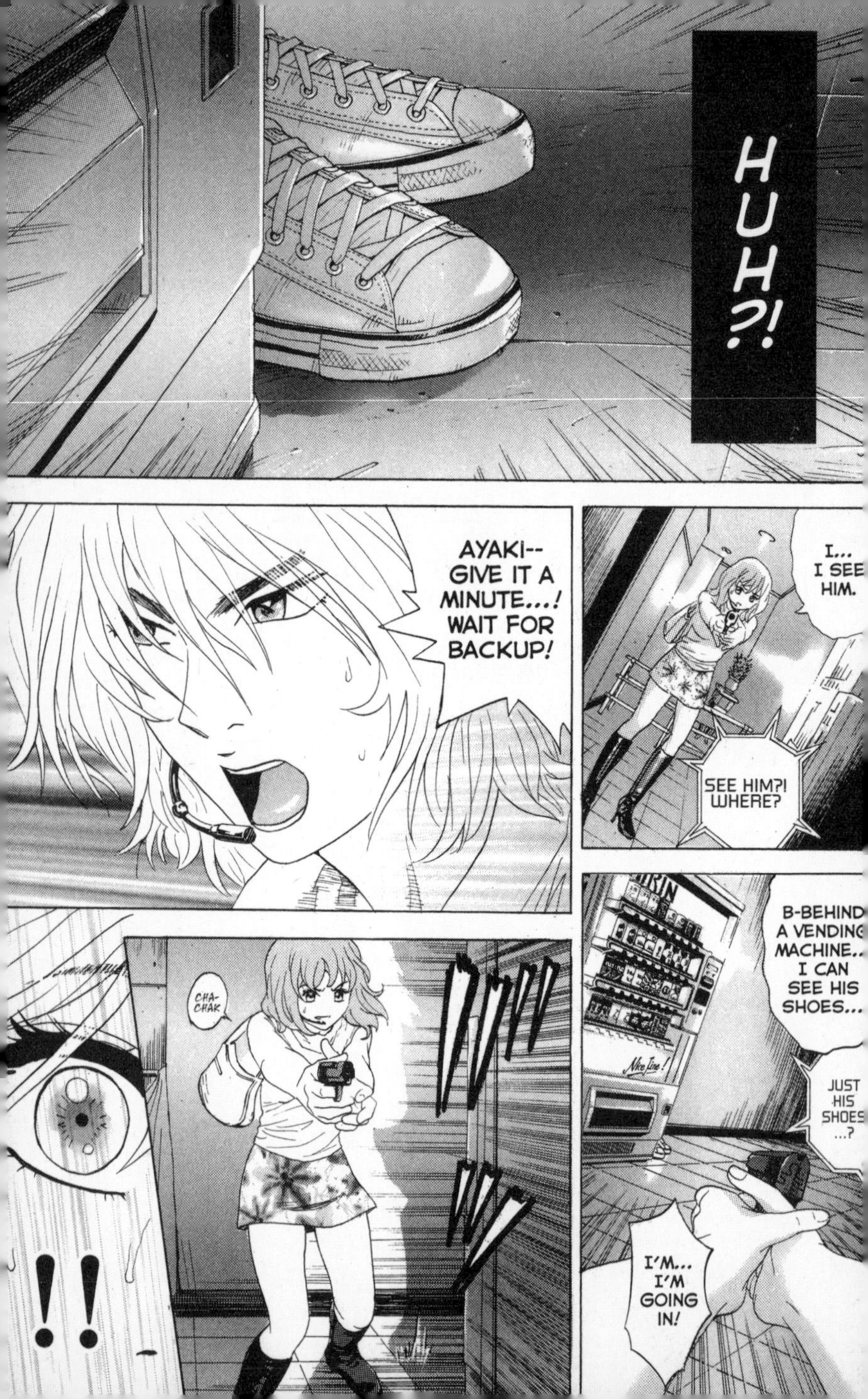
HUH?!
I... I SEE HIM.
SEE HIM?! WHERE?
B-BEHIND A VENDING MACHINE... I CAN SEE HIS SHOES...
JUST HIS SHOES ...?
I'M... I'M GOING IN!
AYAKI-- GIVE IT A MINUTE...! WAIT FOR BACKUP!
CHA-CHAK
!!

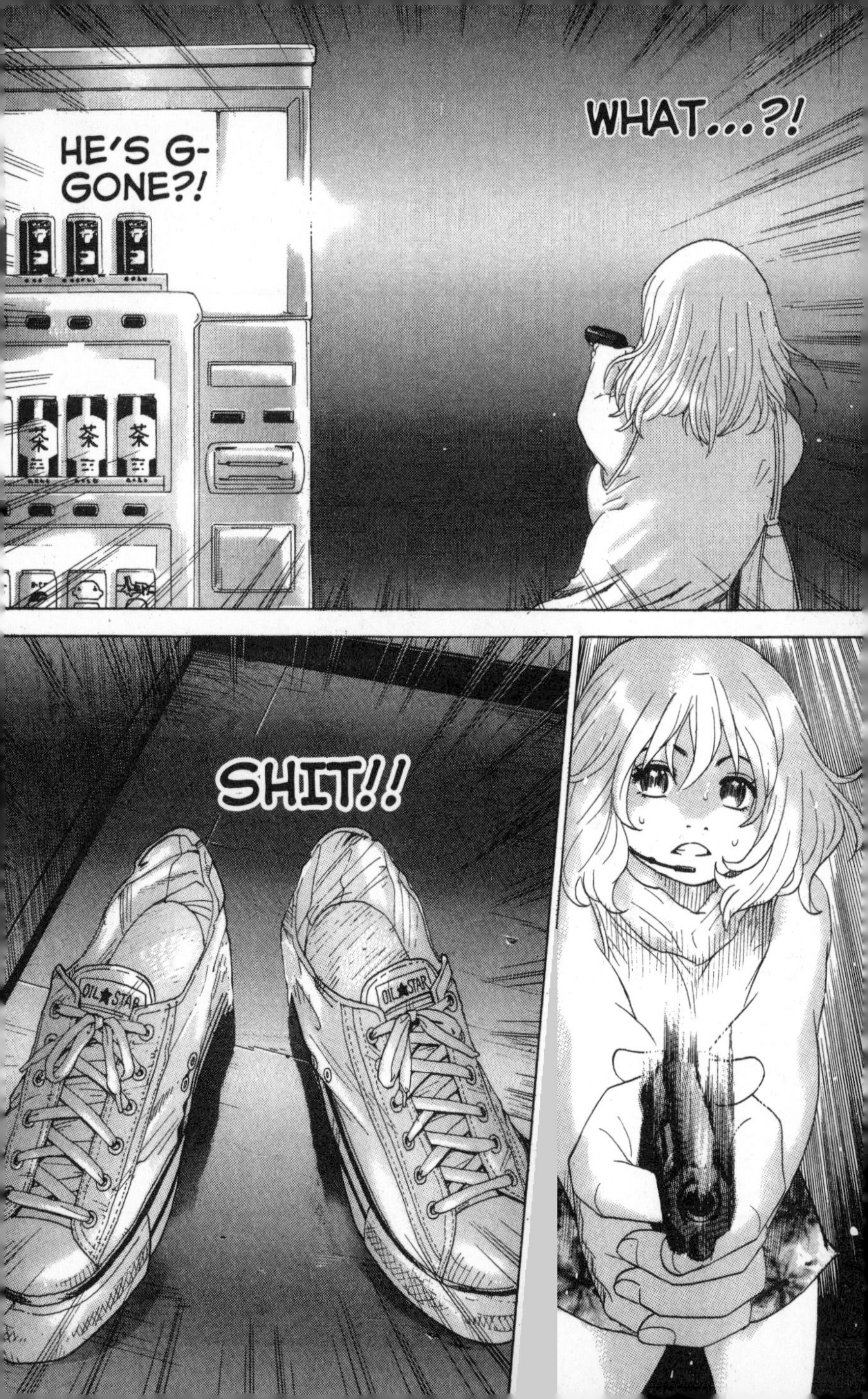
WHAT...?!
HE'S G-GONE?!
SHIT!!

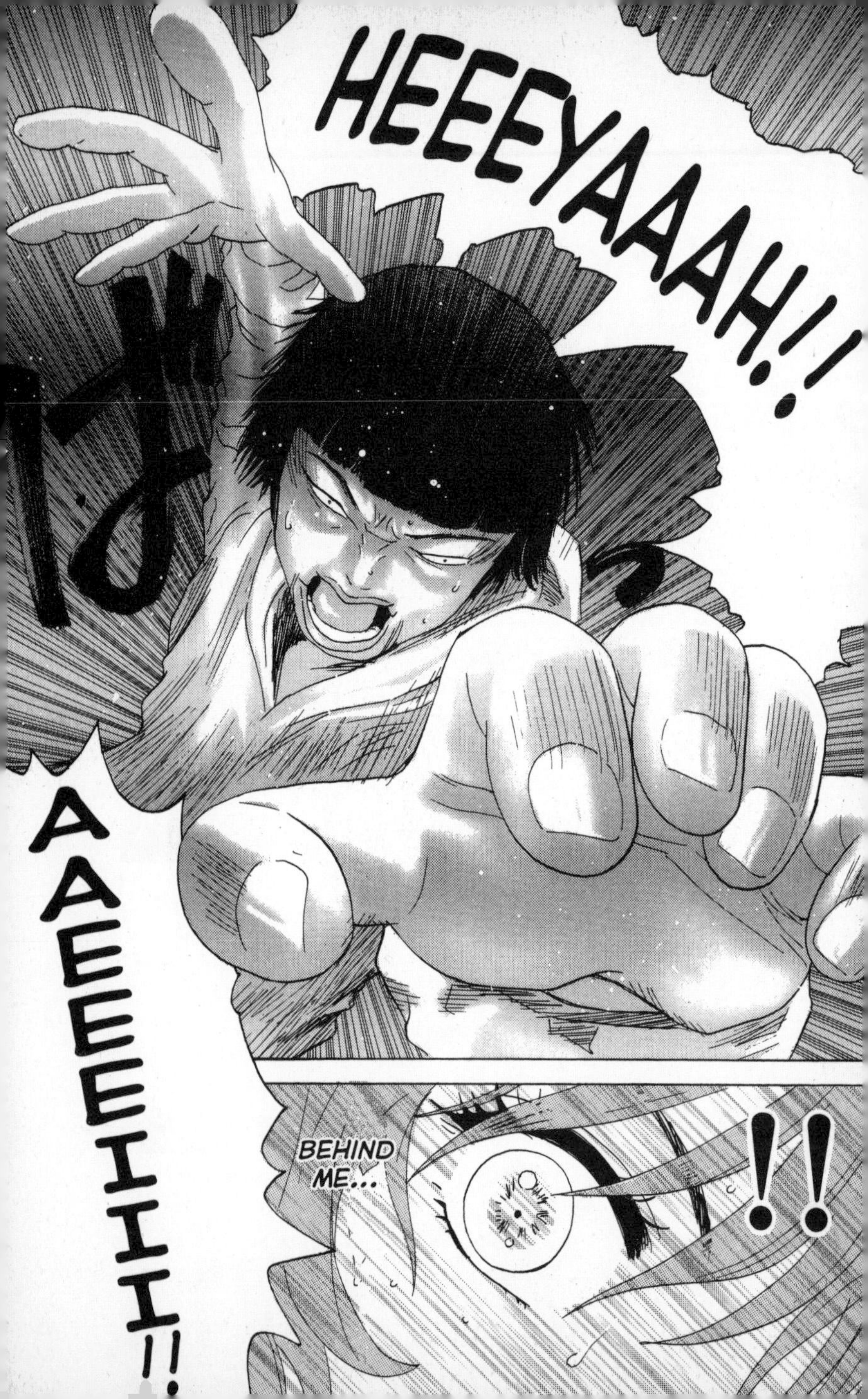
HEEEYAAAH!!
AAEEEIII!!
BEHIND ME...
!!

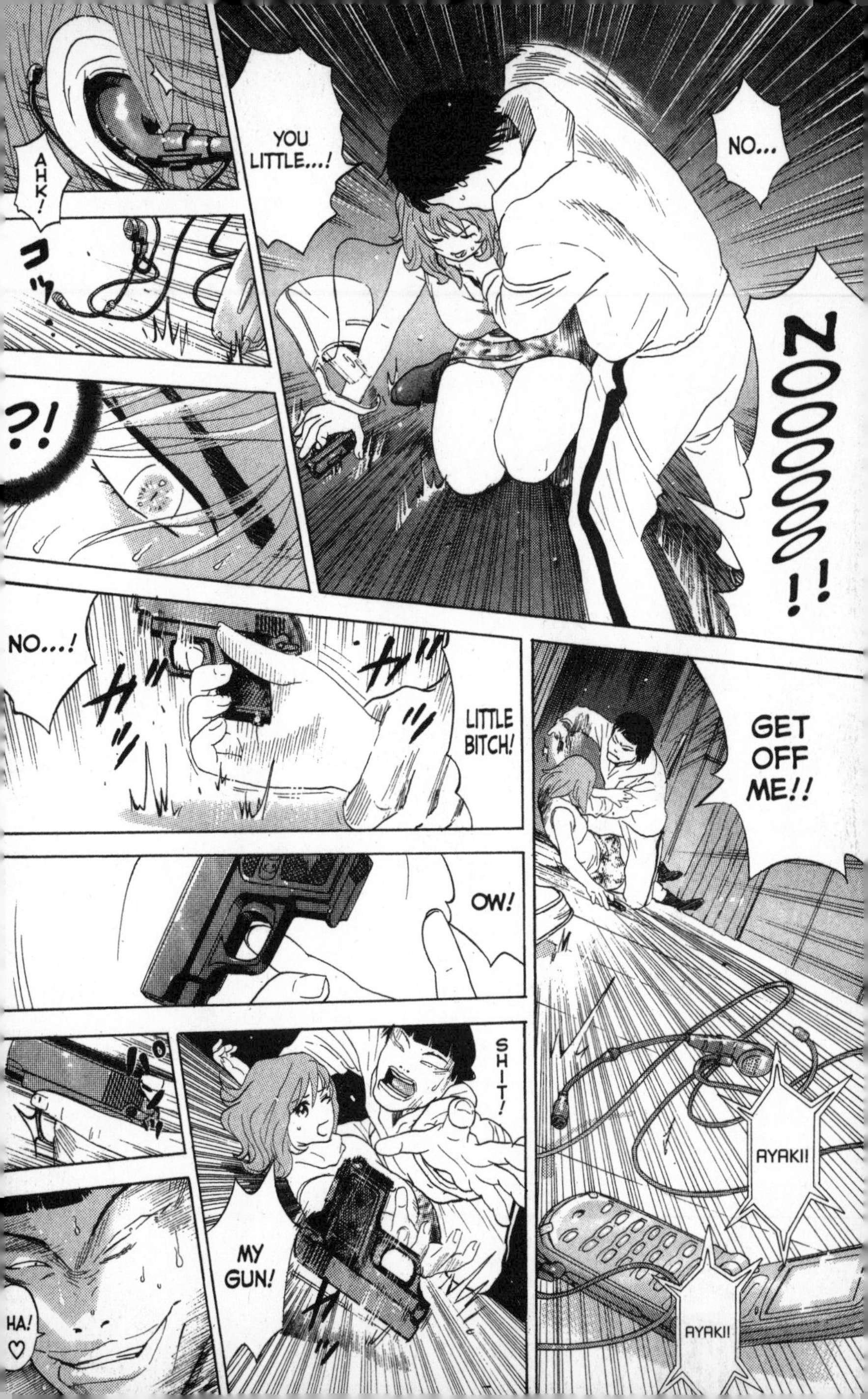
NO...
NOOOOOO!!
YOU LITTLE...!
AHK!
コッ
?!
GET OFF ME!!
AYAKI!
AYAKI!
LITTLE BITCH!
NO...!
OW!
SHIT!
MY GUN!
HA! ♡

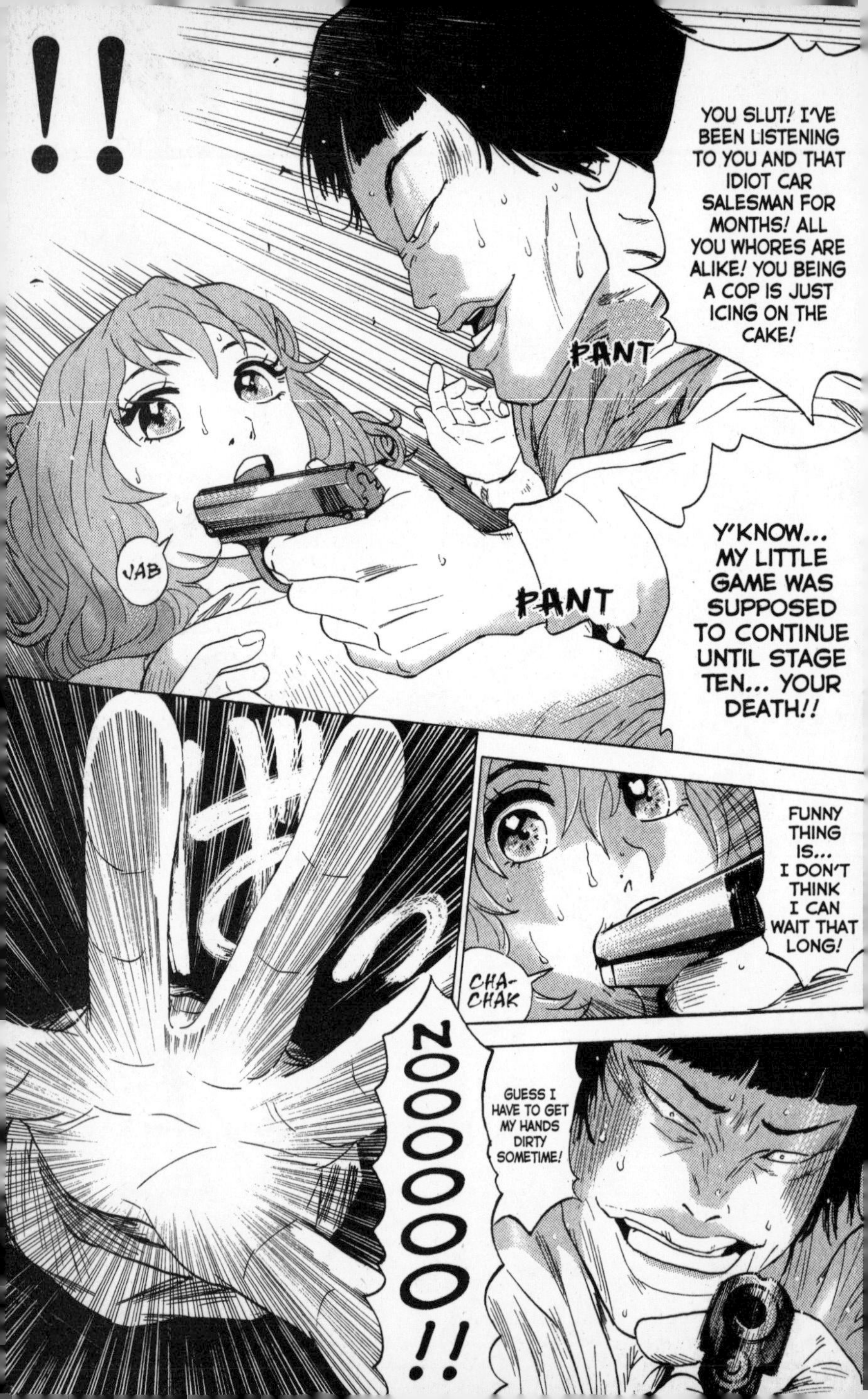
YOU SLUT! I'VE BEEN LISTENING TO YOU AND THAT IDIOT CAR SALESMAN FOR MONTHS! ALL YOU WHORES ARE ALIKE! YOU BEING A COP IS JUST ICING ON THE CAKE!
!!
PANT
Y'KNOW... MY LITTLE GAME WAS SUPPOSED TO CONTINUE UNTIL STAGE TEN... YOUR DEATH!!
PANT
JAB
FUNNY THING IS... I DON'T THINK I CAN WAIT THAT LONG!
CHA-CHAK
GUESS I HAVE TO GET MY HANDS DIRTY SOMETIME!
NOOOOOO!!

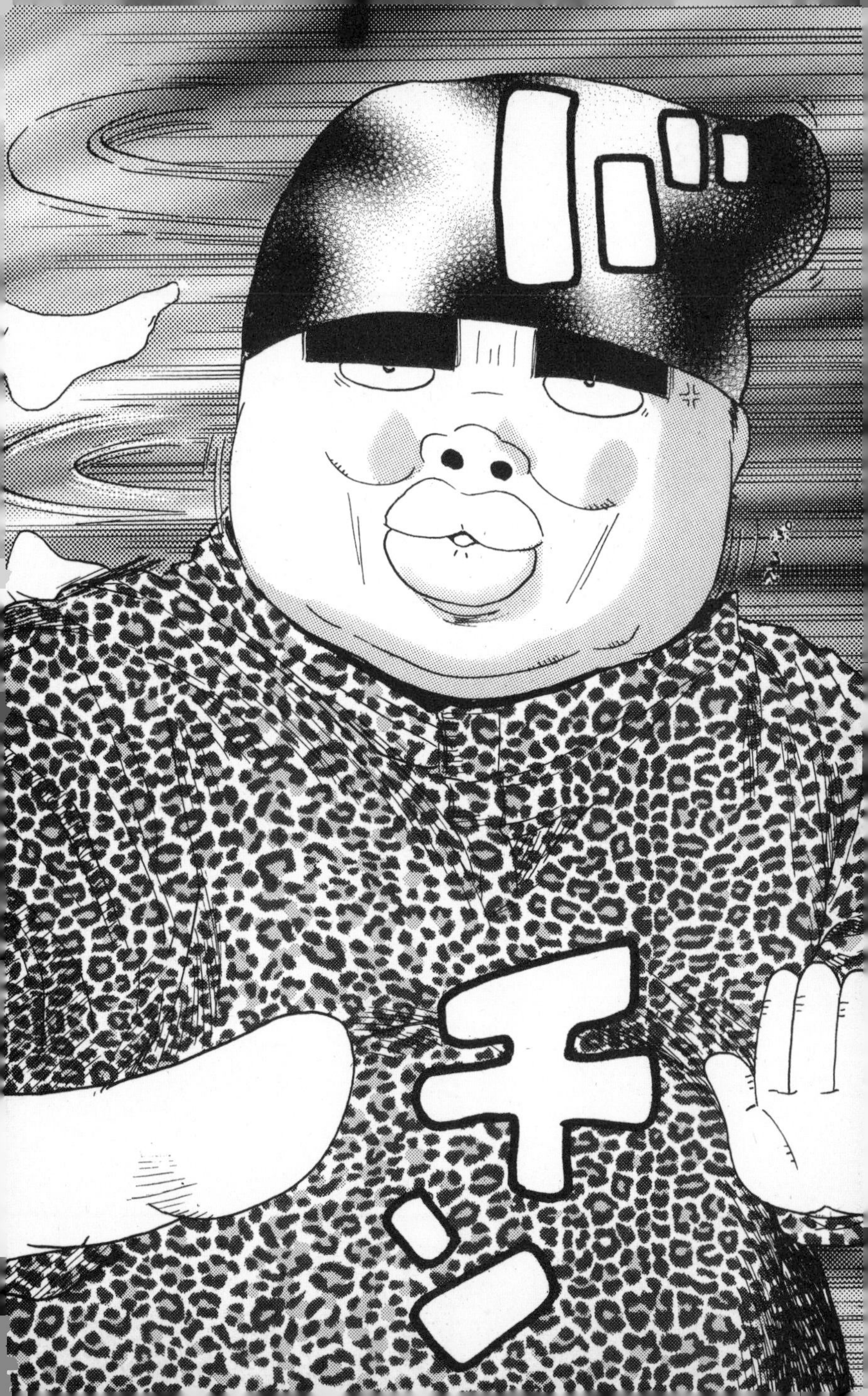
チン

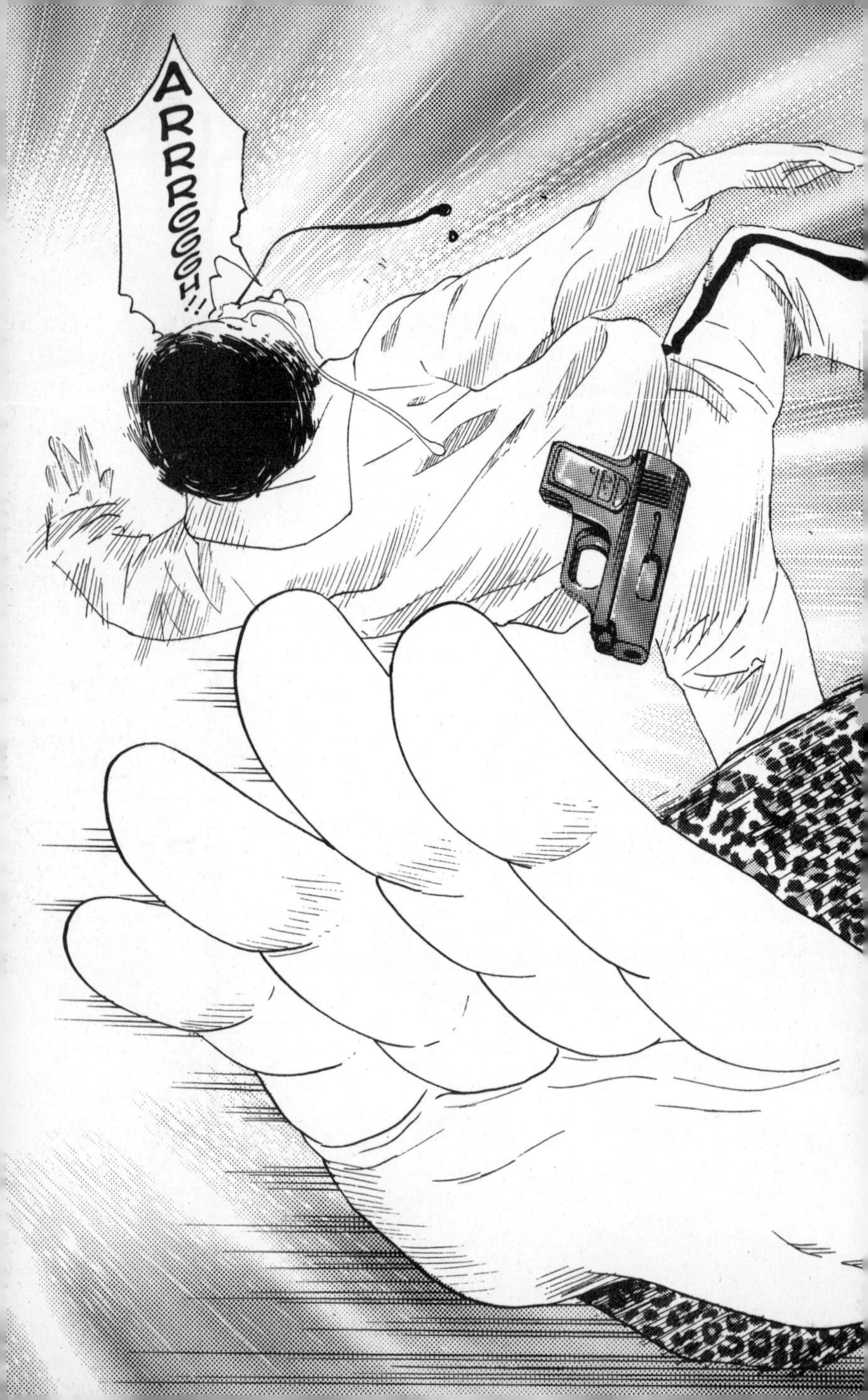
ARRRGGGH!!

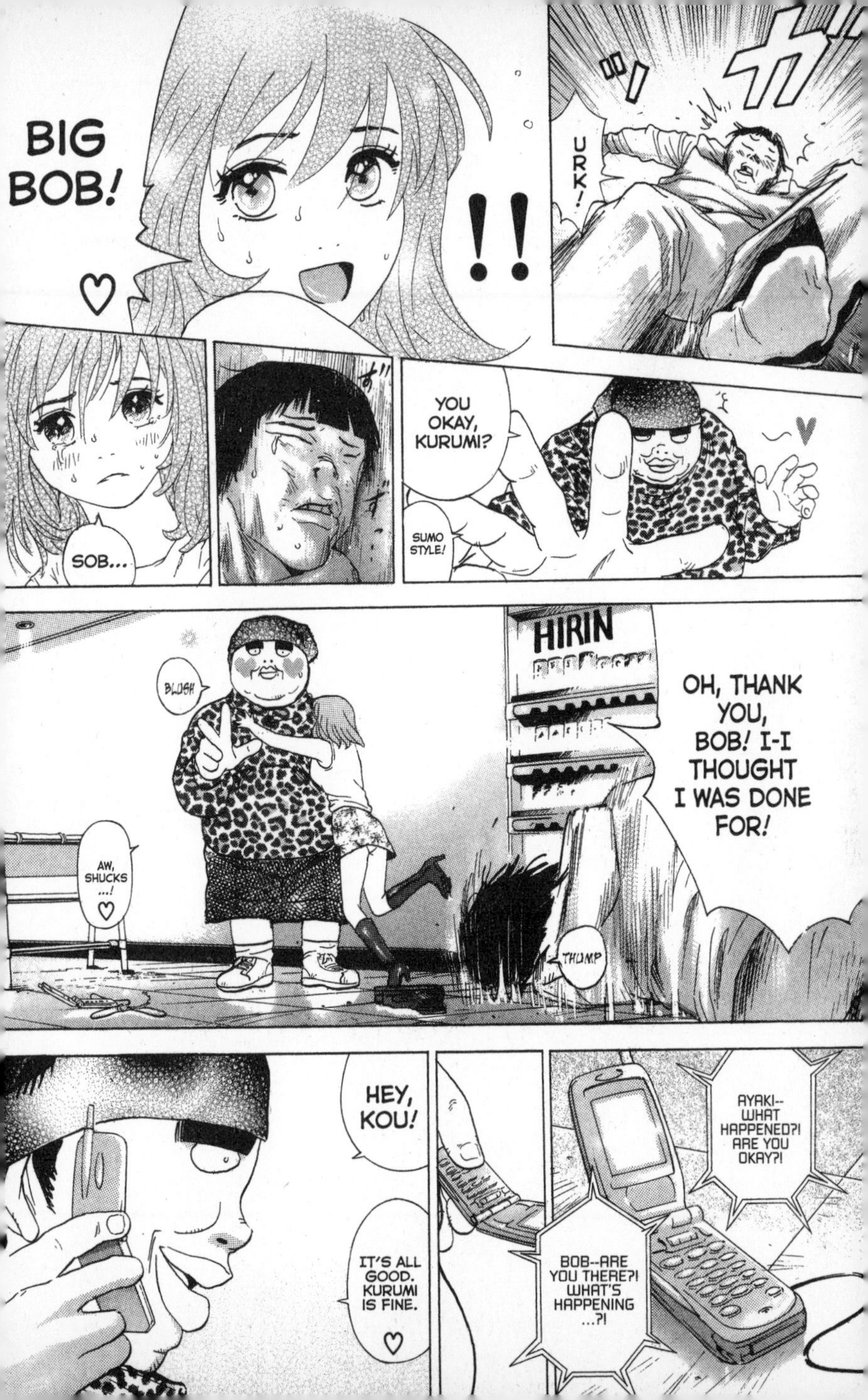
URK!
!!
BIG BOB! ♡
YOU OKAY, KURUMI?
SUMO STYLE!
SOB...
OH, THANK YOU, BOB! I-I THOUGHT I WAS DONE FOR!
HIRIN
THUMP
BLUSH
AW, SHUCKS...! ♡
AYAKI-- WHAT HAPPENED?! ARE YOU OKAY?!
BOB--ARE YOU THERE?! WHAT'S HAPPENING...?!
HEY, KOU!
IT'S ALL GOOD. KURUMI IS FINE. ♡

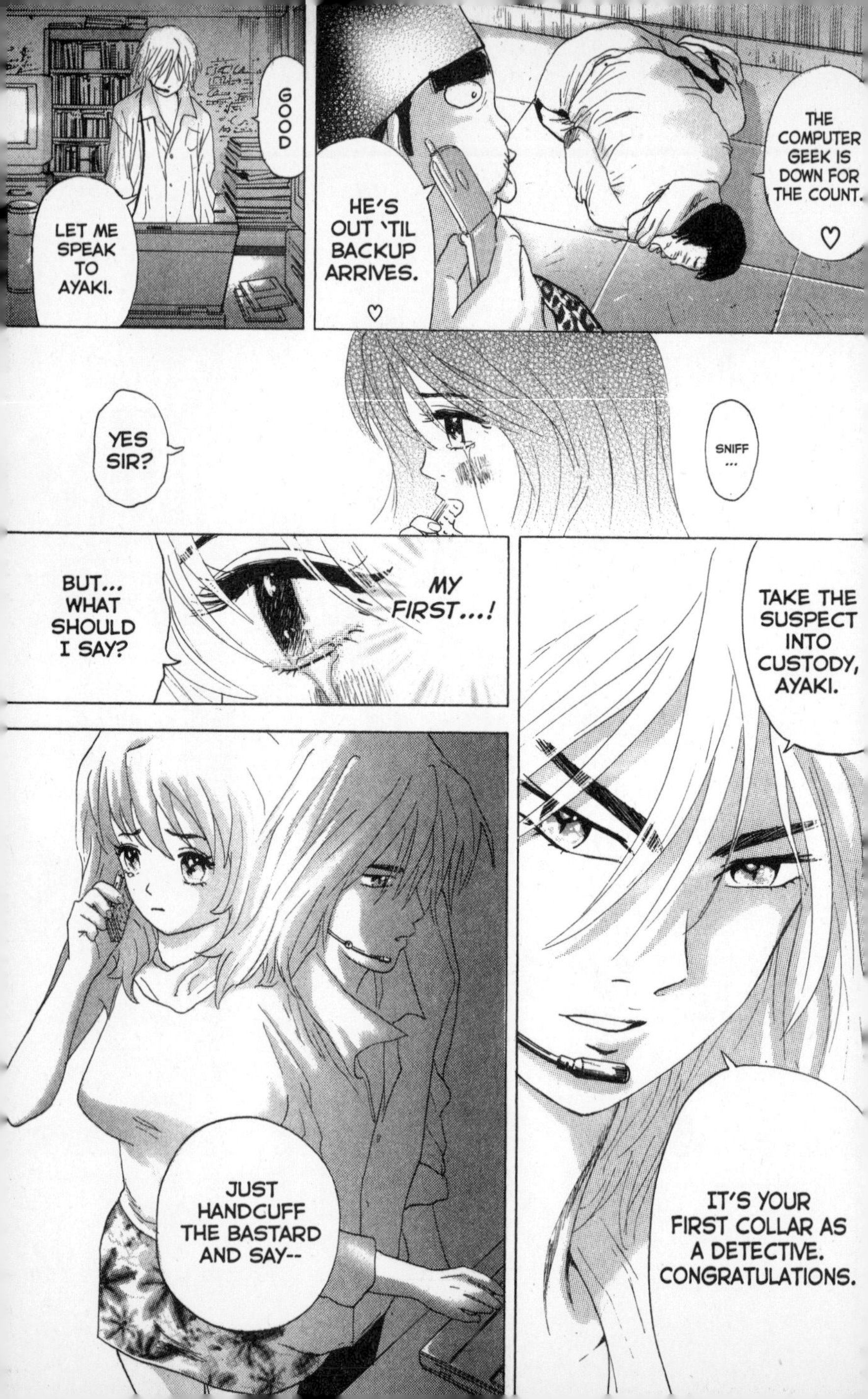
THE COMPUTER GEEK IS DOWN FOR THE COUNT. ♡
HE'S OUT 'TIL BACKUP ARRIVES. ♡
GOOD
LET ME SPEAK TO AYAKI.
SNIFF ...
YES SIR?
TAKE THE SUSPECT INTO CUSTODY, AYAKI.
IT'S YOUR FIRST COLLAR AS A DETECTIVE. CONGRATULATIONS.
MY FIRST...!
BUT... WHAT SHOULD I SAY?
JUST HANDCUFF THE BASTARD AND SAY--

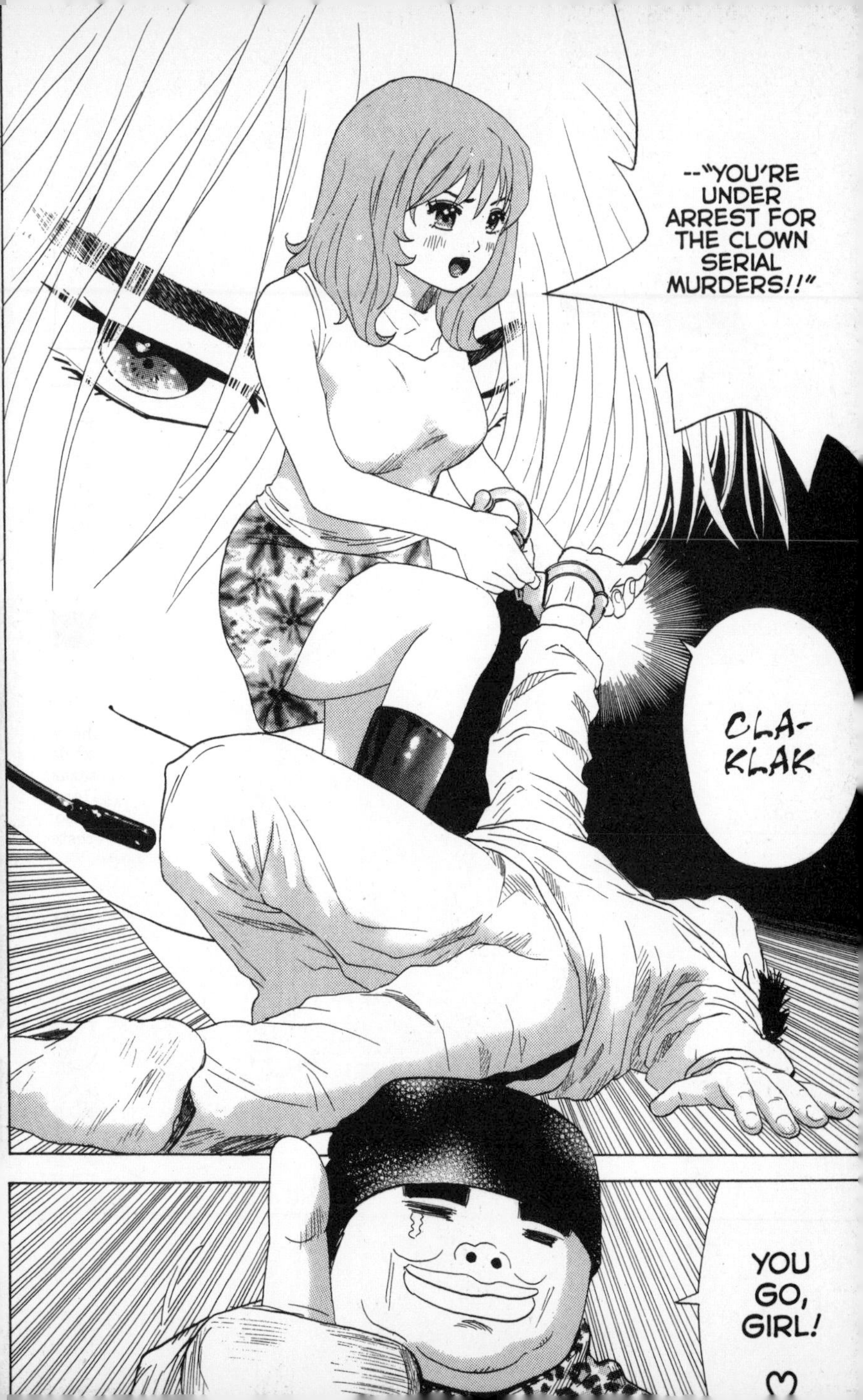
--"YOU'RE UNDER ARREST FOR THE CLOWN SERIAL MURDERS!!"
CLA-KLAK
YOU GO, GIRL! ♡

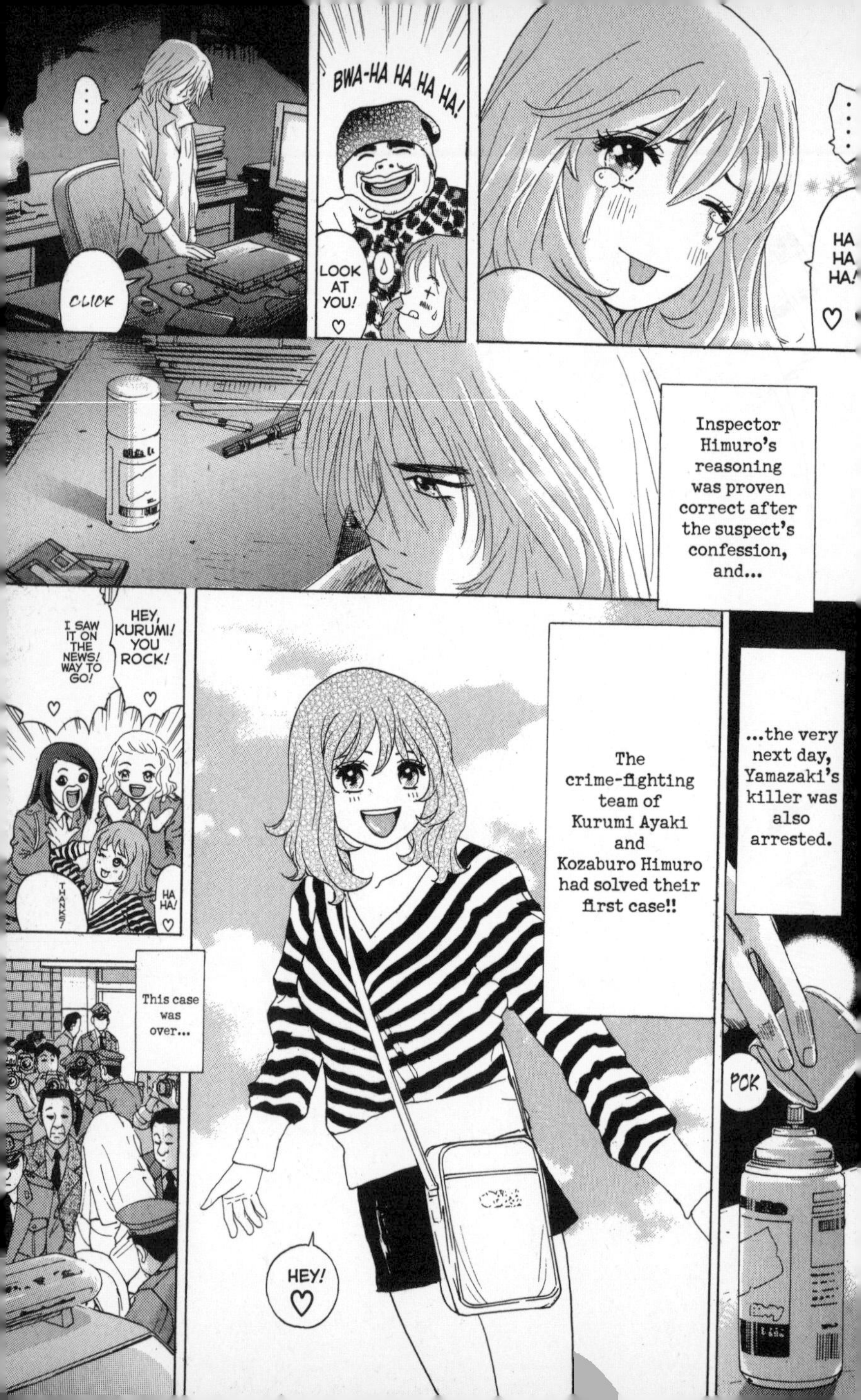
...
HA HA HA! ♡
BWA-HA HA HA HA!
LOOK AT YOU! ♡
...
CLICK
Inspector Himuro's reasoning was proven correct after the suspect's confession, and...
...the very next day, Yamazaki's killer was also arrested.
POK
The crime-fighting team of Kurumi Ayaki and Kozaburo Himuro had solved their first case!!
HEY! ♡
HEY, KURUMI! YOU ROCK!
I SAW IT ON THE NEWS! WAY TO GO!
HA HA! ♡
THANKS!
This case was over...

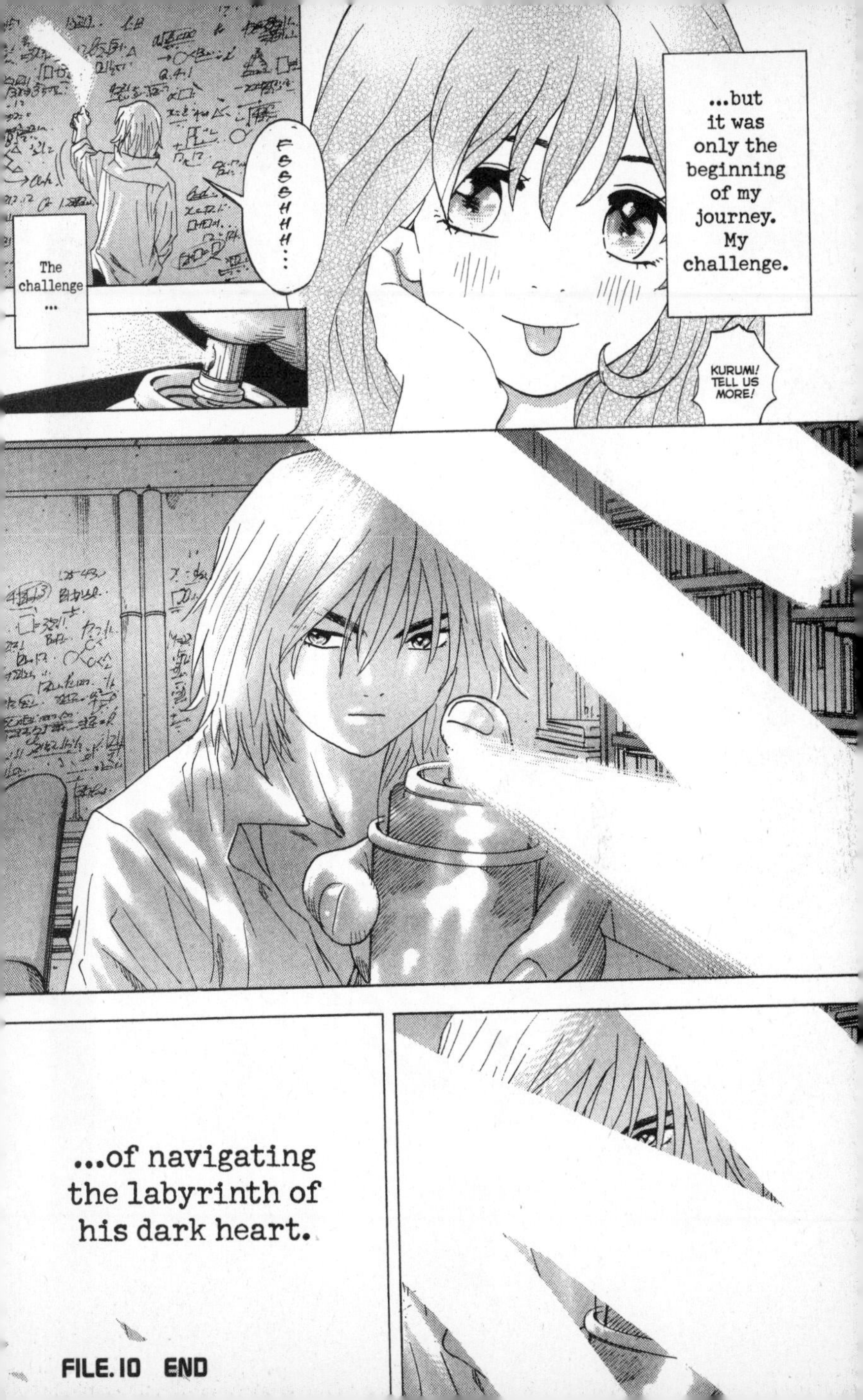
...but it was only the beginning of my journey. My challenge.
KURUMI! TELL US MORE!
FSSSHHH...
The challenge...
...of navigating the labyrinth of his dark heart.
FILE.10 END

case 2:
Survival School

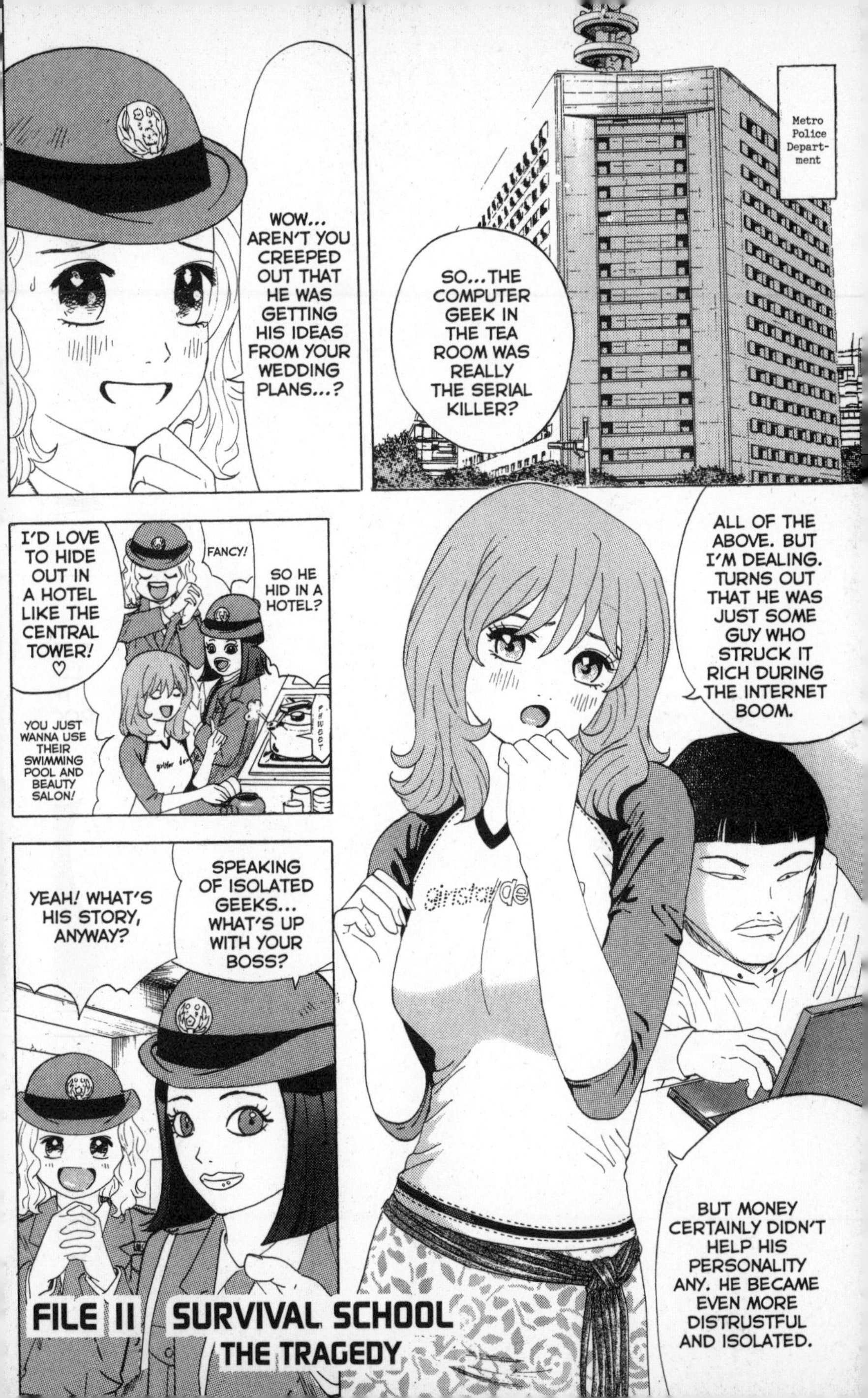
Metro Police Department
SO...THE COMPUTER GEEK IN THE TEA ROOM WAS REALLY THE SERIAL KILLER?
WOW... AREN'T YOU CREEPED OUT THAT HE WAS GETTING HIS IDEAS FROM YOUR WEDDING PLANS...?
ALL OF THE ABOVE. BUT I'M DEALING. TURNS OUT THAT HE WAS JUST SOME GUY WHO STRUCK IT RICH DURING THE INTERNET BOOM.
BUT MONEY CERTAINLY DIDN'T HELP HIS PERSONALITY ANY. HE BECAME EVEN MORE DISTRUSTFUL AND ISOLATED.
SO HE HID IN A HOTEL?
FANCY!
I'D LOVE TO HIDE OUT IN A HOTEL LIKE THE CENTRAL TOWER! ♡
YOU JUST WANNA USE THEIR SWIMMING POOL AND BEAUTY SALON!
SPEAKING OF ISOLATED GEEKS... WHAT'S UP WITH YOUR BOSS?
YEAH! WHAT'S HIS STORY, ANYWAY?
FILE 11 SURVIVAL SCHOOL
THE TRAGEDY

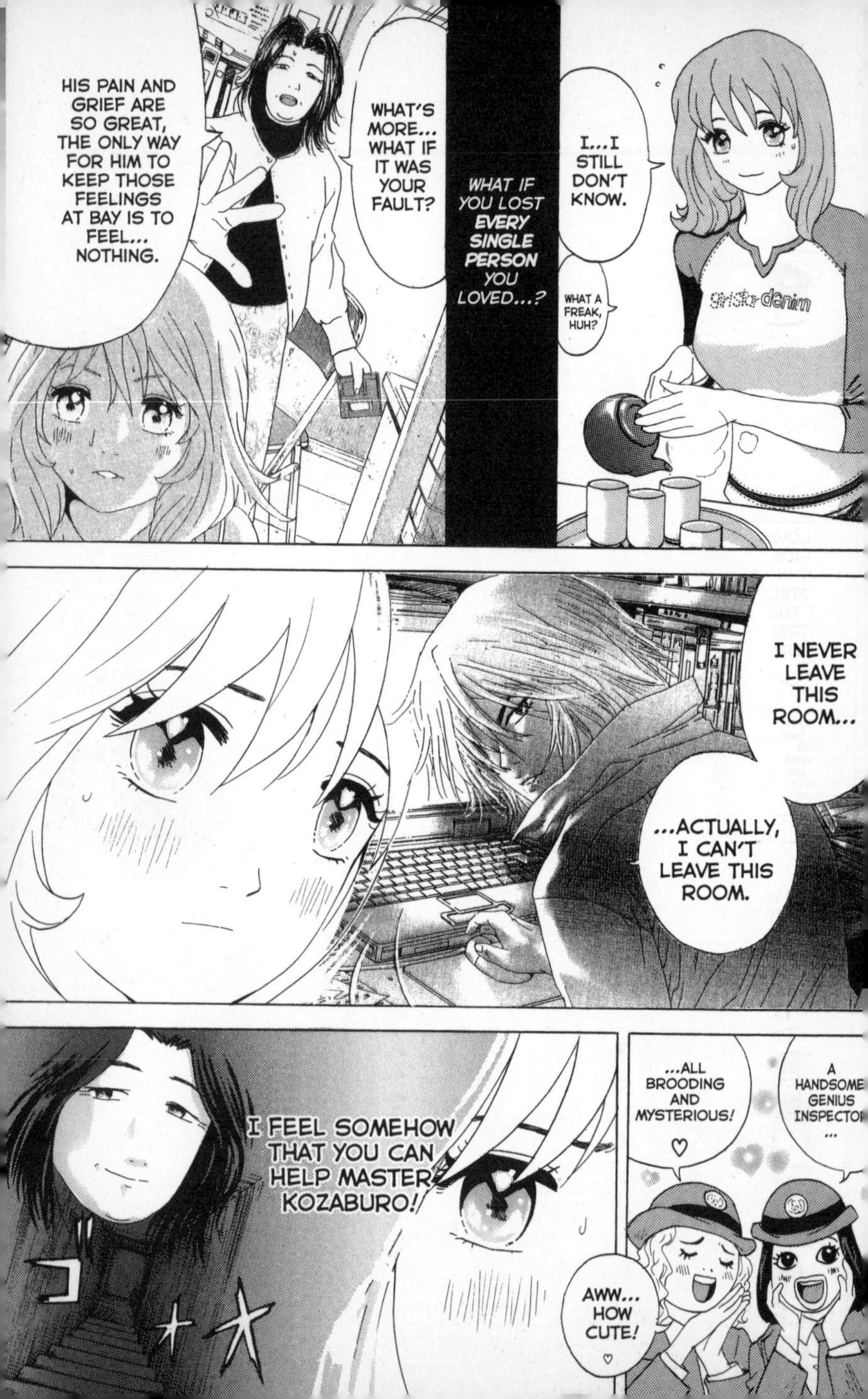
I...I STILL DON'T KNOW.
WHAT A FREAK, HUH?
WHAT IF YOU LOST EVERY SINGLE PERSON YOU LOVED...?
WHAT'S MORE... WHAT IF IT WAS YOUR FAULT?
HIS PAIN AND GRIEF ARE SO GREAT, THE ONLY WAY FOR HIM TO KEEP THOSE FEELINGS AT BAY IS TO FEEL... NOTHING.
I NEVER LEAVE THIS ROOM...
...ACTUALLY, I CAN'T LEAVE THIS ROOM.
A HANDSOME GENIUS INSPECTO ...
...ALL BROODING AND MYSTERIOUS! ♡
AWW... HOW CUTE! ♡
I FEEL SOMEHOW THAT YOU CAN HELP MASTER KOZABURO!

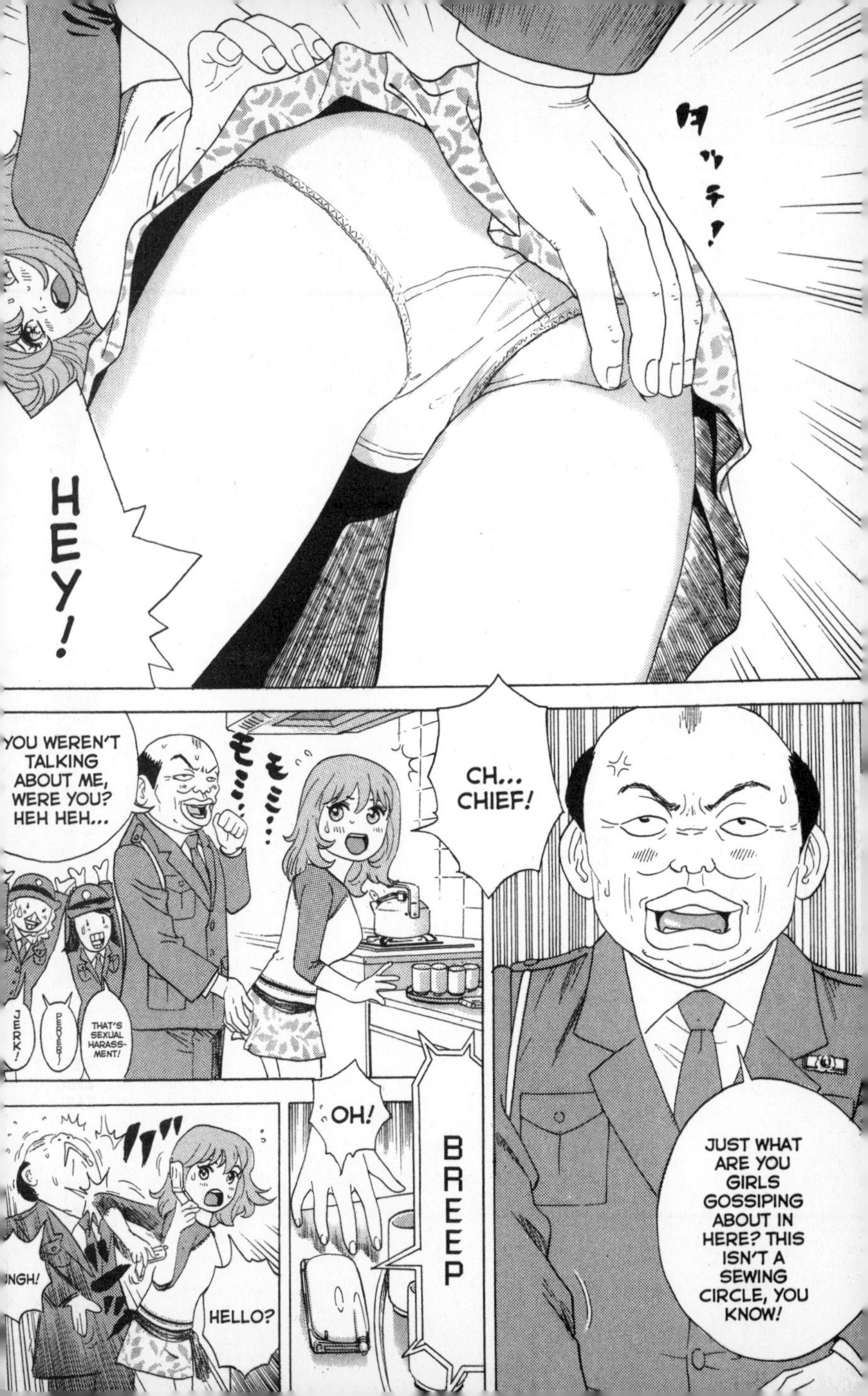
HEY!
JUST WHAT ARE YOU GIRLS GOSSIPING ABOUT IN HERE? THIS ISN'T A SEWING CIRCLE, YOU KNOW!
CH... CHIEF!
YOU WEREN'T TALKING ABOUT ME, WERE YOU? HEH HEH...
THAT'S SEXUAL HARASS-MENT!
PERVERT!
JERK!
OH!
BREEP
HELLO?
UNGH!

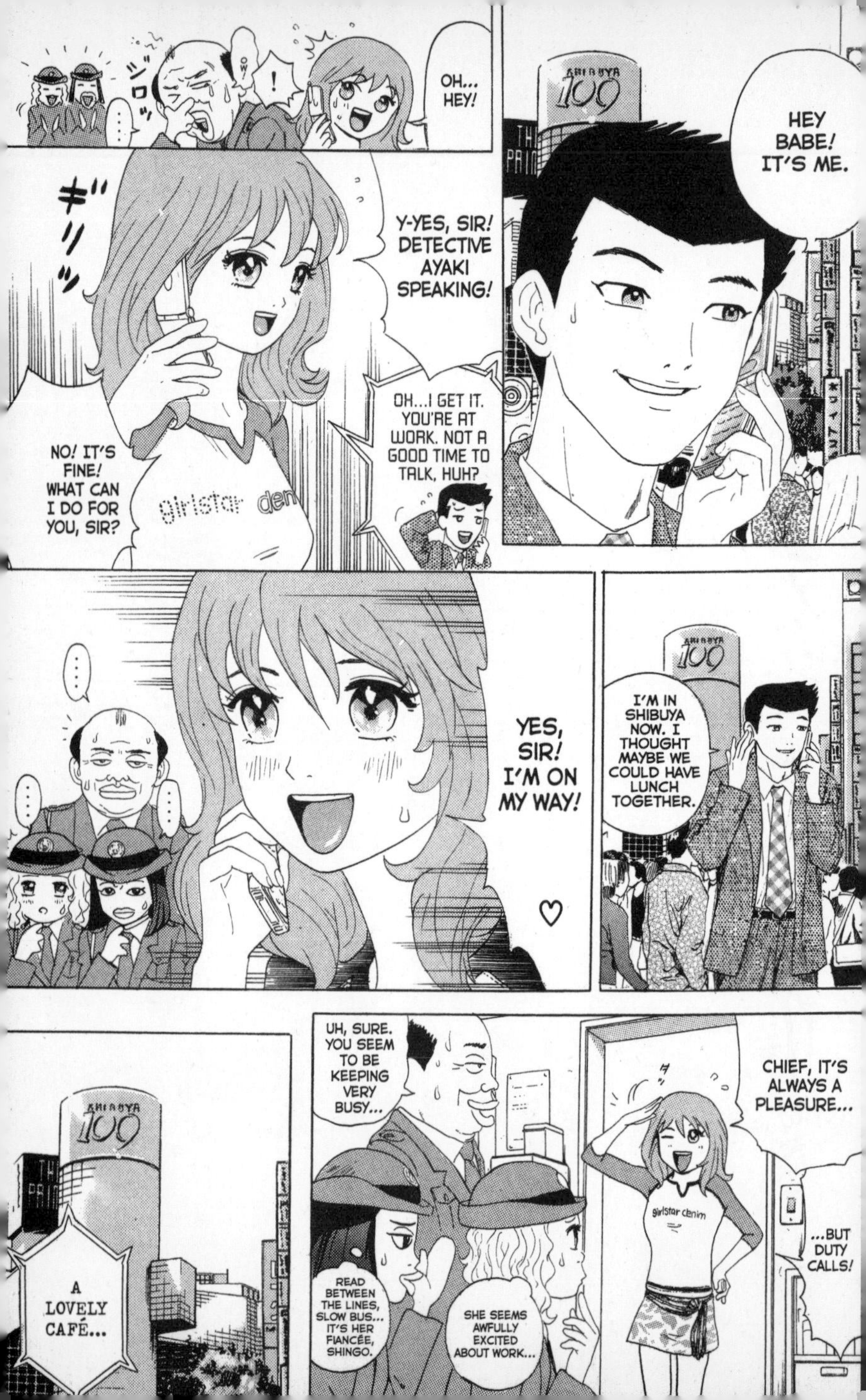
HEY BABE! IT'S ME.
OH... HEY!
!
OW!
ジロッ
. . .
ギリッ
Y-YES, SIR! DETECTIVE AYAKI SPEAKING!
OH...I GET IT. YOU'RE AT WORK. NOT A GOOD TIME TO TALK, HUH?
NO! IT'S FINE! WHAT CAN I DO FOR YOU, SIR?
I'M IN SHIBUYA NOW. I THOUGHT MAYBE WE COULD HAVE LUNCH TOGETHER.
YES, SIR! I'M ON MY WAY!
♡
. . .
. . .
. . .
CHIEF, IT'S ALWAYS A PLEASURE...
...BUT DUTY CALLS!
UH, SURE. YOU SEEM TO BE KEEPING VERY BUSY...
SHE SEEMS AWFULLY EXCITED ABOUT WORK...
READ BETWEEN THE LINES, SLOW BUS... IT'S HER FIANCÉE, SHINGO.
A LOVELY CAFÉ...

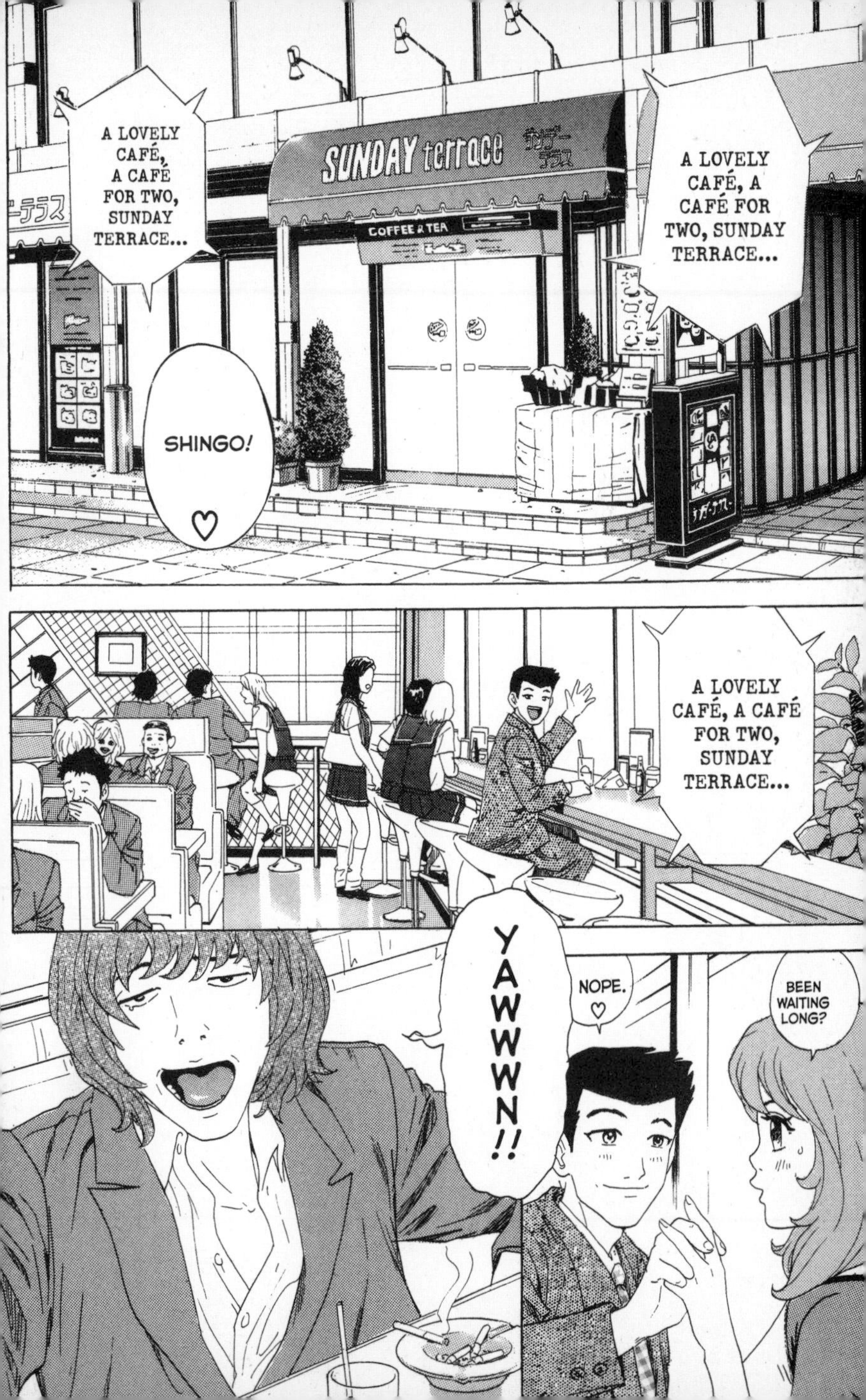
SUNDAY terrace
COFFEE & TEA
A LOVELY CAFÉ, A CAFÉ FOR TWO, SUNDAY TERRACE...
A LOVELY CAFÉ, A CAFÉ FOR TWO, SUNDAY TERRACE...
SHINGO! ♡
A LOVELY CAFÉ, A CAFÉ FOR TWO, SUNDAY TERRACE...
BEEN WAITING LONG?
NOPE. ♡
YAWWWN!!

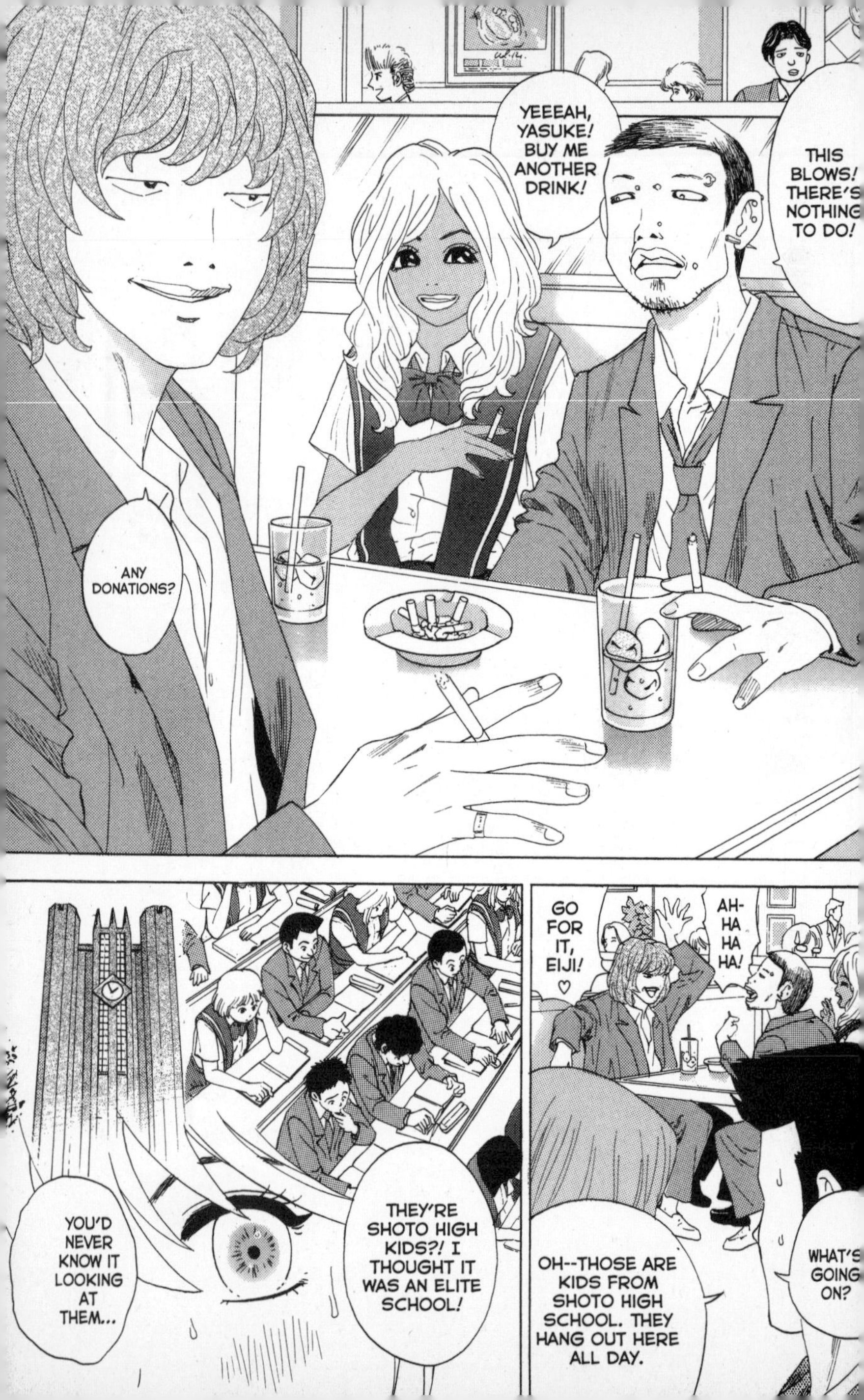
THIS BLOWS! THERE'S NOTHING TO DO!
YEEEAH, YASUKE! BUY ME ANOTHER DRINK!
ANY DONATIONS?
AH-HA HA HA!
GO FOR IT, EIJI! ♡
WHAT'S GOING ON?
OH--THOSE ARE KIDS FROM SHOTO HIGH SCHOOL. THEY HANG OUT HERE ALL DAY.
THEY'RE SHOTO HIGH KIDS?! I THOUGHT IT WAS AN ELITE SCHOOL!
YOU'D NEVER KNOW IT LOOKING AT THEM...

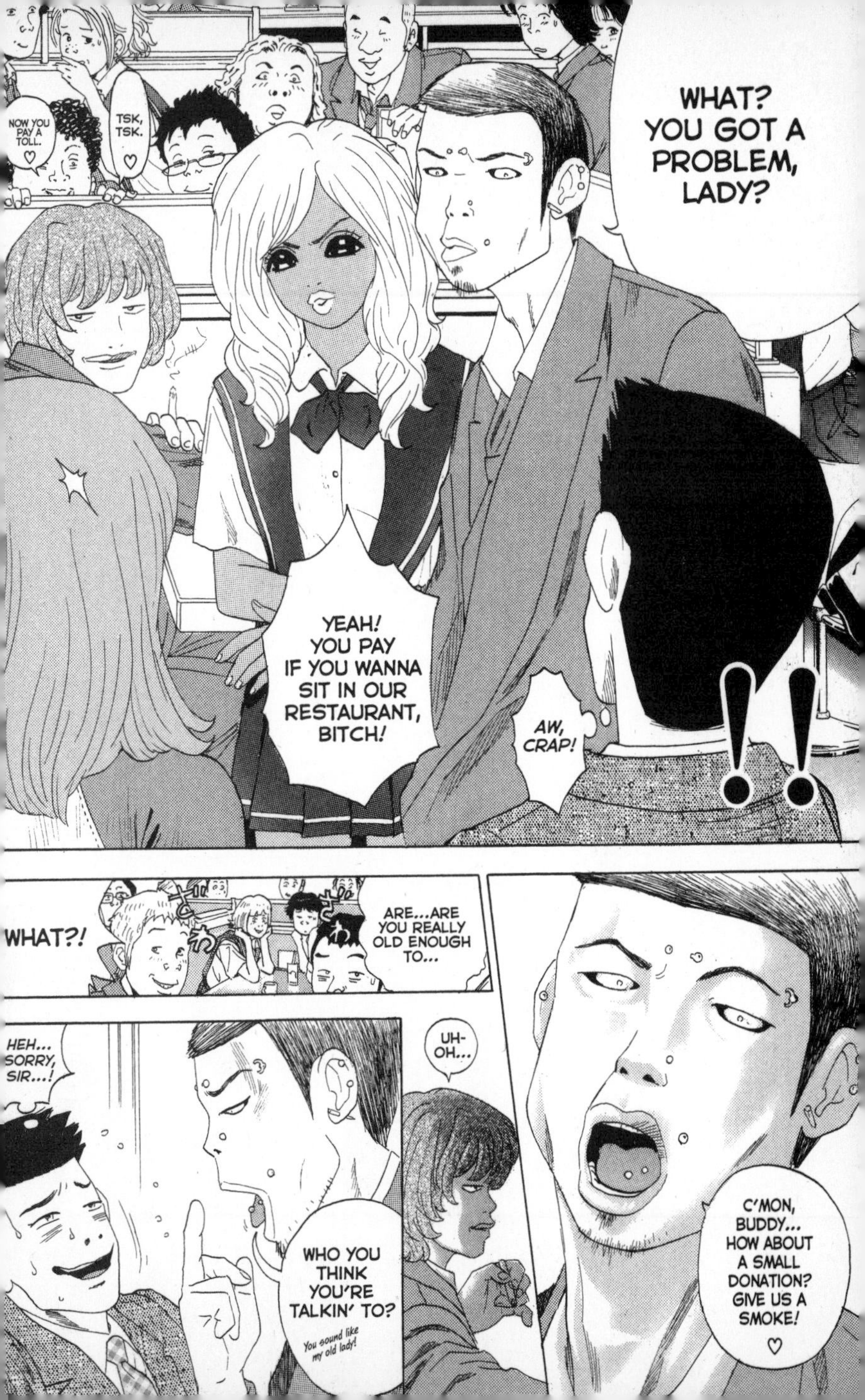
WHAT? YOU GOT A PROBLEM, LADY?
TSK, TSK. ♡
NOW YOU PAY A TOLL. ♡
YEAH! YOU PAY IF YOU WANNA SIT IN OUR RESTAURANT, BITCH!
AW, CRAP!
!!
C'MON, BUDDY... HOW ABOUT A SMALL DONATION? GIVE US A SMOKE! ♡
ARE...ARE YOU REALLY OLD ENOUGH TO...
WHAT?!
UH-OH...
WHO YOU THINK YOU'RE TALKIN' TO?
You sound like my old lady!
HEH... SORRY, SIR...!

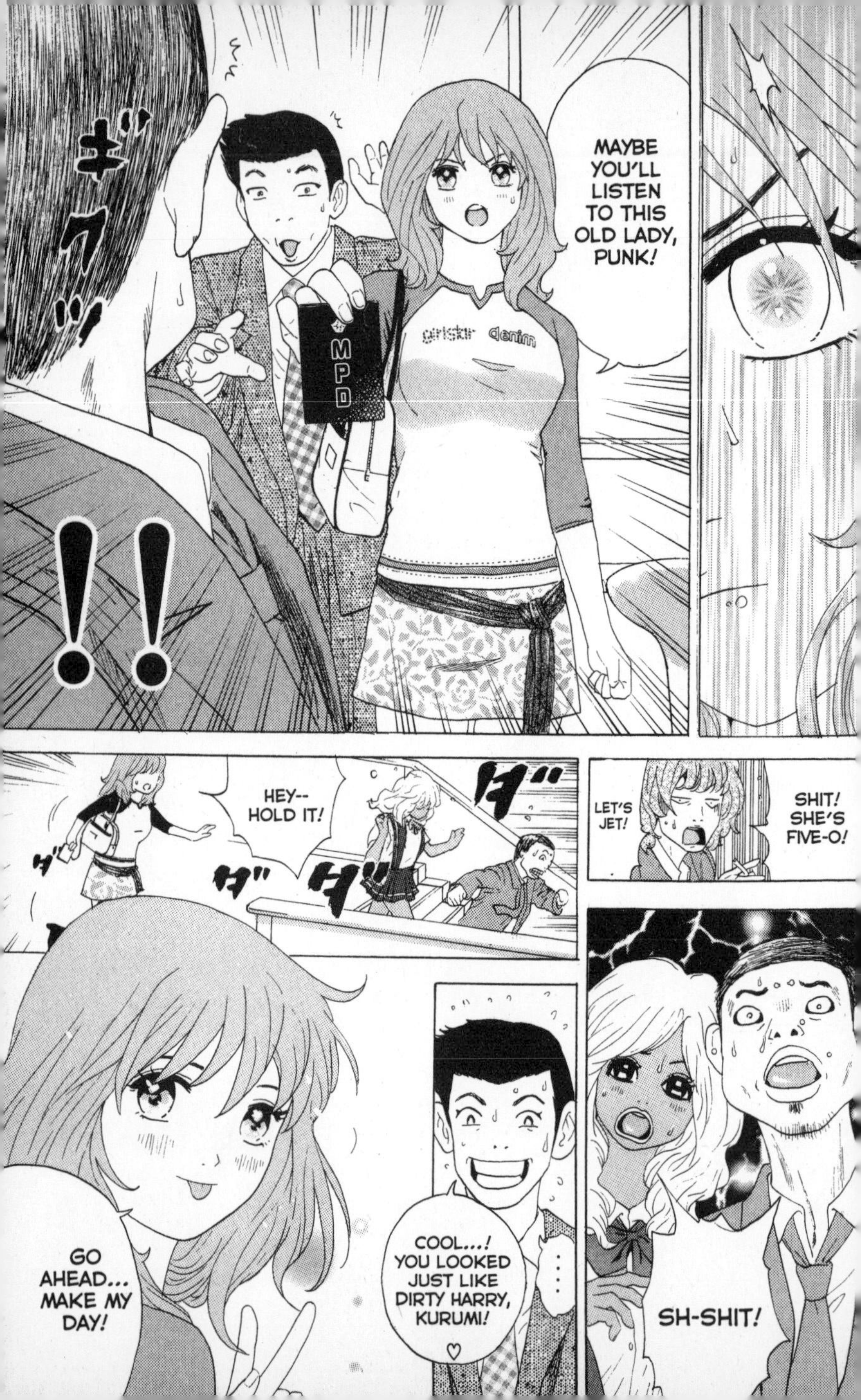
MAYBE YOU'LL LISTEN TO THIS OLD LADY, PUNK!
!!
SHIT! SHE'S FIVE-O!
LET'S JET!
HEY-- HOLD IT!
SH-SHIT!
COOL...! YOU LOOKED JUST LIKE DIRTY HARRY, KURUMI!
....
GO AHEAD... MAKE MY DAY!

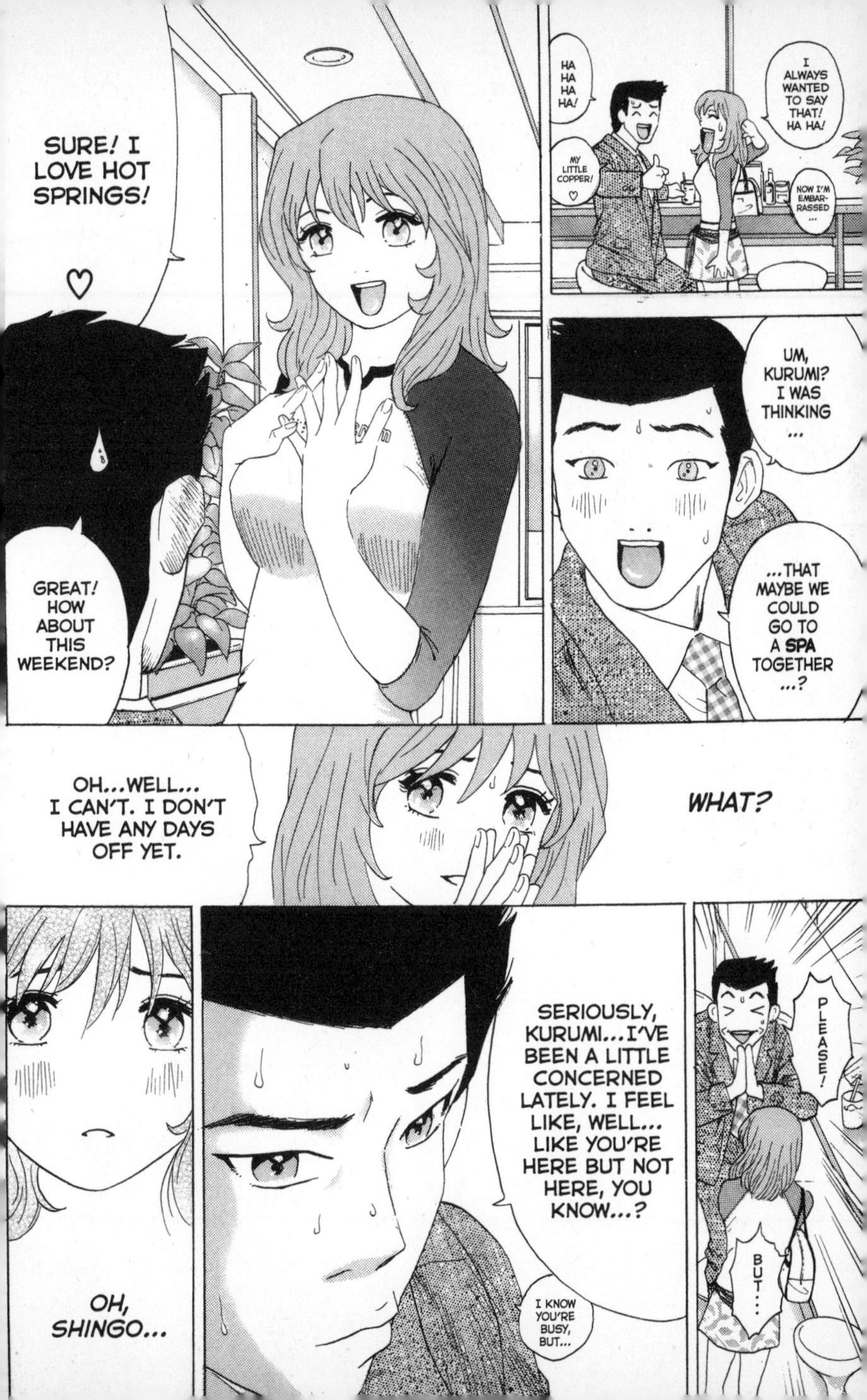

I ALWAYS WANTED TO SAY THAT! HA HA!
HA HA HA HA!
NOW I'M EMBARRASSED...
MY LITTLE COPPER! ♡
UM, KURUMI? I WAS THINKING...
...THAT MAYBE WE COULD GO TO A **SPA** TOGETHER...?
SURE! I LOVE HOT SPRINGS! ♡
GREAT! HOW ABOUT THIS WEEKEND?
WHAT?
OH...WELL... I CAN'T. I DON'T HAVE ANY DAYS OFF YET.
PLEASE!
BUT...
SERIOUSLY, KURUMI...I'VE BEEN A LITTLE CONCERNED LATELY. I FEEL LIKE, WELL... LIKE YOU'RE HERE BUT NOT HERE, YOU KNOW...?
I KNOW YOU'RE BUSY, BUT...
OH, SHINGO...

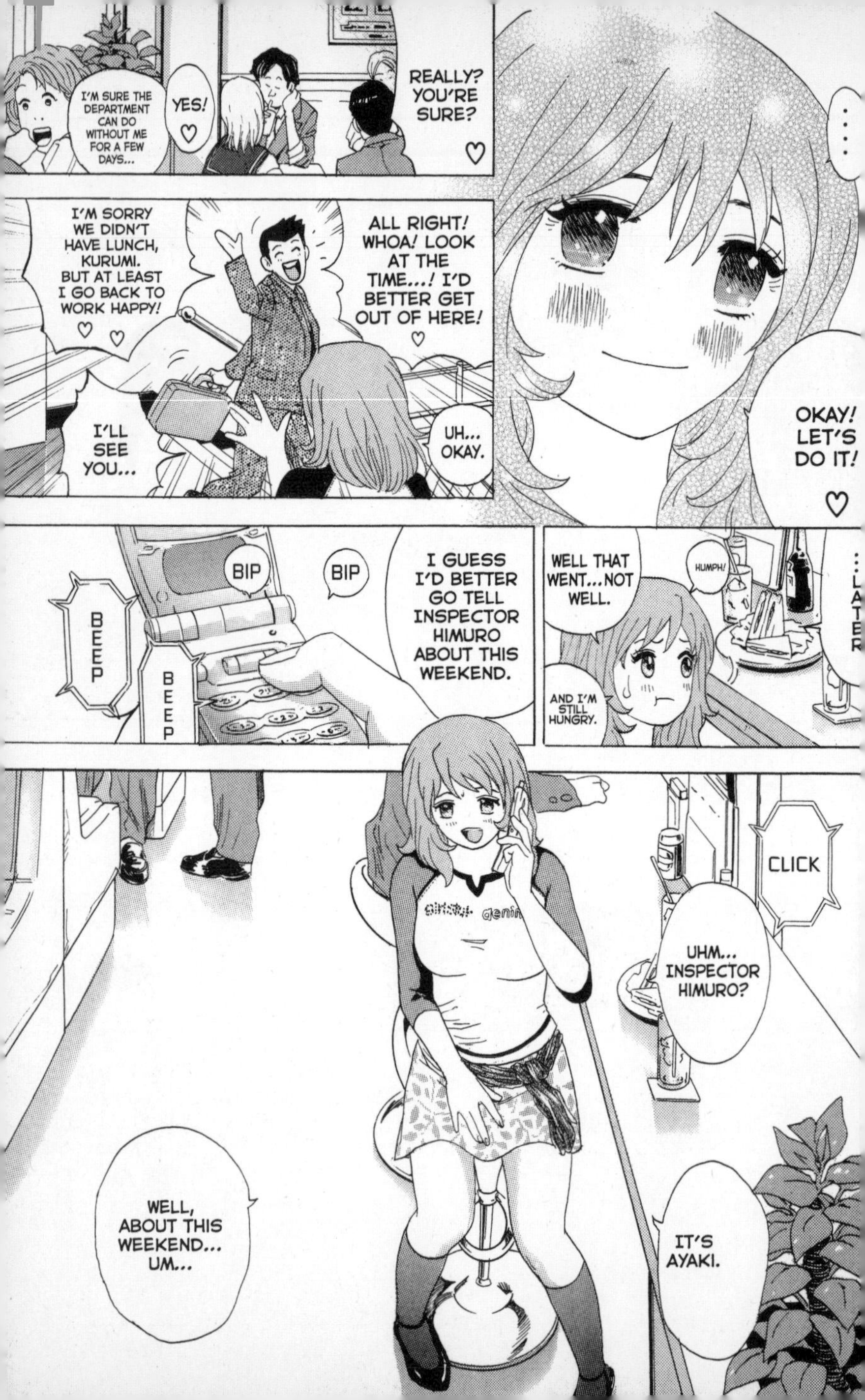
...
OKAY! LET'S DO IT! ♡
REALLY? YOU'RE SURE? ♡
YES! ♡
I'M SURE THE DEPARTMENT CAN DO WITHOUT ME FOR A FEW DAYS...
ALL RIGHT! WHOA! LOOK AT THE TIME...! I'D BETTER GET OUT OF HERE! ♡
I'M SORRY WE DIDN'T HAVE LUNCH, KURUMI. BUT AT LEAST I GO BACK TO WORK HAPPY! ♡ ♡
UH... OKAY.
I'LL SEE YOU...
...LATER
HUMPH!
WELL THAT WENT...NOT WELL.
AND I'M STILL HUNGRY.
I GUESS I'D BETTER GO TELL INSPECTOR HIMURO ABOUT THIS WEEKEND.
BIP
BIP
BEEP
BEEP
CLICK
UHM... INSPECTOR HIMURO?
IT'S AYAKI.
WELL, ABOUT THIS WEEKEND... UM...

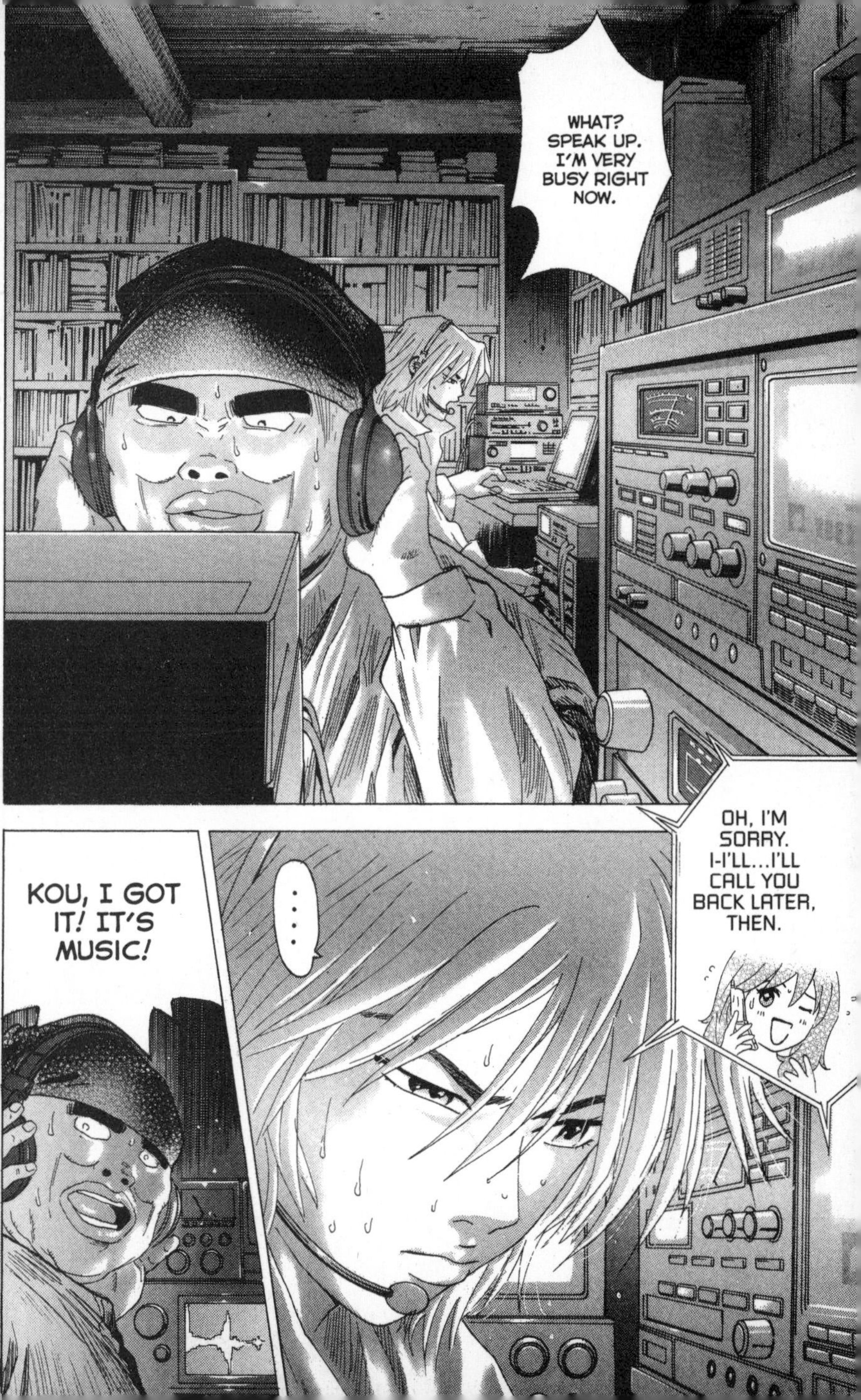
WHAT? SPEAK UP. I'M VERY BUSY RIGHT NOW.
OH, I'M SORRY. I-I'LL...I'LL CALL YOU BACK LATER, THEN.
....
KOU, I GOT IT! IT'S MUSIC!

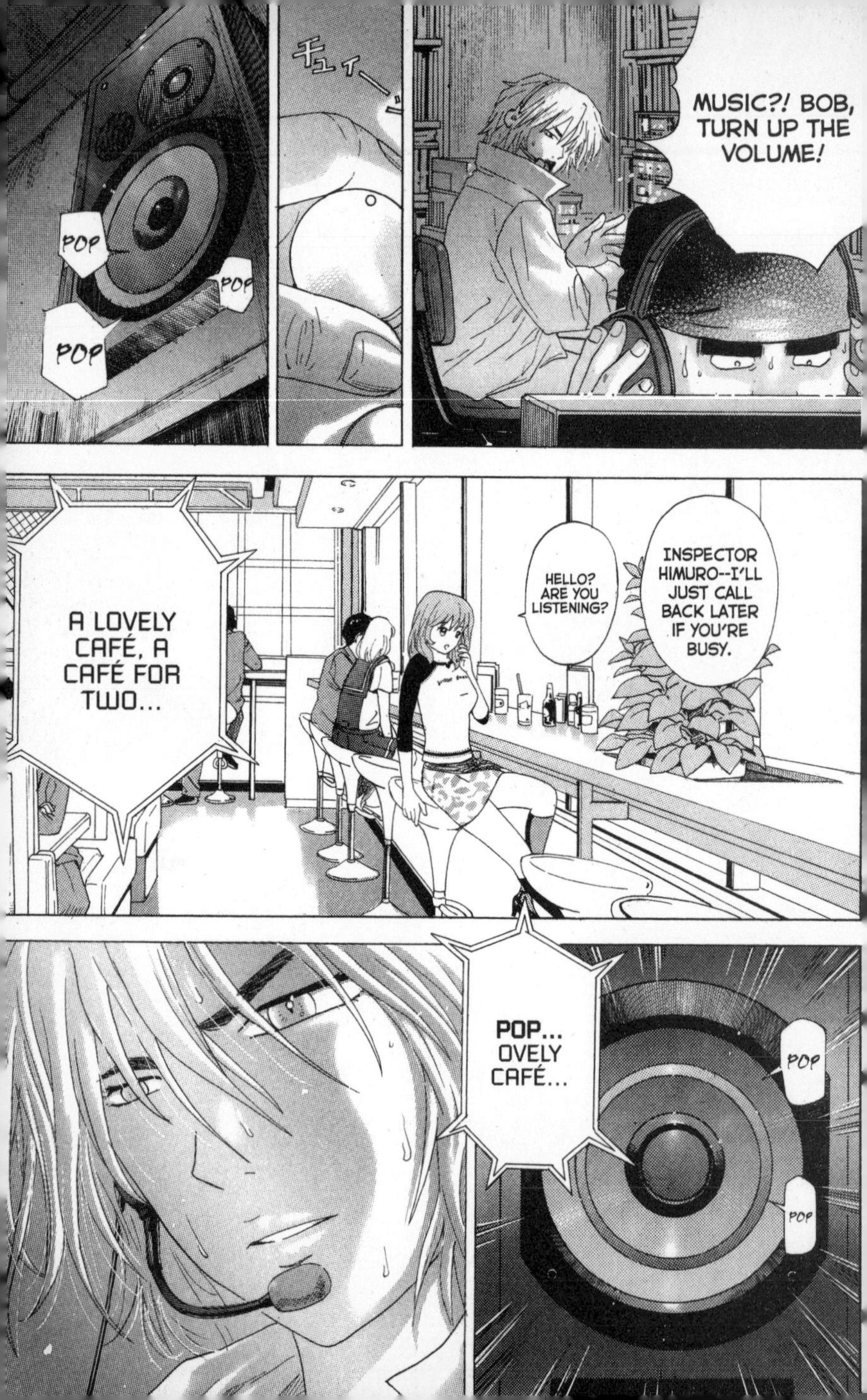
MUSIC?! BOB, TURN UP THE VOLUME!
チュイーー
POP
POP
POP
INSPECTOR HIMURO--I'LL JUST CALL BACK LATER IF YOU'RE BUSY.
HELLO? ARE YOU LISTENING?
A LOVELY CAFÉ, A CAFÉ FOR TWO...
POP
POP... OVELY CAFÉ...
POP

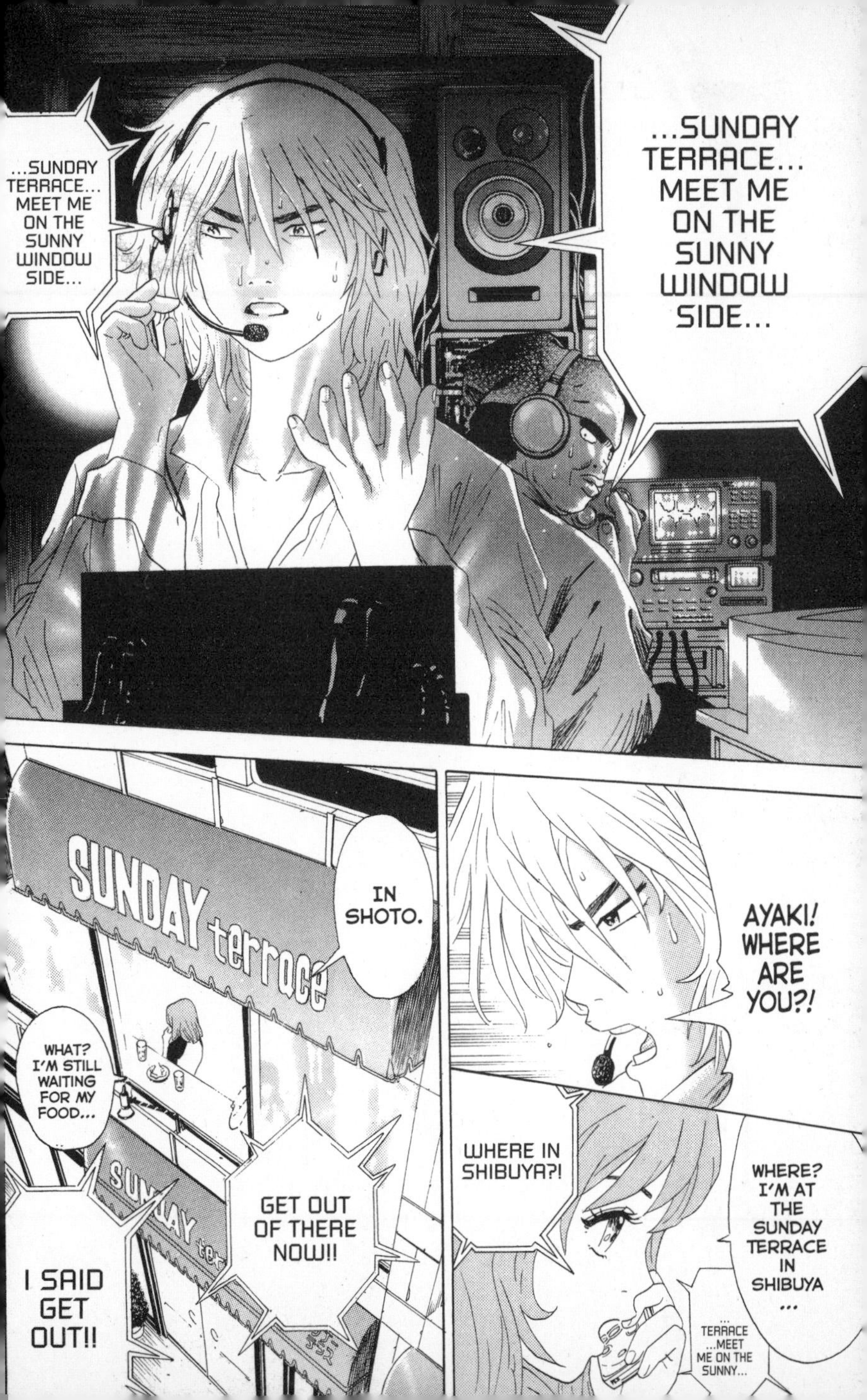
...SUNDAY TERRACE... MEET ME ON THE SUNNY WINDOW SIDE...
...SUNDAY TERRACE... MEET ME ON THE SUNNY WINDOW SIDE...
AYAKI! WHERE ARE YOU?!
WHERE? I'M AT THE SUNDAY TERRACE IN SHIBUYA ...
WHERE IN SHIBUYA?!
... TERRACE ...MEET ME ON THE SUNNY...
SUNDAY terrace
IN SHOTO.
WHAT? I'M STILL WAITING FOR MY FOOD...
GET OUT OF THERE NOW!!
I SAID GET OUT!!

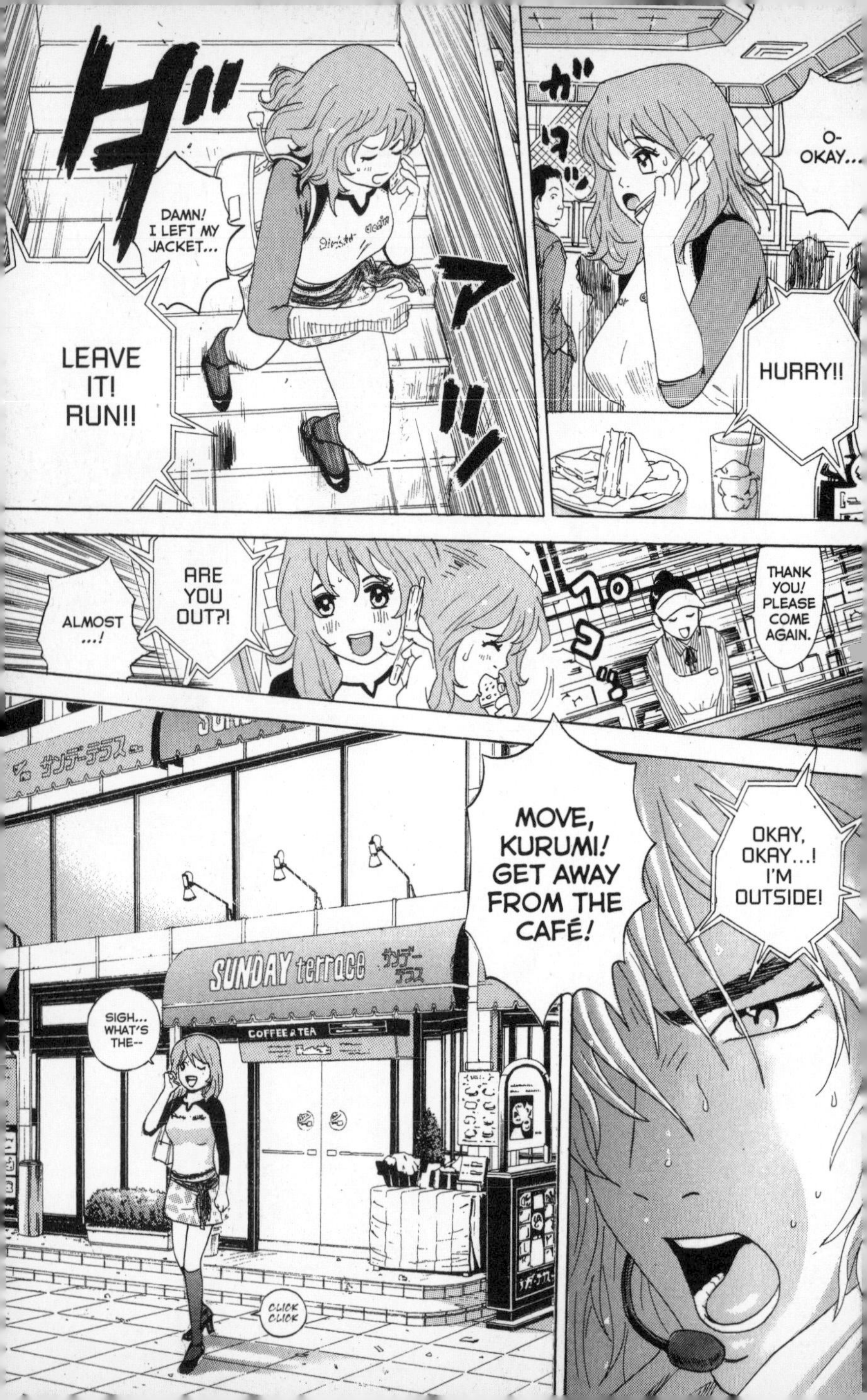
O-
OKAY...
HURRY!!
DAMN! I LEFT MY JACKET...
LEAVE IT! RUN!!
THANK YOU! PLEASE COME AGAIN.
ARE YOU OUT?!
ALMOST ...!
OKAY, OKAY...! I'M OUTSIDE!
MOVE, KURUMI! GET AWAY FROM THE CAFÉ!
SUNDAY terrace
COFFEE & TEA
SIGH... WHAT'S THE--
CLICK CLICK

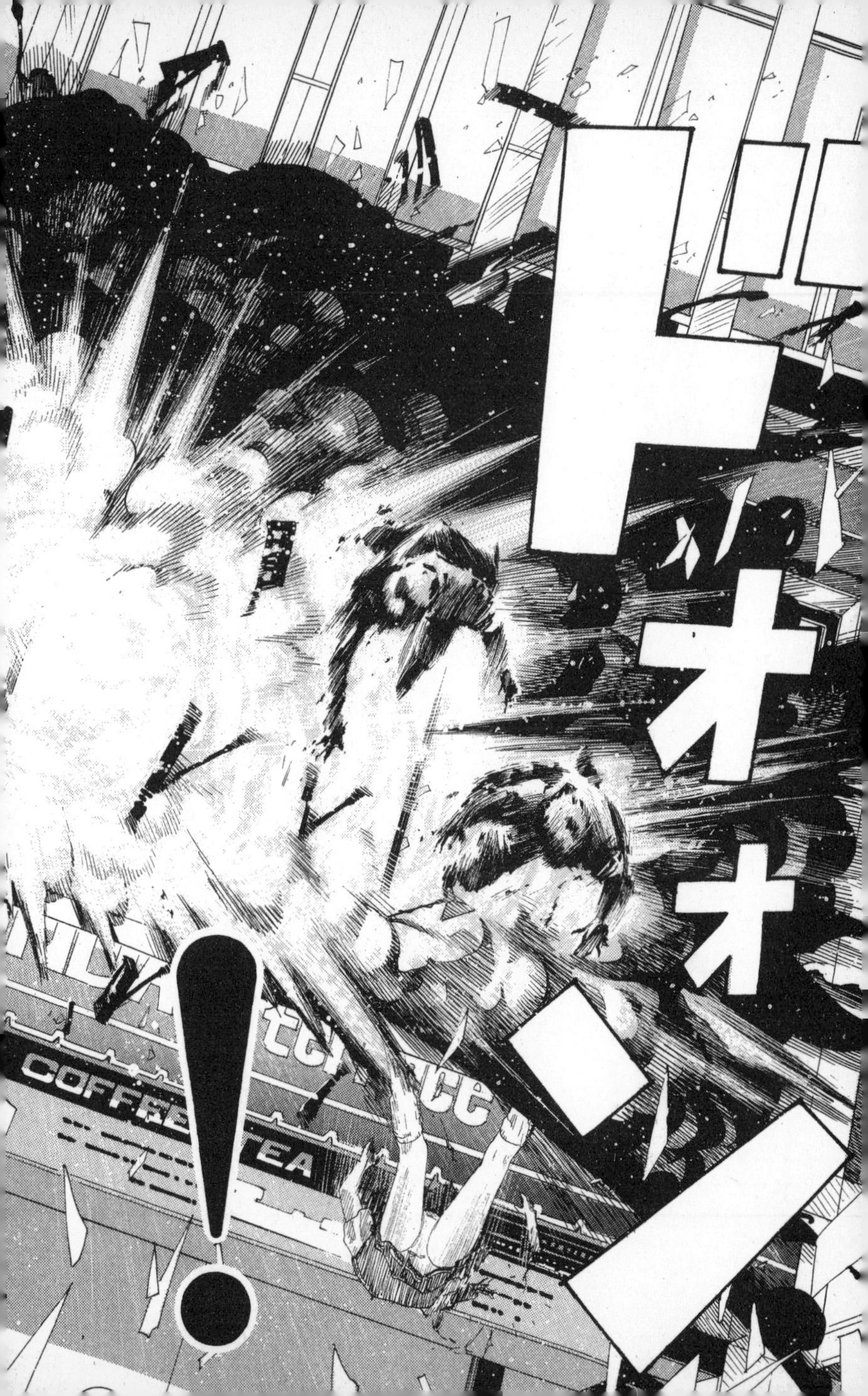
ドオオーン
!
TEA

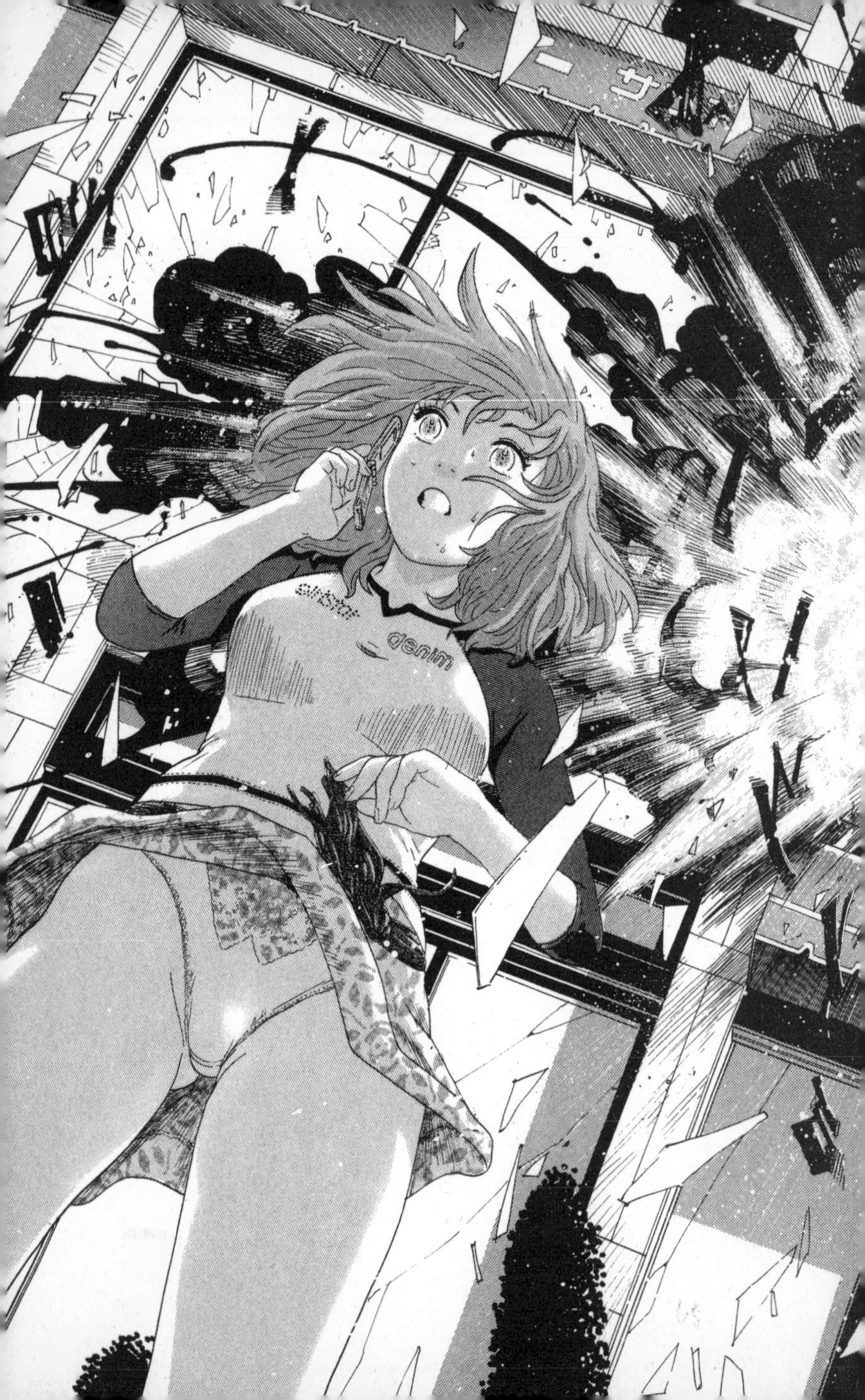
denim

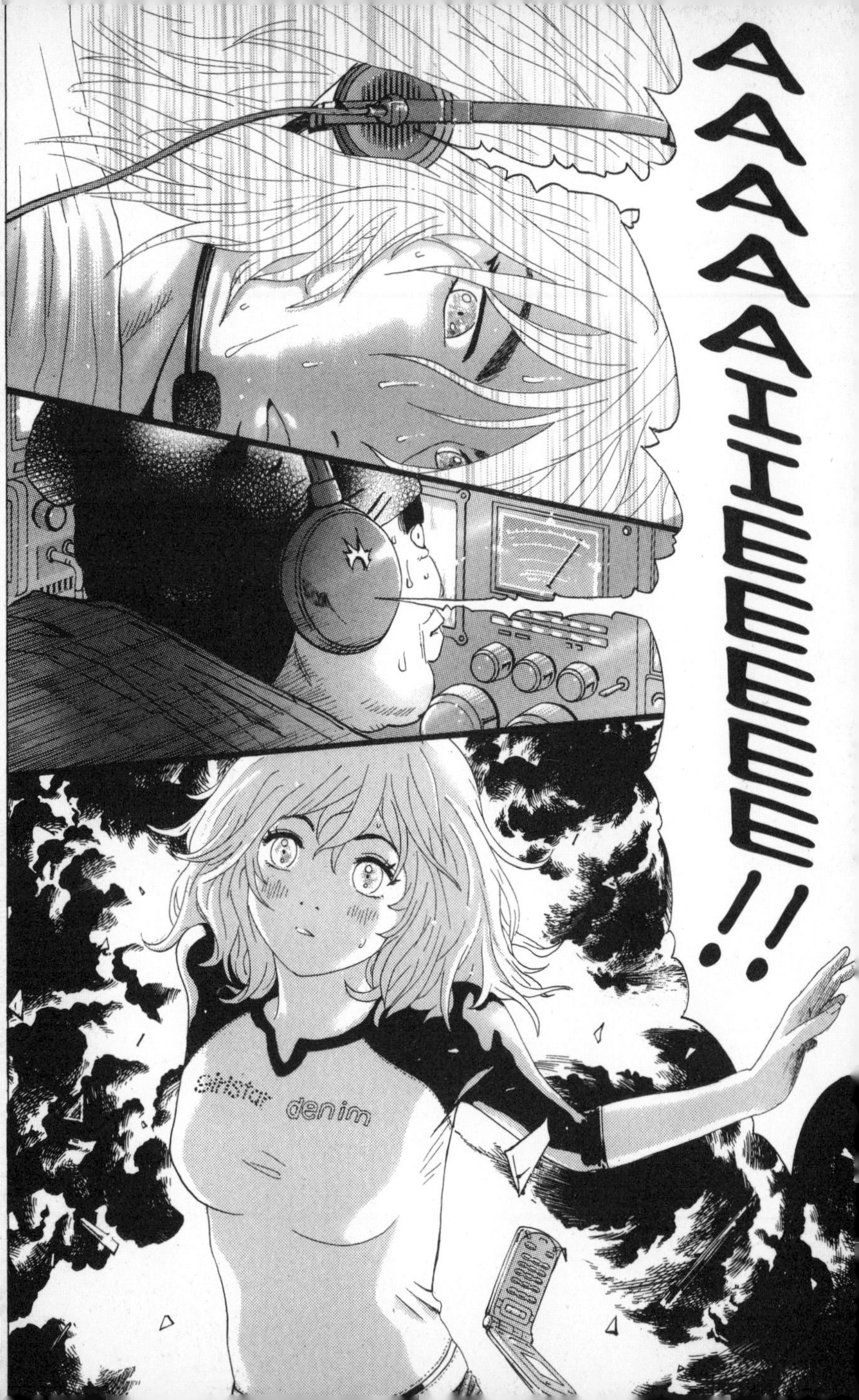
AAAAAIIEEEEE!!
denim

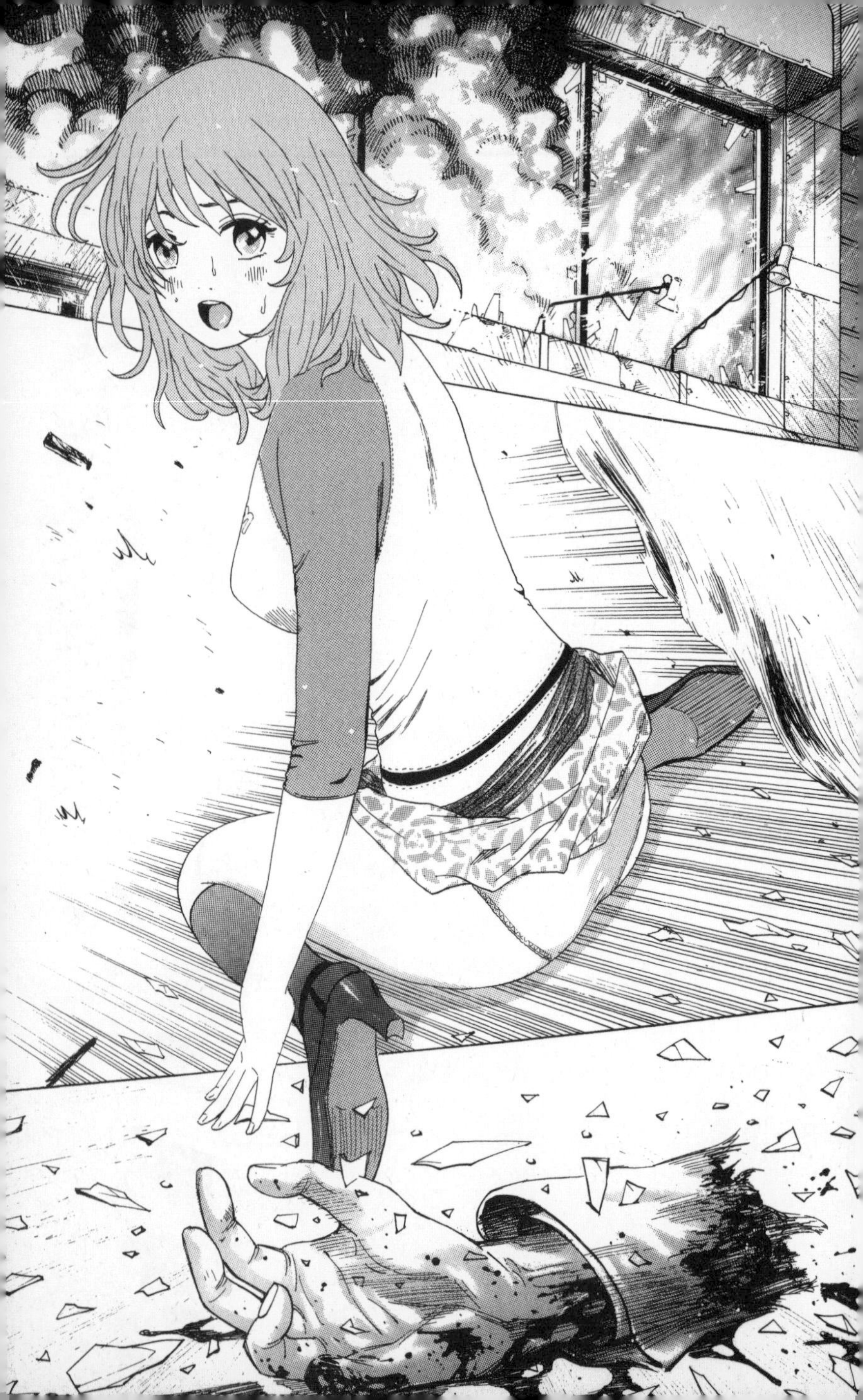

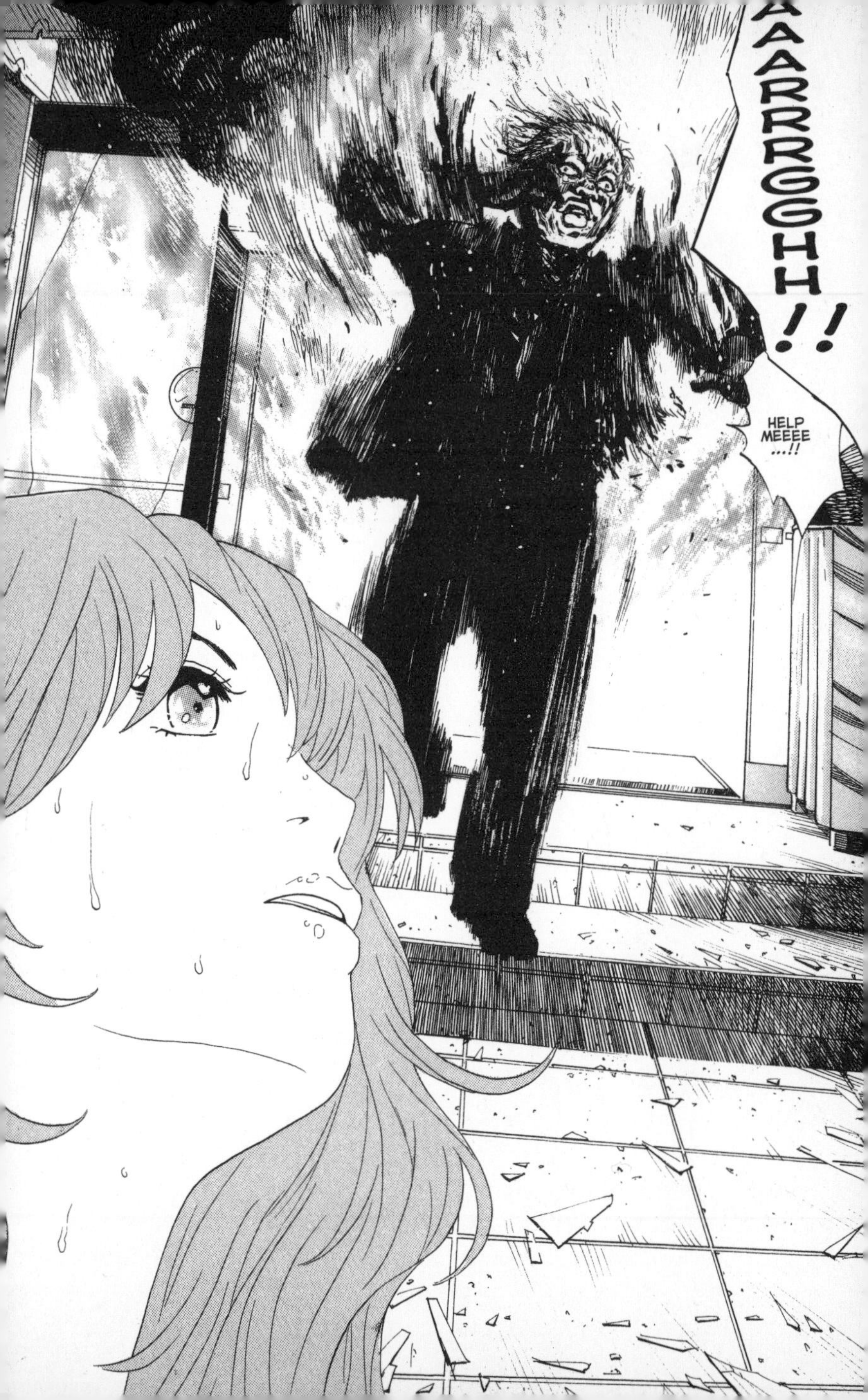
AAARRRGGH!!
HELP MEEEE ...!!

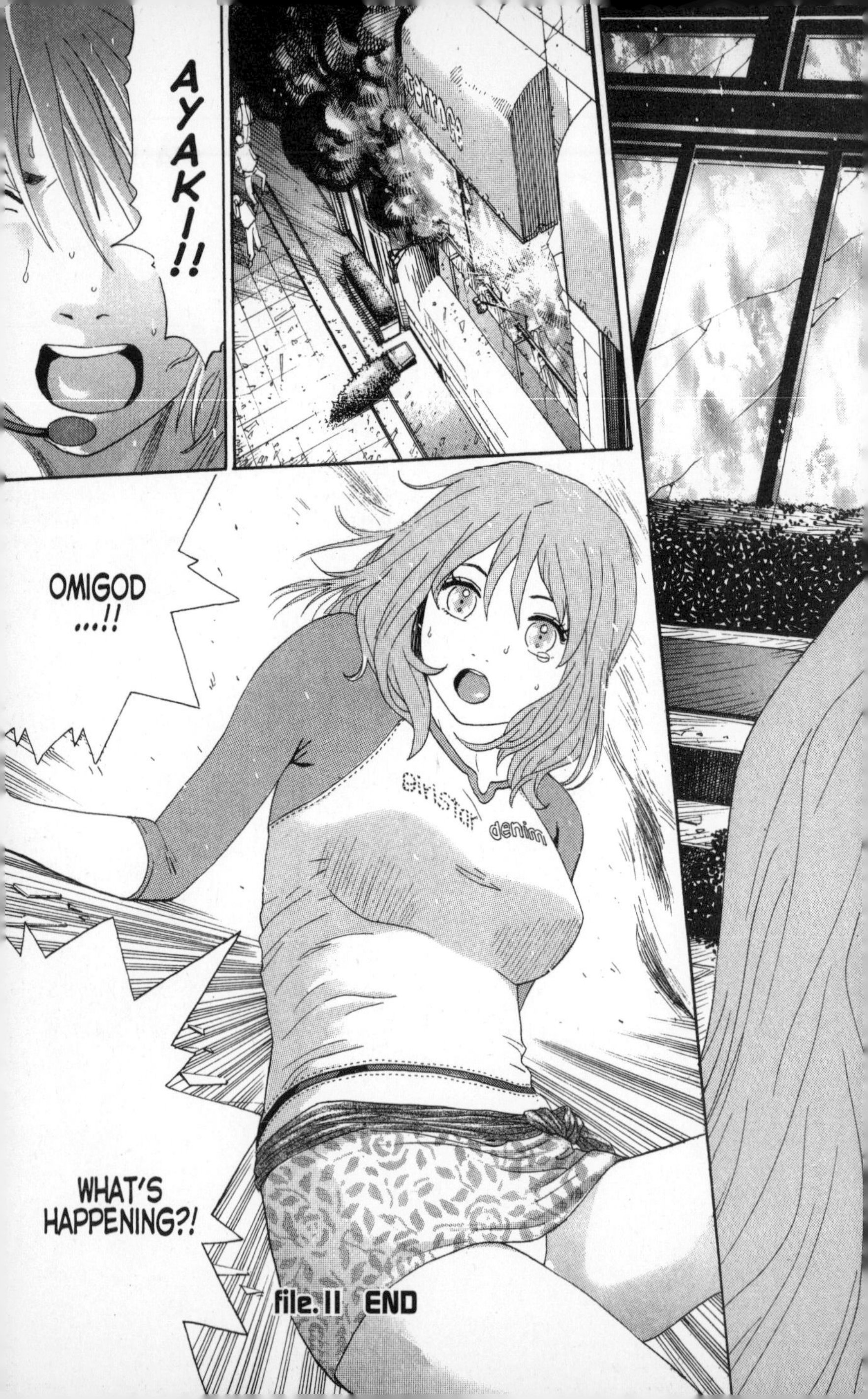
AYAKI!!
OMIGOD ...!!
WHAT'S HAPPENING?!
file.11 END

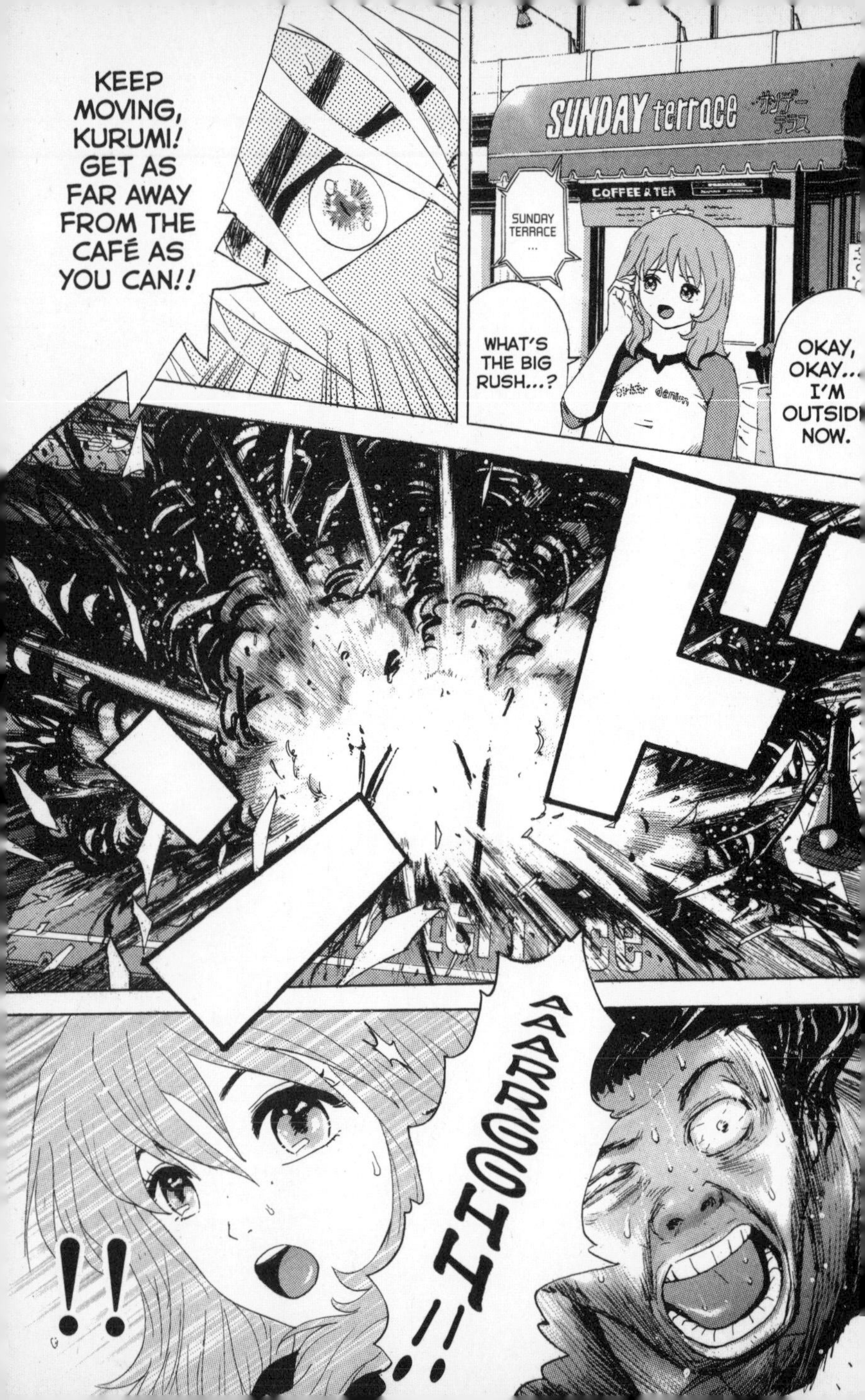
OKAY, OKAY... I'M OUTSID NOW.
SUNDAY TERRACE ...
WHAT'S THE BIG RUSH...?
SUNDAY terrace
COFFEE & TEA
KEEP MOVING, KURUMI! GET AS FAR AWAY FROM THE CAFÉ AS YOU CAN!!
AAARROOII!!
!!

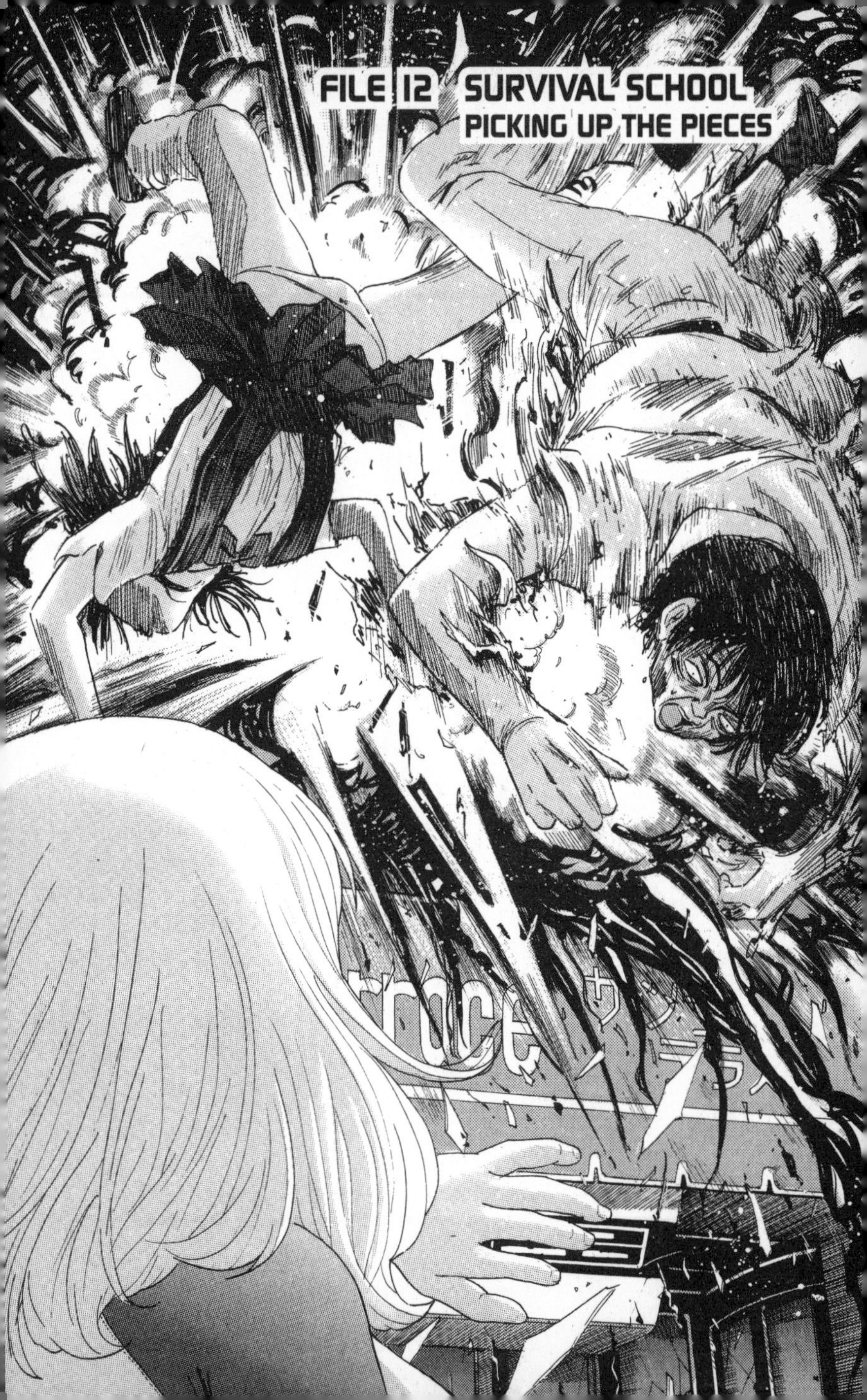
FILE 12 SURVIVAL SCHOOL
PICKING UP THE PIECES

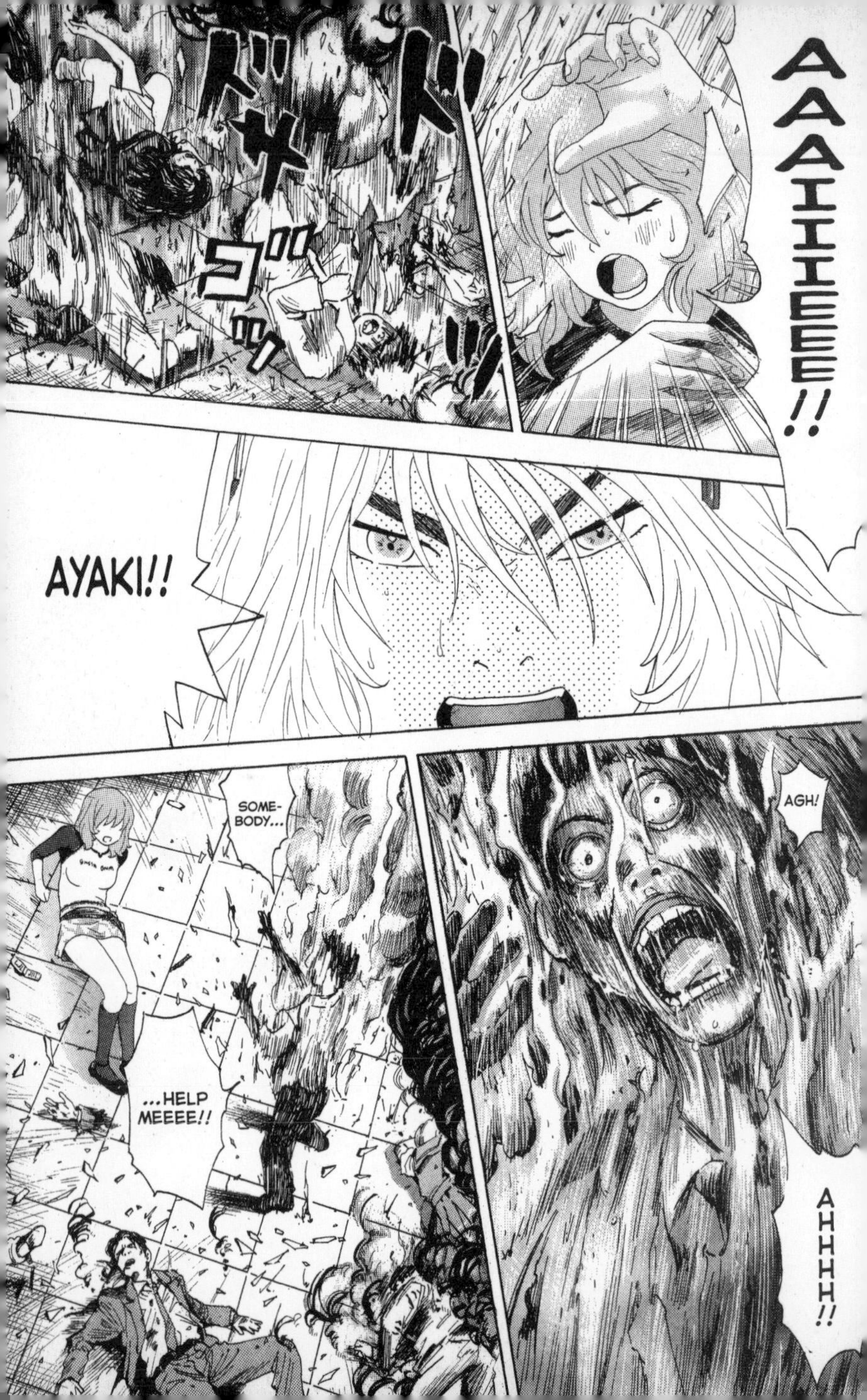
AAAIIIEEE!!
AYAKI!!
AGH!
AHHHH!!
SOME-BODY...
...HELP MEEEE!!

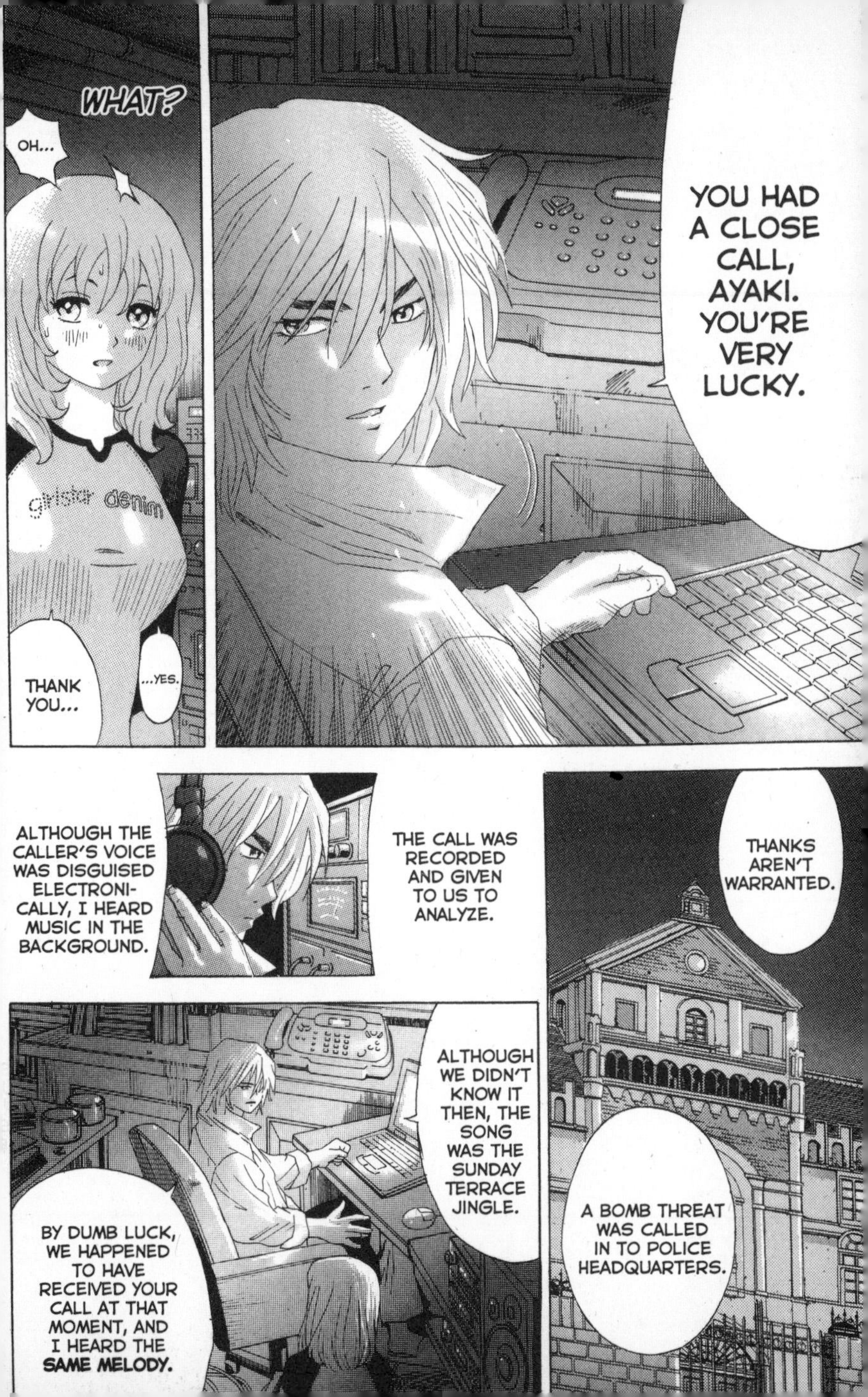
YOU HAD A CLOSE CALL, AYAKI. YOU'RE VERY LUCKY.
WHAT?
OH...
...YES.
THANK YOU...
THANKS AREN'T WARRANTED.
A BOMB THREAT WAS CALLED IN TO POLICE HEADQUARTERS.
THE CALL WAS RECORDED AND GIVEN TO US TO ANALYZE.
ALTHOUGH THE CALLER'S VOICE WAS DISGUISED ELECTRONI-CALLY, I HEARD MUSIC IN THE BACKGROUND.
ALTHOUGH WE DIDN'T KNOW IT THEN, THE SONG WAS THE SUNDAY TERRACE JINGLE.
BY DUMB LUCK, WE HAPPENED TO HAVE RECEIVED YOUR CALL AT THAT MOMENT, AND I HEARD THE **SAME MELODY**.

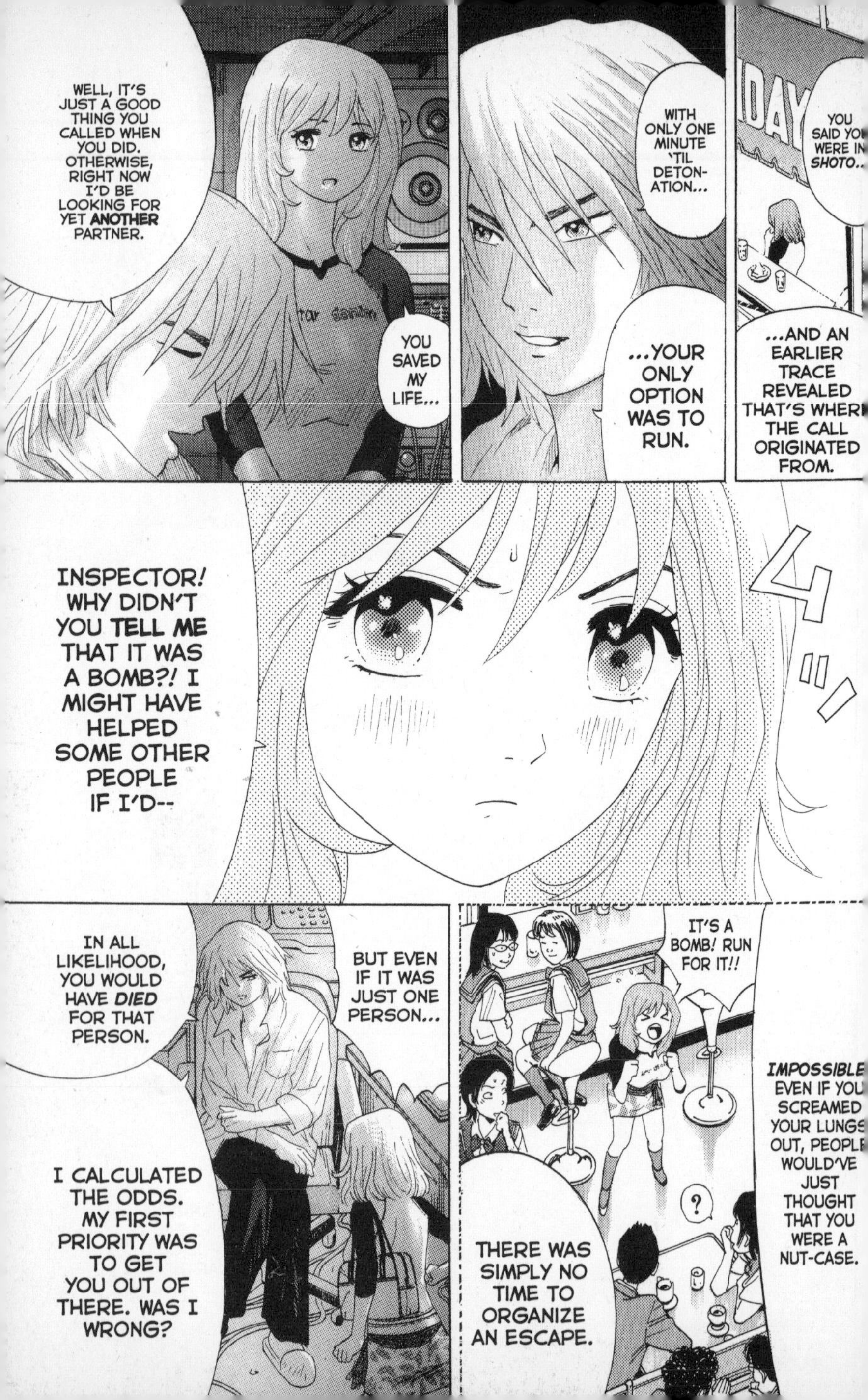
YOU SAID YOU WERE IN *SHOTO*...
...AND AN EARLIER TRACE REVEALED THAT'S WHERE THE CALL ORIGINATED FROM.
WITH ONLY ONE MINUTE 'TIL DETON-ATION...
...YOUR ONLY OPTION WAS TO RUN.
YOU SAVED MY LIFE...
WELL, IT'S JUST A GOOD THING YOU CALLED WHEN YOU DID. OTHERWISE, RIGHT NOW I'D BE LOOKING FOR YET **ANOTHER** PARTNER.
INSPECTOR! WHY DIDN'T YOU **TELL ME** THAT IT WAS A BOMB?! I MIGHT HAVE HELPED SOME OTHER PEOPLE IF I'D--
IT'S A BOMB! RUN FOR IT!!
IMPOSSIBLE. EVEN IF YOU SCREAMED YOUR LUNGS OUT, PEOPLE WOULD'VE JUST THOUGHT THAT YOU WERE A NUT-CASE.
?
THERE WAS SIMPLY NO TIME TO ORGANIZE AN ESCAPE.
BUT EVEN IF IT WAS JUST ONE PERSON...
IN ALL LIKELIHOOD, YOU WOULD HAVE *DIED* FOR THAT PERSON.
I CALCULATED THE ODDS. MY FIRST PRIORITY WAS TO GET YOU OUT OF THERE. WAS I WRONG?

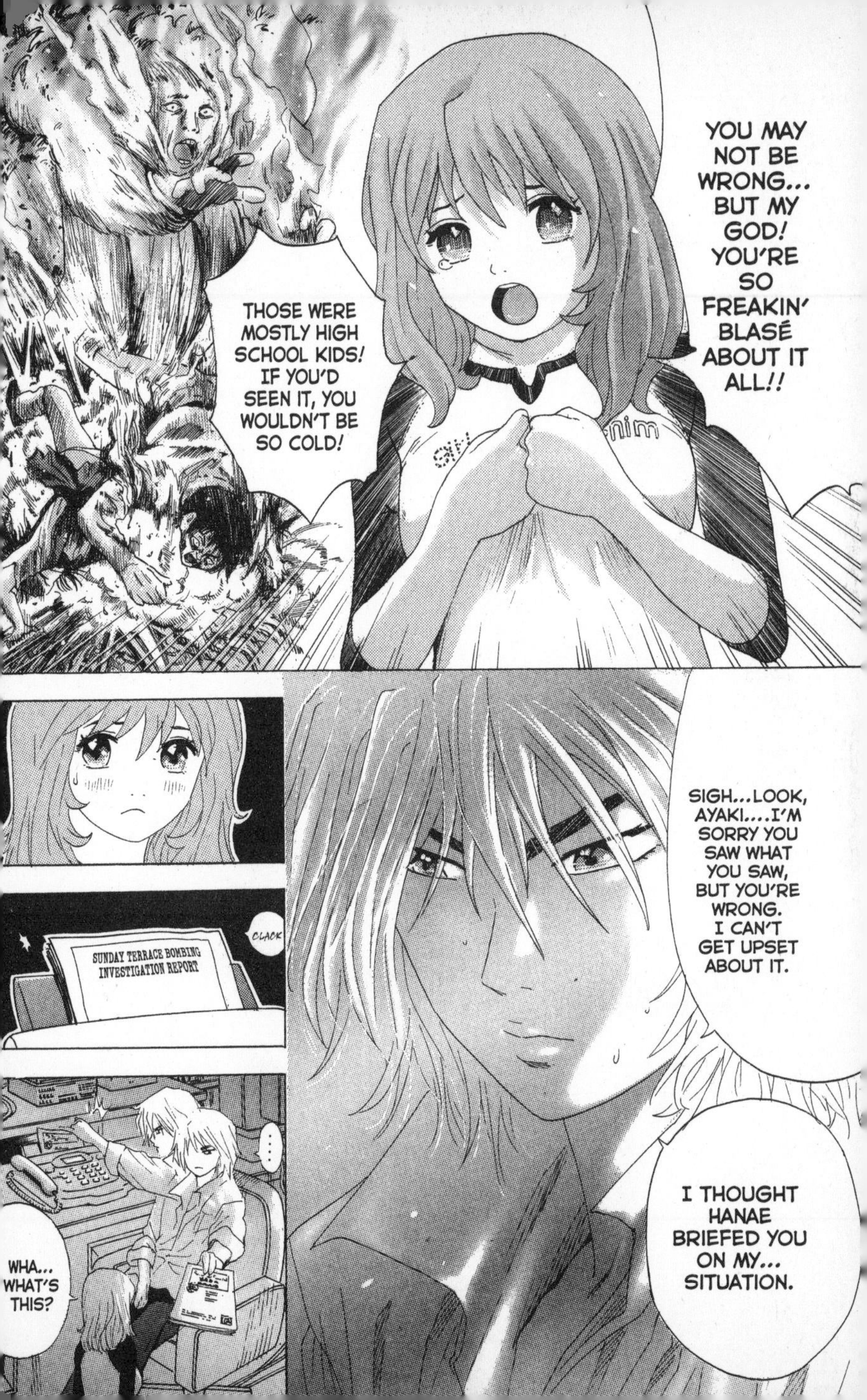
YOU MAY NOT BE WRONG... BUT MY GOD! YOU'RE SO FREAKIN' BLASÉ ABOUT IT ALL!!
THOSE WERE MOSTLY HIGH SCHOOL KIDS! IF YOU'D SEEN IT, YOU WOULDN'T BE SO COLD!
SIGH...LOOK, AYAKI....I'M SORRY YOU SAW WHAT YOU SAW, BUT YOU'RE WRONG. I CAN'T GET UPSET ABOUT IT.
I THOUGHT HANAE BRIEFED YOU ON MY... SITUATION.
CLACK
SUNDAY TERRACE BOMBING INVESTIGATION REPORT
....
WHA... WHAT'S THIS?

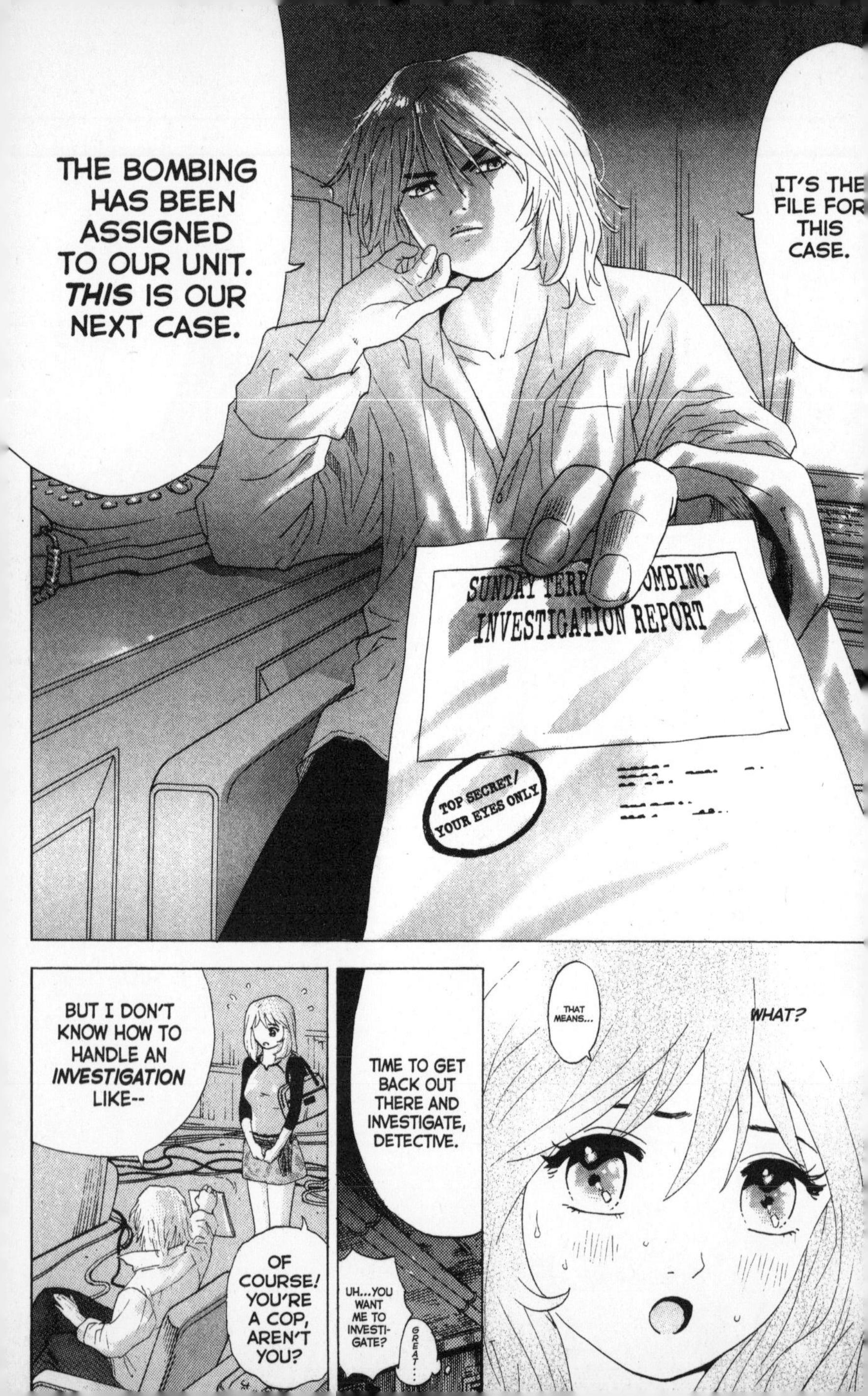
IT'S THE FILE FOR THIS CASE.
THE BOMBING HAS BEEN ASSIGNED TO OUR UNIT. *THIS* IS OUR NEXT CASE.
INVESTIGATION REPORT
TOP SECRET/ YOUR EYES ONLY
WHAT?
THAT MEANS...
TIME TO GET BACK OUT THERE AND INVESTIGATE, DETECTIVE.
UH...YOU WANT ME TO INVESTI-GATE?
GREAT...
BUT I DON'T KNOW HOW TO HANDLE AN *INVESTIGATION* LIKE--
OF COURSE! YOU'RE A COP, AREN'T YOU?

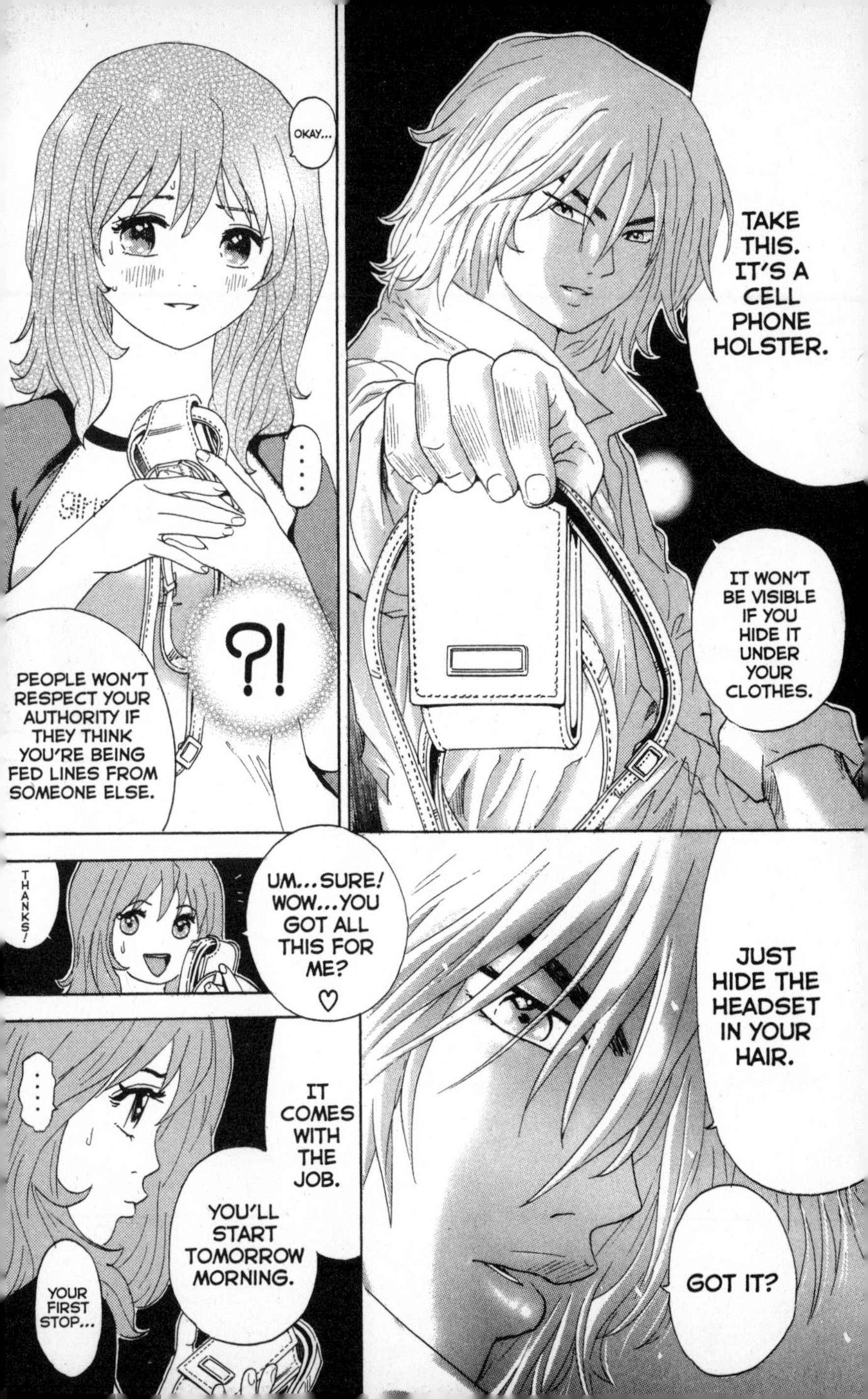
TAKE THIS. IT'S A CELL PHONE HOLSTER.
IT WON'T BE VISIBLE IF YOU HIDE IT UNDER YOUR CLOTHES.
OKAY...
....
?!
PEOPLE WON'T RESPECT YOUR AUTHORITY IF THEY THINK YOU'RE BEING FED LINES FROM SOMEONE ELSE.
JUST HIDE THE HEADSET IN YOUR HAIR.
GOT IT?
UM...SURE! WOW...YOU GOT ALL THIS FOR ME? ♡
THANKS!
IT COMES WITH THE JOB.
YOU'LL START TOMORROW MORNING.
....
YOUR FIRST STOP...

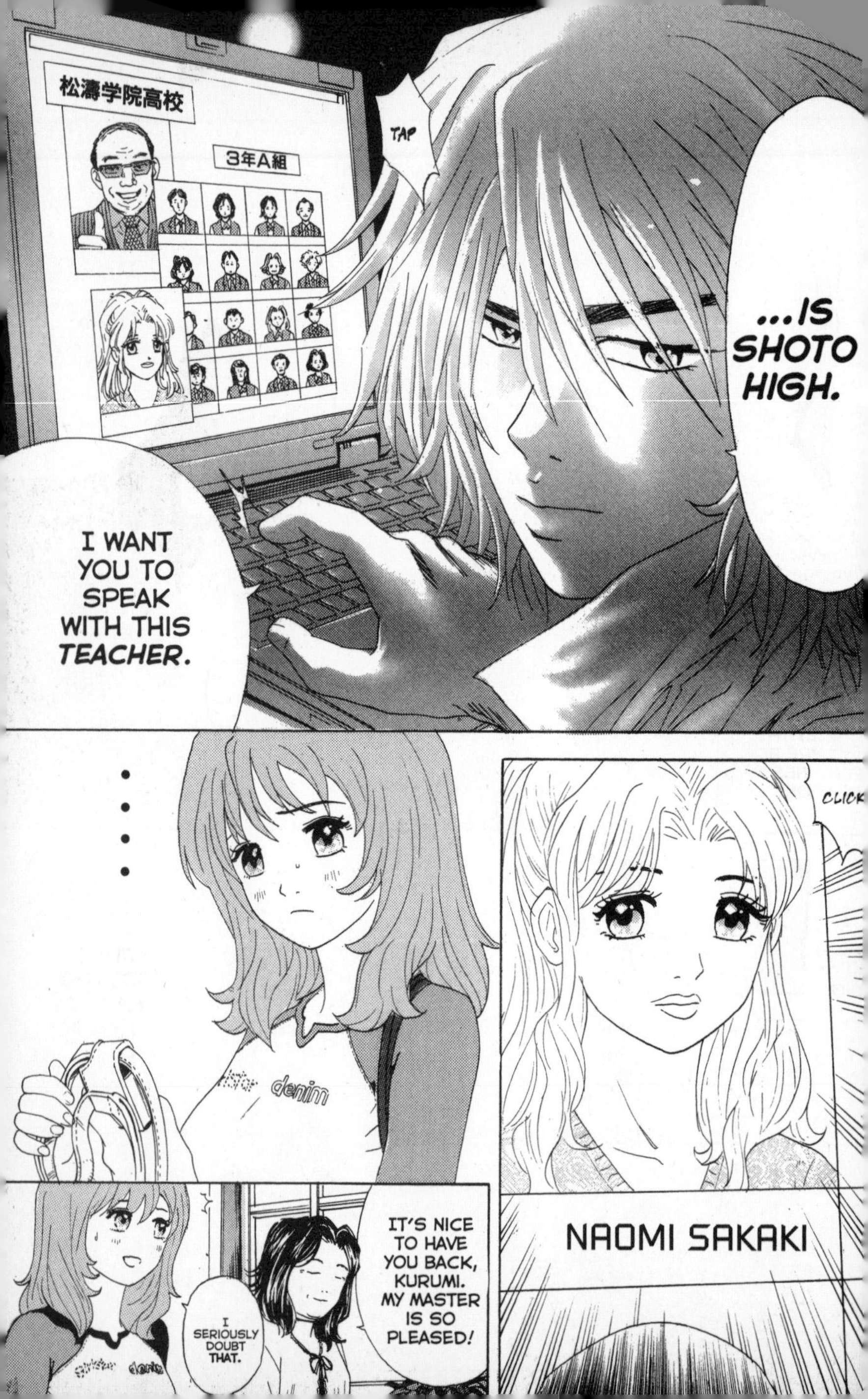
...IS SHOTO HIGH.
TAP
松濤学院高校
3年A組
I WANT YOU TO SPEAK WITH THIS *TEACHER*.
CLICK
NAOMI SAKAKI
....
IT'S NICE TO HAVE YOU BACK, KURUMI. MY MASTER IS SO PLEASED!
I SERIOUSLY DOUBT THAT.

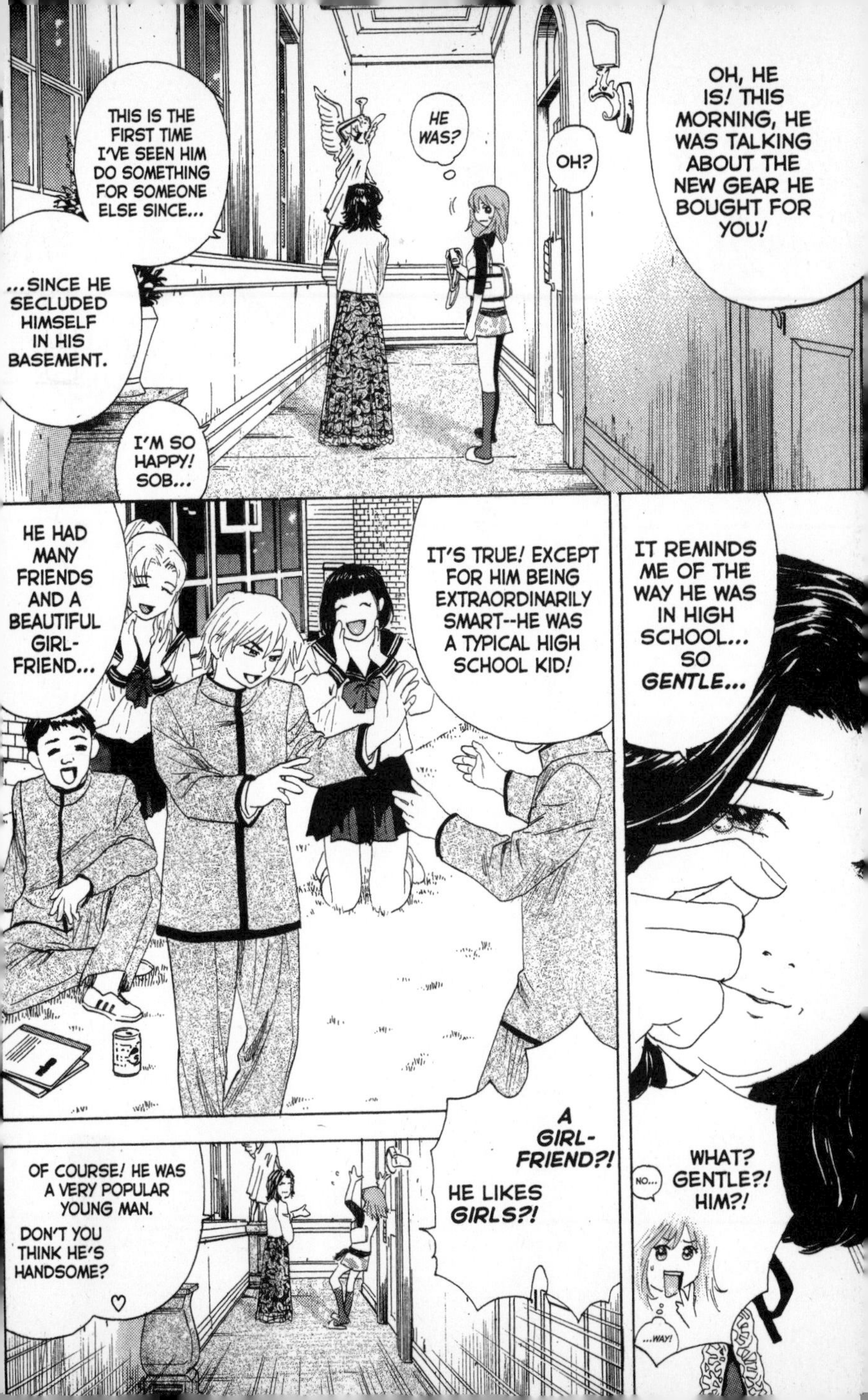
OH, HE IS! THIS MORNING, HE WAS TALKING ABOUT THE NEW GEAR HE BOUGHT FOR YOU!
OH?
HE WAS?
THIS IS THE FIRST TIME I'VE SEEN HIM DO SOMETHING FOR SOMEONE ELSE SINCE...
...SINCE HE SECLUDED HIMSELF IN HIS BASEMENT.
I'M SO HAPPY! SOB...
IT REMINDS ME OF THE WAY HE WAS IN HIGH SCHOOL... SO GENTLE...
IT'S TRUE! EXCEPT FOR HIM BEING EXTRAORDINARILY SMART--HE WAS A TYPICAL HIGH SCHOOL KID!
HE HAD MANY FRIENDS AND A BEAUTIFUL GIRL-FRIEND...
WHAT? GENTLE?! HIM?!
NO...
...WAY!
A GIRL-FRIEND?!
HE LIKES GIRLS?!
OF COURSE! HE WAS A VERY POPULAR YOUNG MAN.
DON'T YOU THINK HE'S HANDSOME? ♡

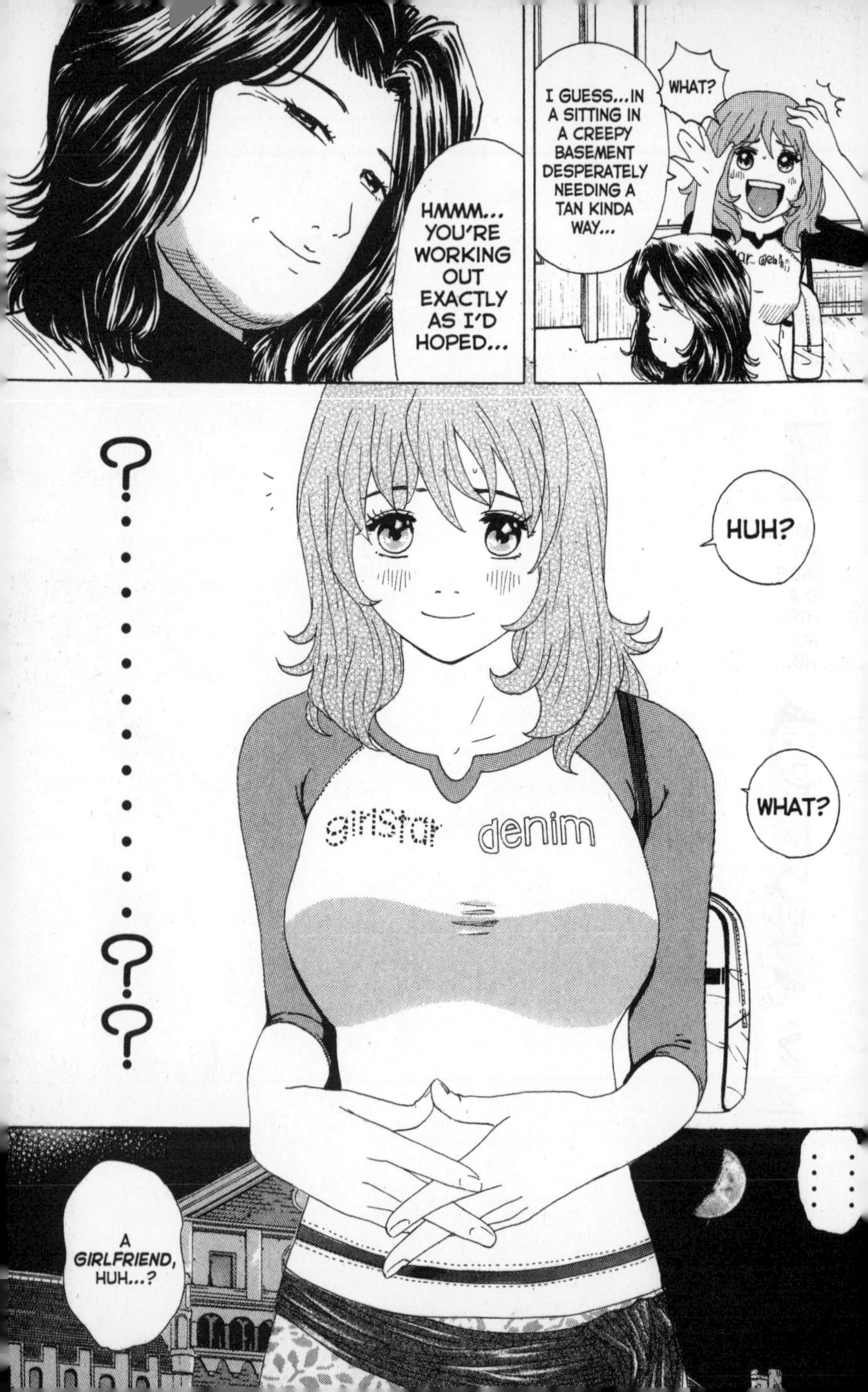
WHAT?
I GUESS...IN A SITTING IN A CREEPY BASEMENT DESPERATELY NEEDING A TAN KINDA WAY...
HMMM... YOU'RE WORKING OUT EXACTLY AS I'D HOPED...
HUH?
WHAT?
?..........??
girlstar denim
.....
A GIRLFRIEND, HUH...?

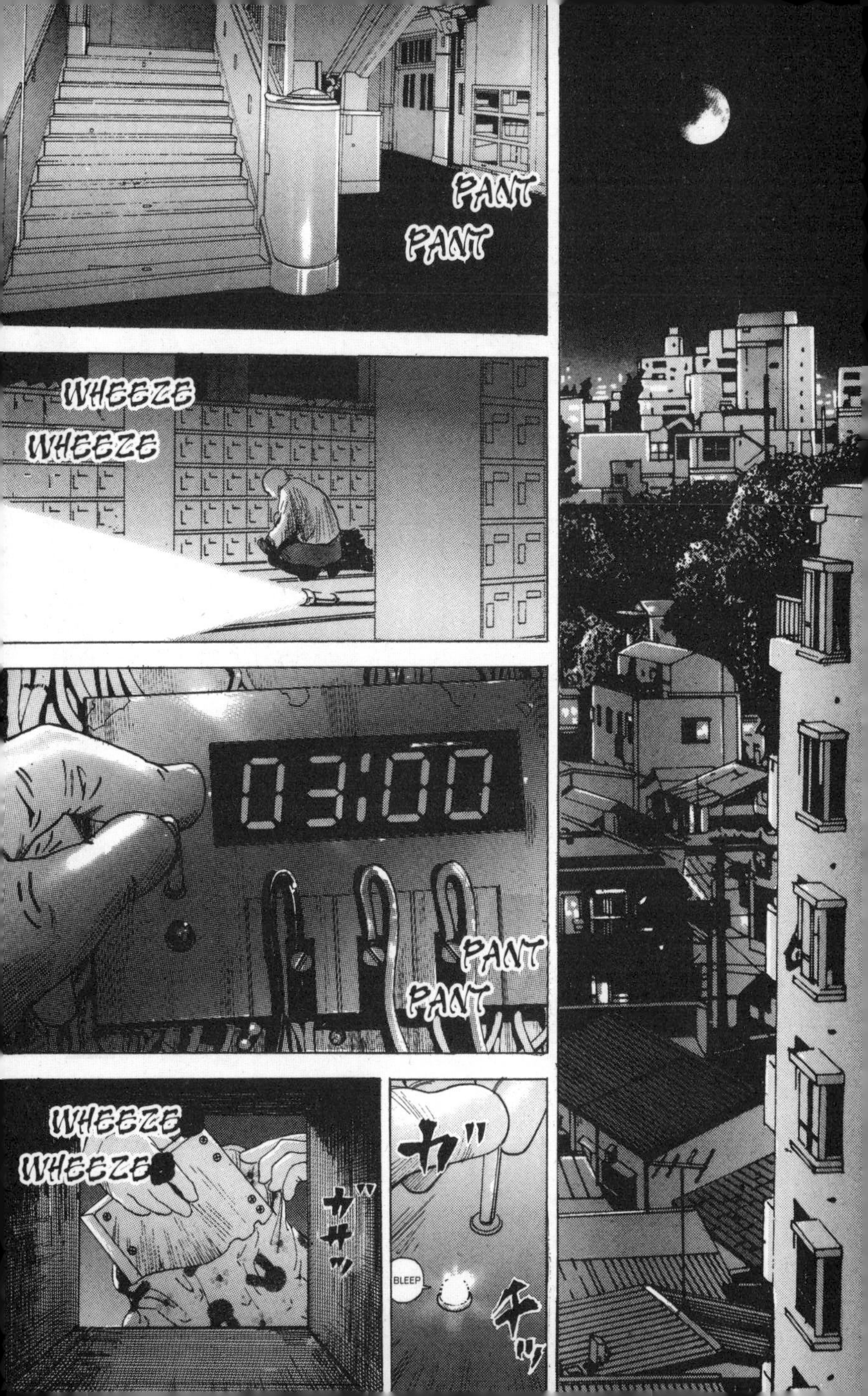
PANT
PANT
WHEEZE
WHEEZE
03:00
PANT
PANT
ガ
BLEEP
チッ
WHEEZE
WHEEZE
ガサッ

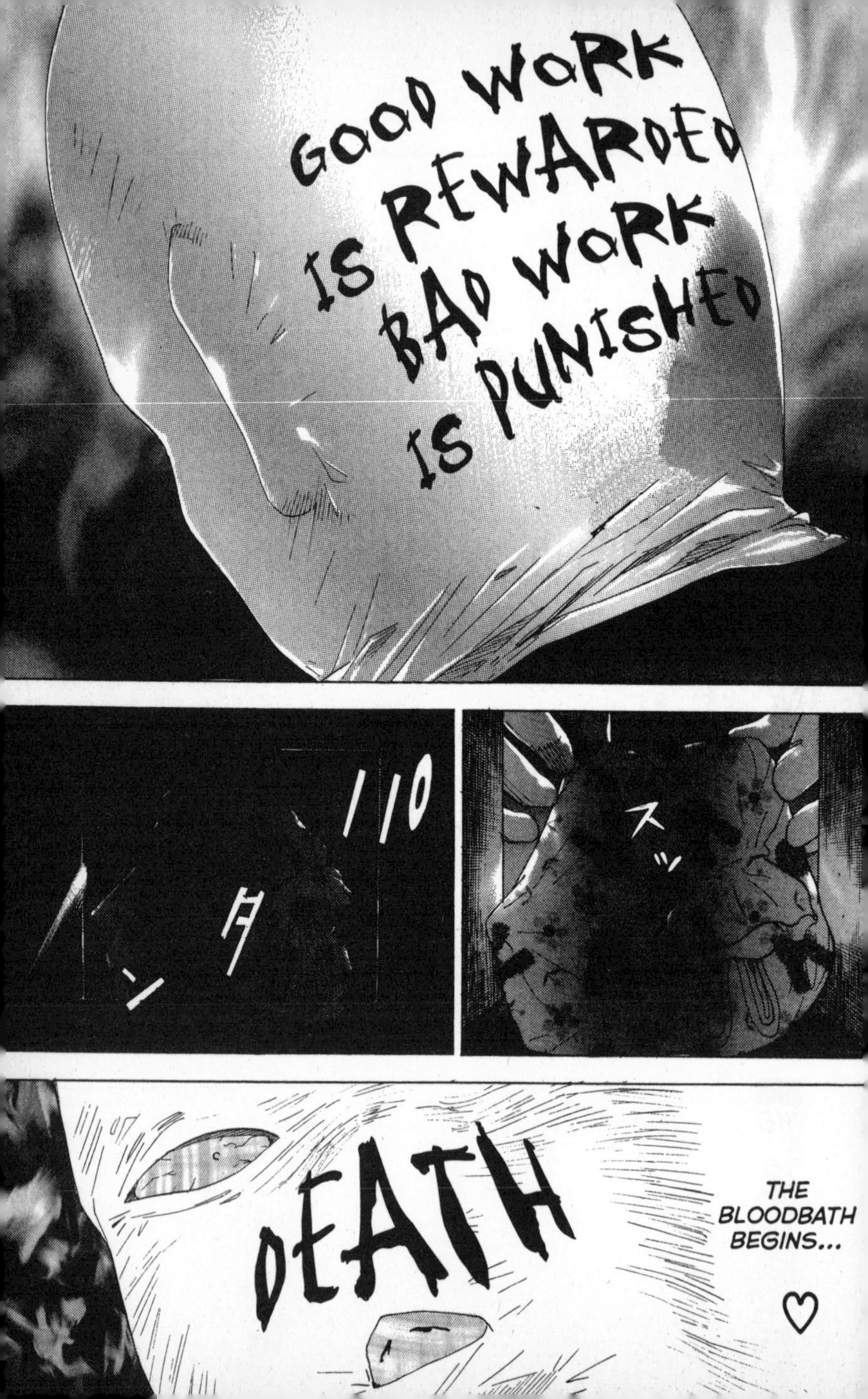
GOOD WORK IS REWARDED BAD WORK IS PUNISHED
スッ
DEATH
THE BLOODBATH BEGINS... ♡

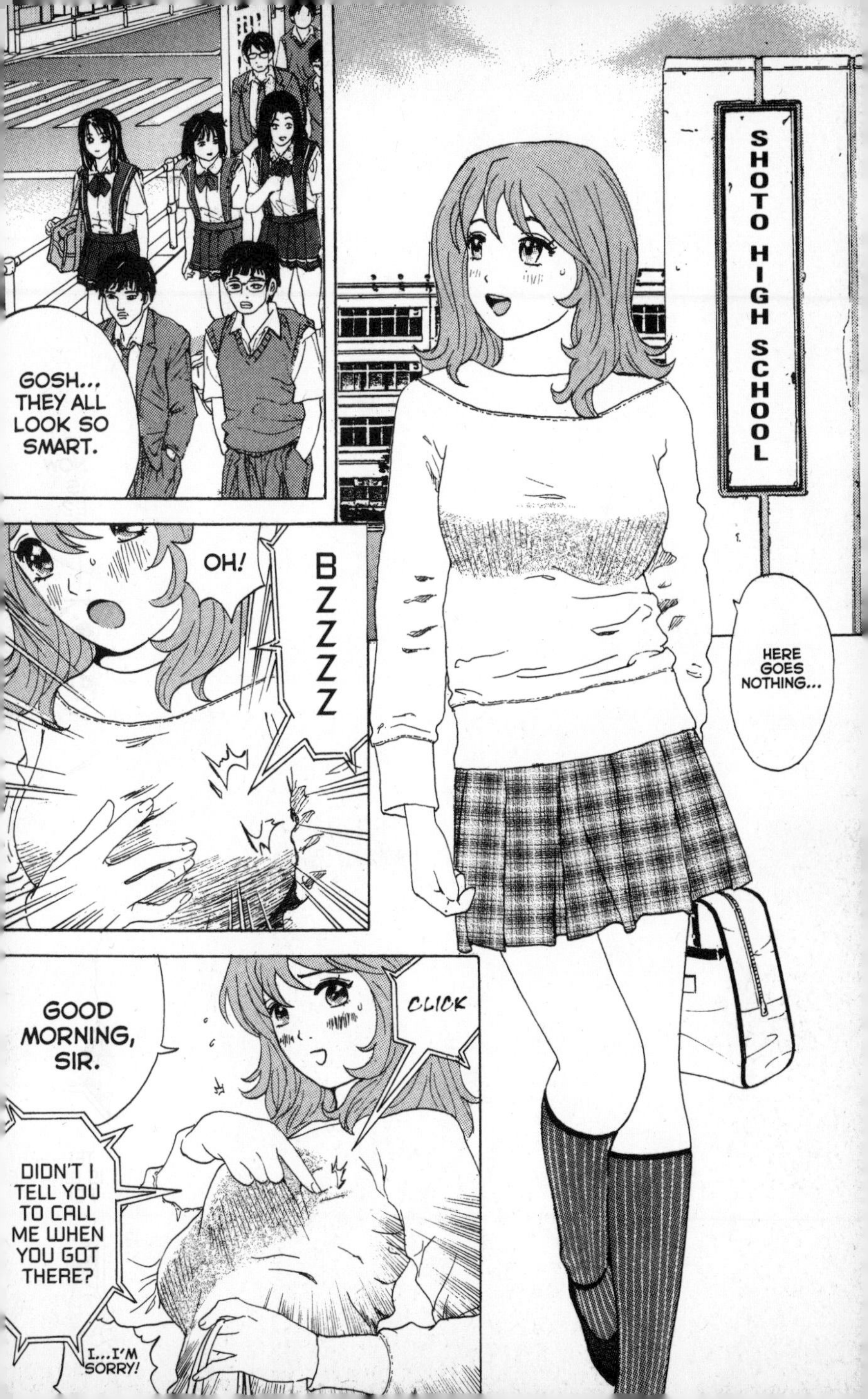
SHOTO HIGH SCHOOL
HERE GOES NOTHING...
GOSH... THEY ALL LOOK SO SMART.
BZZZZZ
OH!
CLICK
GOOD MORNING, SIR.
DIDN'T I TELL YOU TO CALL ME WHEN YOU GOT THERE?
I...I'M SORRY!

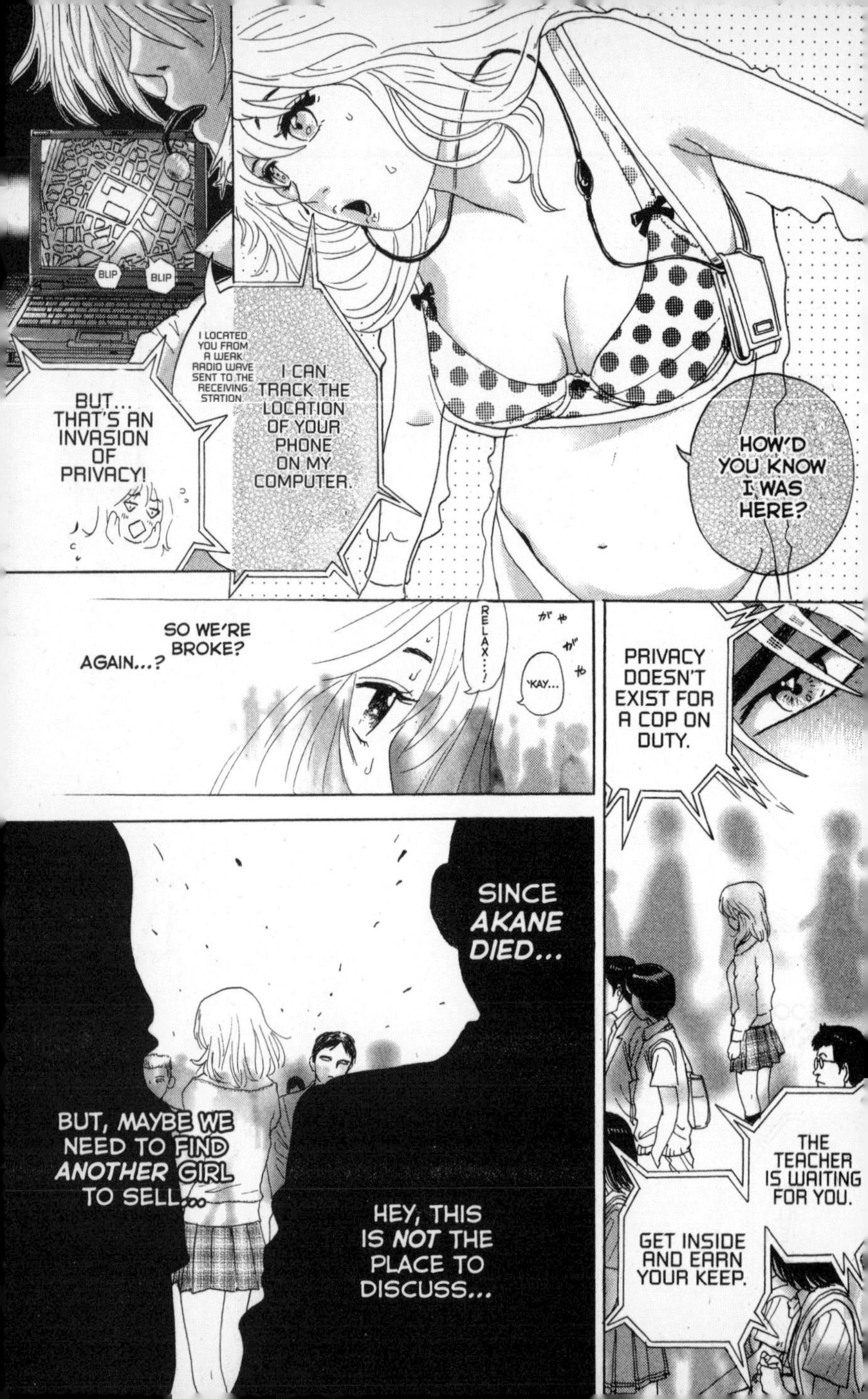
HOW'D YOU KNOW I WAS HERE?
I CAN TRACK THE LOCATION OF YOUR PHONE ON MY COMPUTER.
I LOCATED YOU FROM A WEAK RADIO WAVE SENT TO THE RECEIVING STATION.
BLIP
BLIP
BUT... THAT'S AN INVASION OF PRIVACY!
PRIVACY DOESN'T EXIST FOR A COP ON DUTY.
RELAX...!
'KAY...
SO WE'RE BROKE?
AGAIN...?
THE TEACHER IS WAITING FOR YOU.
GET INSIDE AND EARN YOUR KEEP.
SINCE *AKANE* DIED...
BUT, MAYBE WE NEED TO FIND *ANOTHER* GIRL TO SELL...
HEY, THIS IS *NOT* THE PLACE TO DISCUSS...

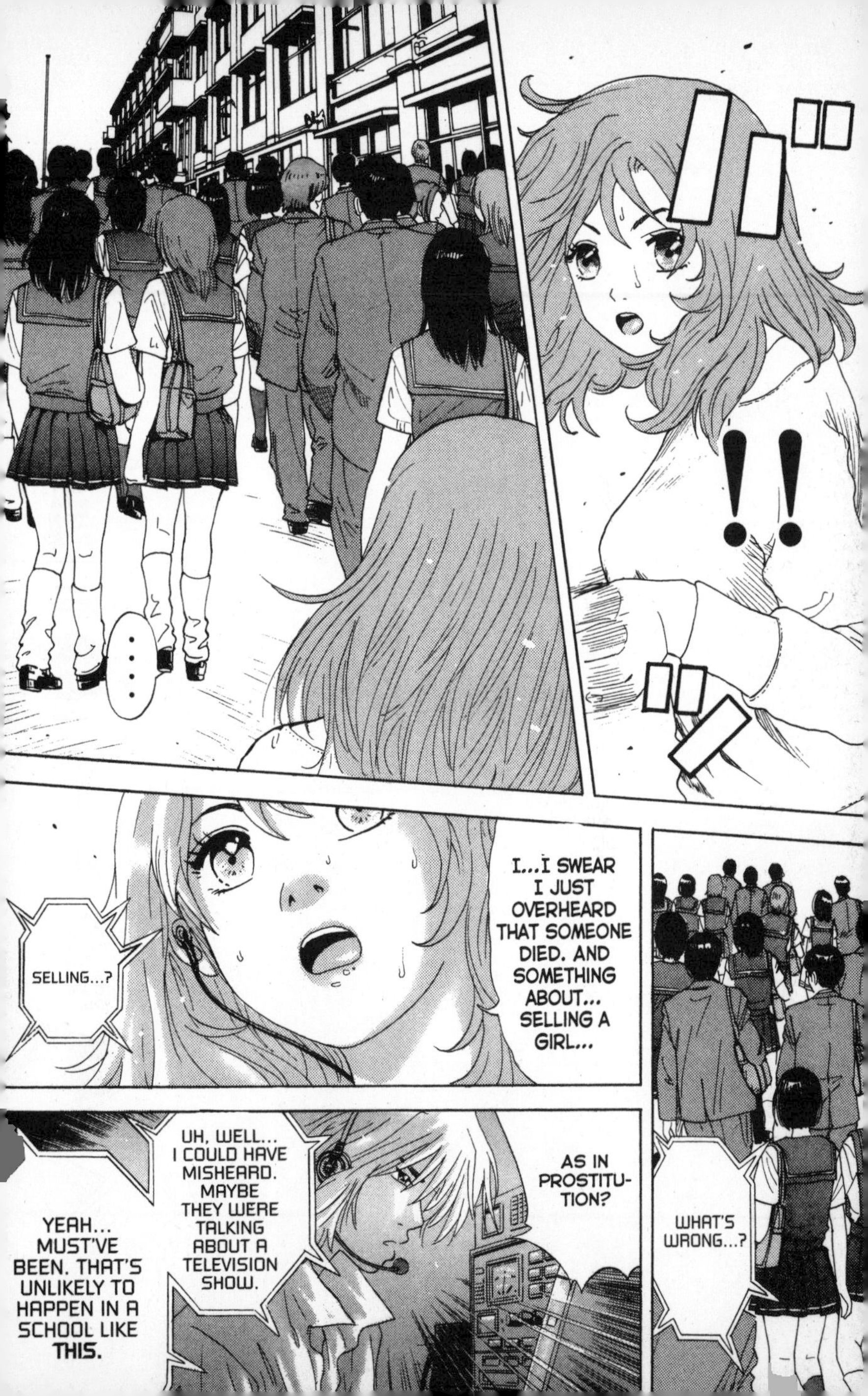
!!
.....
WHAT'S WRONG...?
I...I SWEAR I JUST OVERHEARD THAT SOMEONE DIED. AND SOMETHING ABOUT... SELLING A GIRL...
SELLING...?
AS IN PROSTITU-TION?
UH, WELL... I COULD HAVE MISHEARD. MAYBE THEY WERE TALKING ABOUT A TELEVISION SHOW.
YEAH... MUST'VE BEEN. THAT'S UNLIKELY TO HAPPEN IN A SCHOOL LIKE **THIS.**

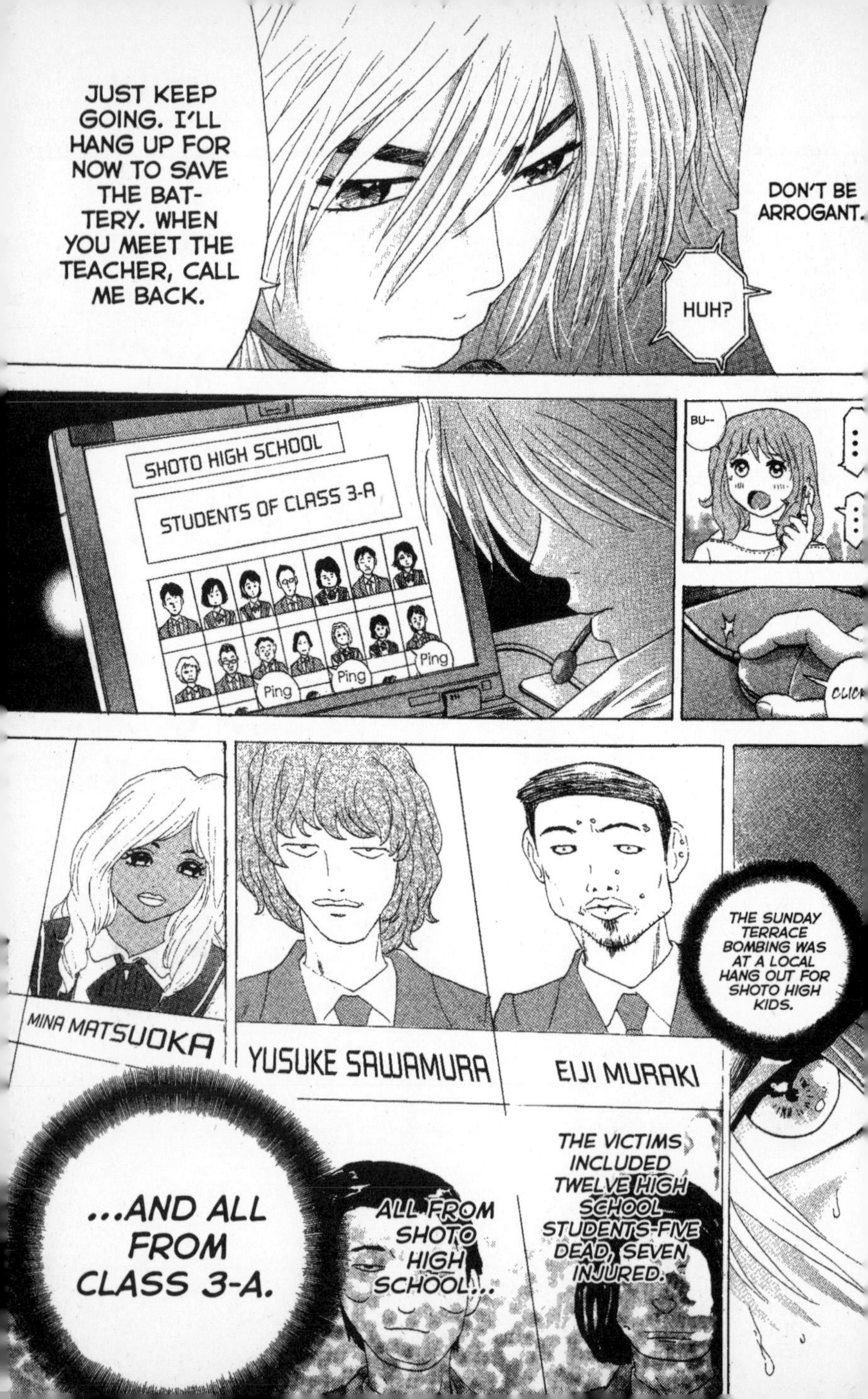
DON'T BE ARROGANT.
HUH?
JUST KEEP GOING. I'LL HANG UP FOR NOW TO SAVE THE BAT-TERY. WHEN YOU MEET THE TEACHER, CALL ME BACK.
BU--
...
...
CLIC
SHOTO HIGH SCHOOL
STUDENTS OF CLASS 3-A
Ping
Ping
Ping
THE SUNDAY TERRACE BOMBING WAS AT A LOCAL HANG OUT FOR SHOTO HIGH KIDS.
EIJI MURAKI
YUSUKE SAWAMURA
MINA MATSUOKA
THE VICTIMS INCLUDED TWELVE HIGH SCHOOL STUDENTS-FIVE DEAD, SEVEN INJURED.
ALL FROM SHOTO HIGH SCHOOL...
...AND ALL FROM CLASS 3-A.

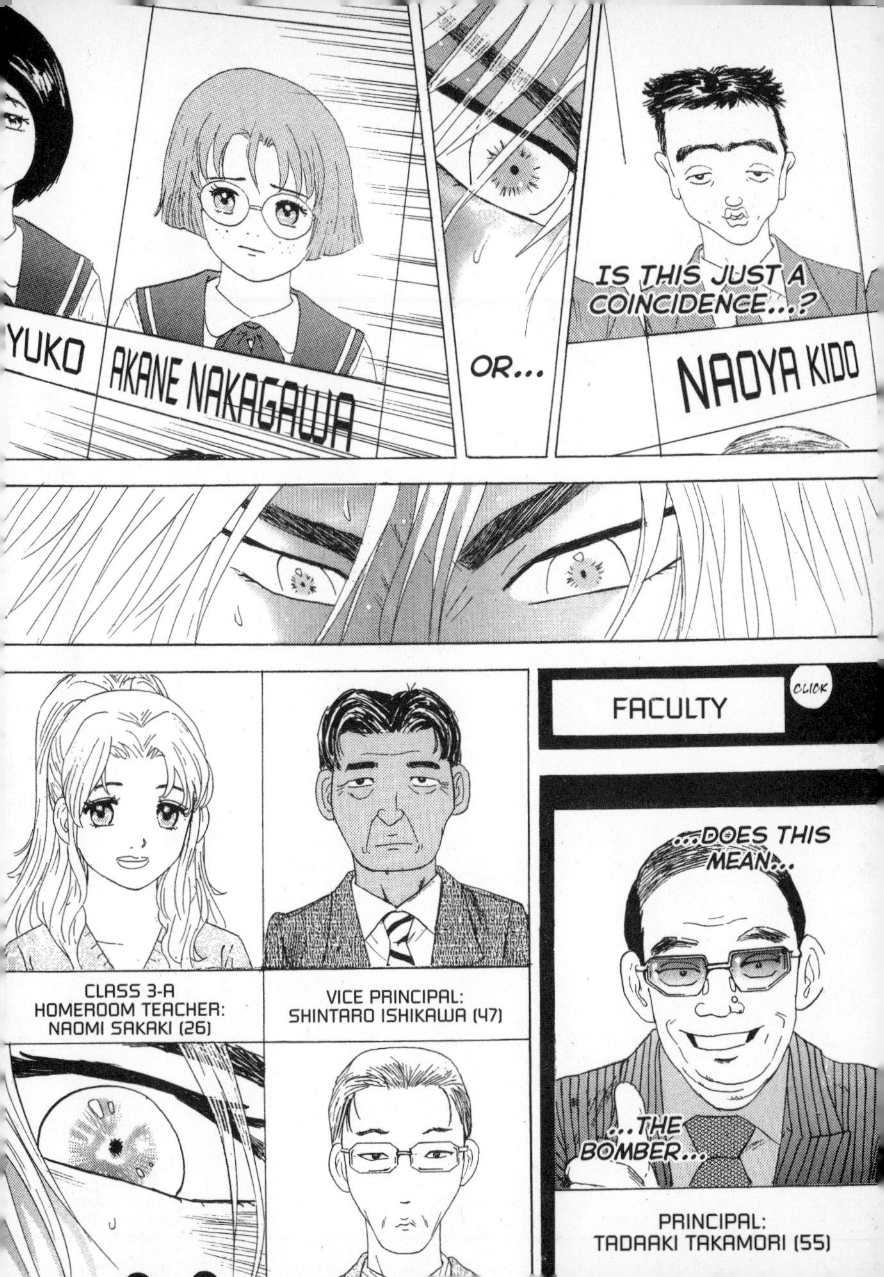
IS THIS JUST A COINCIDENCE...?
NAOYA KIDO
OR...
AKANE NAKAGAWA
YUKO
FACULTY
CLICK
...DOES THIS MEAN...
...THE BOMBER...
PRINCIPAL: TADAAKI TAKAMORI (55)
VICE PRINCIPAL: SHINTARO ISHIKAWA (47)
CLASS 3-A HOMEROOM TEACHER: NAOMI SAKAKI (26)

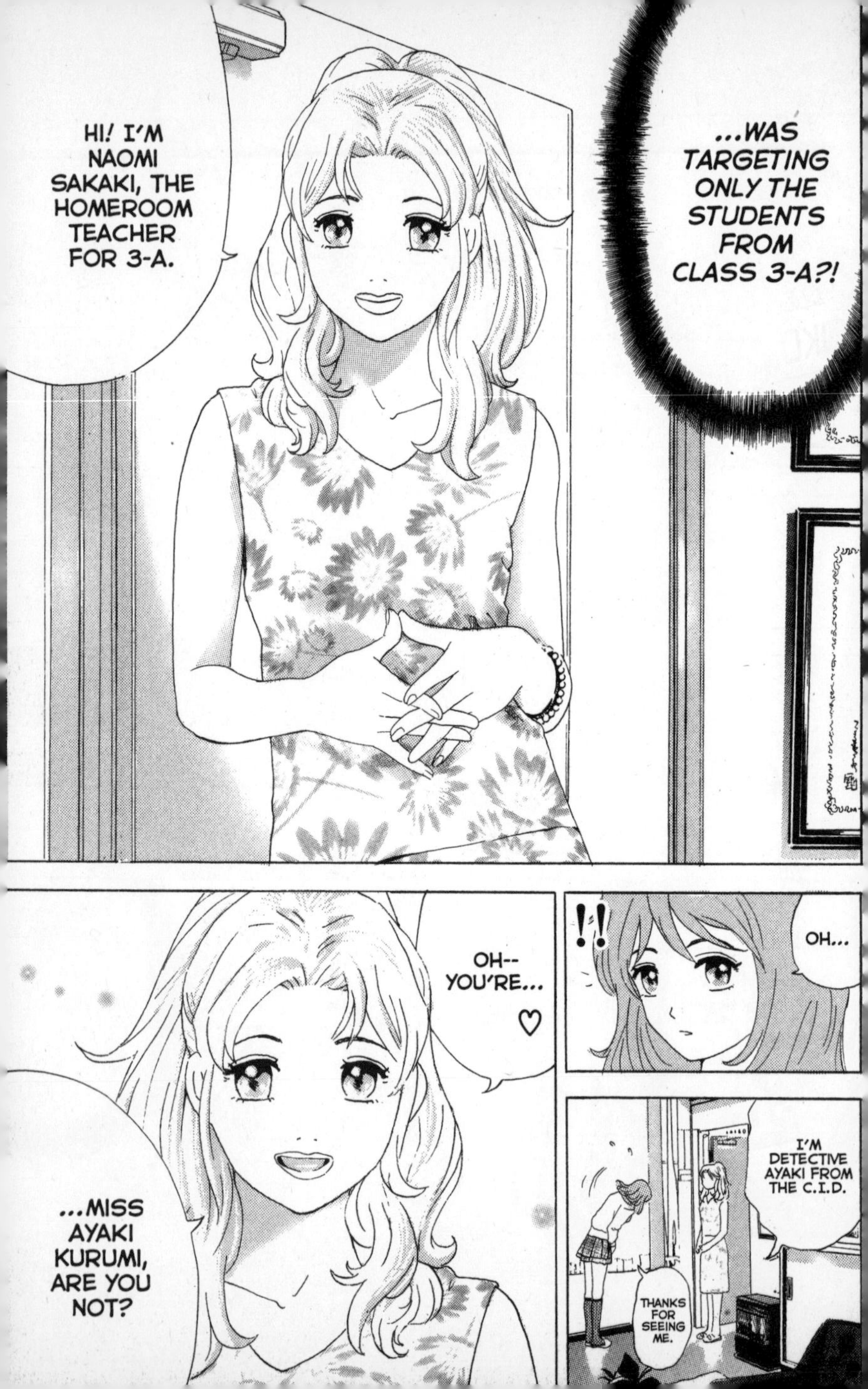
...WAS TARGETING ONLY THE STUDENTS FROM CLASS 3-A?!
HI! I'M NAOMI SAKAKI, THE HOMEROOM TEACHER FOR 3-A.
!!
OH...
I'M DETECTIVE AYAKI FROM THE C.I.D.
THANKS FOR SEEING ME.
OH-- YOU'RE... ♡
...MISS AYAKI KURUMI, ARE YOU NOT?

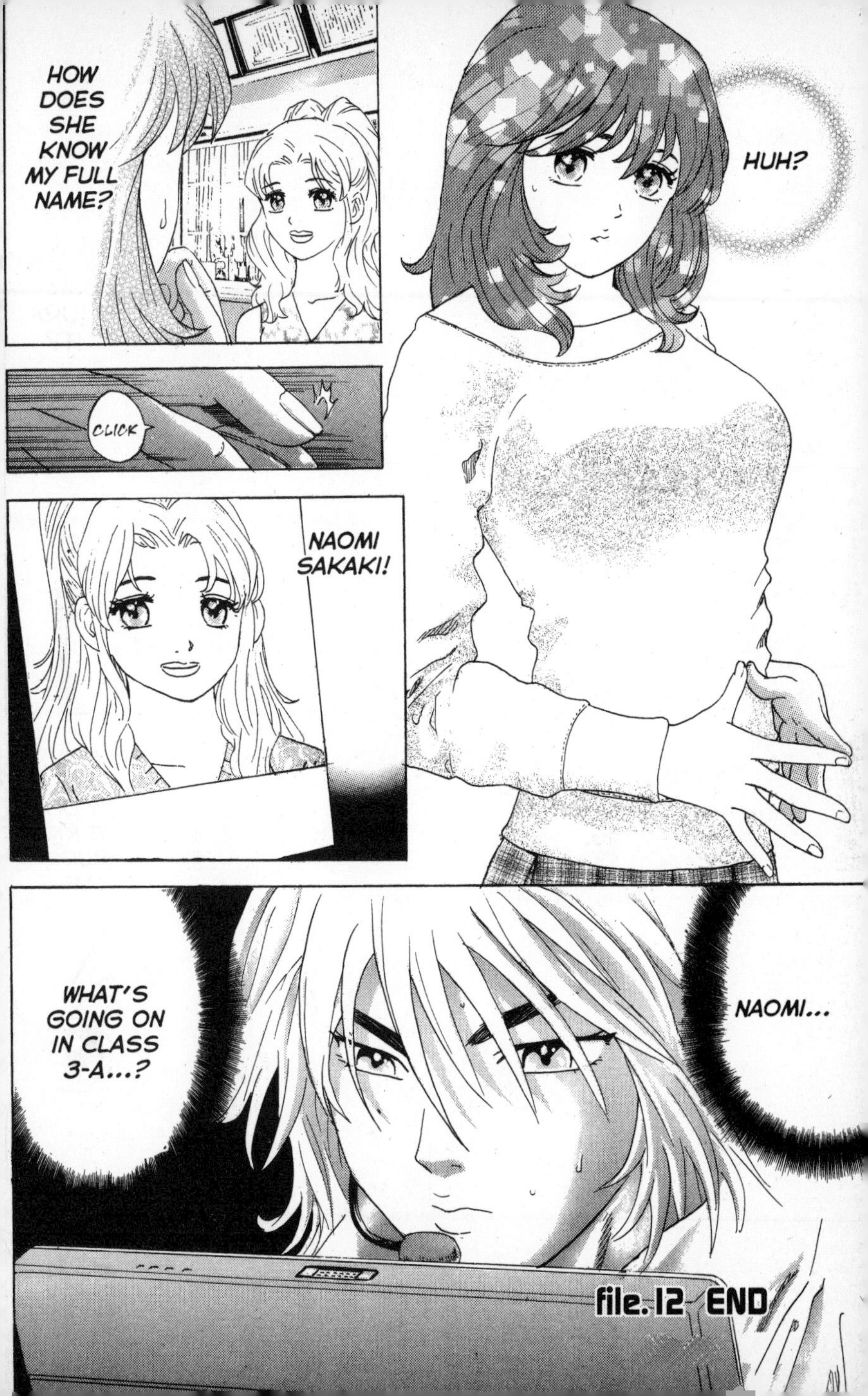
HUH?
HOW DOES SHE KNOW MY FULL NAME?
CLICK
NAOMI SAKAKI!
NAOMI...
WHAT'S GOING ON IN CLASS 3-A...?
file. 12 END

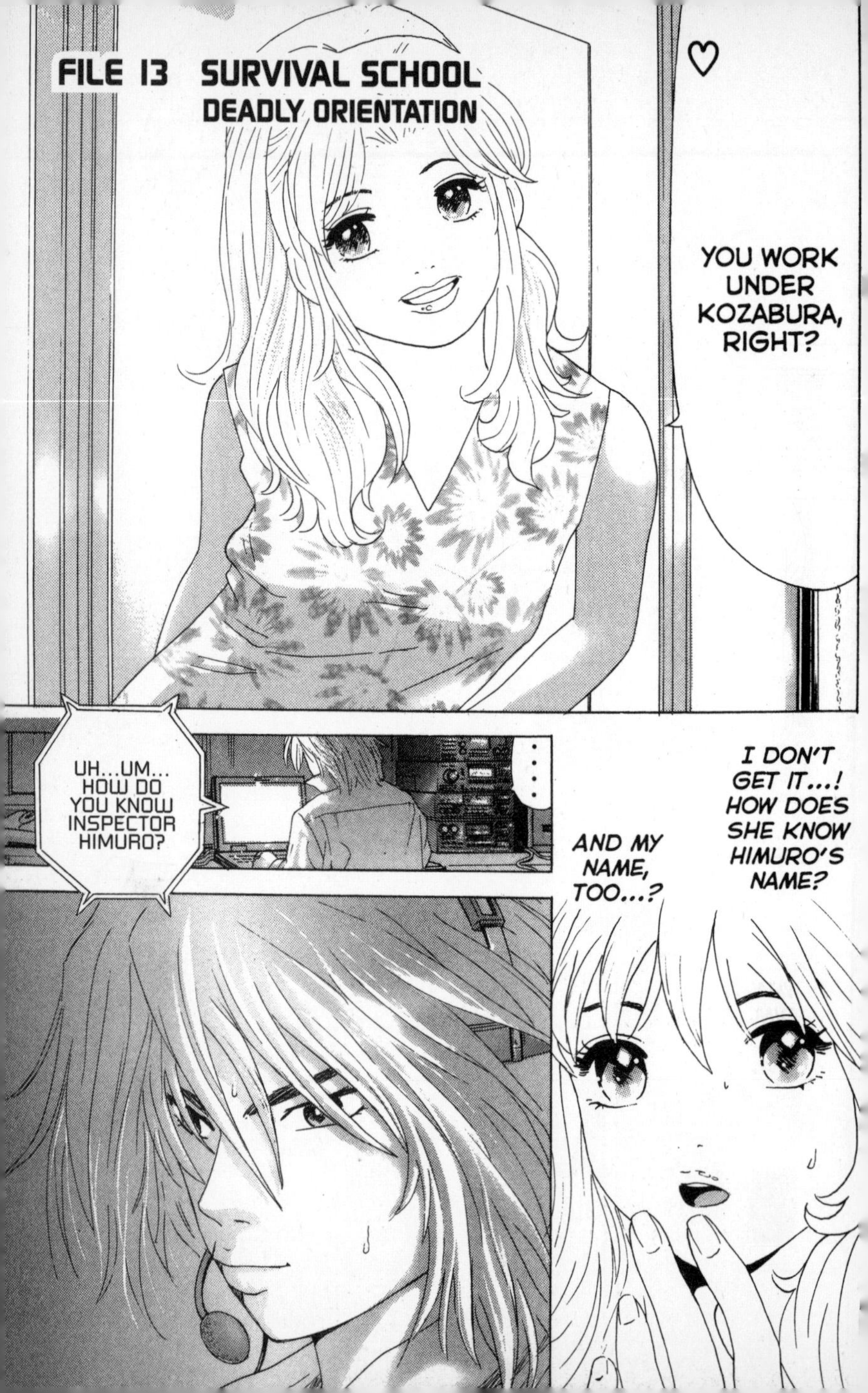
FILE 13 SURVIVAL SCHOOL
DEADLY ORIENTATION
♡
YOU WORK UNDER KOZABURA, RIGHT?
....
UH...UM... HOW DO YOU KNOW INSPECTOR HIMURO?
I DON'T GET IT...! HOW DOES SHE KNOW HIMURO'S NAME?
AND MY NAME, TOO...?

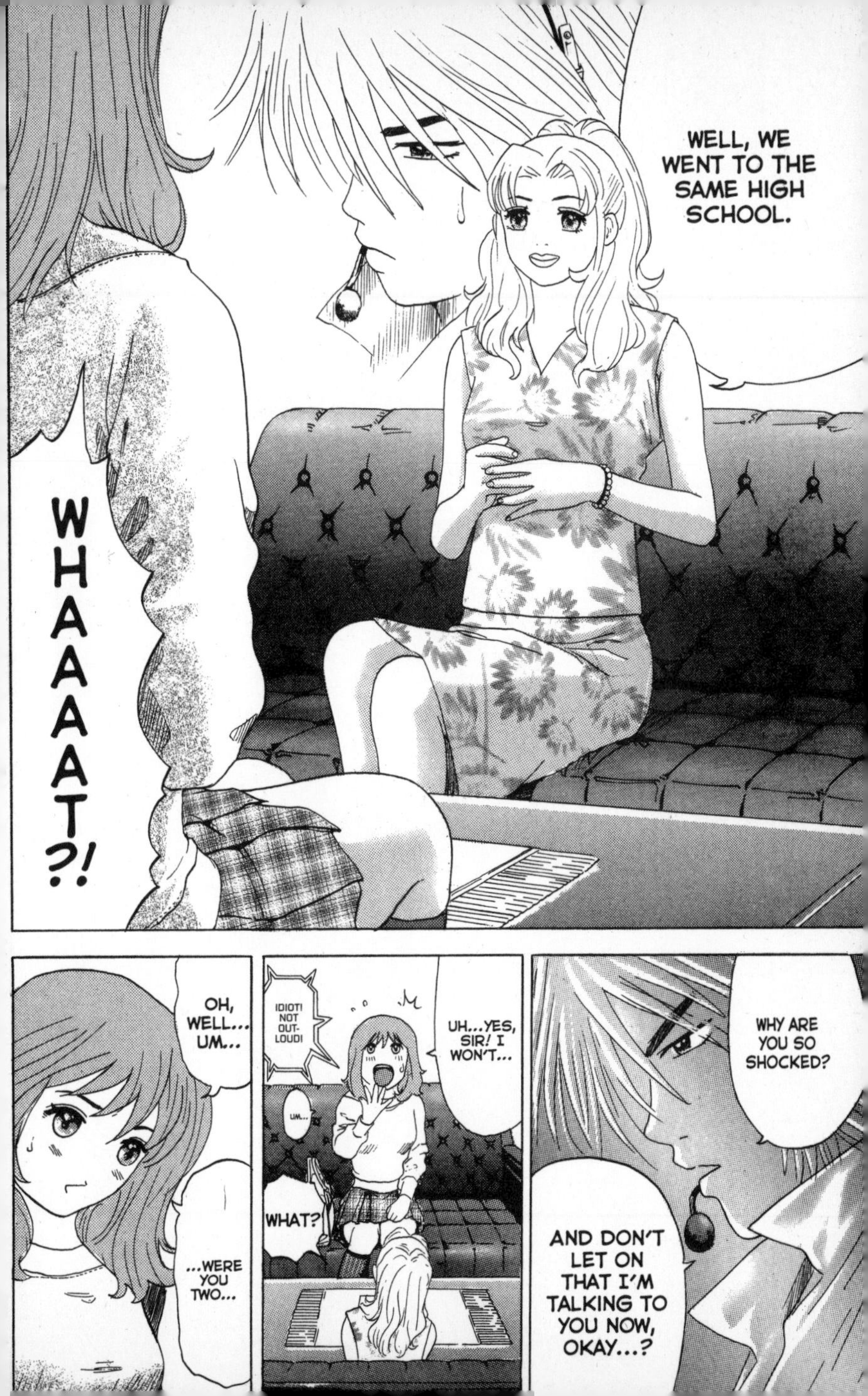
WELL, WE WENT TO THE SAME HIGH SCHOOL.
WHAAAAAT?!
WHY ARE YOU SO SHOCKED?
AND DON'T LET ON THAT I'M TALKING TO YOU NOW, OKAY...?
UH...YES, SIR! I WON'T...
IDIOT! NOT OUT-LOUD!
UM...
WHAT?
OH, WELL... UM...
...WERE YOU TWO...

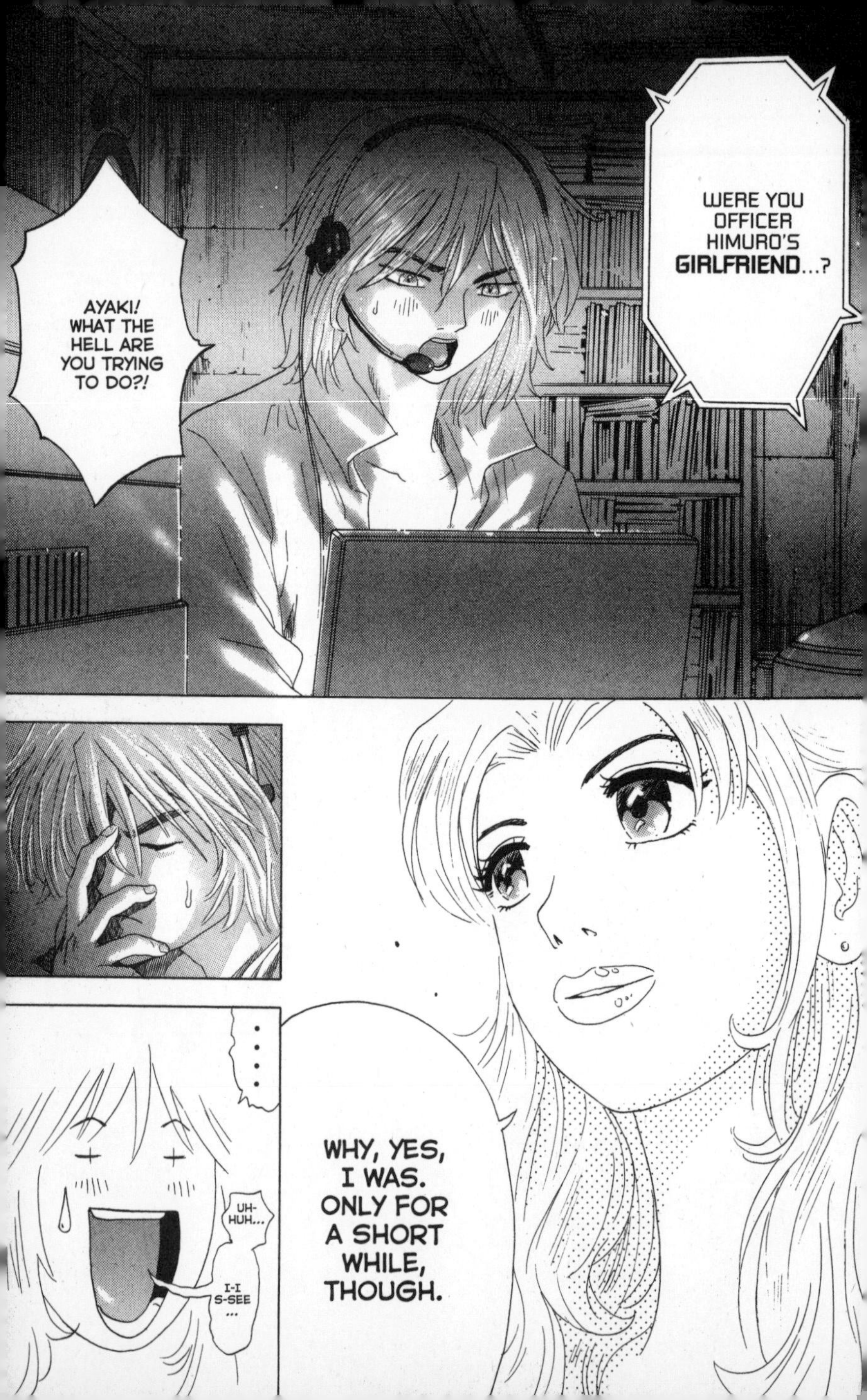
WERE YOU OFFICER HIMURO'S **GIRLFRIEND**...?
AYAKI! WHAT THE HELL ARE YOU TRYING TO DO?!
WHY, YES, I WAS. ONLY FOR A SHORT WHILE, THOUGH.
....
UH-HUH...
I-I S-SEE ...

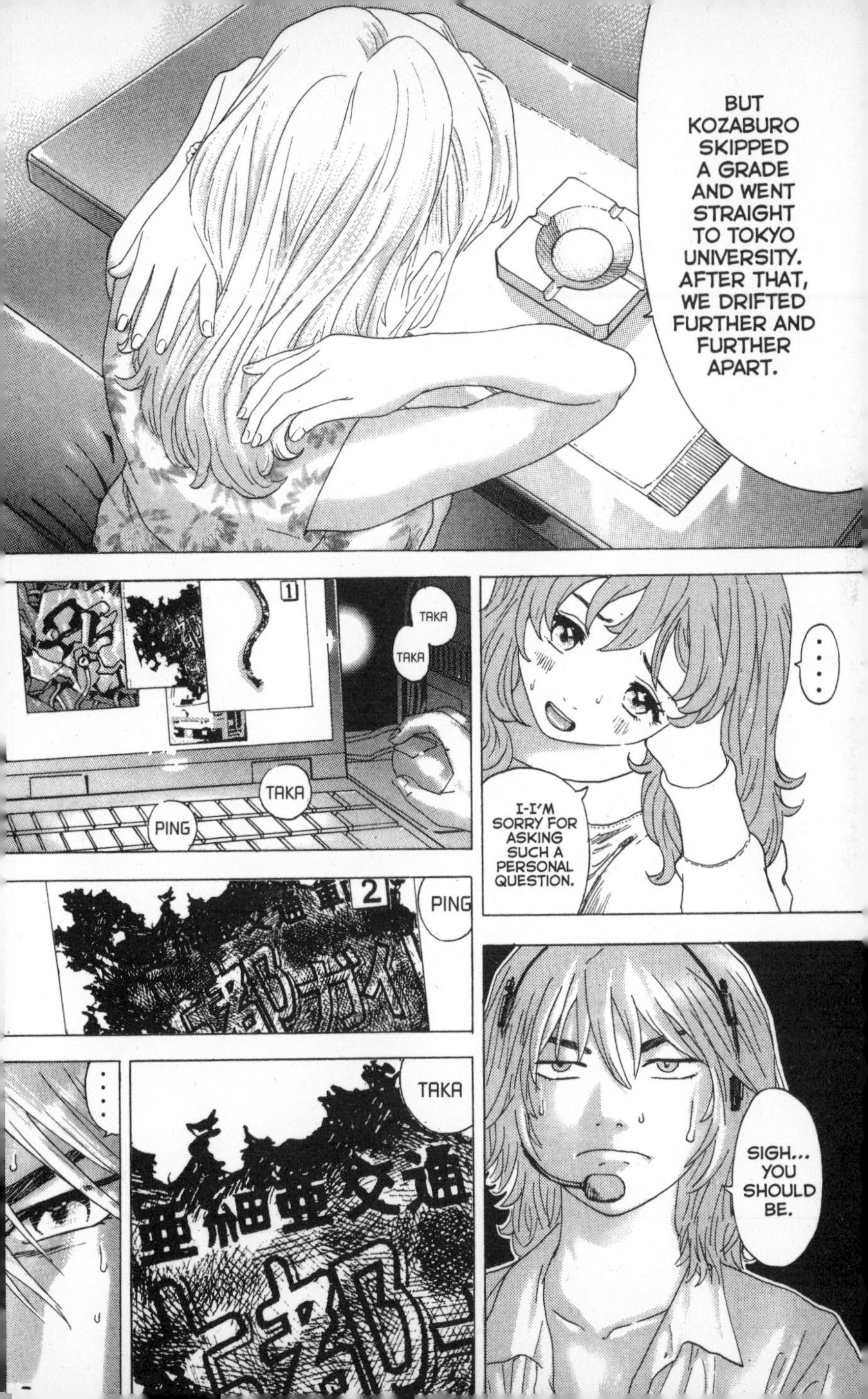

BUT KOZABURO SKIPPED A GRADE AND WENT STRAIGHT TO TOKYO UNIVERSITY. AFTER THAT, WE DRIFTED FURTHER AND FURTHER APART.
....
I-I'M SORRY FOR ASKING SUCH A PERSONAL QUESTION.
1
TAKA
TAKA
TAKA
PING
2
PING
SIGH... YOU SHOULD BE.
TAKA
亜細亜文通
....

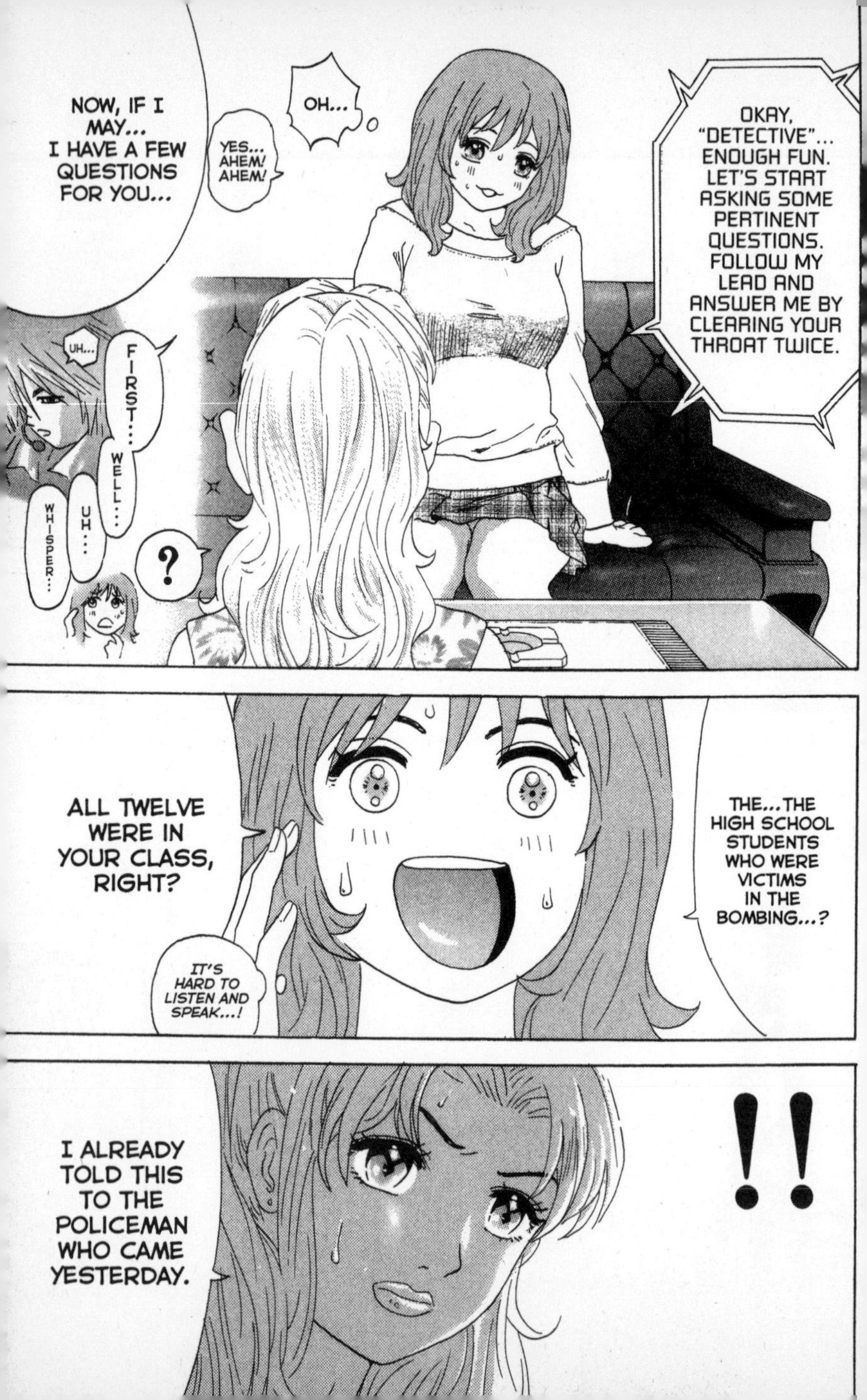
OKAY, "DETECTIVE"... ENOUGH FUN. LET'S START ASKING SOME PERTINENT QUESTIONS. FOLLOW MY LEAD AND ANSWER ME BY CLEARING YOUR THROAT TWICE.
OH...
YES... AHEM! AHEM!
NOW, IF I MAY... I HAVE A FEW QUESTIONS FOR YOU...
FIRST... WELL...
UH...
UH...
WHISPER...
?
THE...THE HIGH SCHOOL STUDENTS WHO WERE VICTIMS IN THE BOMBING...?
ALL TWELVE WERE IN YOUR CLASS, RIGHT?
IT'S HARD TO LISTEN AND SPEAK...!
!!
I ALREADY TOLD THIS TO THE POLICEMAN WHO CAME YESTERDAY.

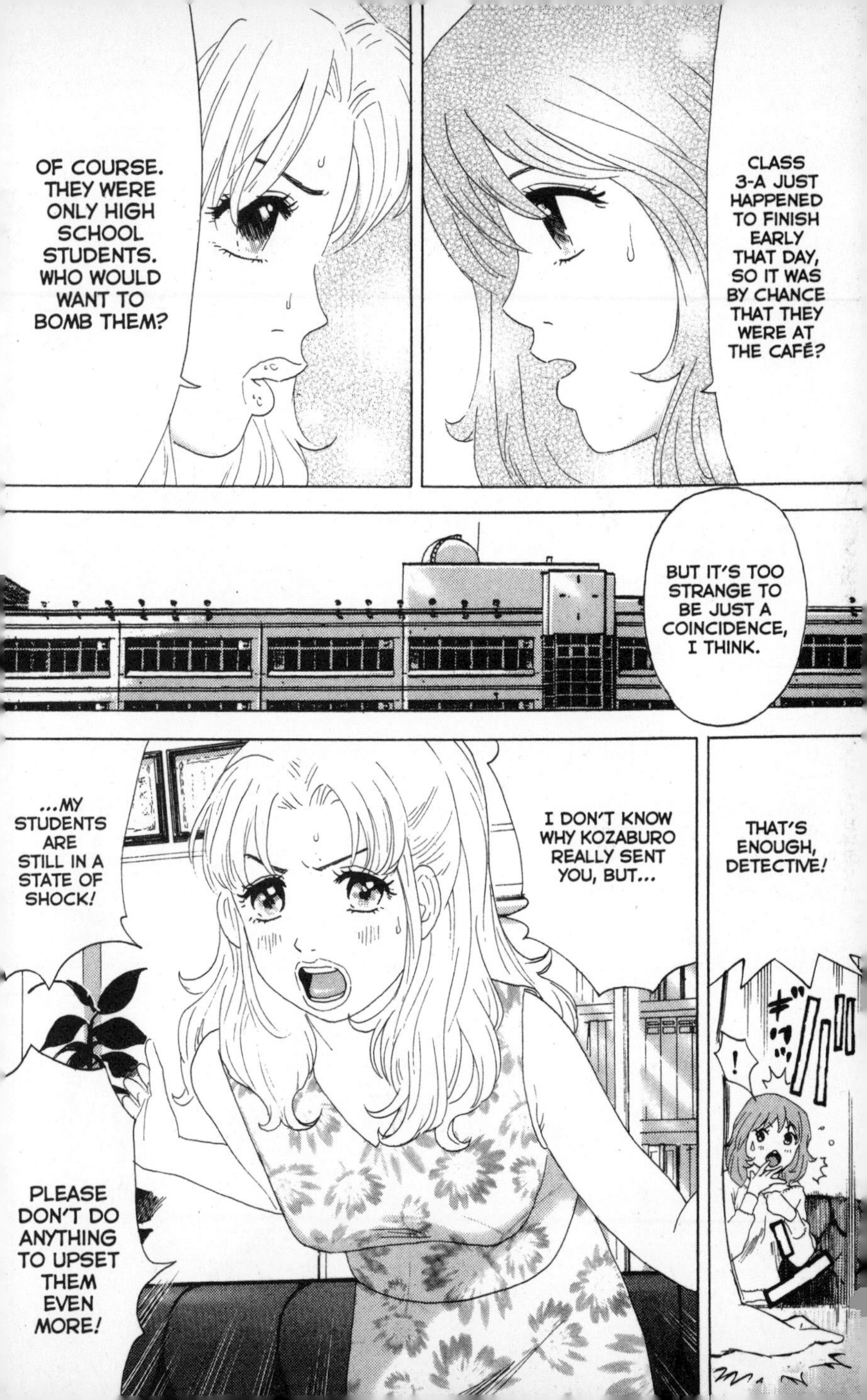
CLASS 3-A JUST HAPPENED TO FINISH EARLY THAT DAY, SO IT WAS BY CHANCE THAT THEY WERE AT THE CAFÉ?
OF COURSE. THEY WERE ONLY HIGH SCHOOL STUDENTS. WHO WOULD WANT TO BOMB THEM?
BUT IT'S TOO STRANGE TO BE JUST A COINCIDENCE, I THINK.
THAT'S ENOUGH, DETECTIVE!
!
I DON'T KNOW WHY KOZABURO REALLY SENT YOU, BUT...
...MY STUDENTS ARE STILL IN A STATE OF SHOCK!
PLEASE DON'T DO ANYTHING TO UPSET THEM EVEN MORE!

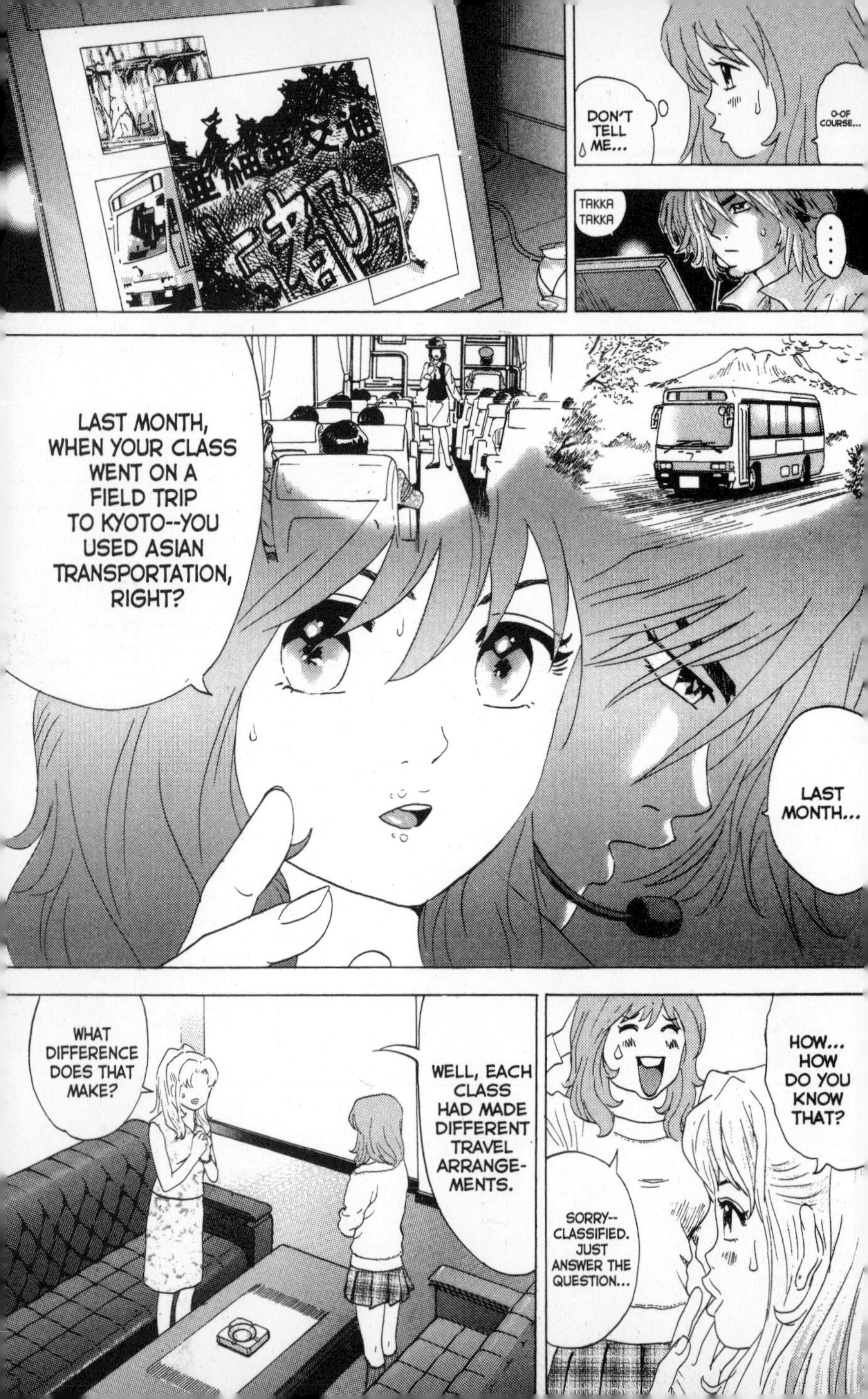
DON'T TELL ME...
O-OF COURSE...
TAKKA TAKKA
....
LAST MONTH, WHEN YOUR CLASS WENT ON A FIELD TRIP TO KYOTO--YOU USED ASIAN TRANSPORTATION, RIGHT?
LAST MONTH...
WHAT DIFFERENCE DOES THAT MAKE?
WELL, EACH CLASS HAD MADE DIFFERENT TRAVEL ARRANGE-MENTS.
HOW... HOW DO YOU KNOW THAT?
SORRY--CLASSIFIED. JUST ANSWER THE QUESTION...

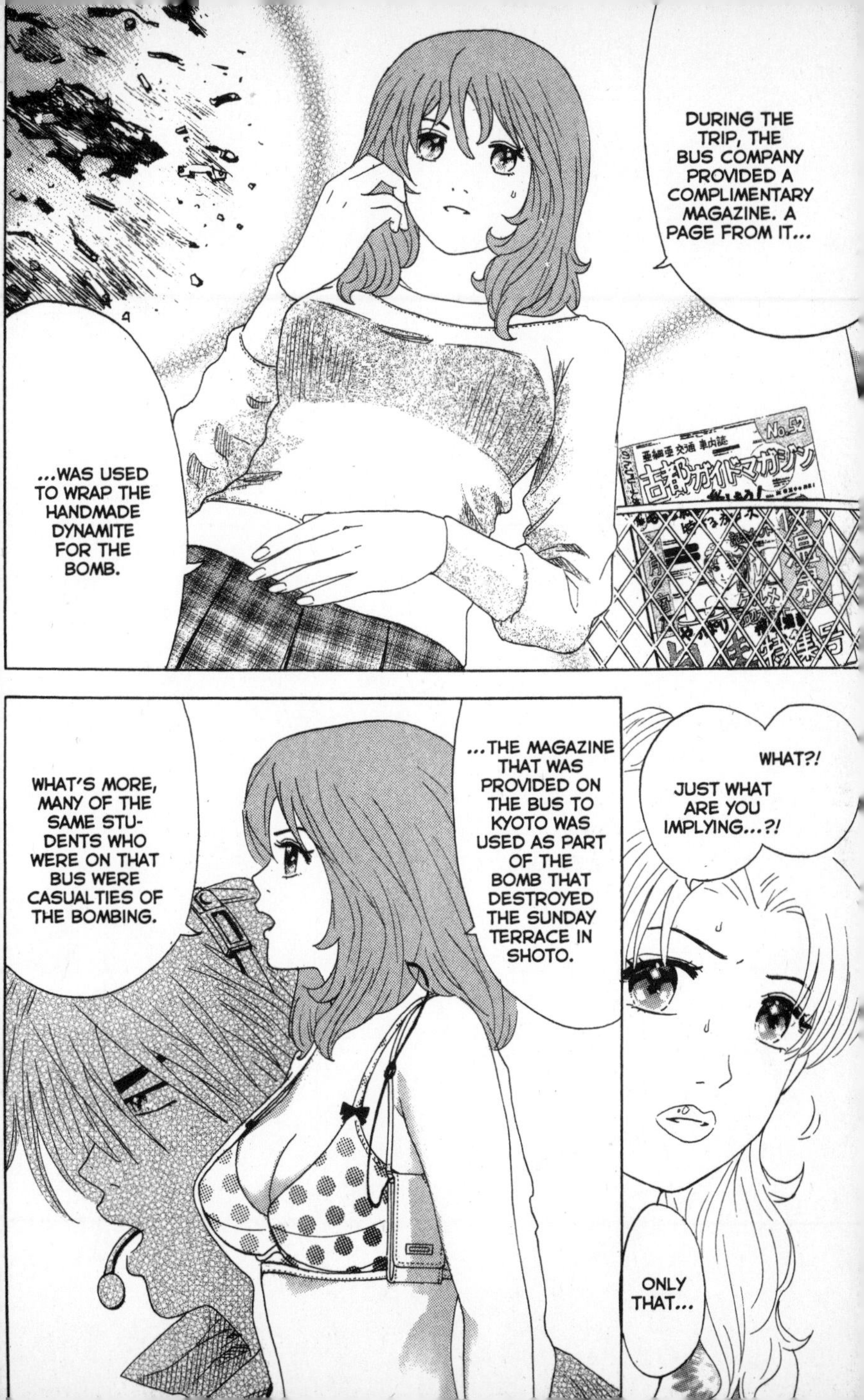
DURING THE TRIP, THE BUS COMPANY PROVIDED A COMPLIMENTARY MAGAZINE. A PAGE FROM IT...
No.52
古都ガイドマガジン
...WAS USED TO WRAP THE HANDMADE DYNAMITE FOR THE BOMB.
WHAT?!
JUST WHAT ARE YOU IMPLYING...?!
ONLY THAT...
...THE MAGAZINE THAT WAS PROVIDED ON THE BUS TO KYOTO WAS USED AS PART OF THE BOMB THAT DESTROYED THE SUNDAY TERRACE IN SHOTO.
WHAT'S MORE, MANY OF THE SAME STUDENTS WHO WERE ON THAT BUS WERE CASUALTIES OF THE BOMBING.

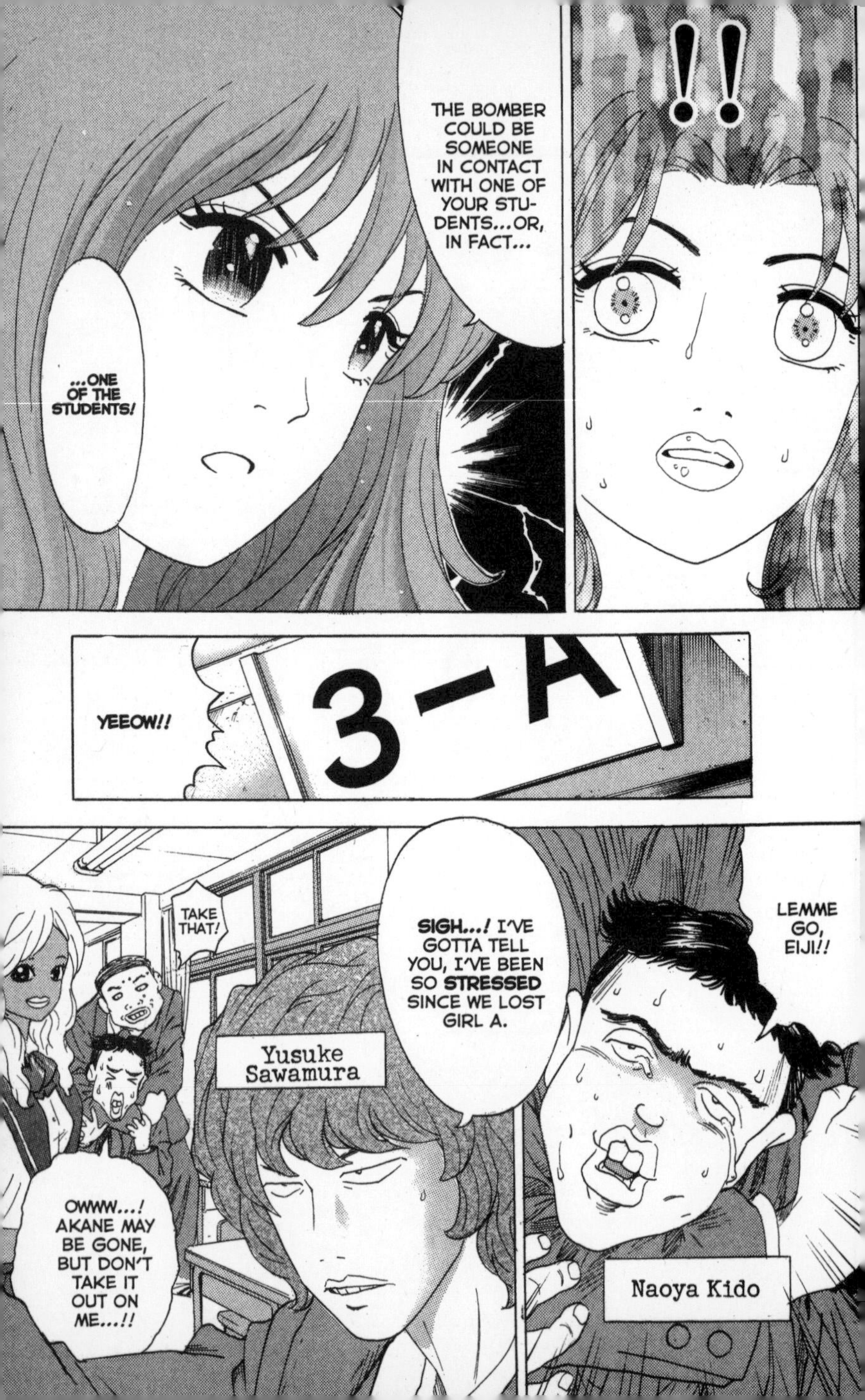
!!
THE BOMBER COULD BE SOMEONE IN CONTACT WITH ONE OF YOUR STU-DENTS...OR, IN FACT...
...ONE OF THE STUDENTS!
3-A
YEEOW!!
LEMME GO, EIJI!!
SIGH...! I'VE GOTTA TELL YOU, I'VE BEEN SO STRESSED SINCE WE LOST GIRL A.
Naoya Kido
TAKE THAT!
Yusuke Sawamura
OWWW...! AKANE MAY BE GONE, BUT DON'T TAKE IT OUT ON ME...!!

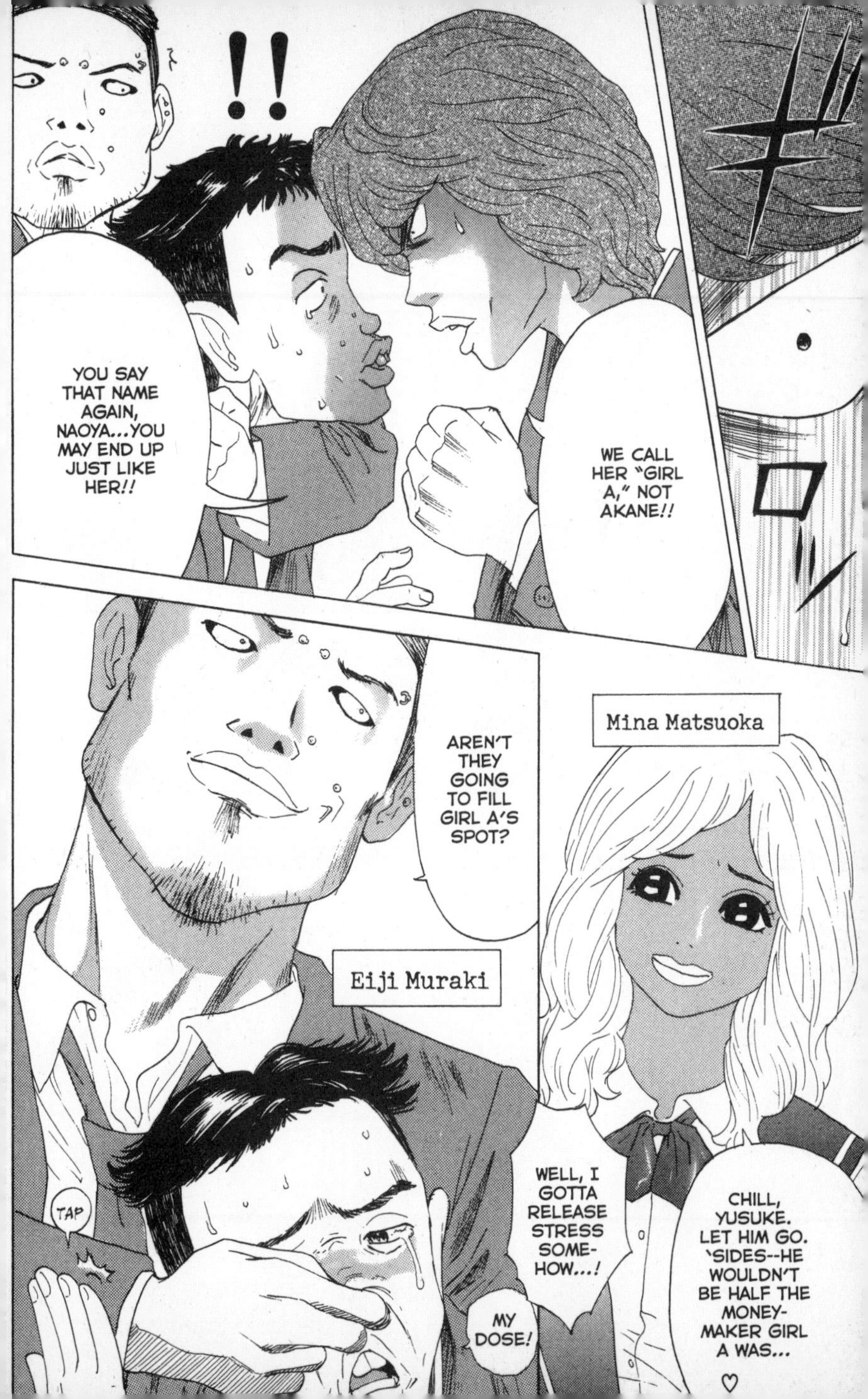
!!
WE CALL HER "GIRL A," NOT AKANE!!
YOU SAY THAT NAME AGAIN, NAOYA...YOU MAY END UP JUST LIKE HER!!
Mina Matsuoka
AREN'T THEY GOING TO FILL GIRL A'S SPOT?
Eiji Muraki
CHILL, YUSUKE. LET HIM GO. 'SIDES--HE WOULDN'T BE HALF THE MONEY-MAKER GIRL A WAS... ♡
WELL, I GOTTA RELEASE STRESS SOME-HOW...!
MY DOSE!
TAP

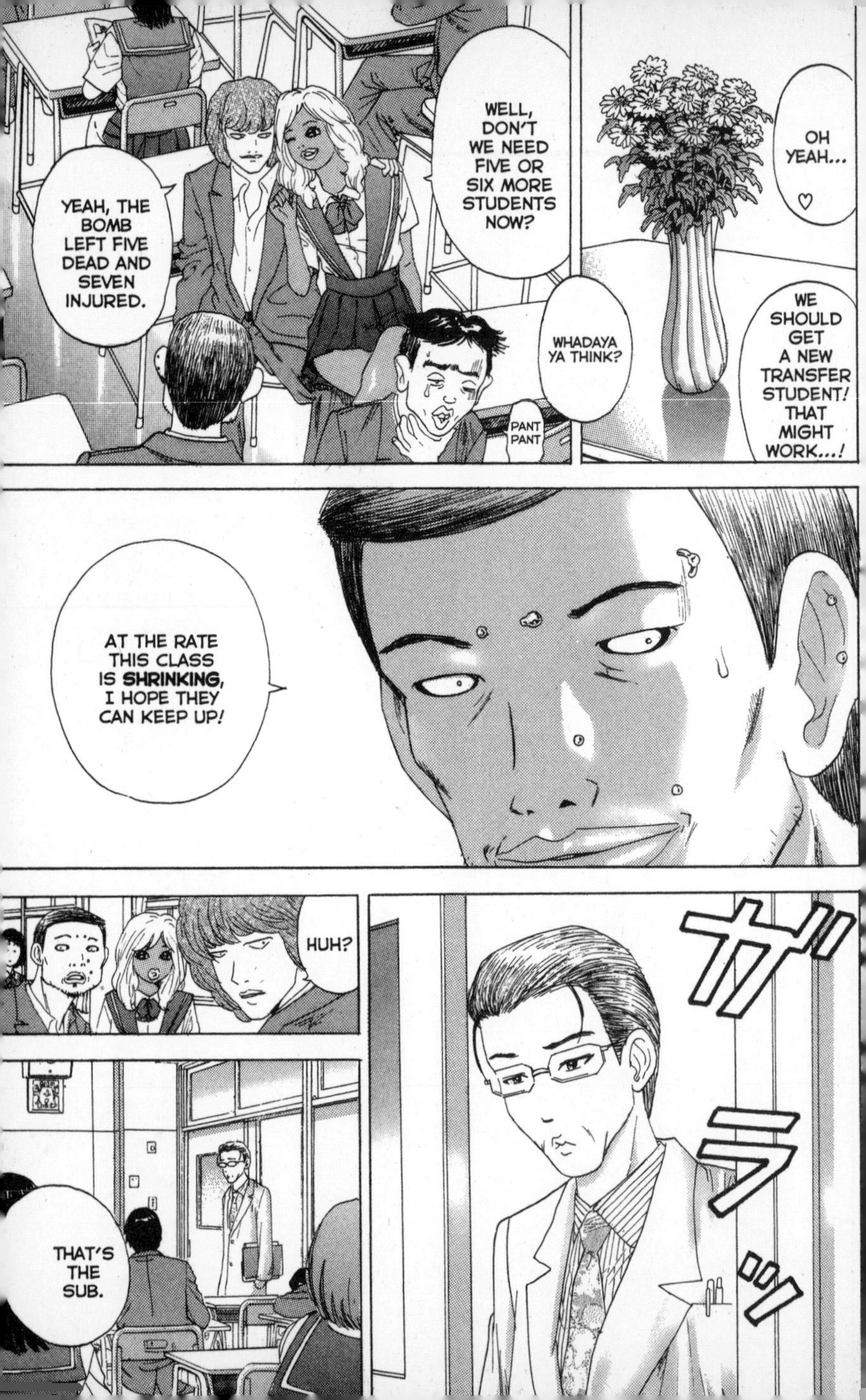
OH YEAH... ♡
WE SHOULD GET A NEW TRANSFER STUDENT! THAT MIGHT WORK...!
WHADAYA YA THINK?
PANT PANT
WELL, DON'T WE NEED FIVE OR SIX MORE STUDENTS NOW?
YEAH, THE BOMB LEFT FIVE DEAD AND SEVEN INJURED.
AT THE RATE THIS CLASS IS **SHRINKING**, I HOPE THEY CAN KEEP UP!
ガラッ
HUH?
THAT'S THE SUB.

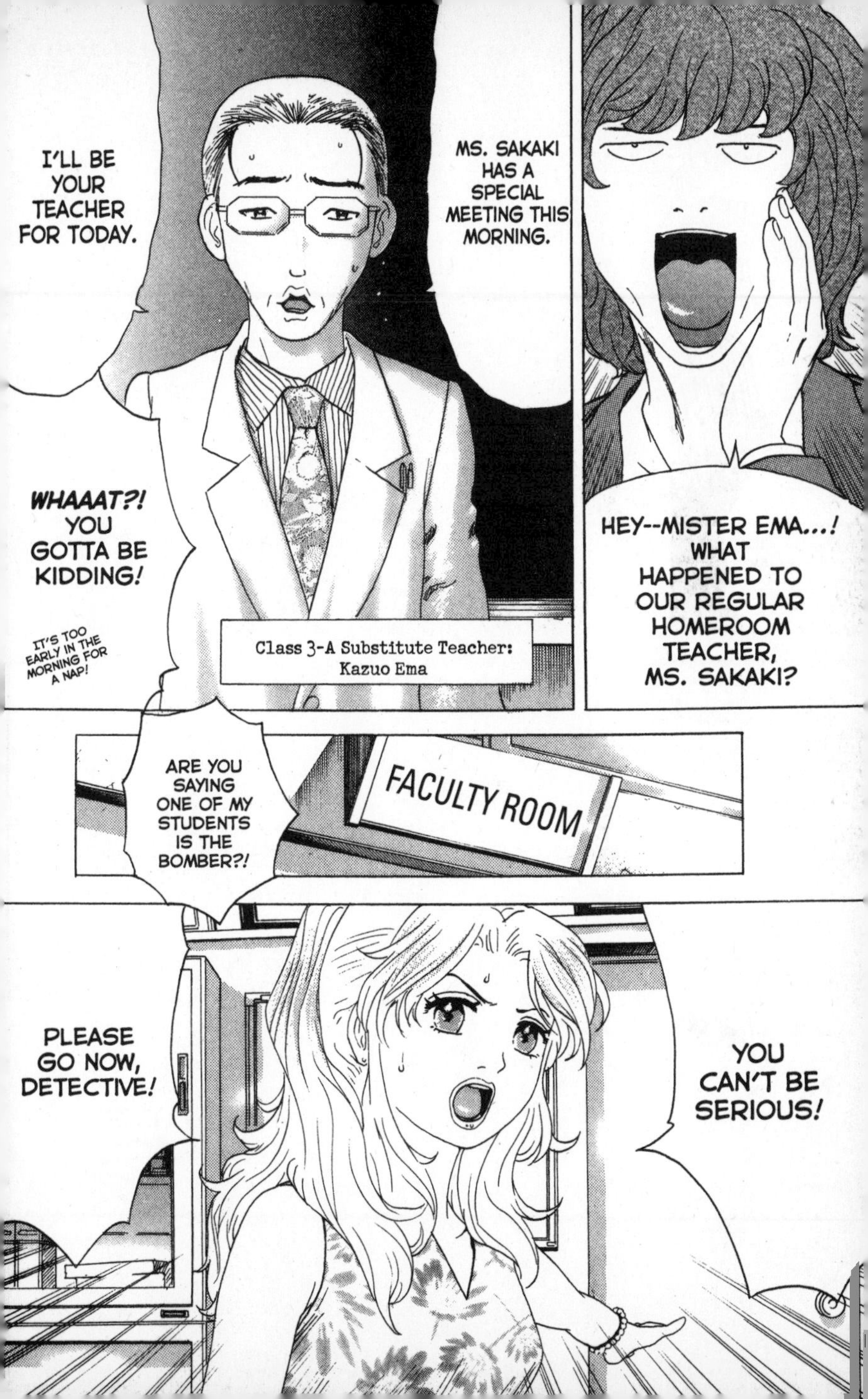
HEY--MISTER EMA...! WHAT HAPPENED TO OUR REGULAR HOMEROOM TEACHER, MS. SAKAKI?
MS. SAKAKI HAS A SPECIAL MEETING THIS MORNING.
I'LL BE YOUR TEACHER FOR TODAY.
Class 3-A Substitute Teacher: Kazuo Ema
WHAAAT?! YOU GOTTA BE KIDDING!
IT'S TOO EARLY IN THE MORNING FOR A NAP!
FACULTY ROOM
ARE YOU SAYING ONE OF MY STUDENTS IS THE BOMBER?!
YOU CAN'T BE SERIOUS!
PLEASE GO NOW, DETECTIVE!

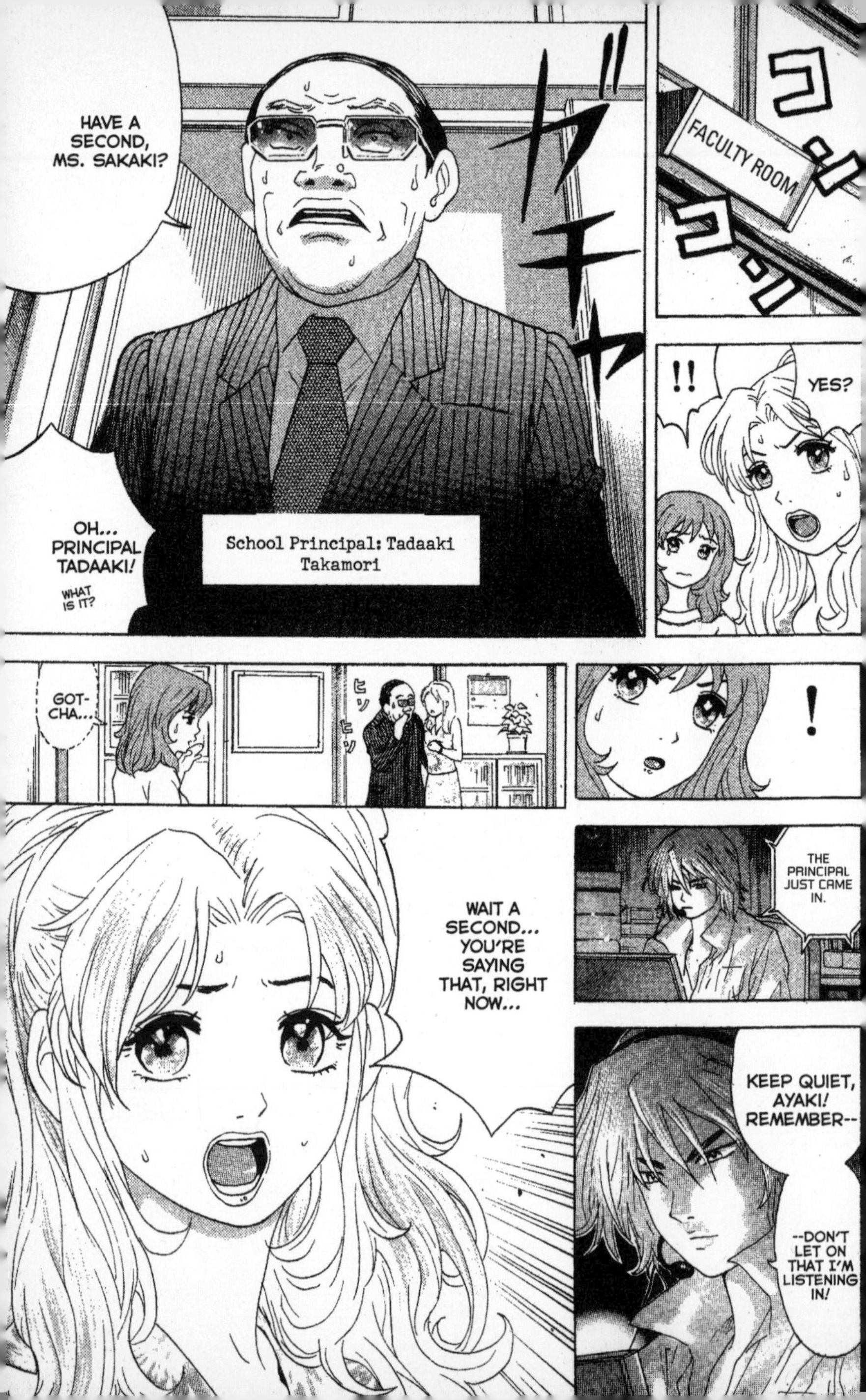
FACULTY ROOM
!!
YES?
ガチャ
HAVE A SECOND, MS. SAKAKI?
School Principal: Tadaaki Takamori
OH... PRINCIPAL TADAAKI!
WHAT IS IT?
!
ヒソ ヒソ
GOT-CHA...
THE PRINCIPAL JUST CAME IN.
KEEP QUIET, AYAKI! REMEMBER--
--DON'T LET ON THAT I'M LISTENING IN!
WAIT A SECOND... YOU'RE SAYING THAT, RIGHT NOW...

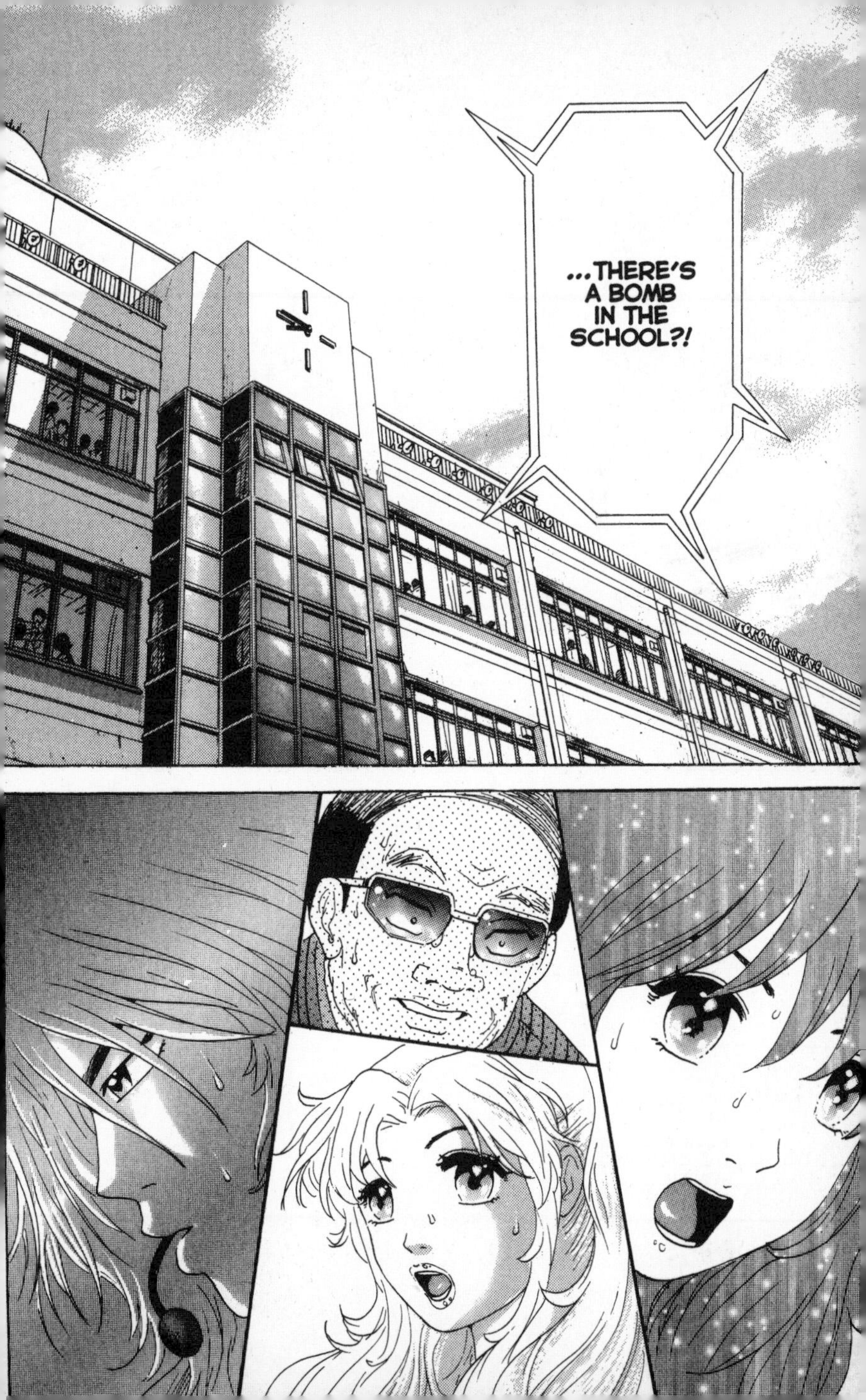
...THERE'S A BOMB IN THE SCHOOL?!

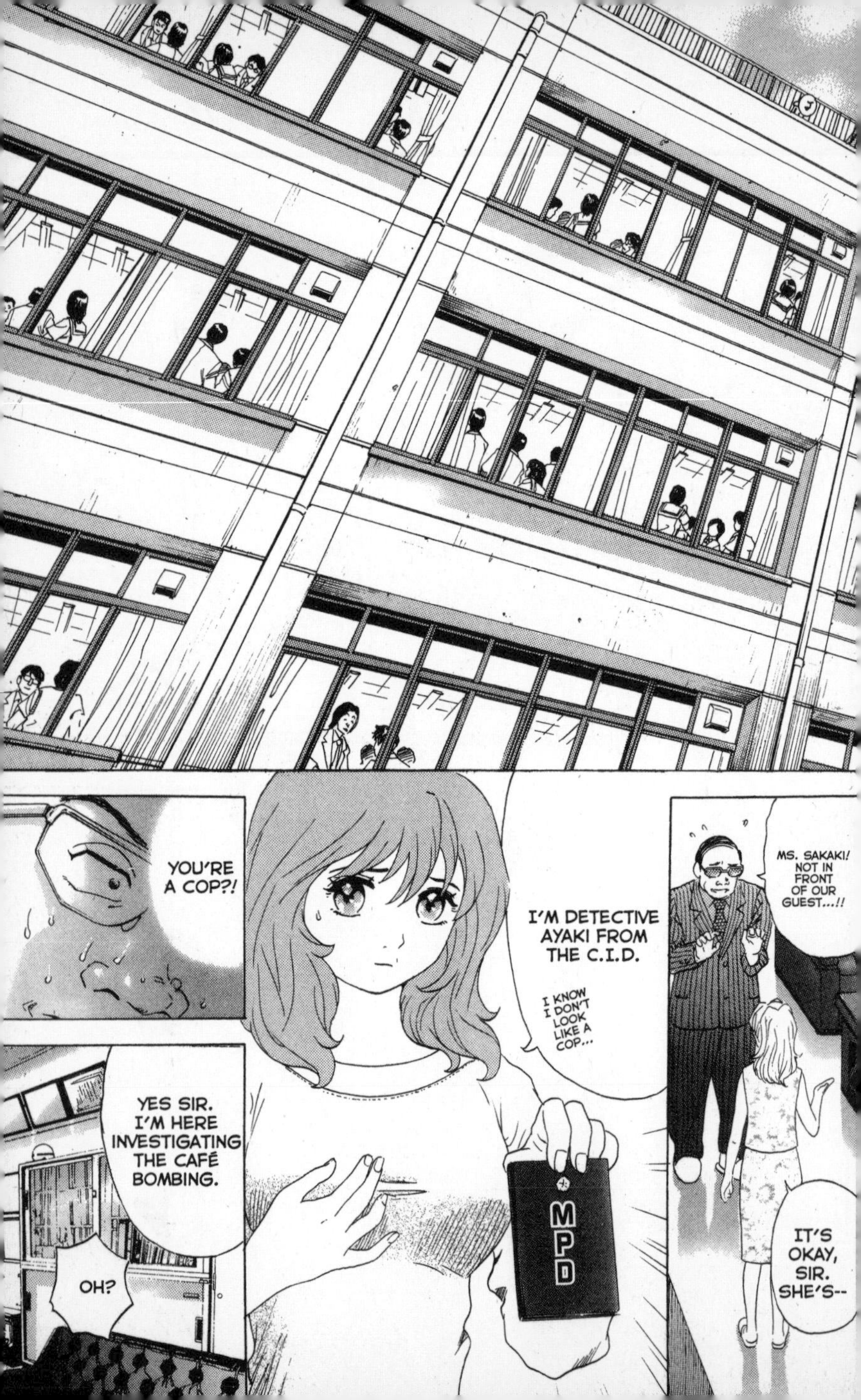
MS. SAKAKI! NOT IN FRONT OF OUR GUEST...!!
IT'S OKAY, SIR. SHE'S--
I'M DETECTIVE AYAKI FROM THE C.I.D.
I KNOW I DON'T LOOK LIKE A COP...
MPD
YOU'RE A COP?!
YES SIR. I'M HERE INVESTIGATING THE CAFÉ BOMBING.
OH?

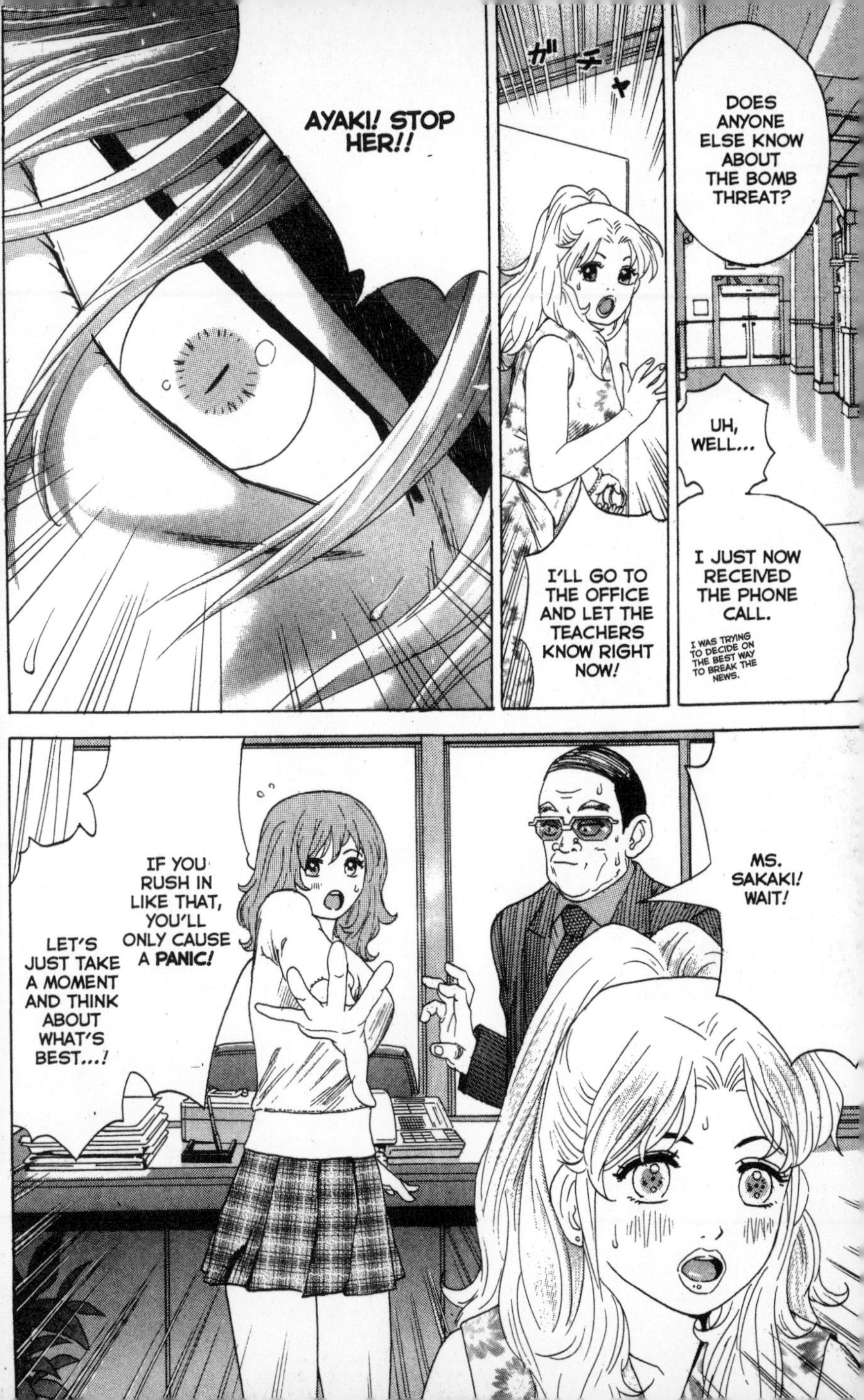
DOES ANYONE ELSE KNOW ABOUT THE BOMB THREAT?
UH, WELL...
I JUST NOW RECEIVED THE PHONE CALL.
I WAS TRYING TO DECIDE ON THE BEST WAY TO BREAK THE NEWS.
ガチャ
I'LL GO TO THE OFFICE AND LET THE TEACHERS KNOW RIGHT NOW!
AYAKI! STOP HER!!
MS. SAKAKI! WAIT!
IF YOU RUSH IN LIKE THAT, YOU'LL ONLY CAUSE A **PANIC**!
LET'S JUST TAKE A MOMENT AND THINK ABOUT WHAT'S BEST...!

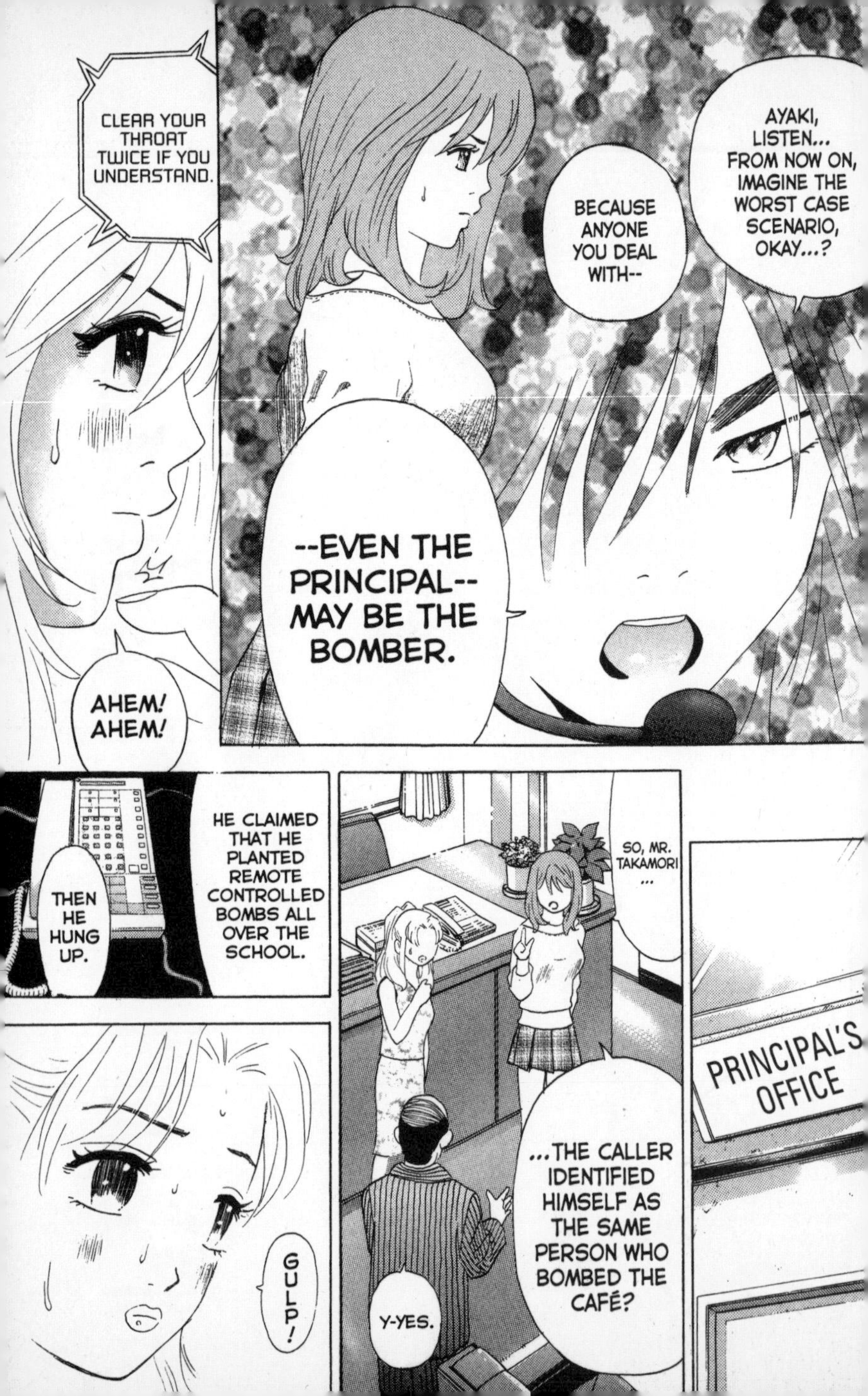
AYAKI, LISTEN... FROM NOW ON, IMAGINE THE WORST CASE SCENARIO, OKAY...?
BECAUSE ANYONE YOU DEAL WITH--
--EVEN THE PRINCIPAL-- MAY BE THE BOMBER.
CLEAR YOUR THROAT TWICE IF YOU UNDERSTAND.
AHEM! AHEM!
PRINCIPAL'S OFFICE
SO, MR. TAKAMORI ...
...THE CALLER IDENTIFIED HIMSELF AS THE SAME PERSON WHO BOMBED THE CAFÉ?
Y-YES.
HE CLAIMED THAT HE PLANTED REMOTE CONTROLLED BOMBS ALL OVER THE SCHOOL.
THEN HE HUNG UP.
GULP!

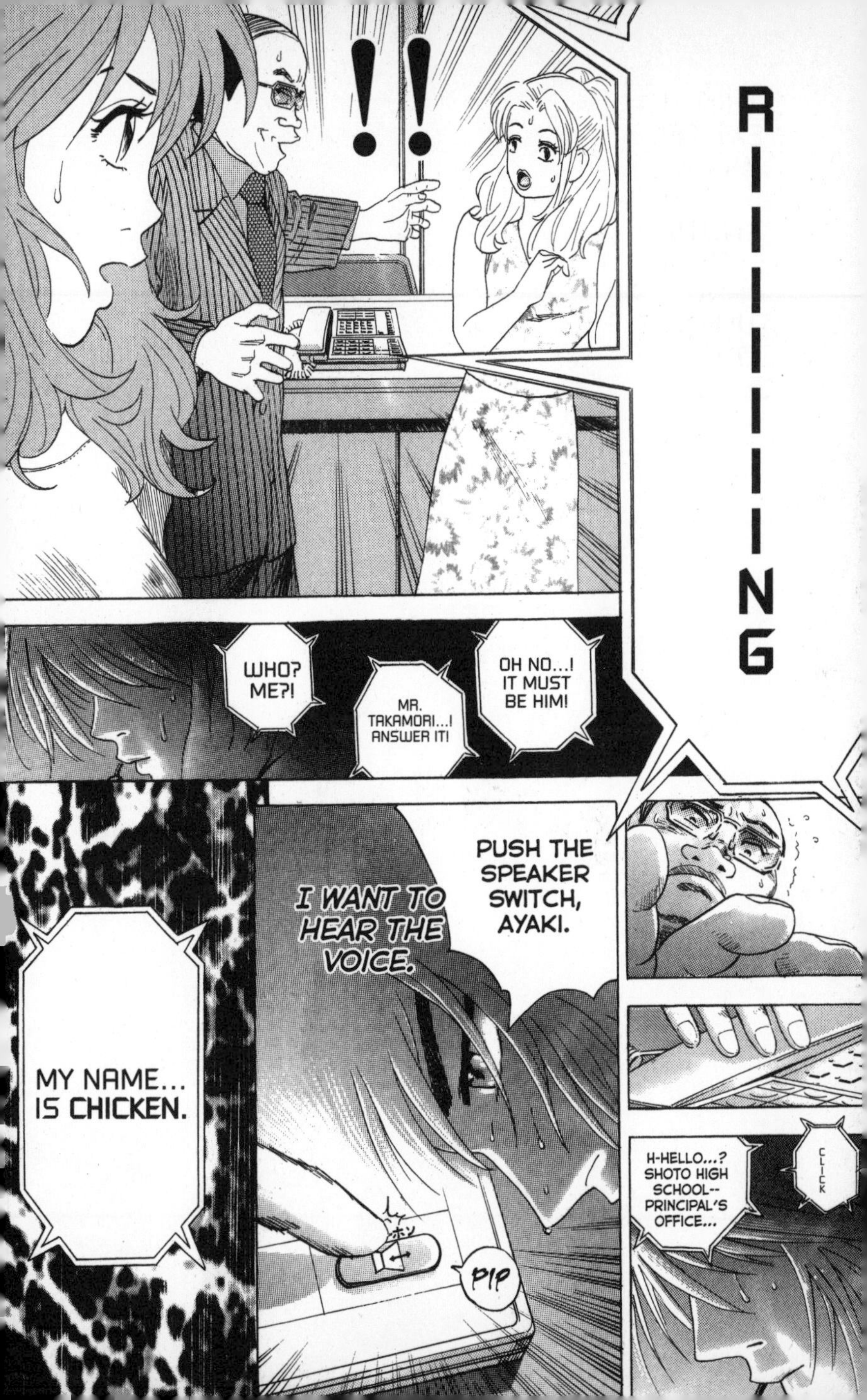
RIIIIIING
!!
OH NO...! IT MUST BE HIM!
MR. TAKAMORI...! ANSWER IT!
WHO? ME?!
CLICK
H-HELLO...? SHOTO HIGH SCHOOL-- PRINCIPAL'S OFFICE...
PUSH THE SPEAKER SWITCH, AYAKI.
I WANT TO HEAR THE VOICE.
PIP
MY NAME... IS CHICKEN.

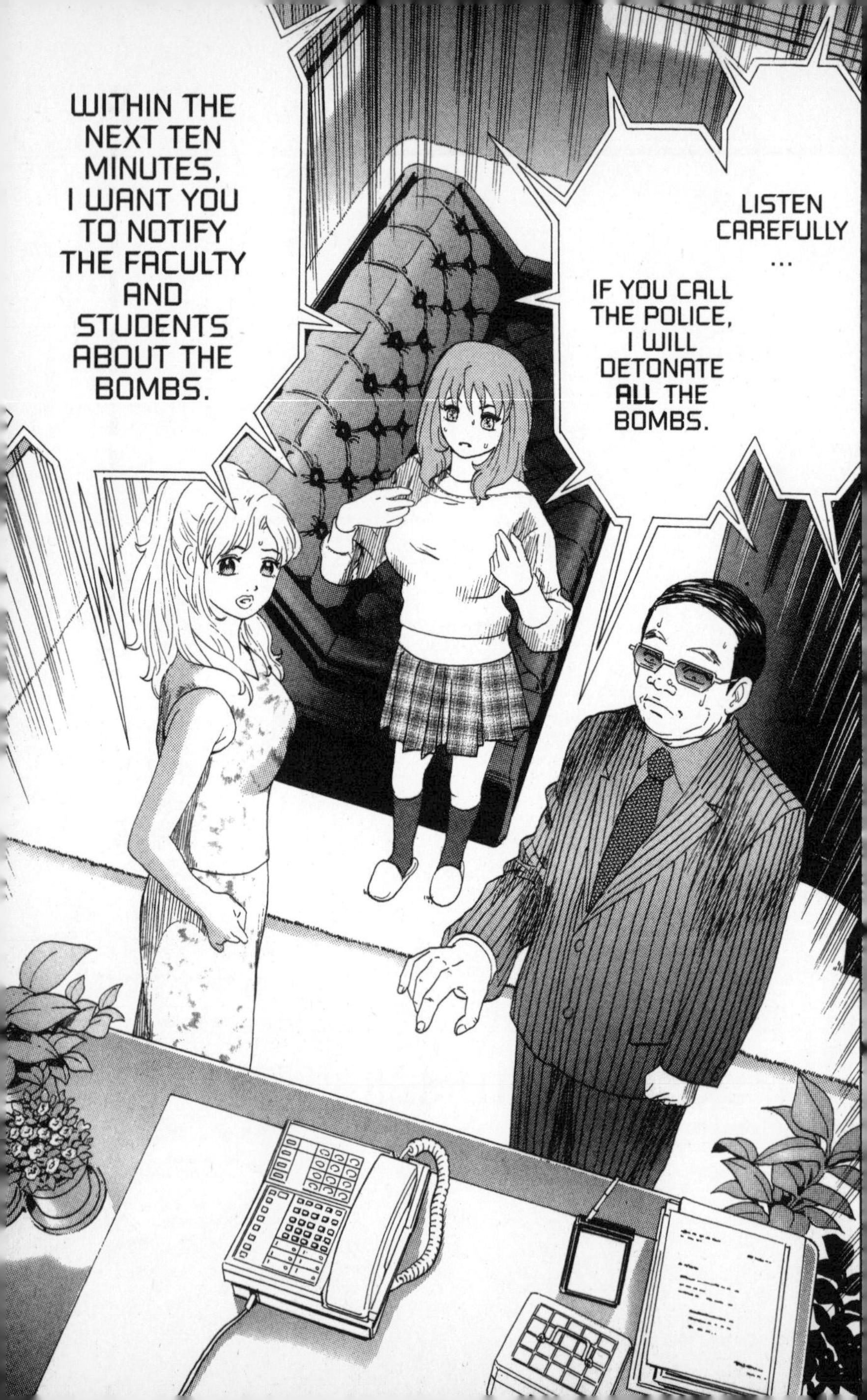
LISTEN CAREFULLY ...
IF YOU CALL THE POLICE, I WILL DETONATE **ALL** THE BOMBS.
WITHIN THE NEXT TEN MINUTES, I WANT YOU TO NOTIFY THE FACULTY AND STUDENTS ABOUT THE BOMBS.

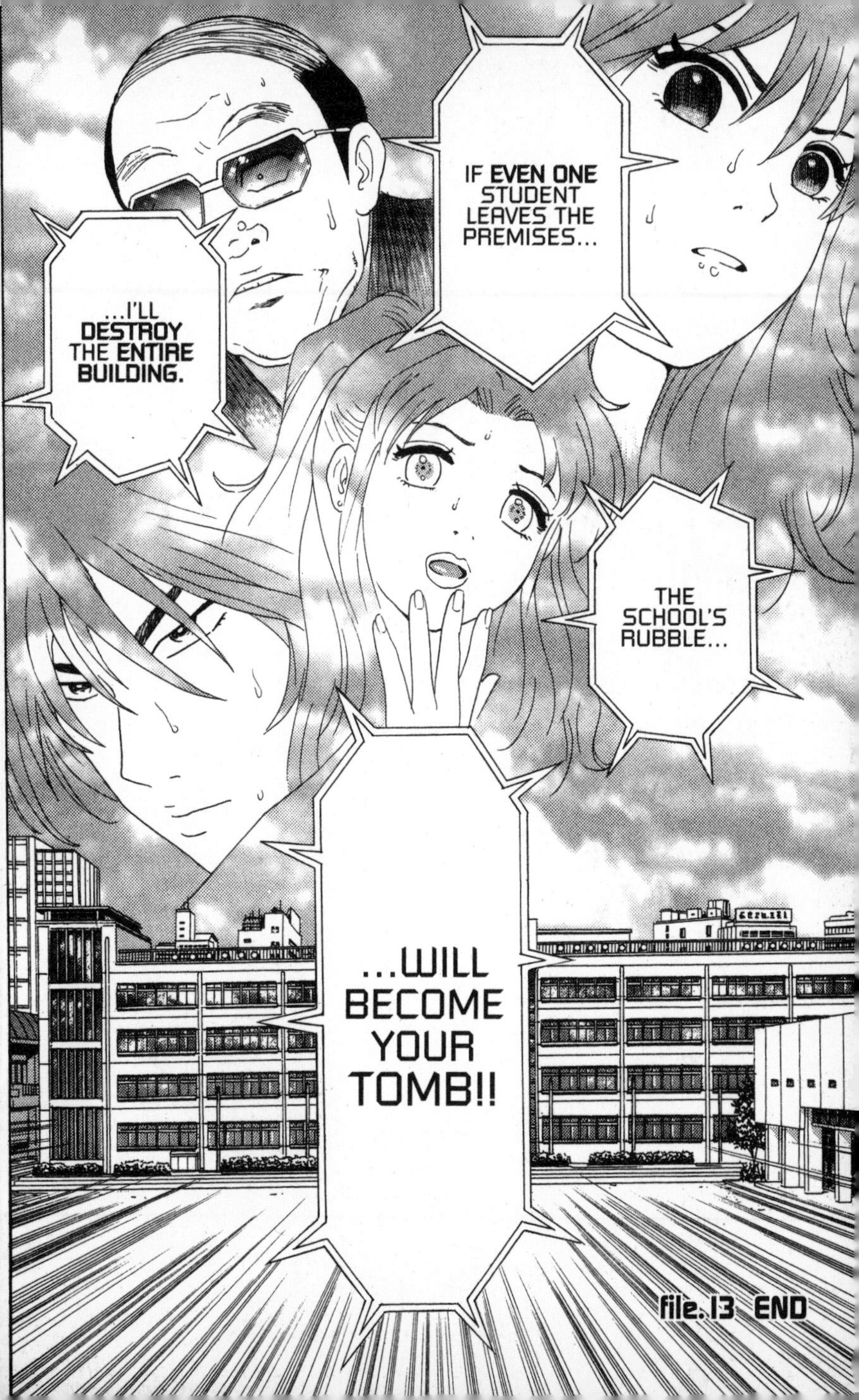
IF EVEN ONE STUDENT LEAVES THE PREMISES...
...I'LL DESTROY THE ENTIRE BUILDING.
THE SCHOOL'S RUBBLE...
...WILL BECOME YOUR TOMB!!
file.13 END

FILE 14 SURVIVAL SCHOOL
AN UNUSUAL TRANSFER STUDENT

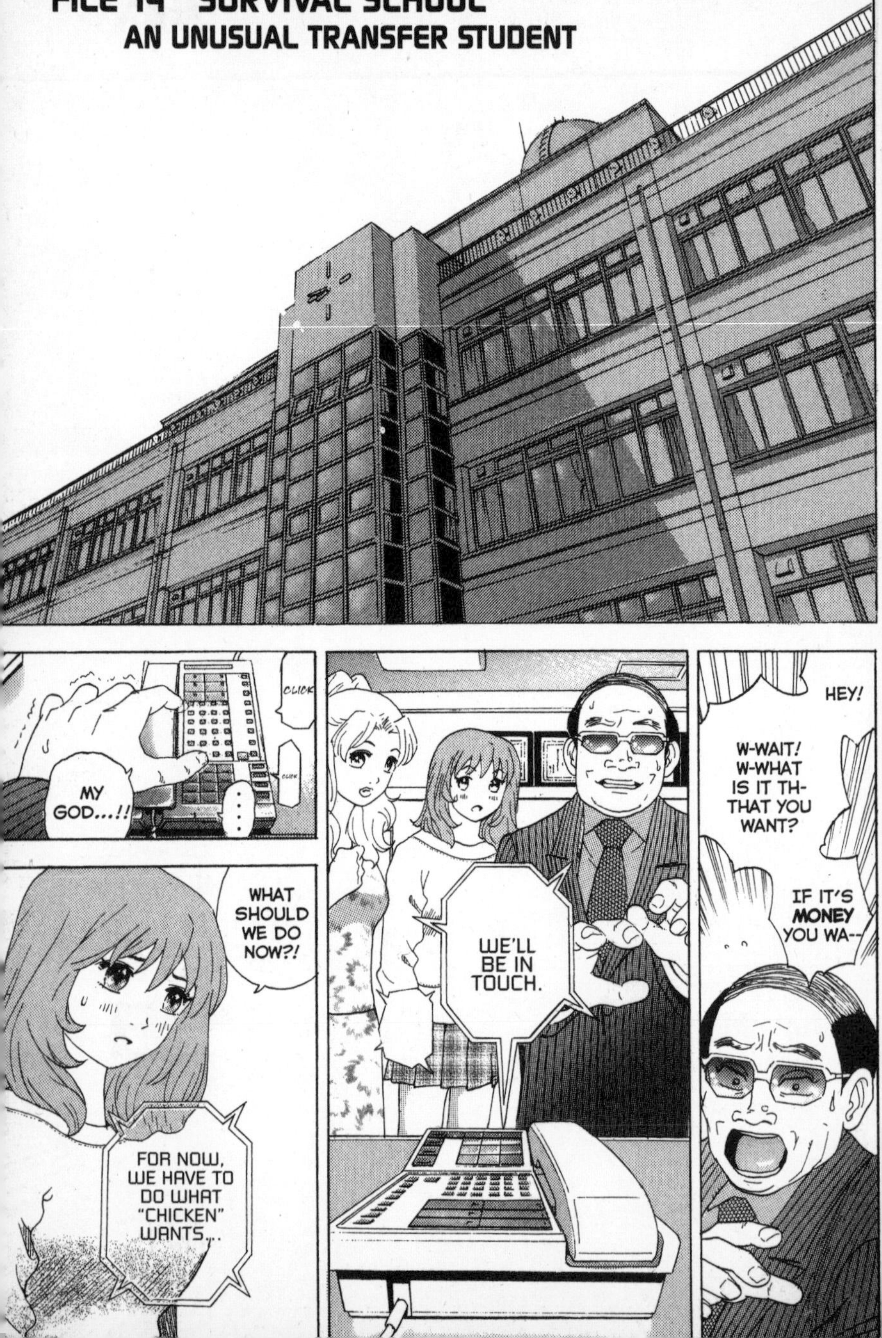
HEY!
W-WAIT! W-WHAT IS IT TH- THAT YOU WANT?
IF IT'S **MONEY** YOU WA--
WE'LL BE IN TOUCH.
CLICK
CLICK
MY GOD...!!
...
WHAT SHOULD WE DO NOW?!
FOR NOW, WE HAVE TO DO WHAT "CHICKEN" WANTS...

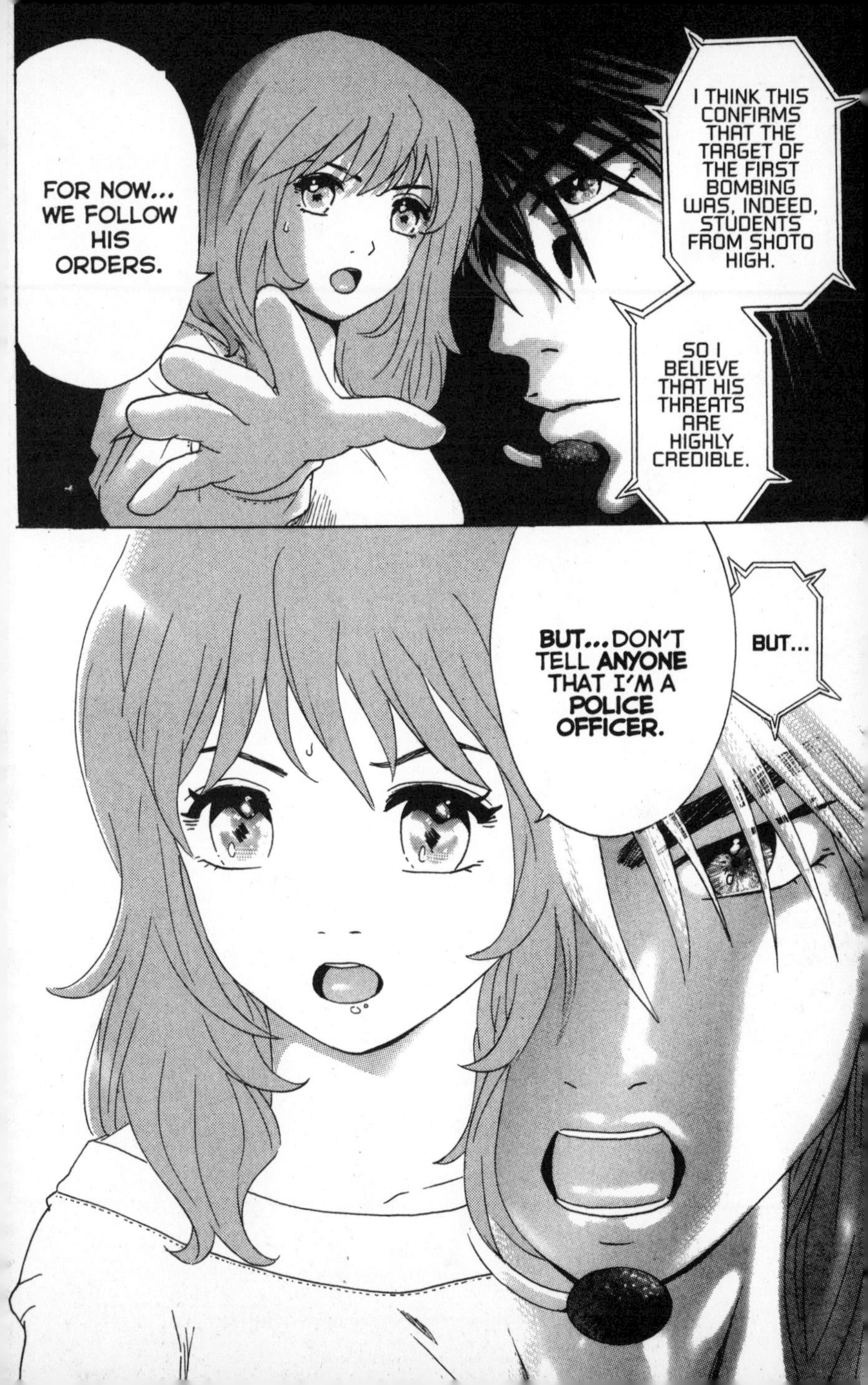
I THINK THIS CONFIRMS THAT THE TARGET OF THE FIRST BOMBING WAS, INDEED, STUDENTS FROM SHOTO HIGH.
SO I BELIEVE THAT HIS THREATS ARE HIGHLY CREDIBLE.
FOR NOW... WE FOLLOW HIS ORDERS.
BUT...
BUT... DON'T TELL ANYONE THAT I'M A POLICE OFFICER.

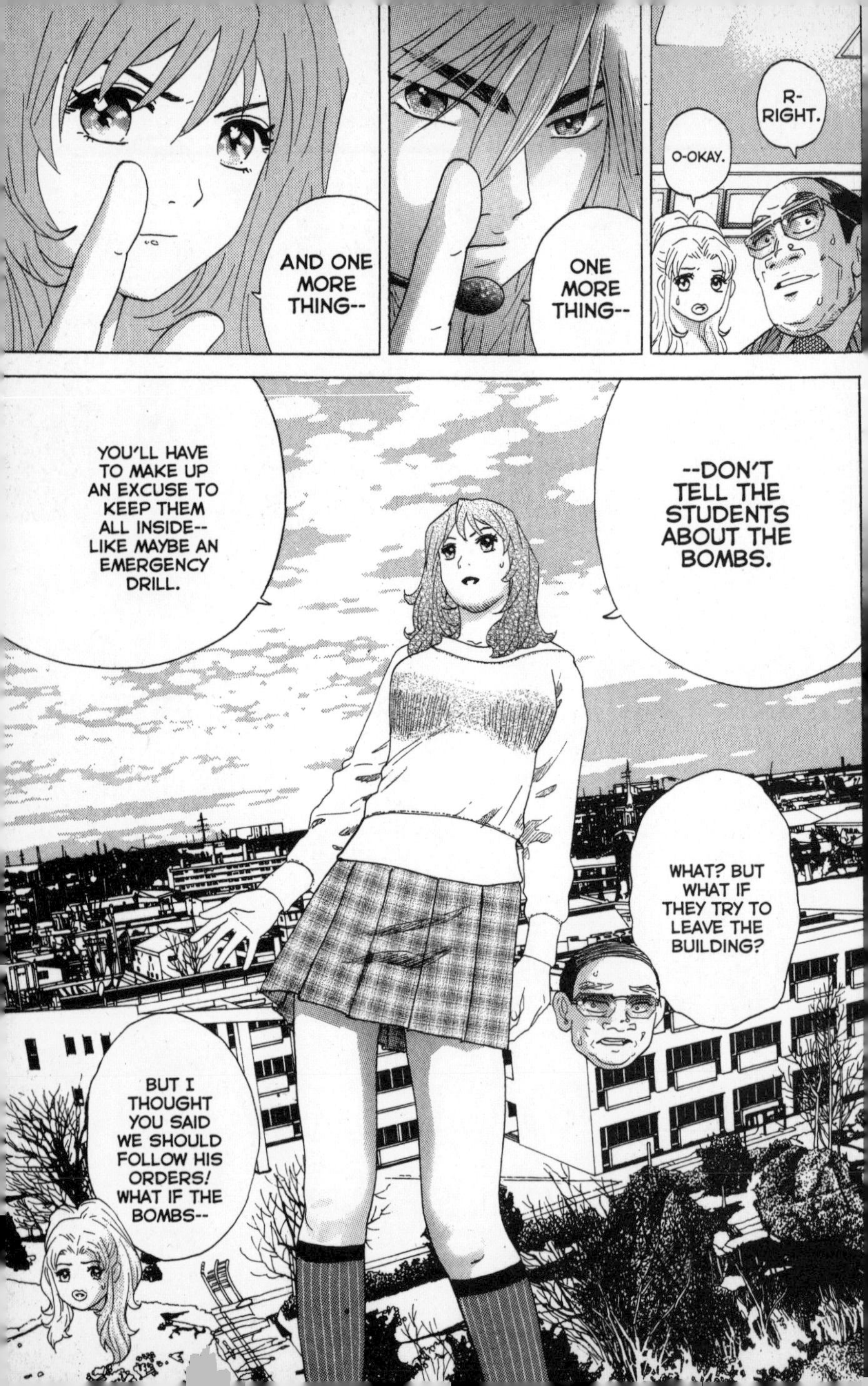
R-RIGHT.
O-OKAY.
ONE MORE THING--
AND ONE MORE THING--
--DON'T TELL THE STUDENTS ABOUT THE BOMBS.
YOU'LL HAVE TO MAKE UP AN EXCUSE TO KEEP THEM ALL INSIDE-- LIKE MAYBE AN EMERGENCY DRILL.
WHAT? BUT WHAT IF THEY TRY TO LEAVE THE BUILDING?
BUT I THOUGHT YOU SAID WE SHOULD FOLLOW HIS ORDERS! WHAT IF THE BOMBS--

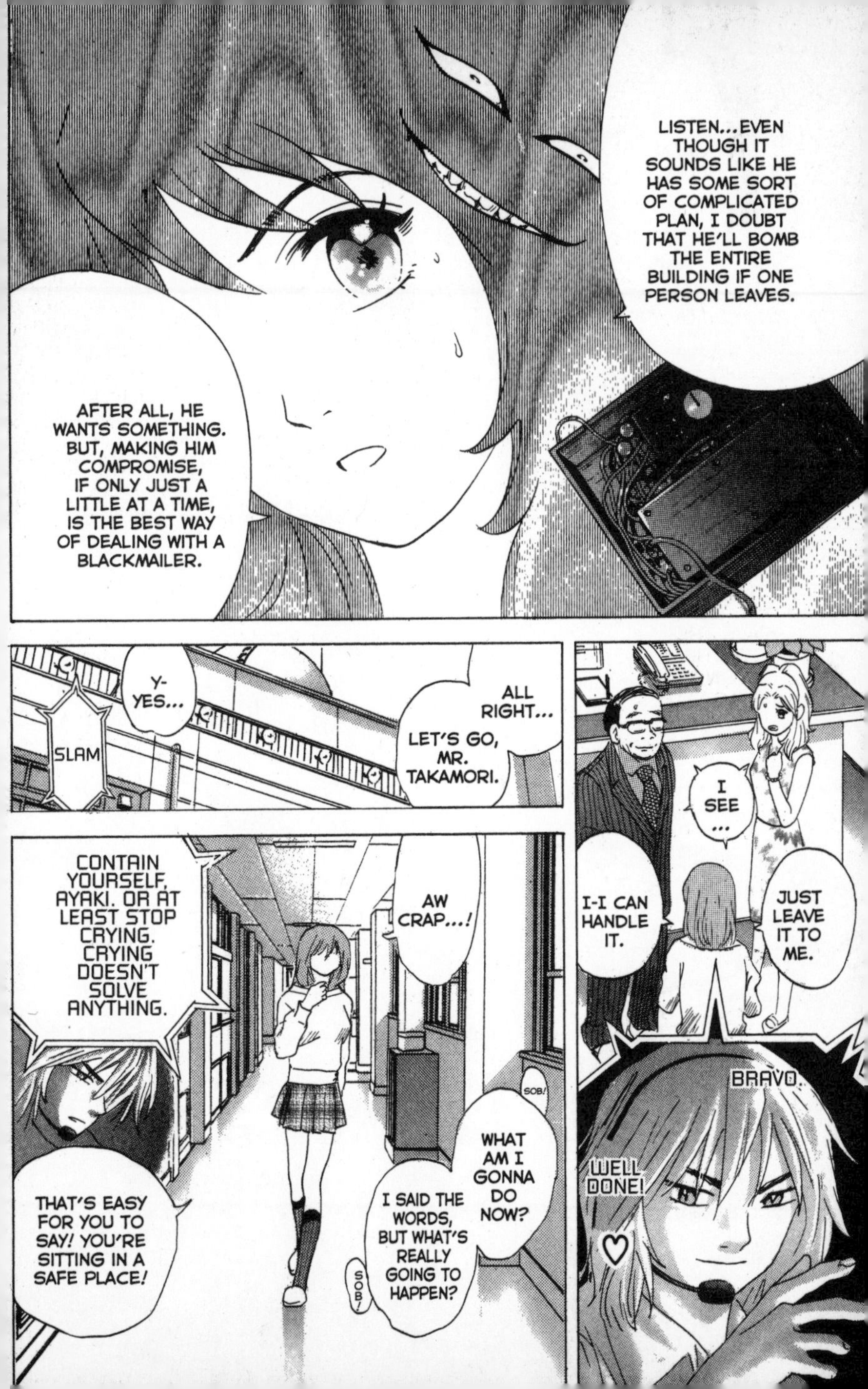
LISTEN...EVEN THOUGH IT SOUNDS LIKE HE HAS SOME SORT OF COMPLICATED PLAN, I DOUBT THAT HE'LL BOMB THE ENTIRE BUILDING IF ONE PERSON LEAVES.
AFTER ALL, HE WANTS SOMETHING. BUT, MAKING HIM COMPROMISE, IF ONLY JUST A LITTLE AT A TIME, IS THE BEST WAY OF DEALING WITH A BLACKMAILER.
I SEE...
JUST LEAVE IT TO ME.
I-I CAN HANDLE IT.
ALL RIGHT...
LET'S GO, MR. TAKAMORI.
Y-YES...
SLAM
BRAVO.
WELL DONE!
AW CRAP...!
CONTAIN YOURSELF, AYAKI. OR AT LEAST STOP CRYING. CRYING DOESN'T SOLVE ANYTHING.
SOB!
WHAT AM I GONNA DO NOW?
I SAID THE WORDS, BUT WHAT'S REALLY GOING TO HAPPEN?
SOB!
THAT'S EASY FOR YOU TO SAY! YOU'RE SITTING IN A SAFE PLACE!

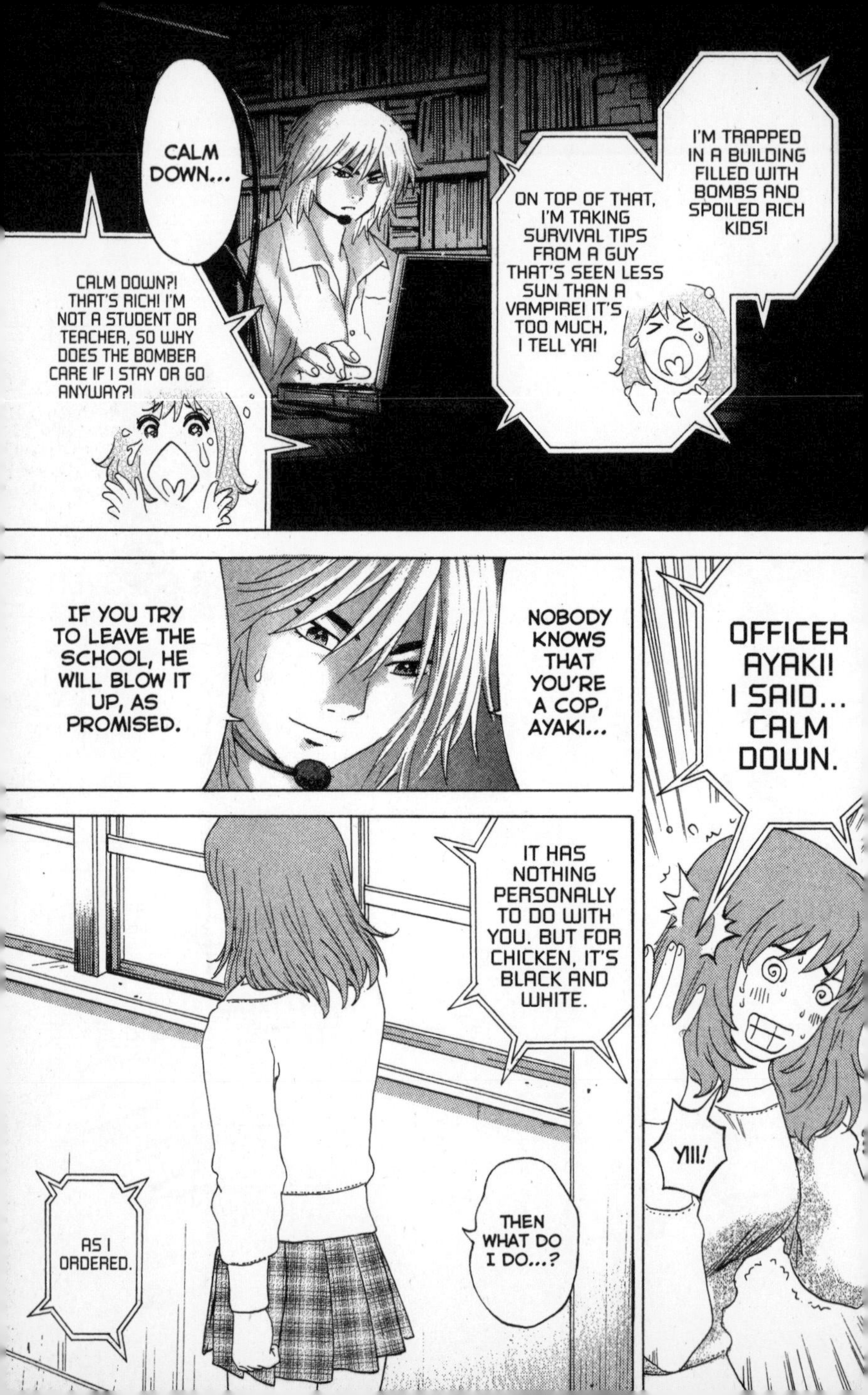

I'M TRAPPED IN A BUILDING FILLED WITH BOMBS AND SPOILED RICH KIDS!
ON TOP OF THAT, I'M TAKING SURVIVAL TIPS FROM A GUY THAT'S SEEN LESS SUN THAN A VAMPIRE! IT'S TOO MUCH, I TELL YA!
CALM DOWN...
CALM DOWN?! THAT'S RICH! I'M NOT A STUDENT OR TEACHER, SO WHY DOES THE BOMBER CARE IF I STAY OR GO ANYWAY?!
OFFICER AYAKI! I SAID... CALM DOWN.
YIII!
NOBODY KNOWS THAT YOU'RE A COP, AYAKI...
IF YOU TRY TO LEAVE THE SCHOOL, HE WILL BLOW IT UP, AS PROMISED.
IT HAS NOTHING PERSONALLY TO DO WITH YOU. BUT FOR CHICKEN, IT'S BLACK AND WHITE.
THEN WHAT DO I DO...?
AS I ORDERED.

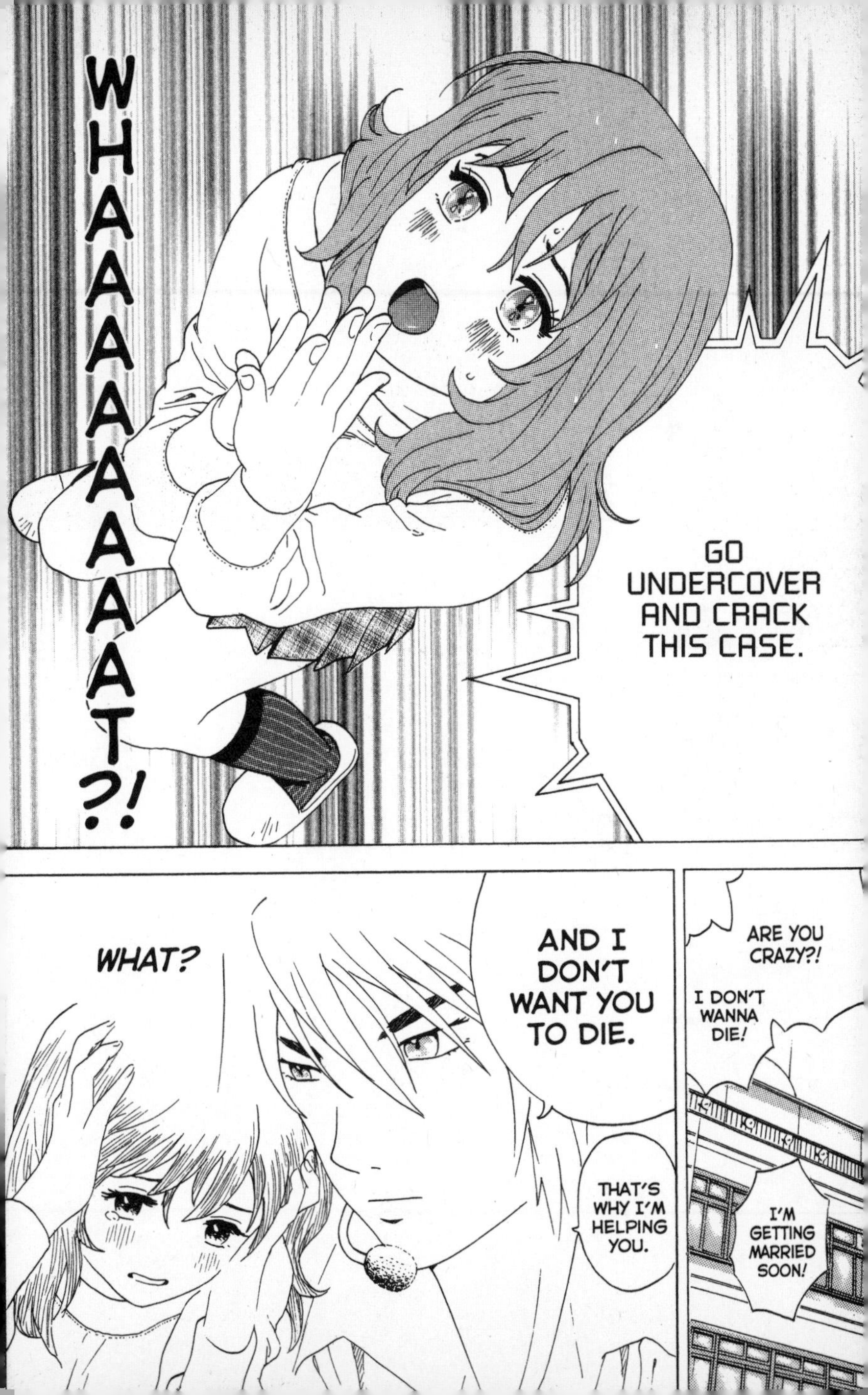
GO UNDERCOVER AND CRACK THIS CASE.
WHAAAAAAAAT?!
ARE YOU CRAZY?!
I DON'T WANNA DIE!
I'M GETTING MARRIED SOON!
AND I DON'T WANT YOU TO DIE.
THAT'S WHY I'M HELPING YOU.
WHAT?

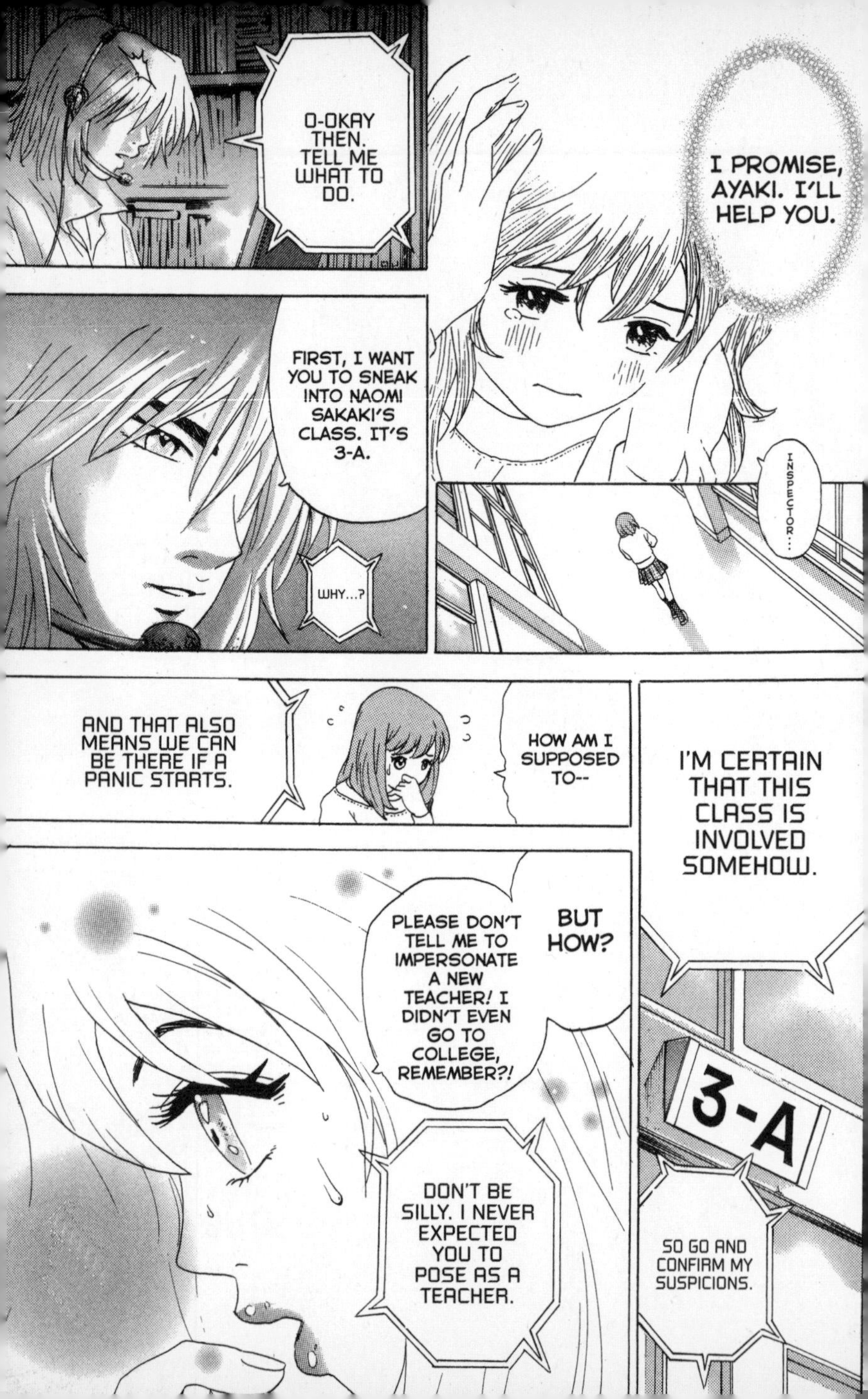
I PROMISE, AYAKI. I'LL HELP YOU.
INSPECTOR...
O-OKAY THEN. TELL ME WHAT TO DO.
FIRST, I WANT YOU TO SNEAK INTO NAOMI SAKAKI'S CLASS. IT'S 3-A.
WHY...?
I'M CERTAIN THAT THIS CLASS IS INVOLVED SOMEHOW.
3-A
SO GO AND CONFIRM MY SUSPICIONS.
HOW AM I SUPPOSED TO--
AND THAT ALSO MEANS WE CAN BE THERE IF A PANIC STARTS.
BUT HOW?
PLEASE DON'T TELL ME TO IMPERSONATE A NEW TEACHER! I DIDN'T EVEN GO TO COLLEGE, REMEMBER?!
DON'T BE SILLY. I NEVER EXPECTED YOU TO POSE AS A TEACHER.

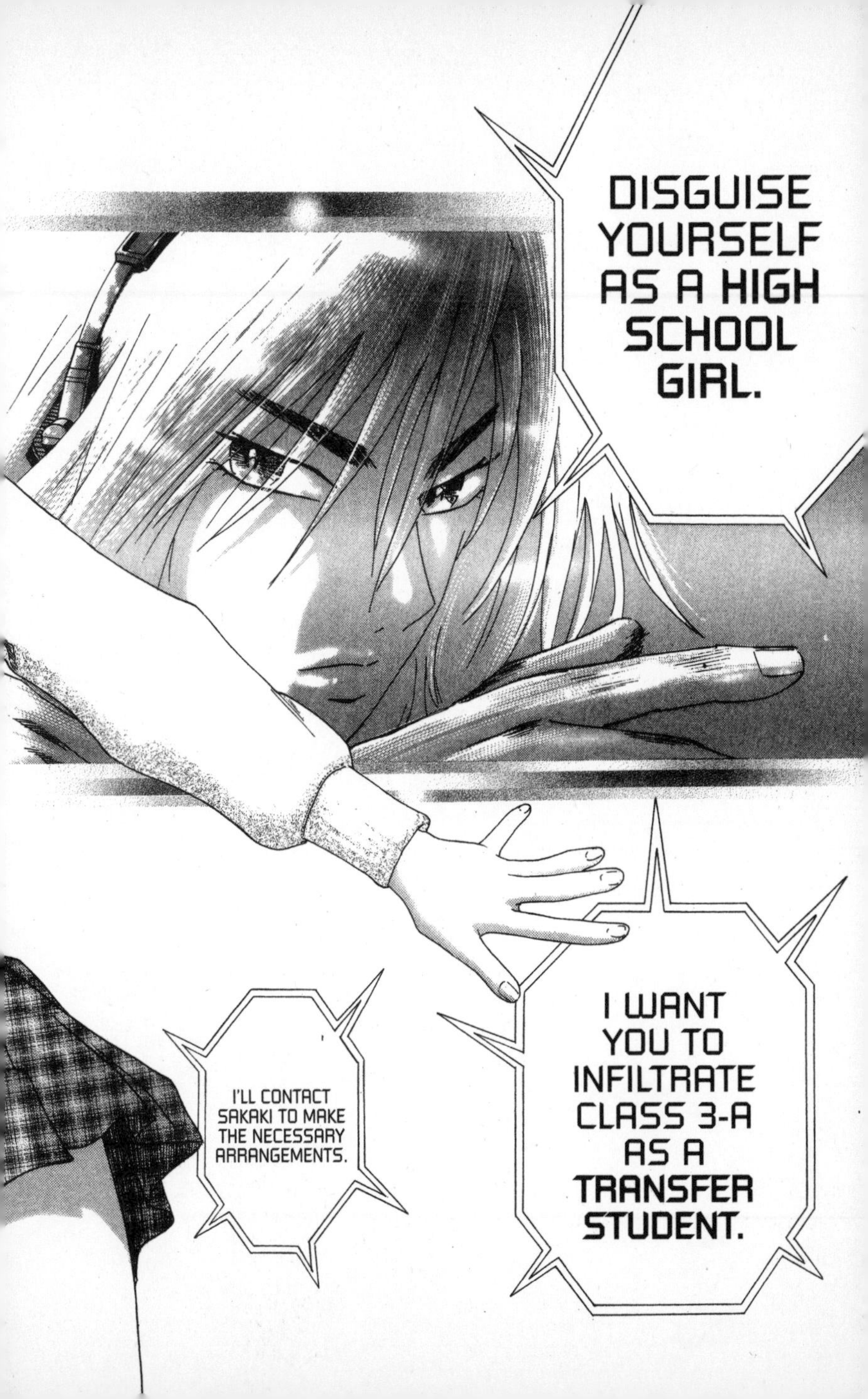
DISGUISE YOURSELF AS A HIGH SCHOOL GIRL.
I WANT YOU TO INFILTRATE CLASS 3-A AS A TRANSFER STUDENT.
I'LL CONTACT SAKAKI TO MAKE THE NECESSARY ARRANGEMENTS.

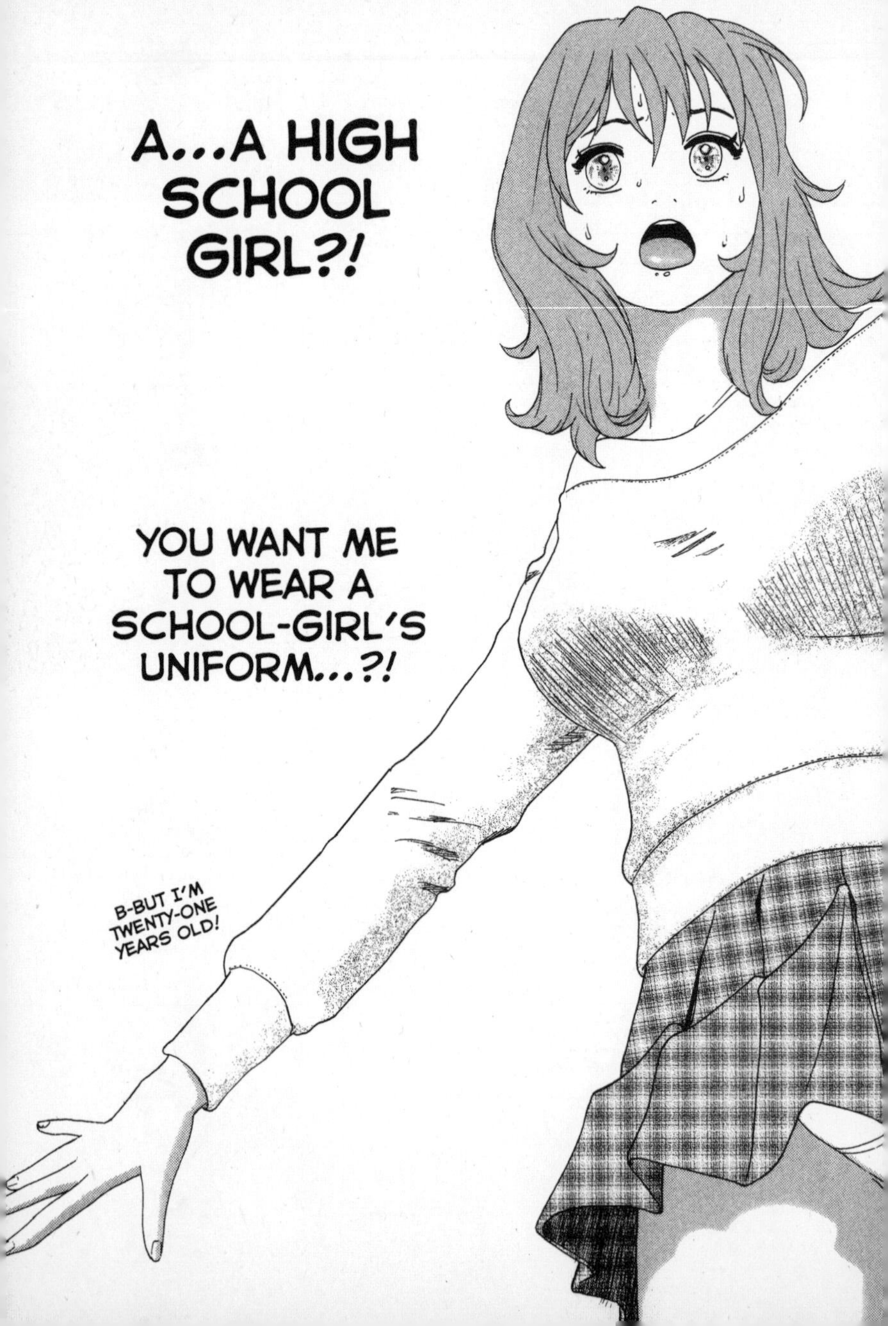
A...A HIGH SCHOOL GIRL?!
YOU WANT ME TO WEAR A SCHOOL-GIRL'S UNIFORM...?!
B-BUT I'M TWENTY-ONE YEARS OLD!

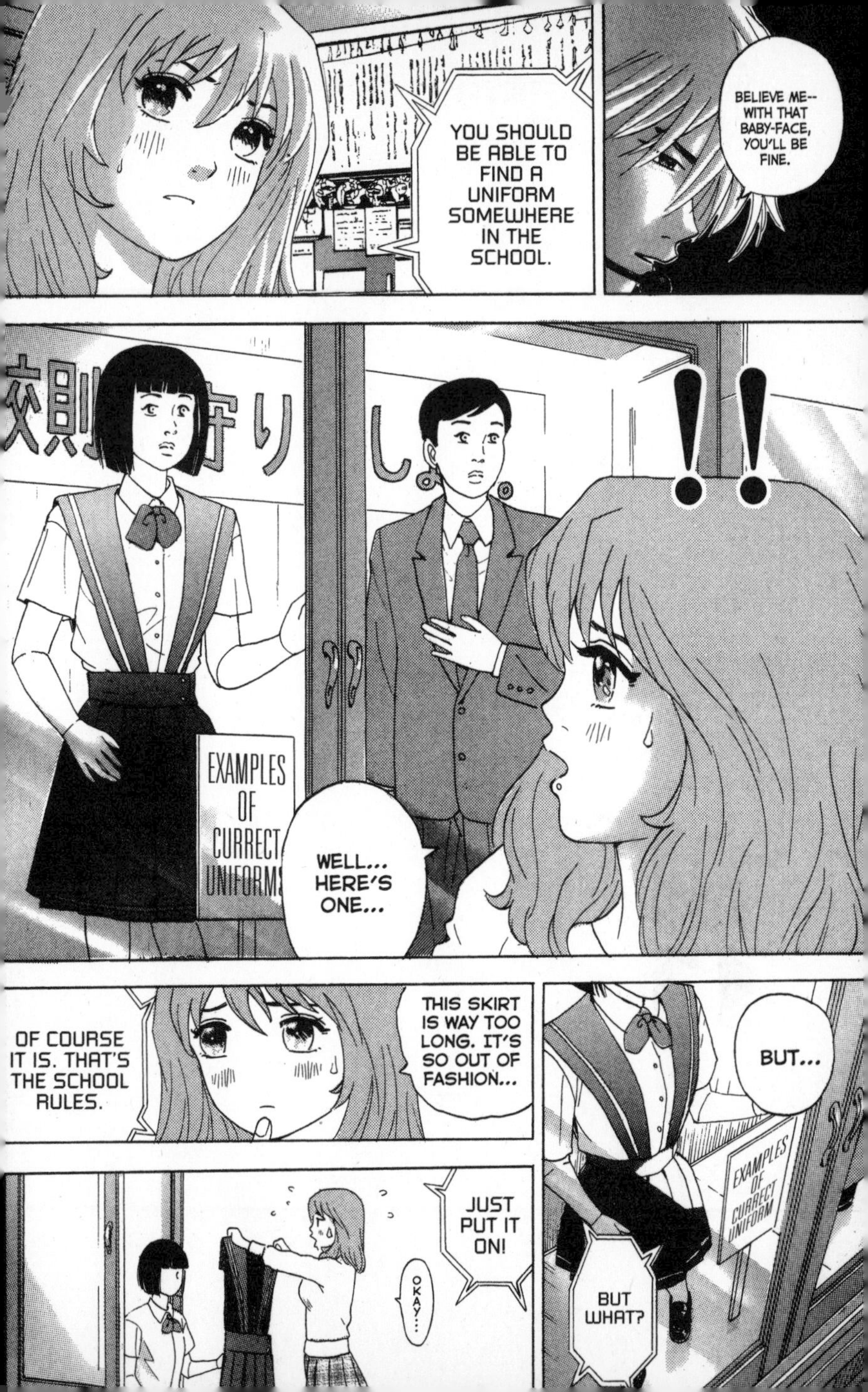
BELIEVE ME-- WITH THAT BABY-FACE, YOU'LL BE FINE.
YOU SHOULD BE ABLE TO FIND A UNIFORM SOMEWHERE IN THE SCHOOL.
EXAMPLES OF CURRECT UNIFORMS
WELL... HERE'S ONE...
BUT...
EXAMPLES OF CURRECT UNIFORM
BUT WHAT?
THIS SKIRT IS WAY TOO LONG. IT'S SO OUT OF FASHION...
OF COURSE IT IS. THAT'S THE SCHOOL RULES.
JUST PUT IT ON!
OKAY...

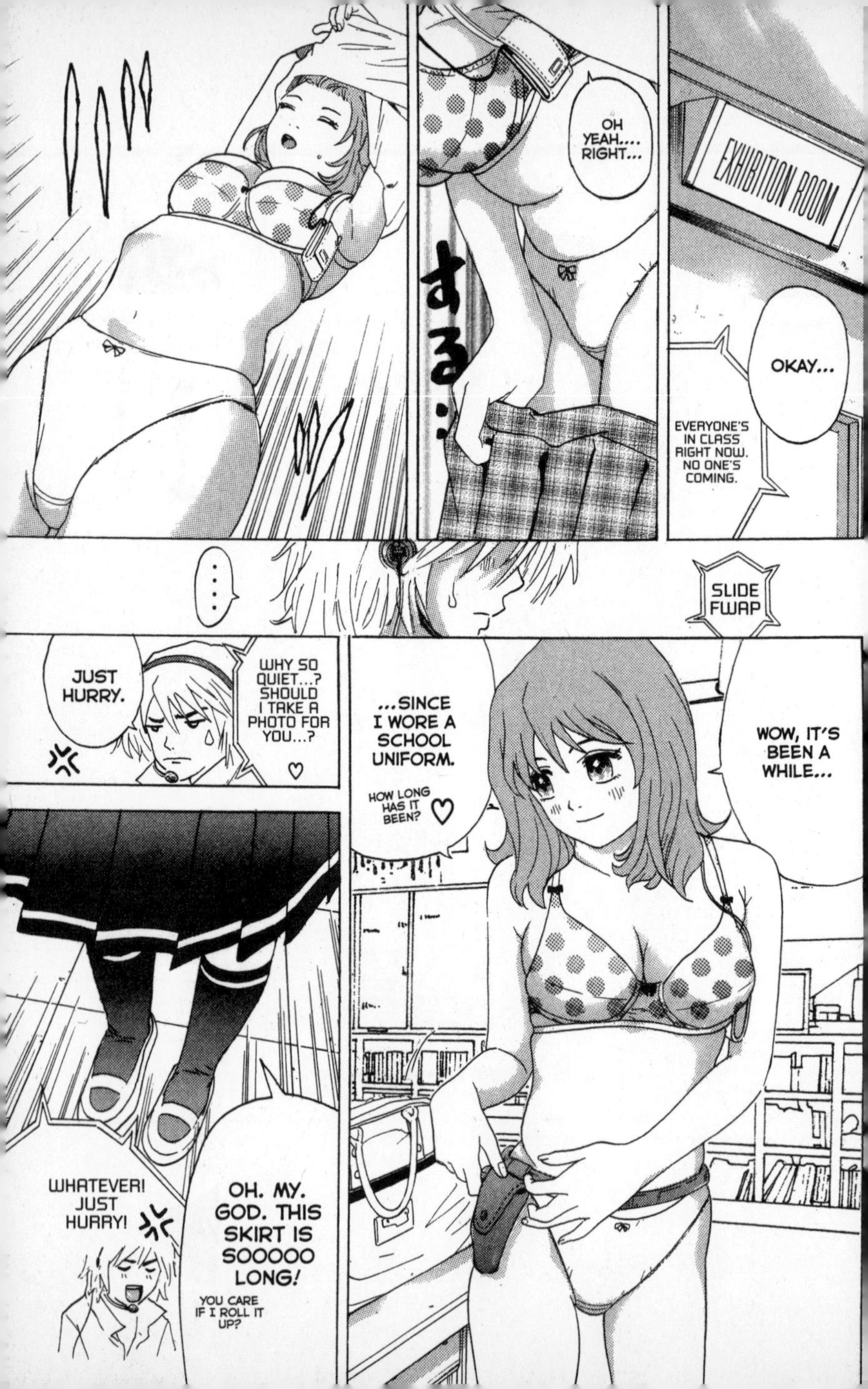

EXHIBITION ROOM
OKAY...
EVERYONE'S IN CLASS RIGHT NOW. NO ONE'S COMING.
OH YEAH.... RIGHT...
する…
SLIDE FWAP
....
WOW, IT'S BEEN A WHILE...
...SINCE I WORE A SCHOOL UNIFORM.
HOW LONG HAS IT BEEN? ♡
WHY SO QUIET...? SHOULD I TAKE A PHOTO FOR YOU...? ♡
JUST HURRY.
OH. MY. GOD. THIS SKIRT IS SOOOOO LONG!
YOU CARE IF I ROLL IT UP?
WHATEVER! JUST HURRY!

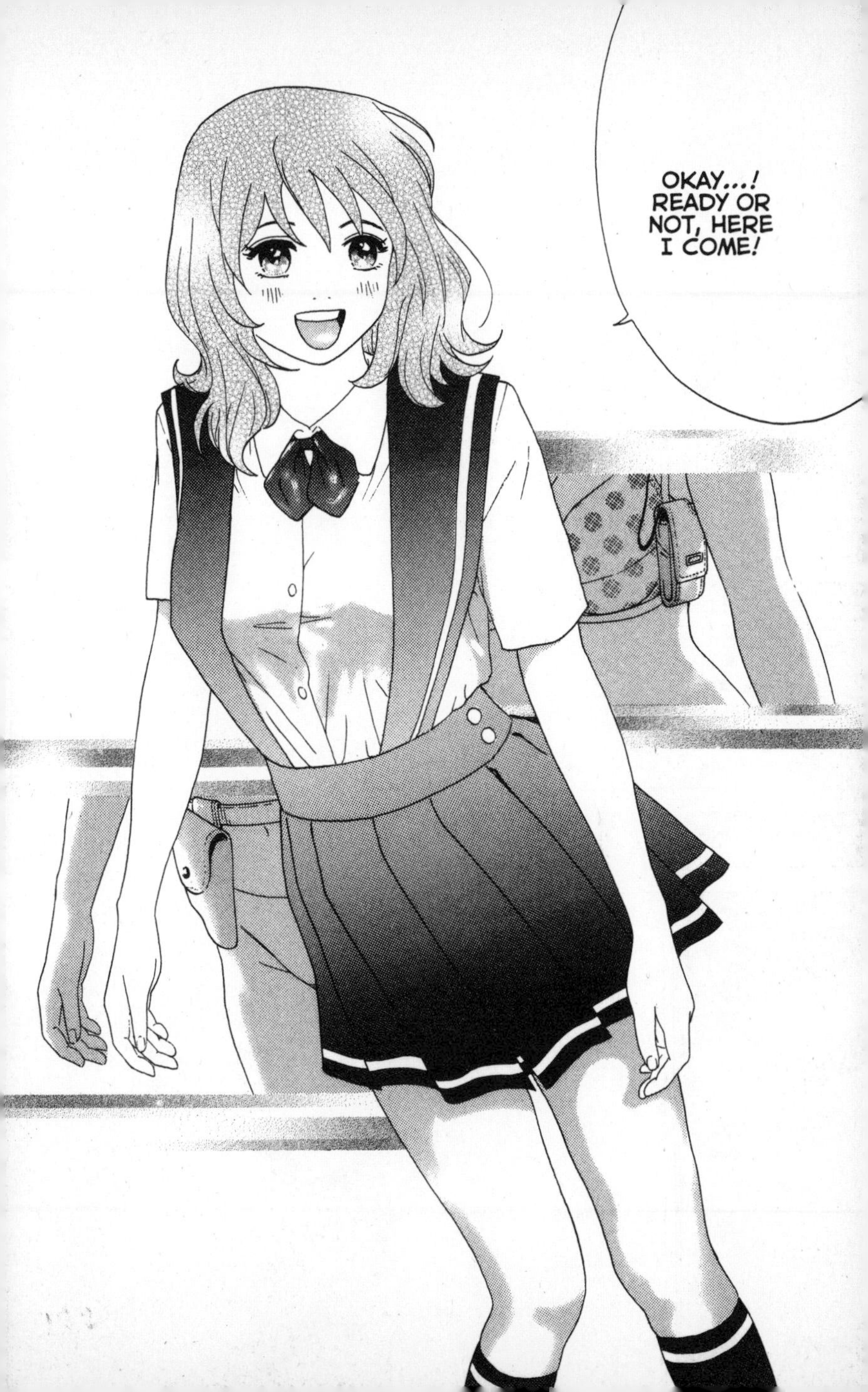
OKAY...! READY OR NOT, HERE I COME!

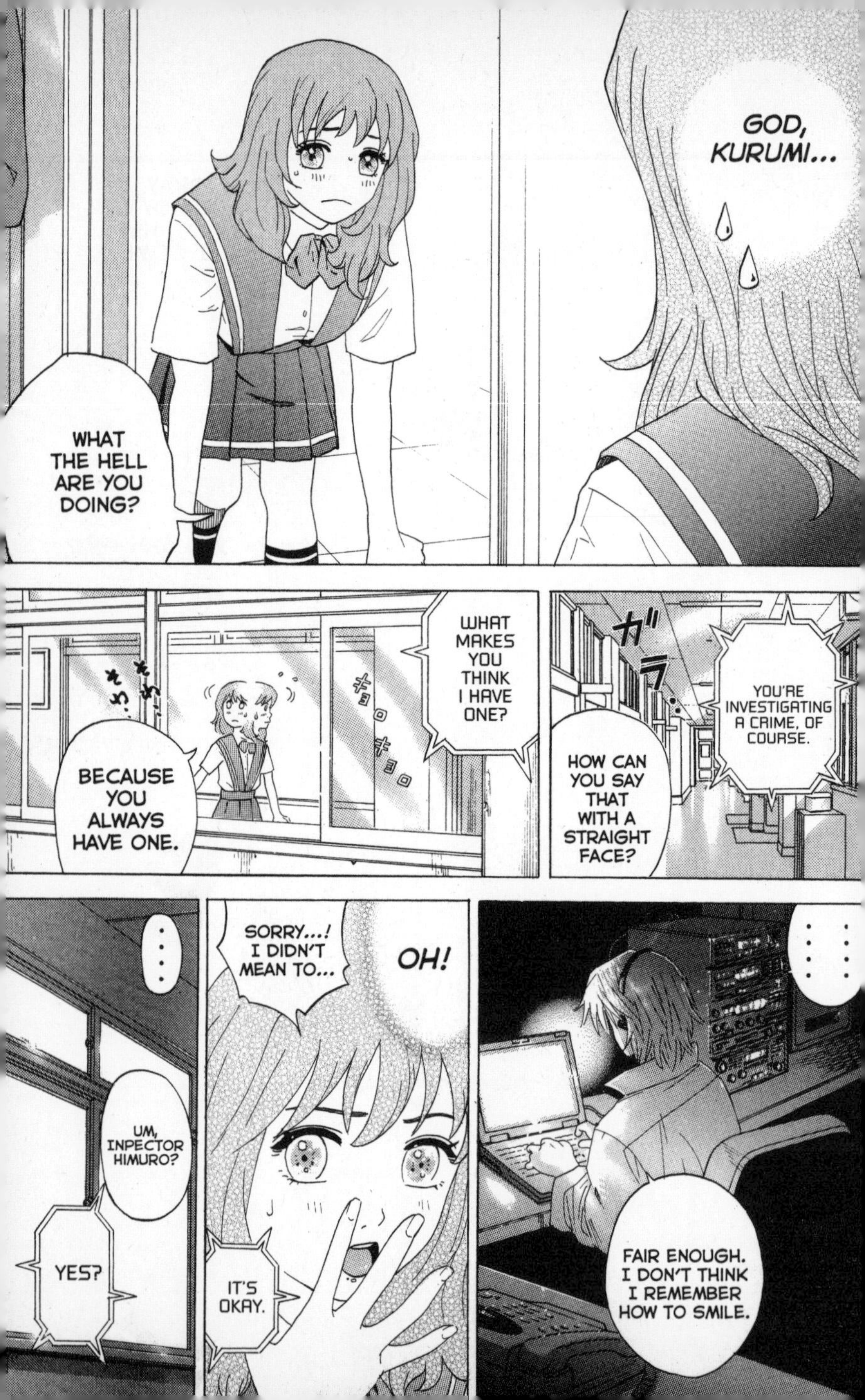
GOD, KURUMI...
WHAT THE HELL ARE YOU DOING?
ガラ
YOU'RE INVESTIGATING A CRIME, OF COURSE.
HOW CAN YOU SAY THAT WITH A STRAIGHT FACE?
WHAT MAKES YOU THINK I HAVE ONE?
キョロキョロ
BECAUSE YOU ALWAYS HAVE ONE.
....
FAIR ENOUGH. I DON'T THINK I REMEMBER HOW TO SMILE.
OH!
SORRY...! I DIDN'T MEAN TO...
IT'S OKAY.
....
UM, INPECTOR HIMURO?
YES?

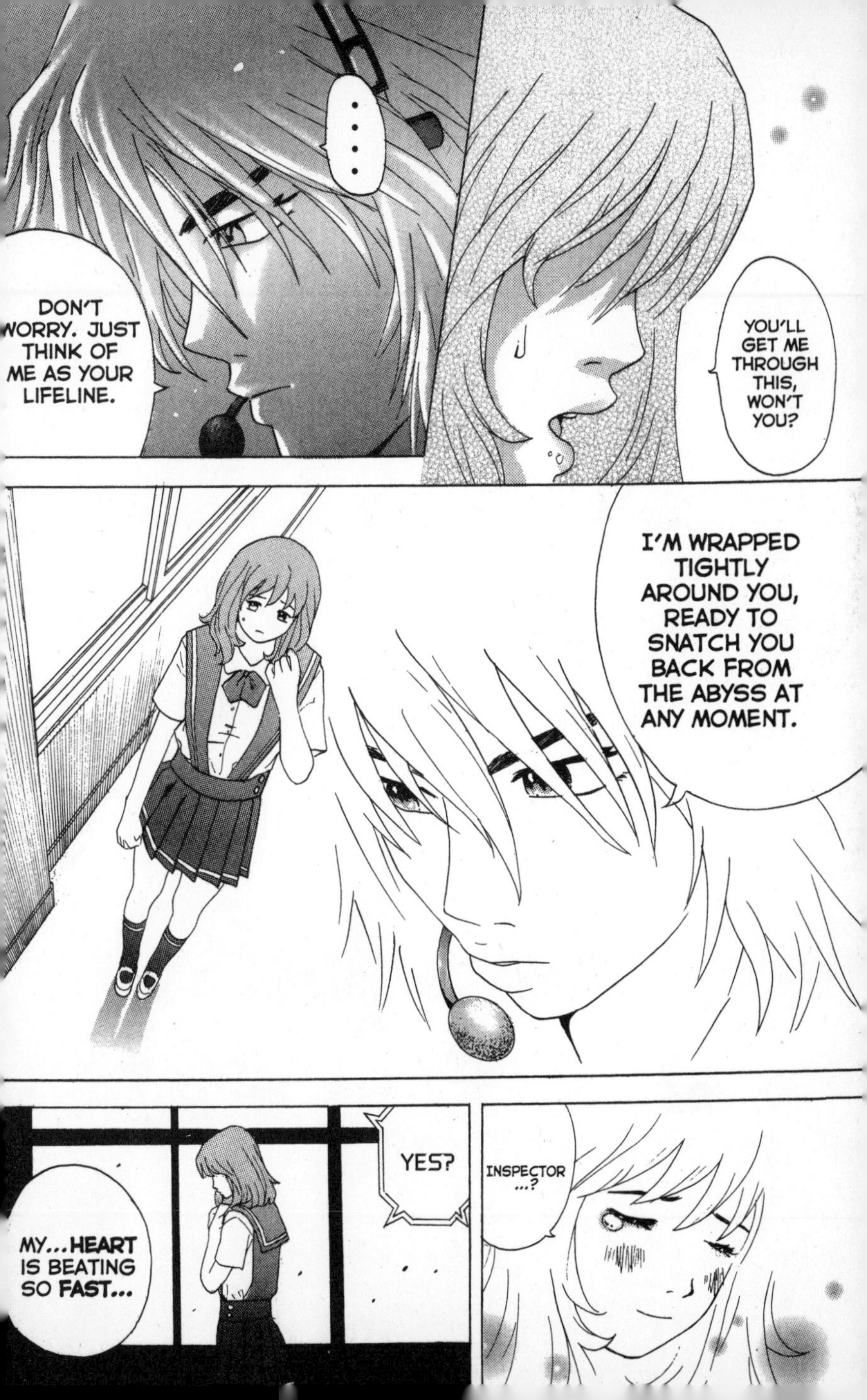
YOU'LL GET ME THROUGH THIS, WON'T YOU?
....
DON'T WORRY. JUST THINK OF ME AS YOUR LIFELINE.
I'M WRAPPED TIGHTLY AROUND YOU, READY TO SNATCH YOU BACK FROM THE ABYSS AT ANY MOMENT.
INSPECTOR ...?
YES?
MY...HEART IS BEATING SO FAST...

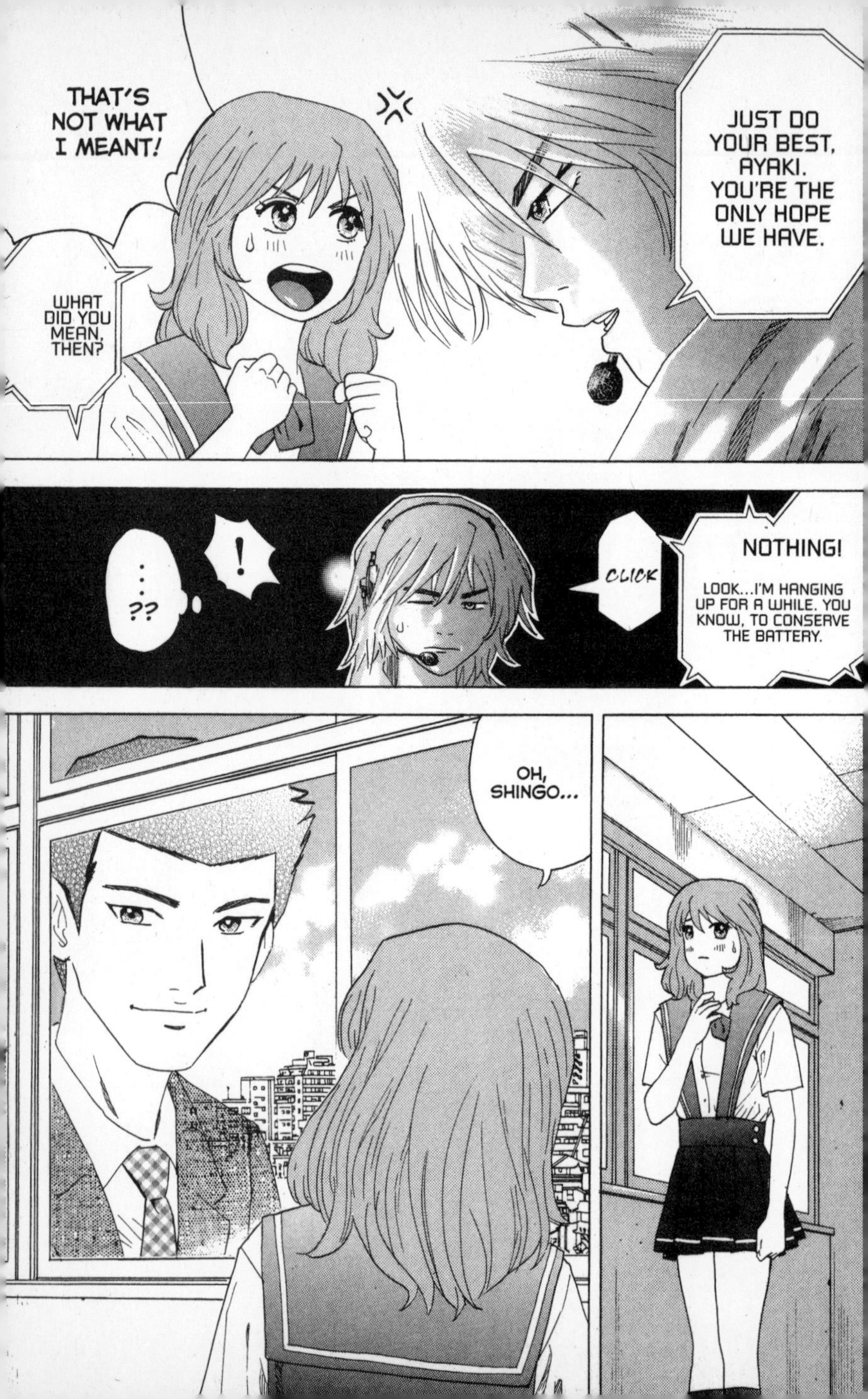
JUST DO YOUR BEST, AYAKI. YOU'RE THE ONLY HOPE WE HAVE.
THAT'S NOT WHAT I MEANT!
WHAT DID YOU MEAN, THEN?
NOTHING!
LOOK...I'M HANGING UP FOR A WHILE. YOU KNOW, TO CONSERVE THE BATTERY.
CLICK
!
...??
OH, SHINGO...

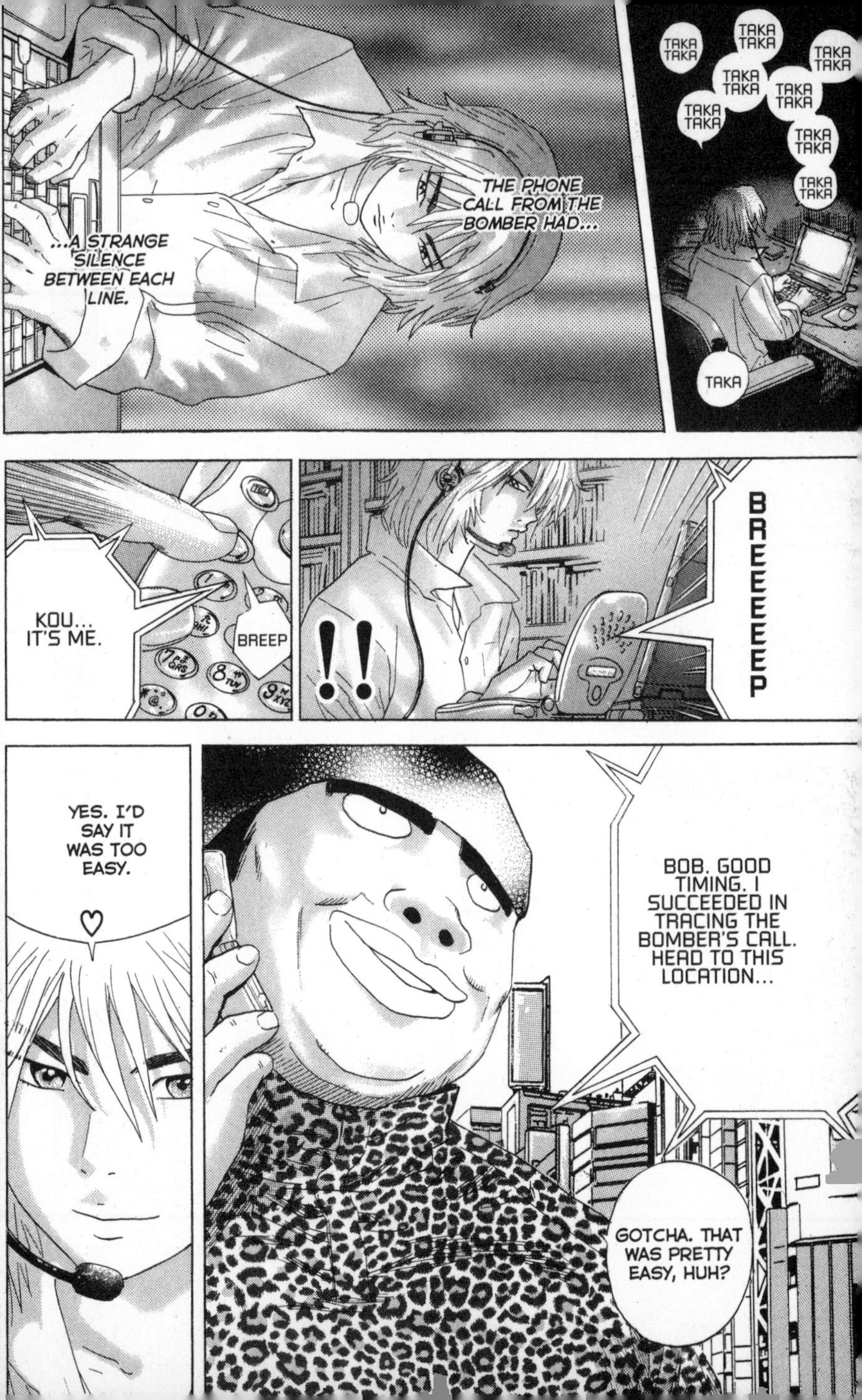

TAKA TAKA
TAKA TAKA
TAKA TAKA
TAKA TAKA
TAKA TAKA
TAKA TAKA
TAKA TAKA
TAKA TAKA
TAKA
THE PHONE CALL FROM THE BOMBER HAD...
...A STRANGE SILENCE BETWEEN EACH LINE.
BREEEEEP
!!
BREEP
KOU... IT'S ME.
BOB. GOOD TIMING. I SUCCEEDED IN TRACING THE BOMBER'S CALL. HEAD TO THIS LOCATION...
GOTCHA. THAT WAS PRETTY EASY, HUH?
YES. I'D SAY IT WAS TOO EASY.
♥

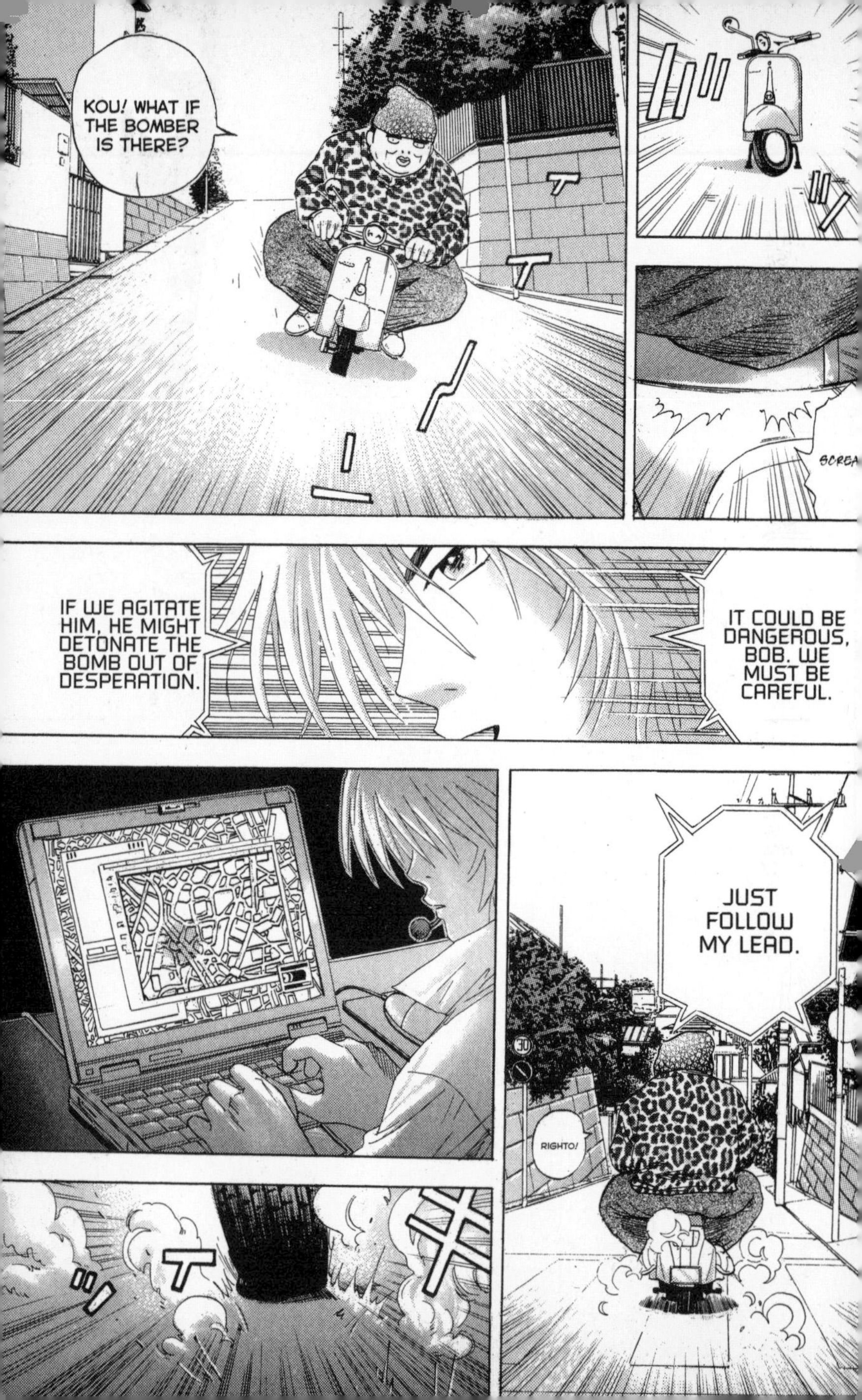
SCREA
KOU! WHAT IF THE BOMBER IS THERE?
IT COULD BE DANGEROUS, BOB. WE MUST BE CAREFUL.
IF WE AGITATE HIM, HE MIGHT DETONATE THE BOMB OUT OF DESPERATION.
JUST FOLLOW MY LEAD.
RIGHTO!

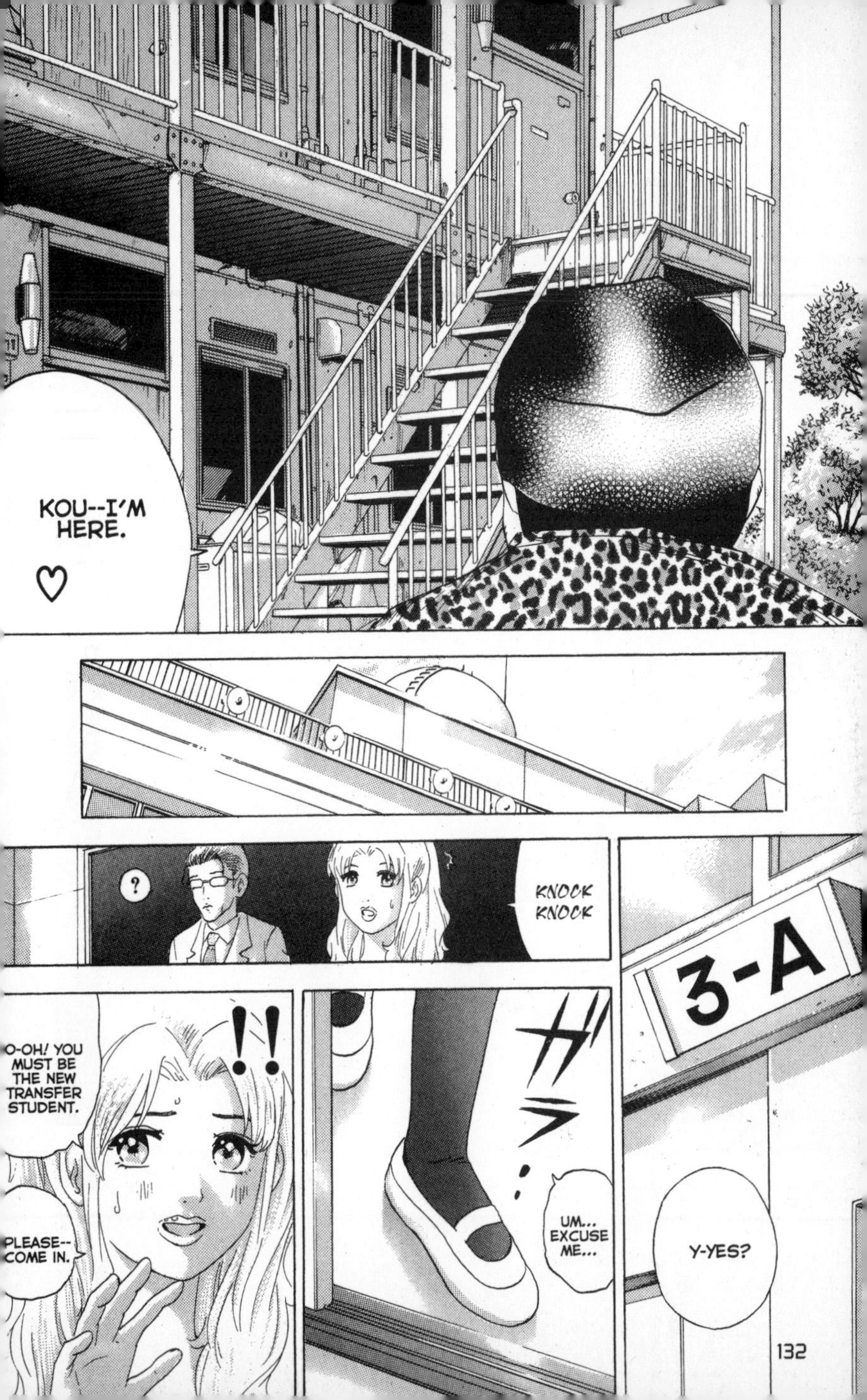
KOU--I'M HERE. ♡
3-A
Y-YES?
KNOCK KNOCK
?
ガラ
UM... EXCUSE ME...
!!
O-OH! YOU MUST BE THE NEW TRANSFER STUDENT.
PLEASE-- COME IN.

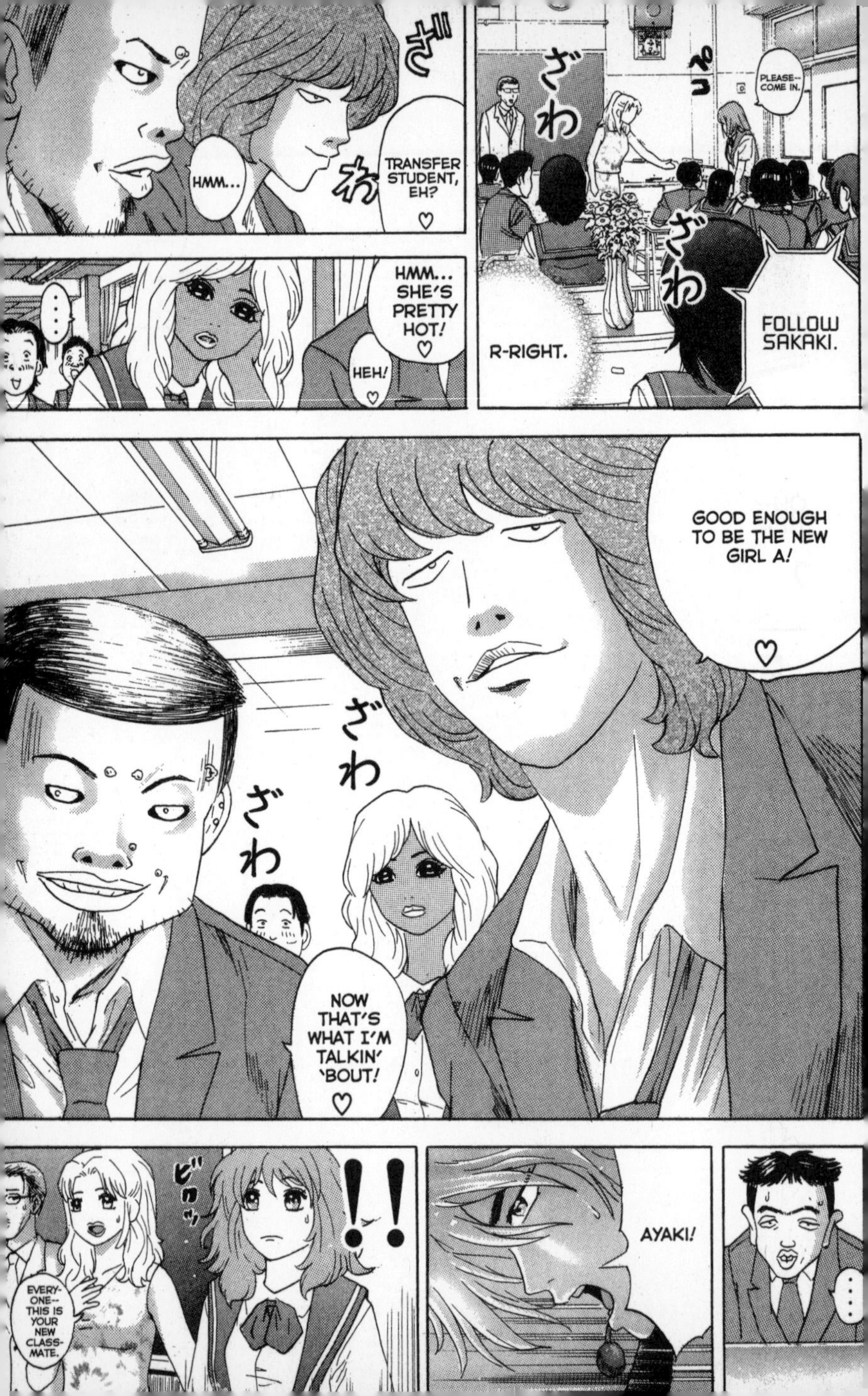
PLEASE-- COME IN.
ぺこ
ざわ
ざわ
FOLLOW SAKAKI.
R-RIGHT.
ざわ
TRANSFER STUDENT, EH? ♡
HMM...
HMM... SHE'S PRETTY HOT! ♡
HEH! ♡
...
GOOD ENOUGH TO BE THE NEW GIRL A! ♡
ざわ
ざわ
NOW THAT'S WHAT I'M TALKIN' 'BOUT! ♡
...
AYAKI!
!!
ビクッ
EVERY-ONE-- THIS IS YOUR NEW CLASS-MATE.

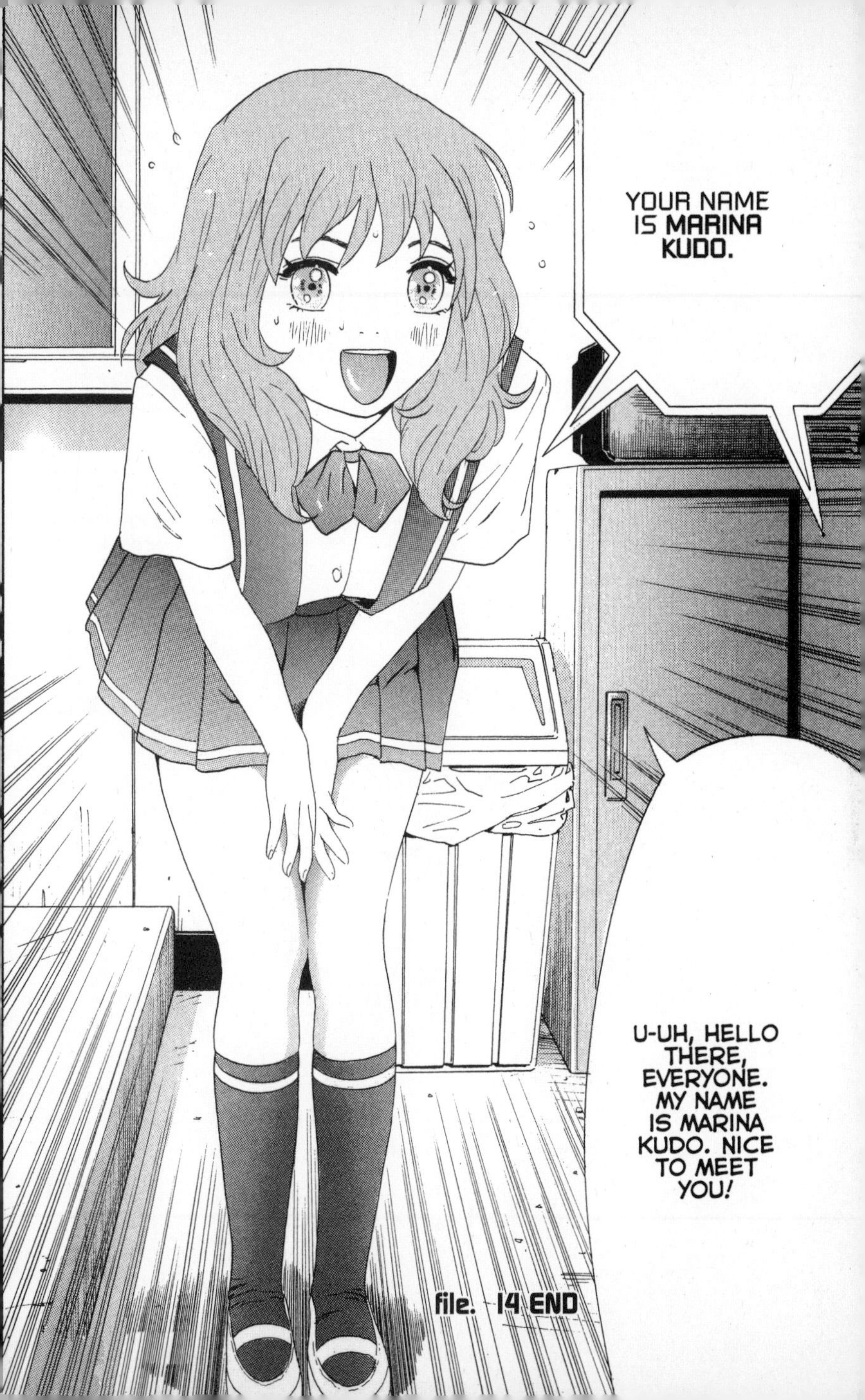
YOUR NAME IS MARINA KUDO.
U-UH, HELLO THERE, EVERYONE. MY NAME IS MARINA KUDO. NICE TO MEET YOU!
file. 14 END

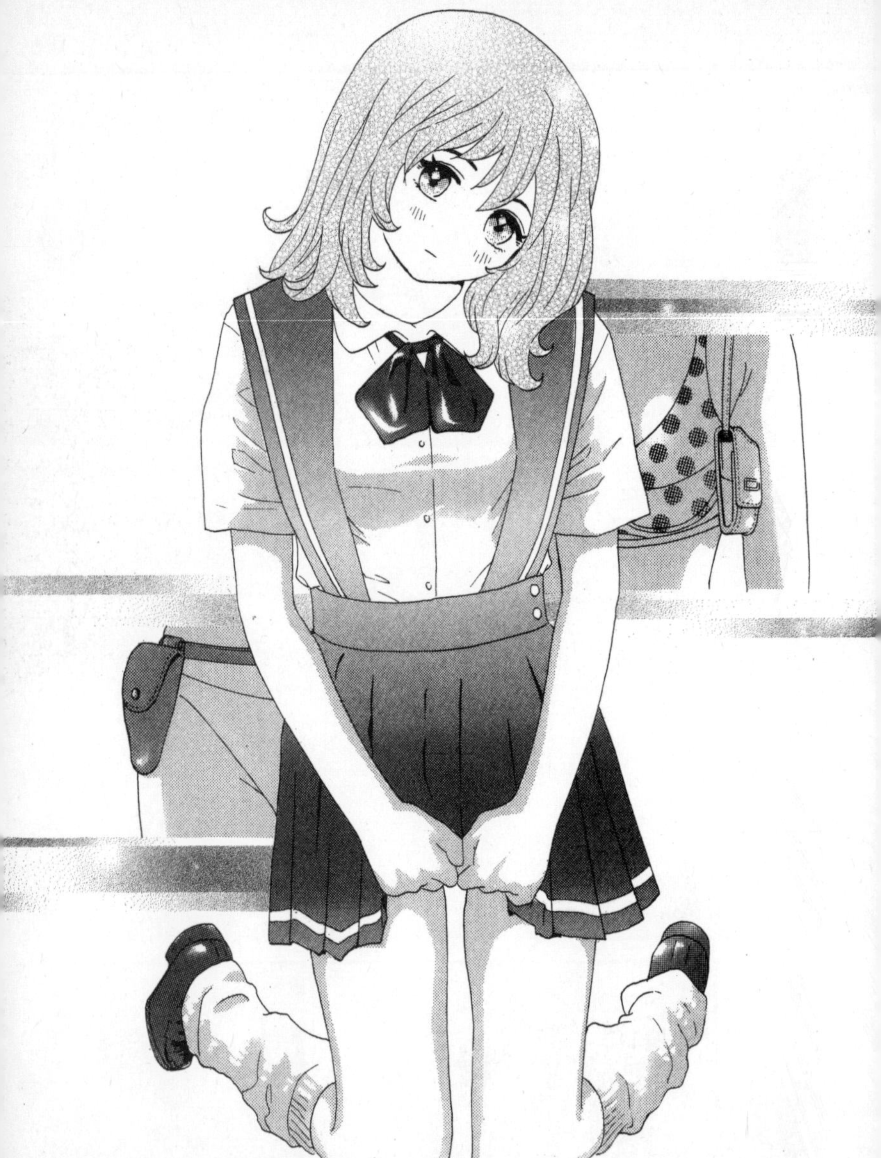

FILE 15 SURVIVAL SCHOOL

NO ESCAPE

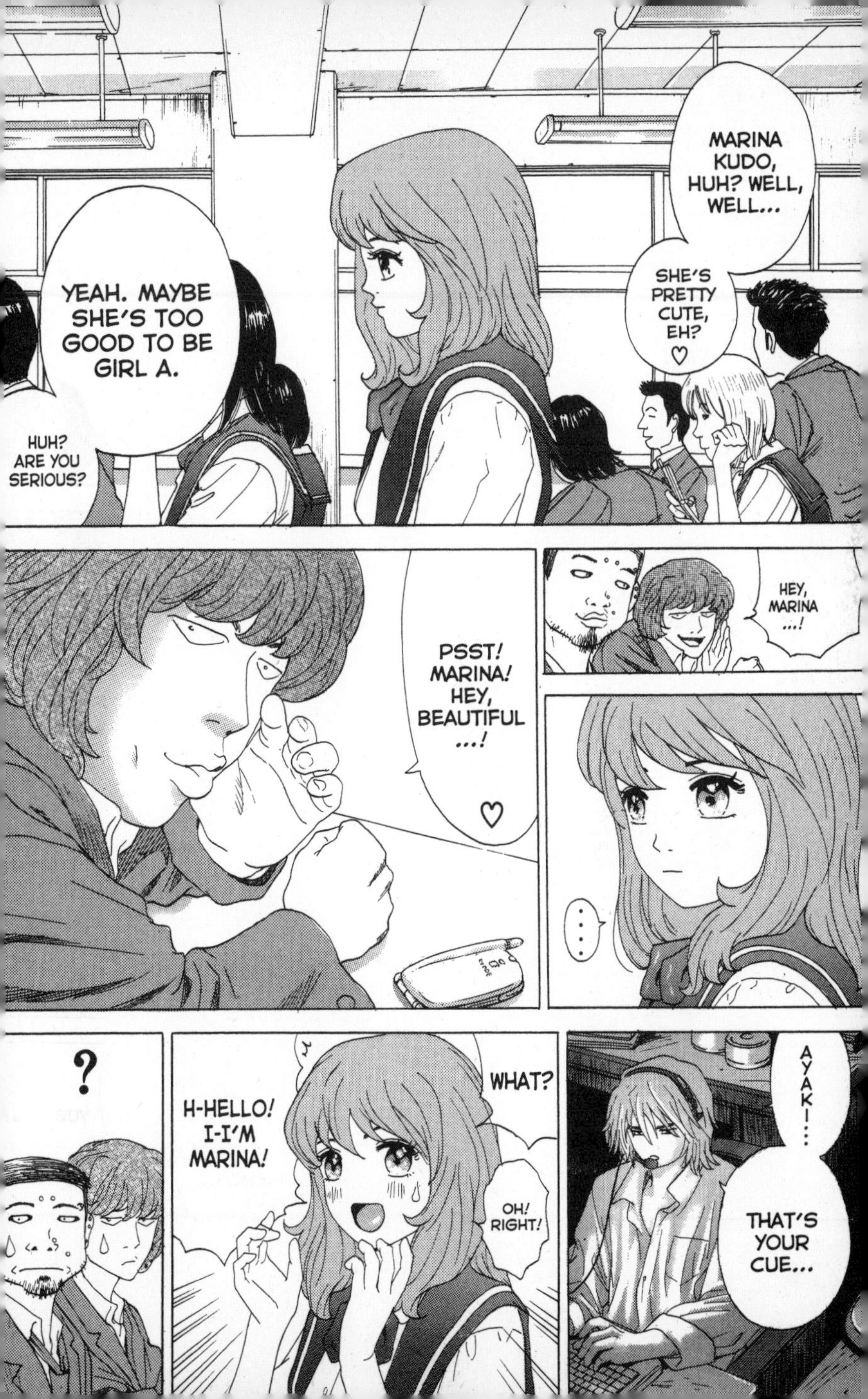
MARINA KUDO, HUH? WELL, WELL...
SHE'S PRETTY CUTE, EH? ♡
YEAH. MAYBE SHE'S TOO GOOD TO BE GIRL A.
HUH? ARE YOU SERIOUS?
HEY, MARINA ...!
....
PSST! MARINA! HEY, BEAUTIFUL ...! ♡
AYAKI...
THAT'S YOUR CUE...
WHAT?
OH! RIGHT!
H-HELLO! I-I'M MARINA!
?

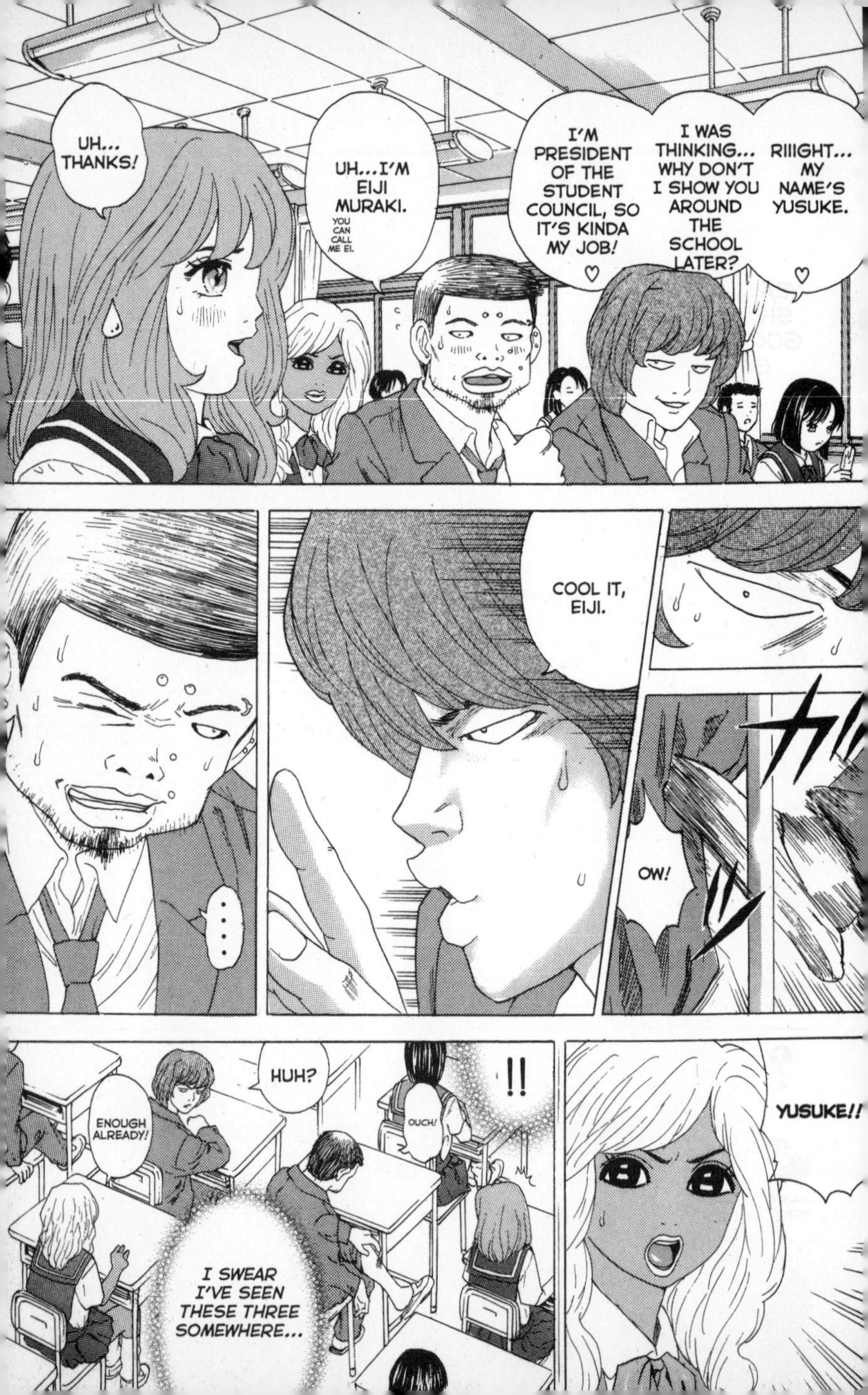
RIIIGHT... MY NAME'S YUSUKE. ♡
I WAS THINKING... WHY DON'T I SHOW YOU AROUND THE SCHOOL LATER?
I'M PRESIDENT OF THE STUDENT COUNCIL, SO IT'S KINDA MY JOB! ♡
UH...I'M EIJI MURAKI.
YOU CAN CALL ME EI.
UH... THANKS!
OW!
COOL IT, EIJI.
....
YUSUKE!!
!!
OUCH!
HUH?
ENOUGH ALREADY!
I SWEAR I'VE SEEN THESE THREE SOMEWHERE...

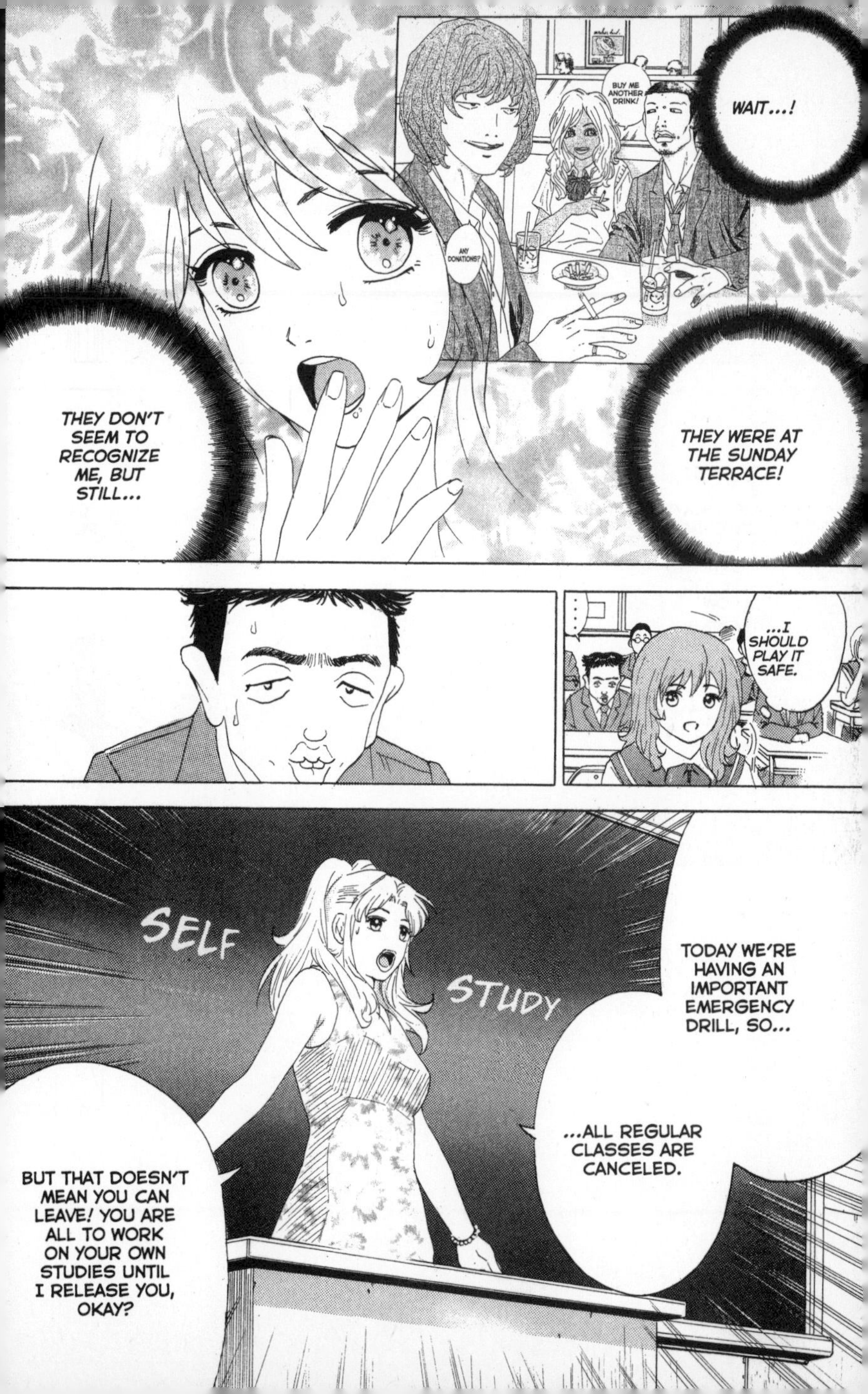
WAIT...!
BUY ME ANOTHER DRINK!
ANY DONATIONS?
THEY WERE AT THE SUNDAY TERRACE!
THEY DON'T SEEM TO RECOGNIZE ME, BUT STILL...
...I SHOULD PLAY IT SAFE.
TODAY WE'RE HAVING AN IMPORTANT EMERGENCY DRILL, SO...
...ALL REGULAR CLASSES ARE CANCELED.
SELF STUDY
BUT THAT DOESN'T MEAN YOU CAN LEAVE! YOU ARE ALL TO WORK ON YOUR OWN STUDIES UNTIL I RELEASE YOU, OKAY?

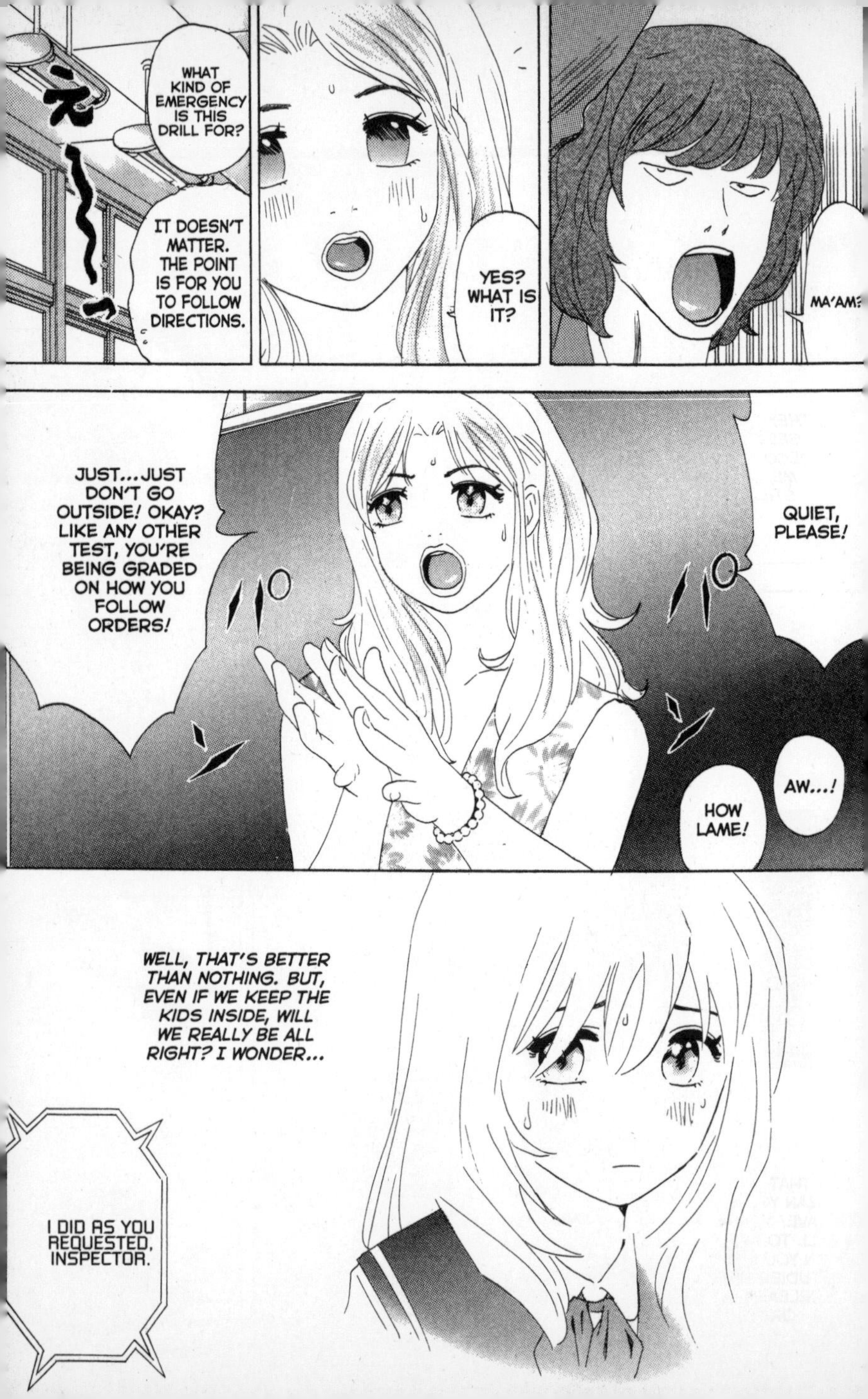
MA'AM?
YES? WHAT IS IT?
え〜〜
WHAT KIND OF EMERGENCY IS THIS DRILL FOR?
IT DOESN'T MATTER. THE POINT IS FOR YOU TO FOLLOW DIRECTIONS.
QUIET, PLEASE!
JUST...JUST DON'T GO OUTSIDE! OKAY? LIKE ANY OTHER TEST, YOU'RE BEING GRADED ON HOW YOU FOLLOW ORDERS!
AW...!
HOW LAME!
WELL, THAT'S BETTER THAN NOTHING. BUT, EVEN IF WE KEEP THE KIDS INSIDE, WILL WE REALLY BE ALL RIGHT? I WONDER...
I DID AS YOU REQUESTED, INSPECTOR.

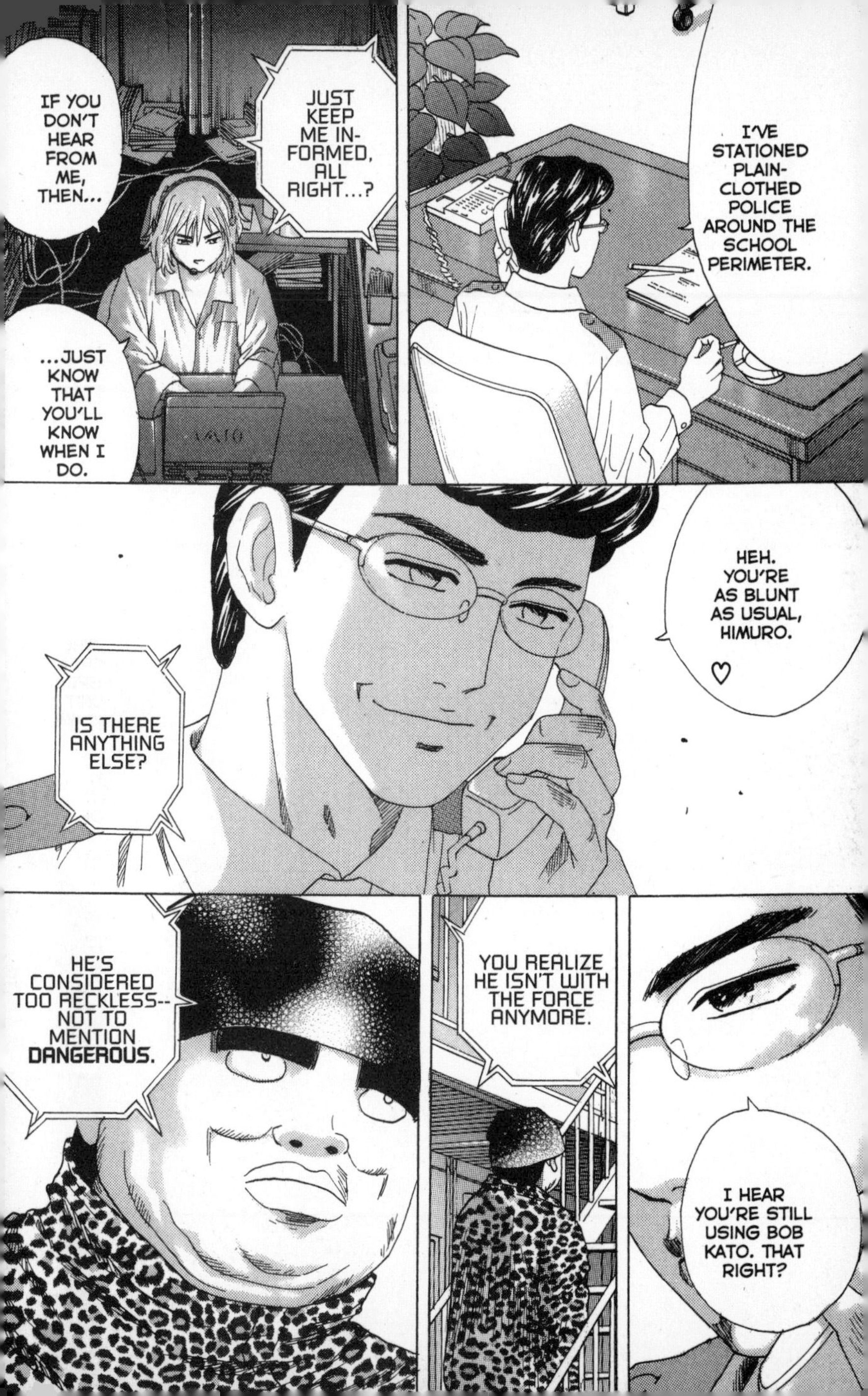
I'VE STATIONED PLAIN-CLOTHED POLICE AROUND THE SCHOOL PERIMETER.
JUST KEEP ME IN-FORMED, ALL RIGHT...?
IF YOU DON'T HEAR FROM ME, THEN...
...JUST KNOW THAT YOU'LL KNOW WHEN I DO.
HEH. YOU'RE AS BLUNT AS USUAL, HIMURO. ♡
IS THERE ANYTHING ELSE?
I HEAR YOU'RE STILL USING BOB KATO. THAT RIGHT?
YOU REALIZE HE ISN'T WITH THE FORCE ANYMORE.
HE'S CONSIDERED TOO RECKLESS-- NOT TO MENTION DANGEROUS.

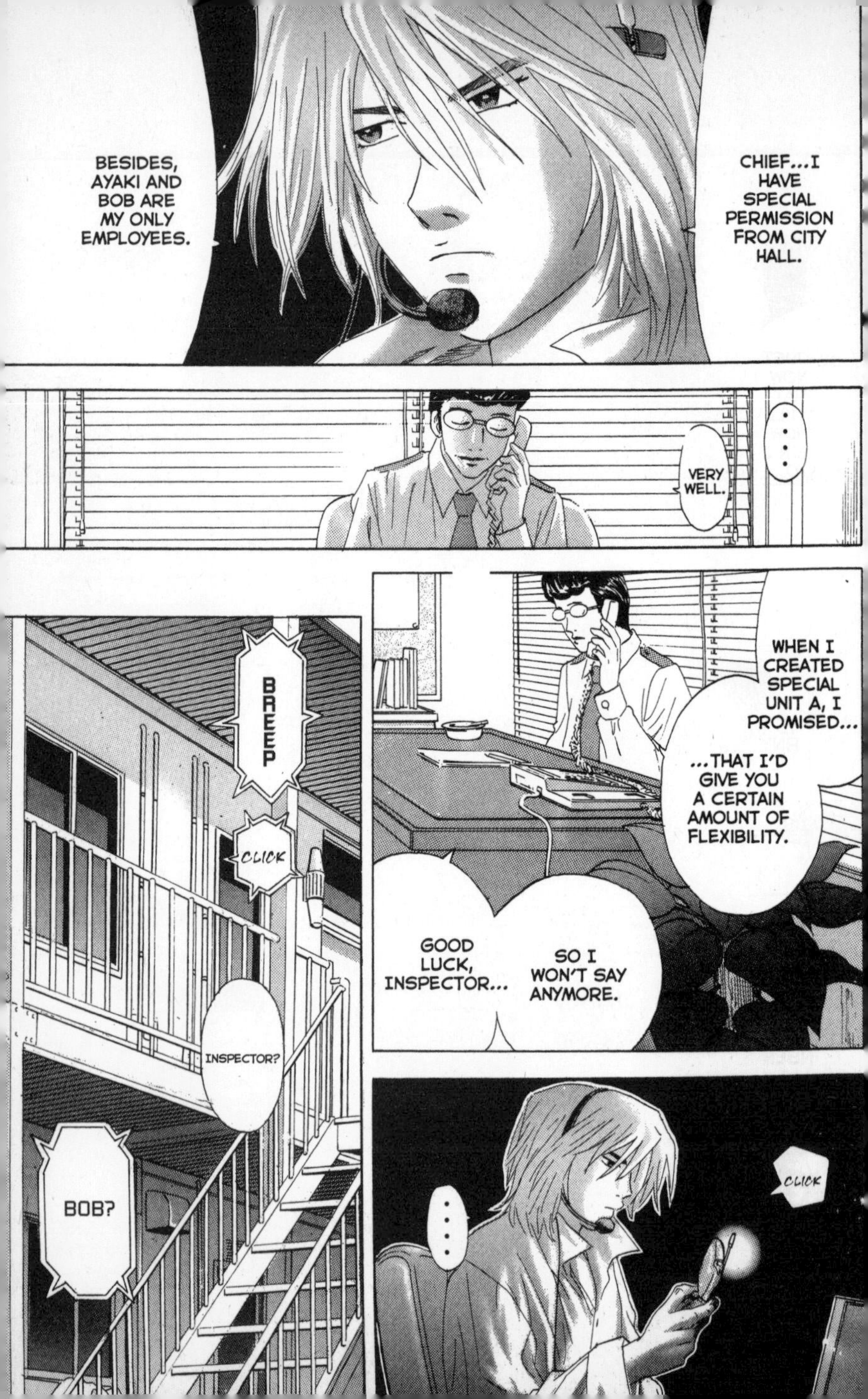
CHIEF...I HAVE SPECIAL PERMISSION FROM CITY HALL.
BESIDES, AYAKI AND BOB ARE MY ONLY EMPLOYEES.
...
VERY WELL.
WHEN I CREATED SPECIAL UNIT A, I PROMISED...
...THAT I'D GIVE YOU A CERTAIN AMOUNT OF FLEXIBILITY.
SO I WON'T SAY ANYMORE.
GOOD LUCK, INSPECTOR...
CLICK
...
BREEP
CLICK
INSPECTOR?
BOB?

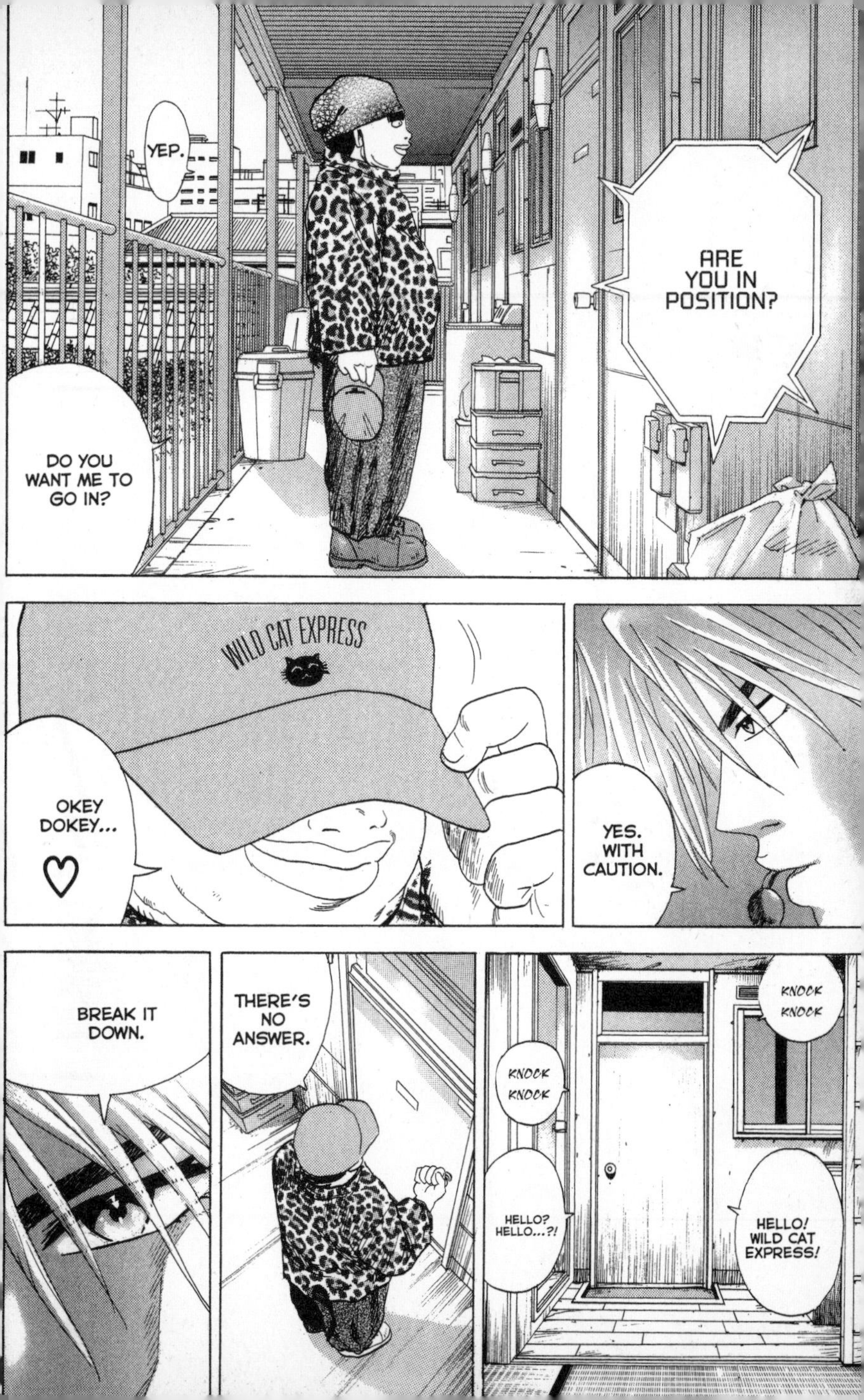
ARE YOU IN POSITION?
YEP.
DO YOU WANT ME TO GO IN?
YES. WITH CAUTION.
WILD CAT EXPRESS
OKEY DOKEY... ♡
KNOCK KNOCK
HELLO! WILD CAT EXPRESS!
KNOCK KNOCK
HELLO? HELLO...?!
THERE'S NO ANSWER.
BREAK IT DOWN.

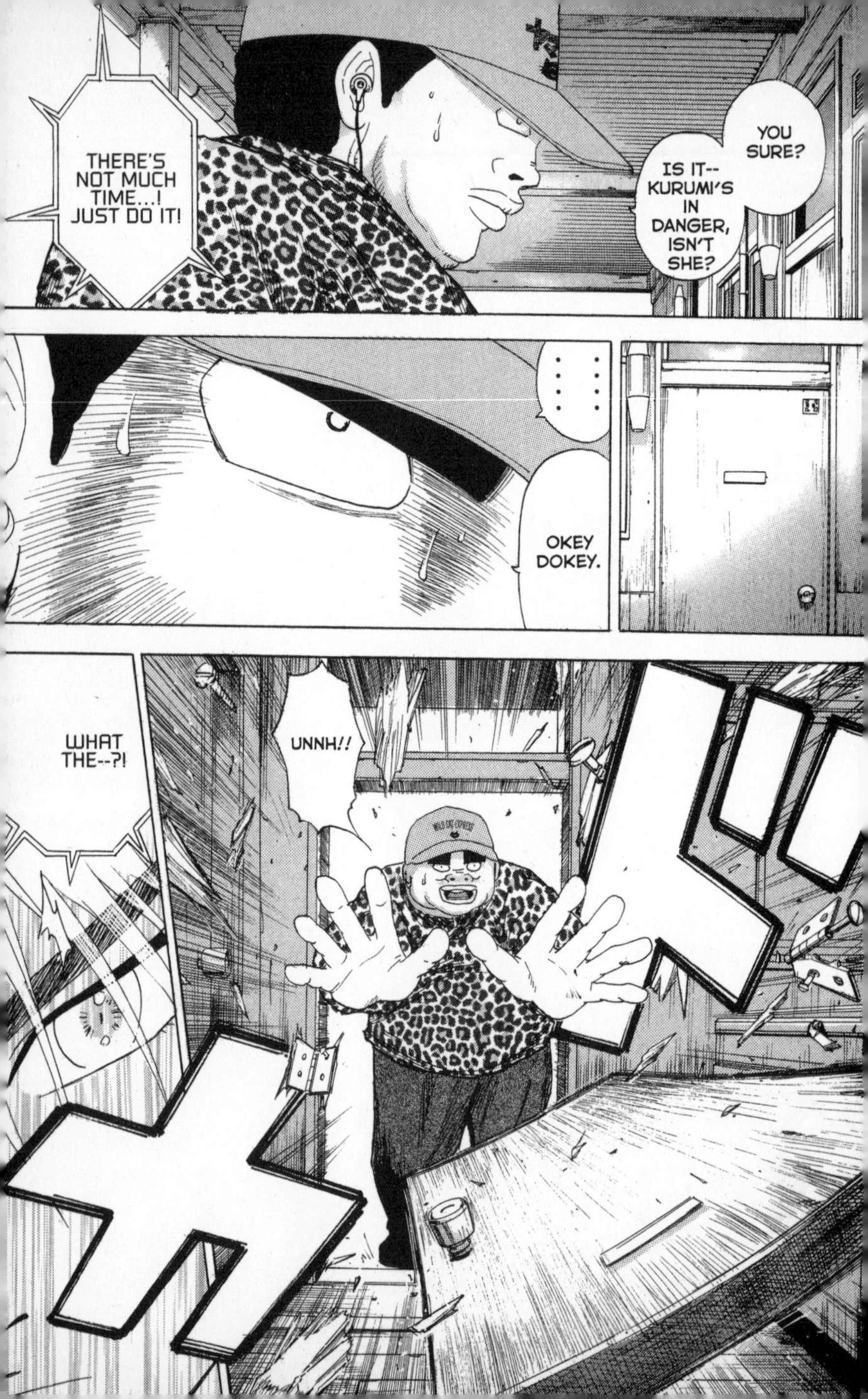
YOU SURE?
IS IT-- KURUMI'S IN DANGER, ISN'T SHE?
THERE'S NOT MUCH TIME...! JUST DO IT!
......
OKEY DOKEY.
UNNH!!
WHAT THE--?!

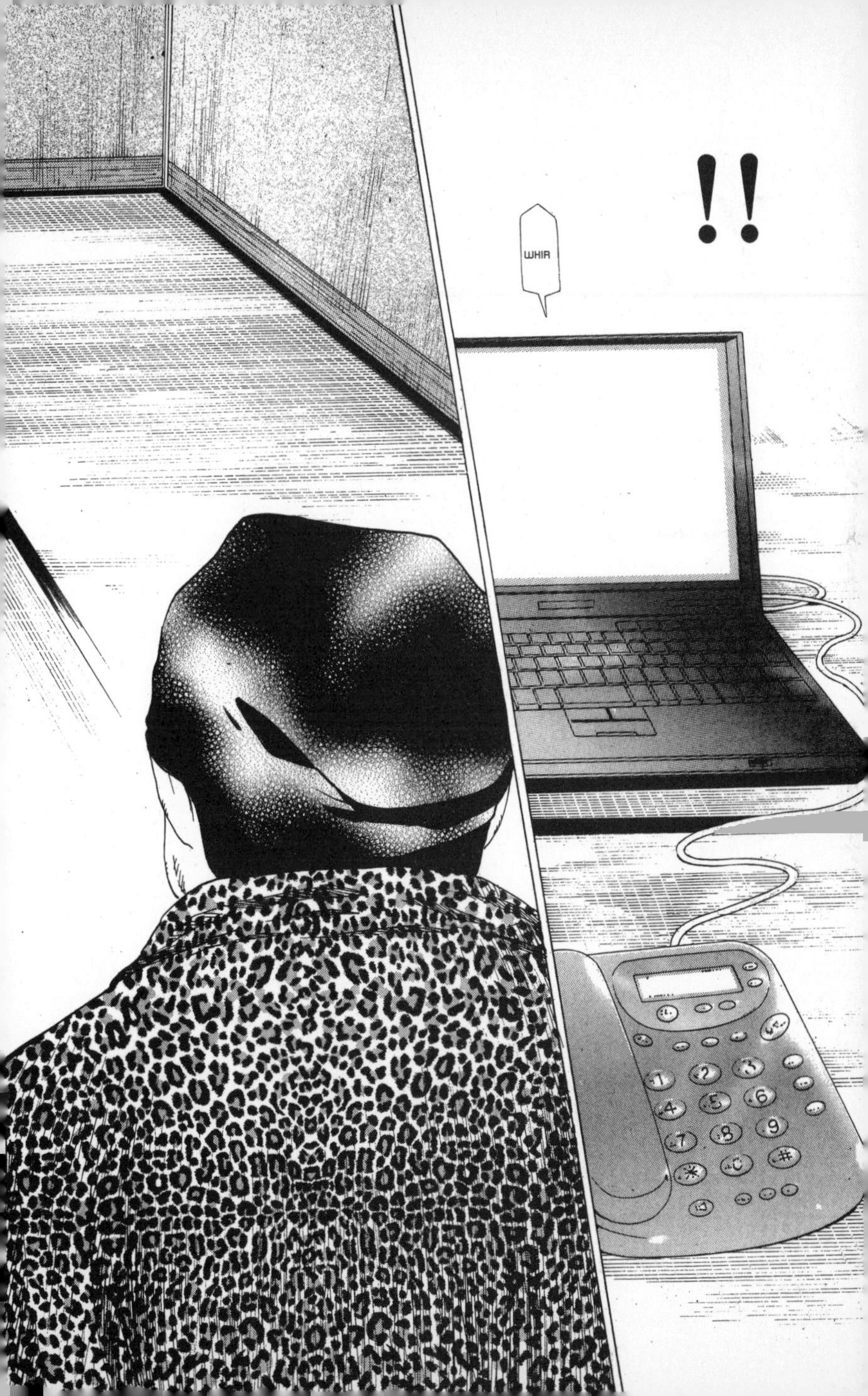
!!
WHIR

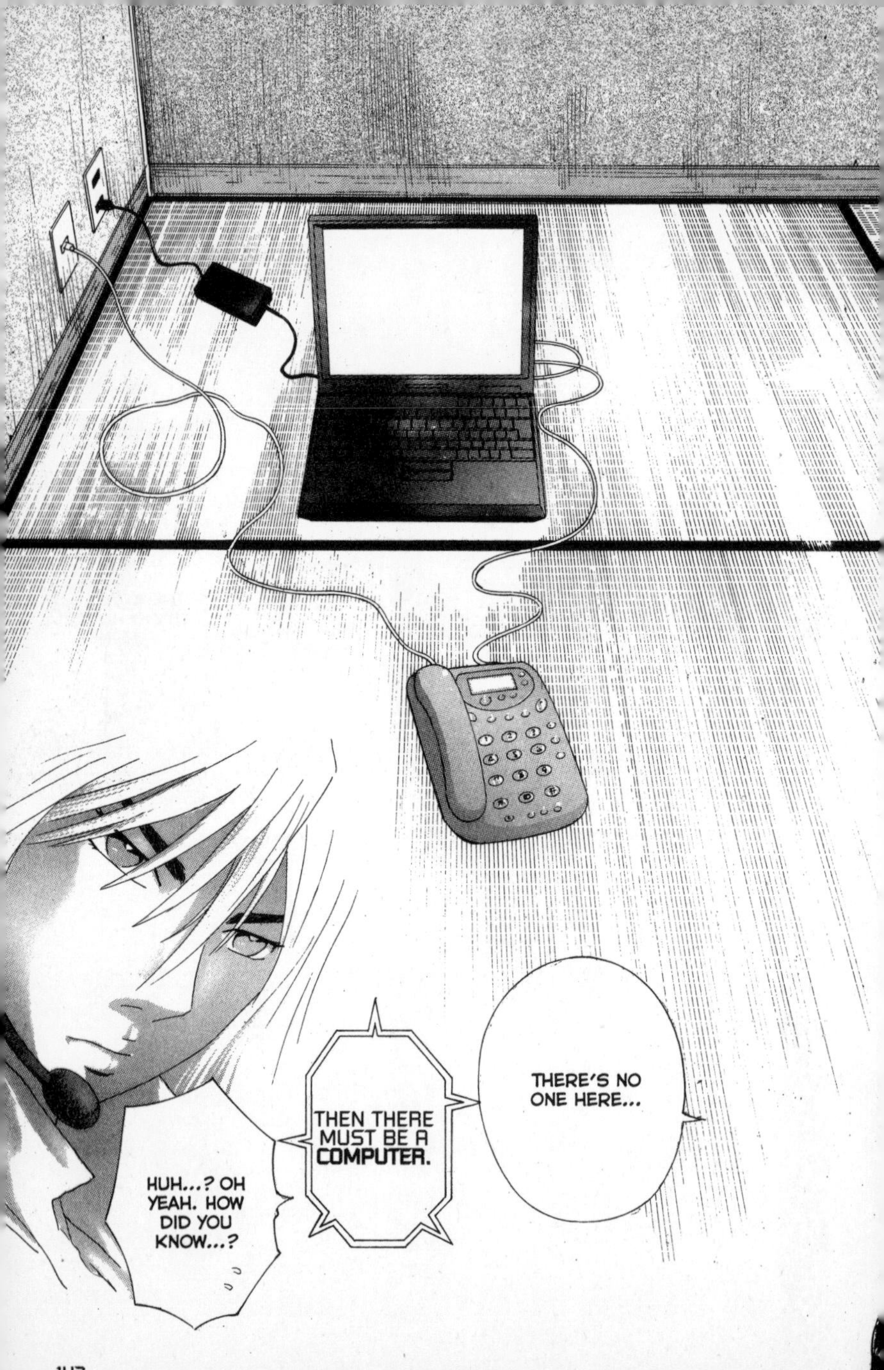
THERE'S NO ONE HERE...
THEN THERE MUST BE A COMPUTER.
HUH...? OH YEAH. HOW DID YOU KNOW...?

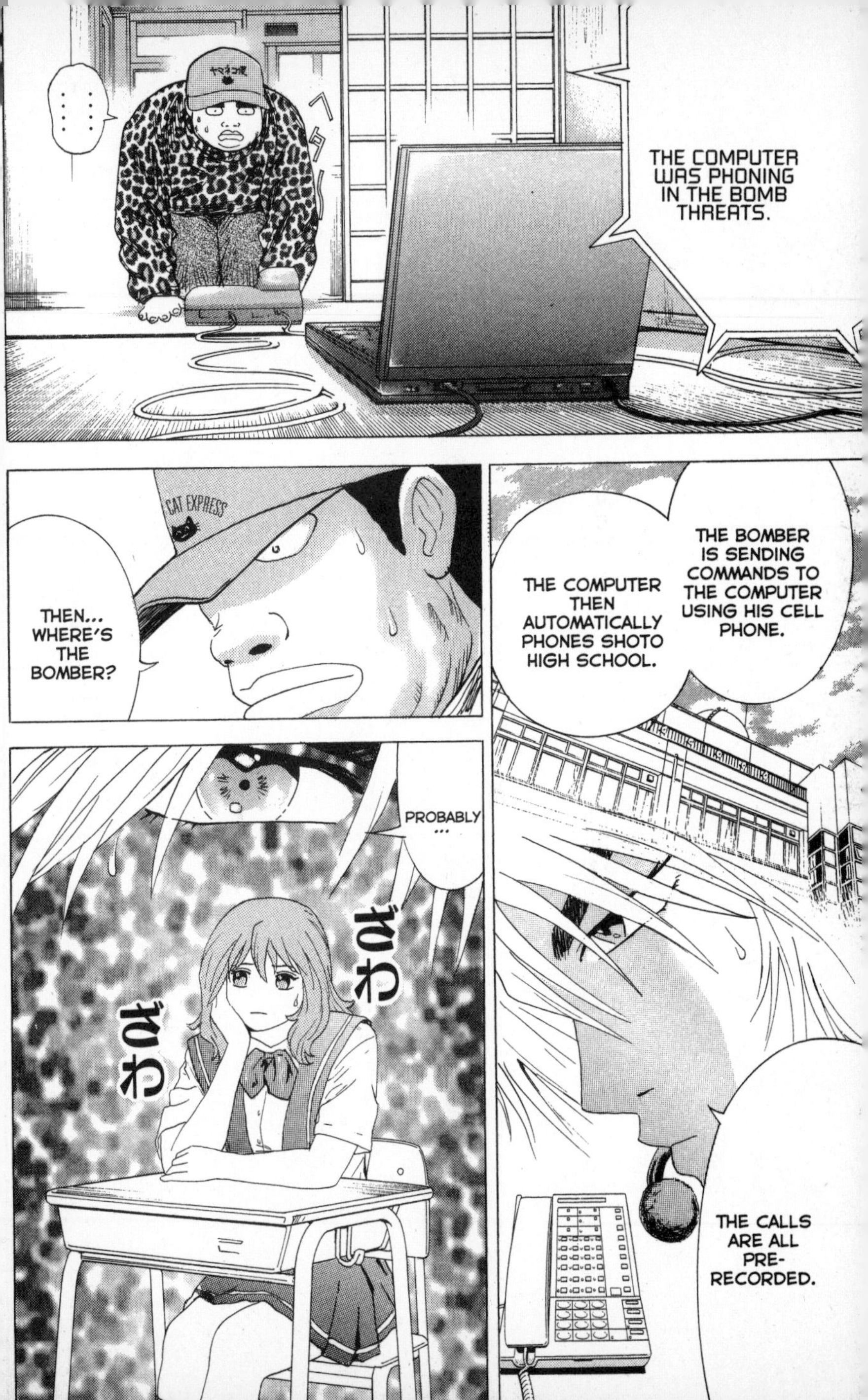
THE COMPUTER WAS PHONING IN THE BOMB THREATS.
......
THE BOMBER IS SENDING COMMANDS TO THE COMPUTER USING HIS CELL PHONE.
THE COMPUTER THEN AUTOMATICALLY PHONES SHOTO HIGH SCHOOL.
THE CALLS ARE ALL PRE-RECORDED.
CAT EXPRESS
THEN... WHERE'S THE BOMBER?
PROBABLY ...
ざわ
ざわ

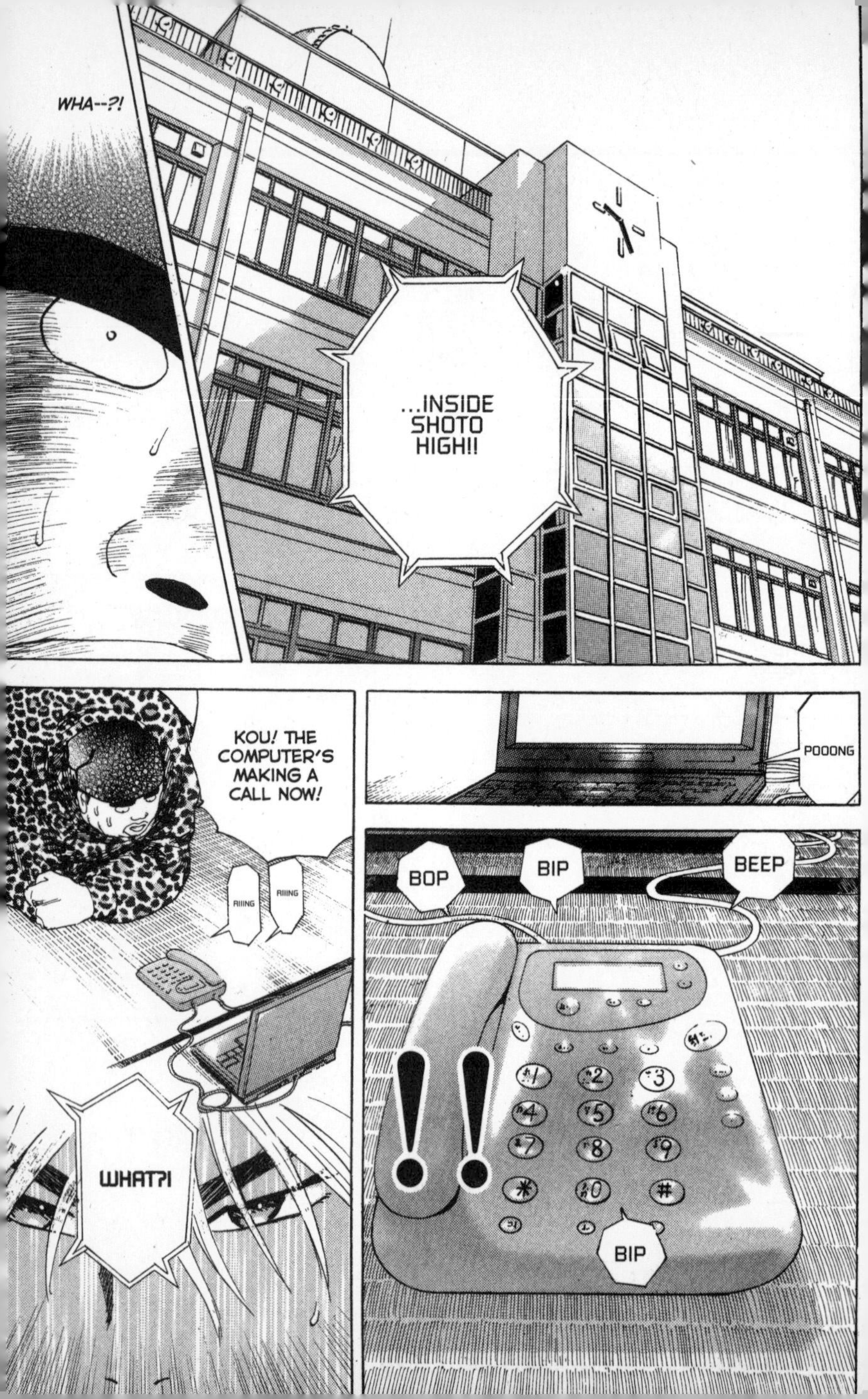
...INSIDE SHOTO HIGH!!
WHA--?!
POOONG
BEEP
BIP
BOP
BIP
KOU! THE COMPUTER'S MAKING A CALL NOW!
RIIING
RIIING
WHAT?!

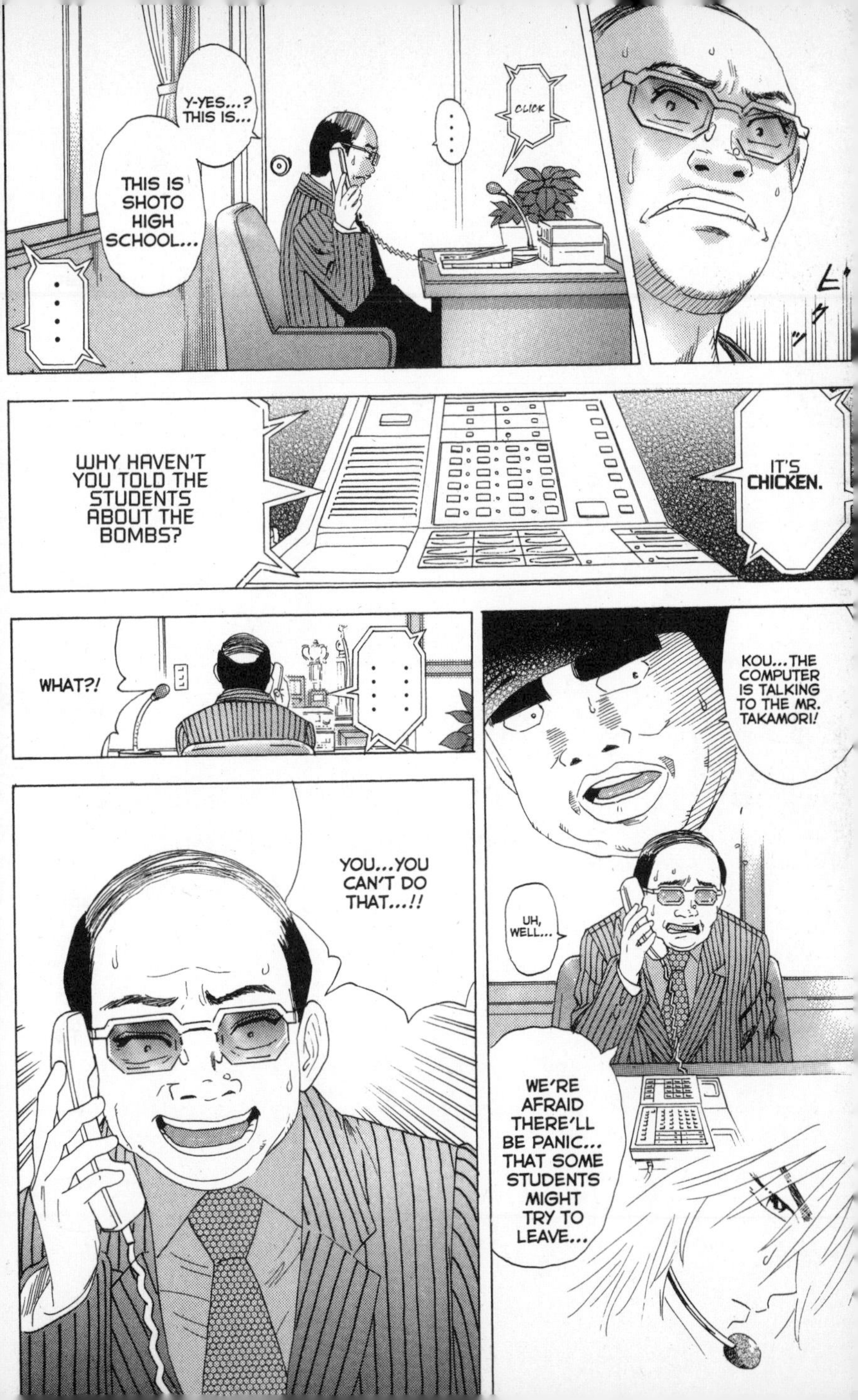
ビクッ
CLICK
....
Y-YES...? THIS IS...
THIS IS SHOTO HIGH SCHOOL...
....
IT'S CHICKEN.
WHY HAVEN'T YOU TOLD THE STUDENTS ABOUT THE BOMBS?
KOU...THE COMPUTER IS TALKING TO THE MR. TAKAMORI!
UH, WELL...
WE'RE AFRAID THERE'LL BE PANIC...THAT SOME STUDENTS MIGHT TRY TO LEAVE...
....
WHAT?!
YOU...YOU CAN'T DO THAT...!!

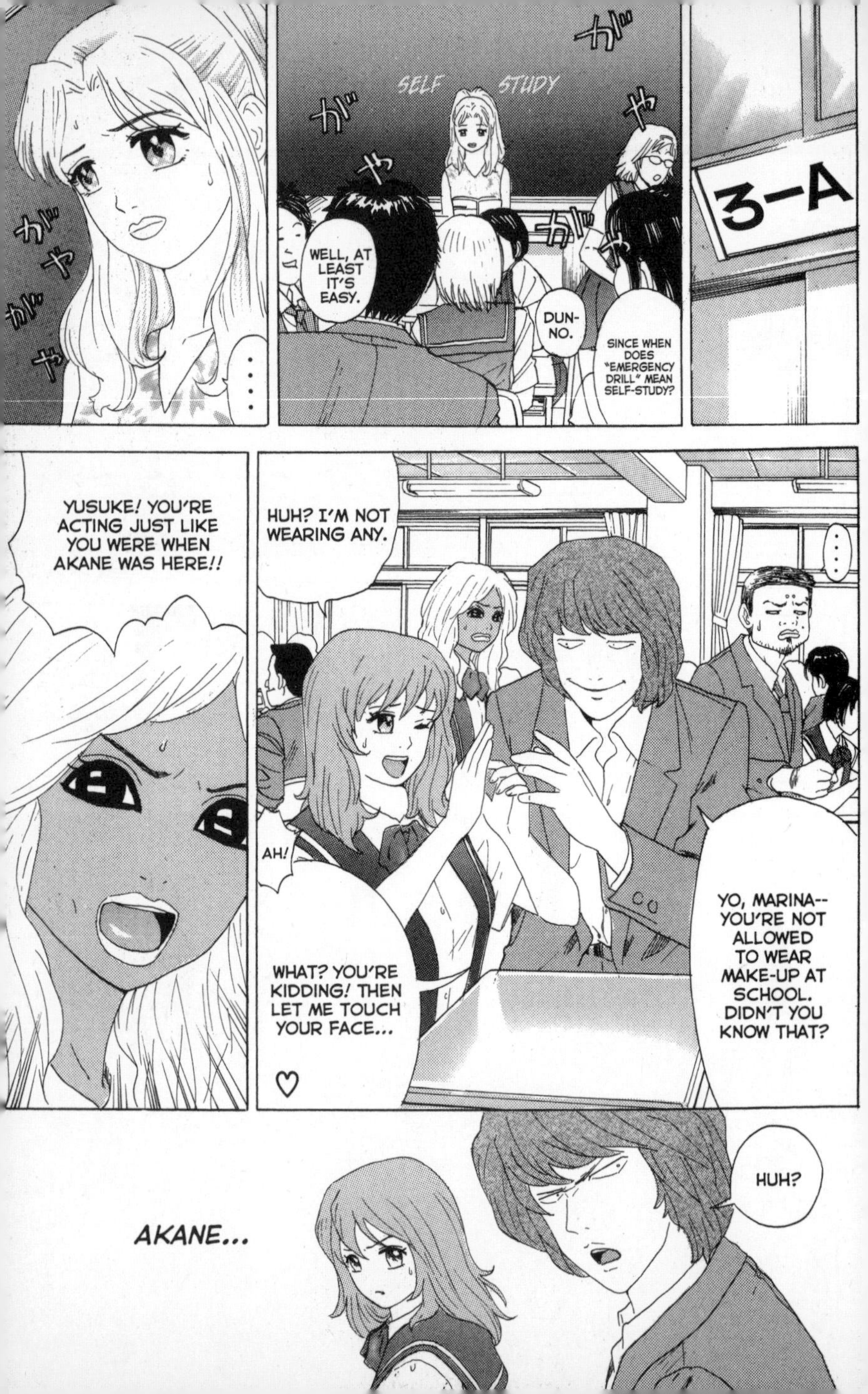
3-A
ガヤ ガヤ
SELF STUDY
ガヤ ガヤ
SINCE WHEN DOES "EMERGENCY DRILL" MEAN SELF-STUDY?
DUN-NO.
WELL, AT LEAST IT'S EASY.
ガヤ ガヤ
....
....
YO, MARINA-- YOU'RE NOT ALLOWED TO WEAR MAKE-UP AT SCHOOL. DIDN'T YOU KNOW THAT?
HUH? I'M NOT WEARING ANY.
WHAT? YOU'RE KIDDING! THEN LET ME TOUCH YOUR FACE... ♡
AH!
YUSUKE! YOU'RE ACTING JUST LIKE YOU WERE WHEN AKANE WAS HERE!!
HUH?
AKANE...

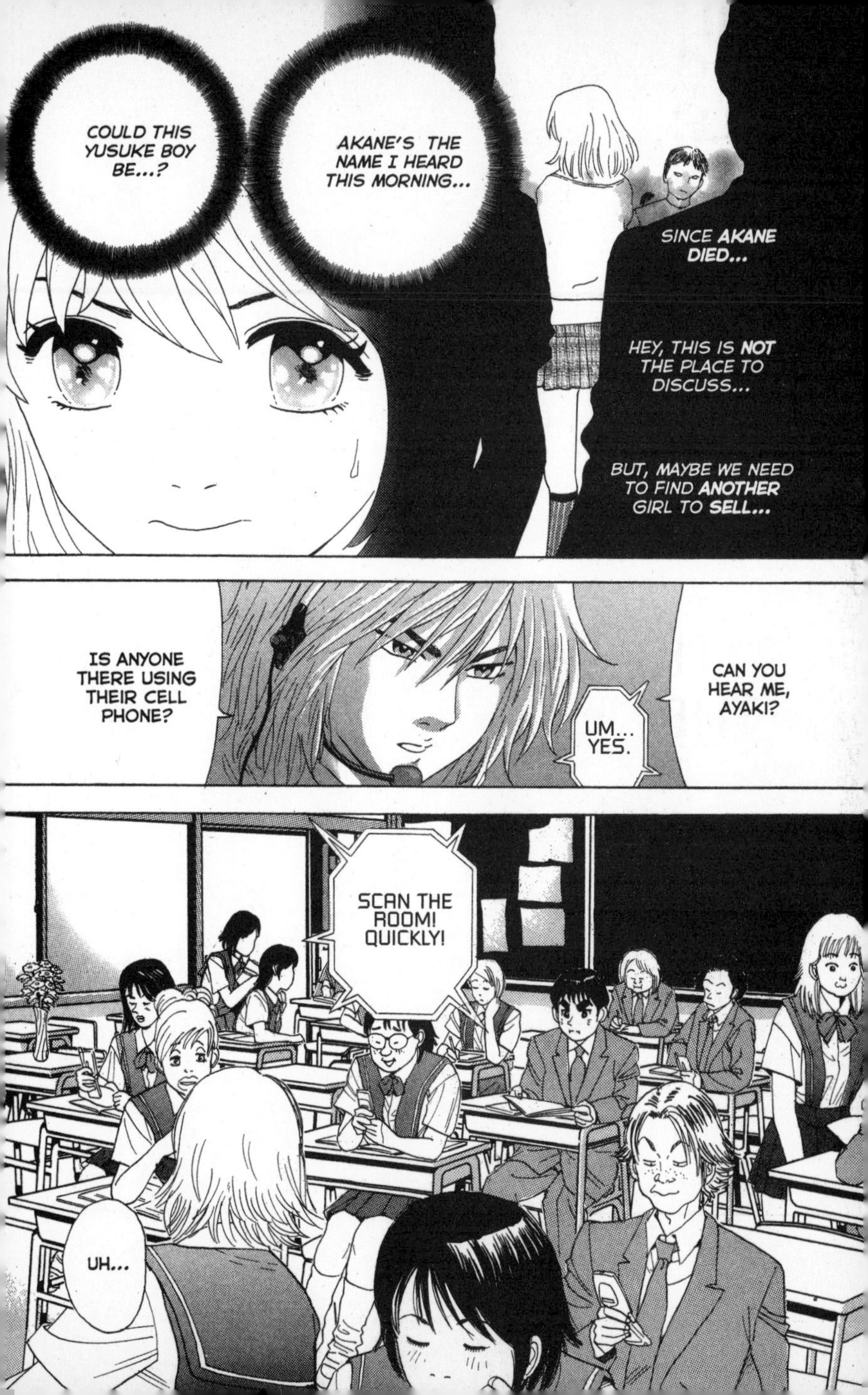
SINCE **AKANE** DIED...
HEY, THIS IS **NOT** THE PLACE TO DISCUSS...
BUT, MAYBE WE NEED TO FIND **ANOTHER** GIRL TO **SELL**...
AKANE'S THE NAME I HEARD THIS MORNING...
COULD THIS YUSUKE BOY BE...?
CAN YOU HEAR ME, AYAKI?
UM... YES.
IS ANYONE THERE USING THEIR CELL PHONE?
SCAN THE ROOM! QUICKLY!
UH...

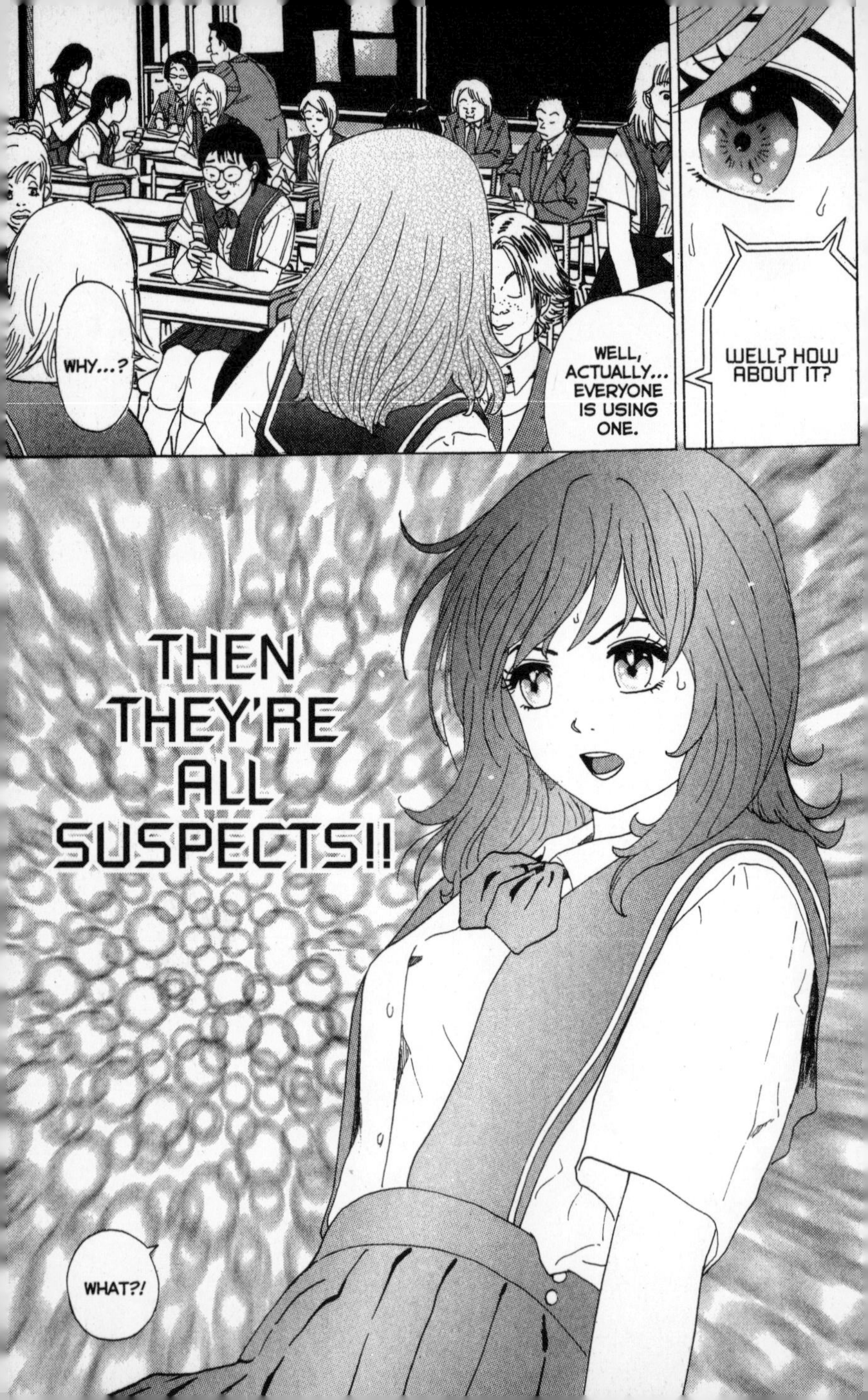
WELL? HOW ABOUT IT?
WELL, ACTUALLY... EVERYONE IS USING ONE.
WHY...?
THEN THEY'RE ALL SUSPECTS!!
WHAT?!

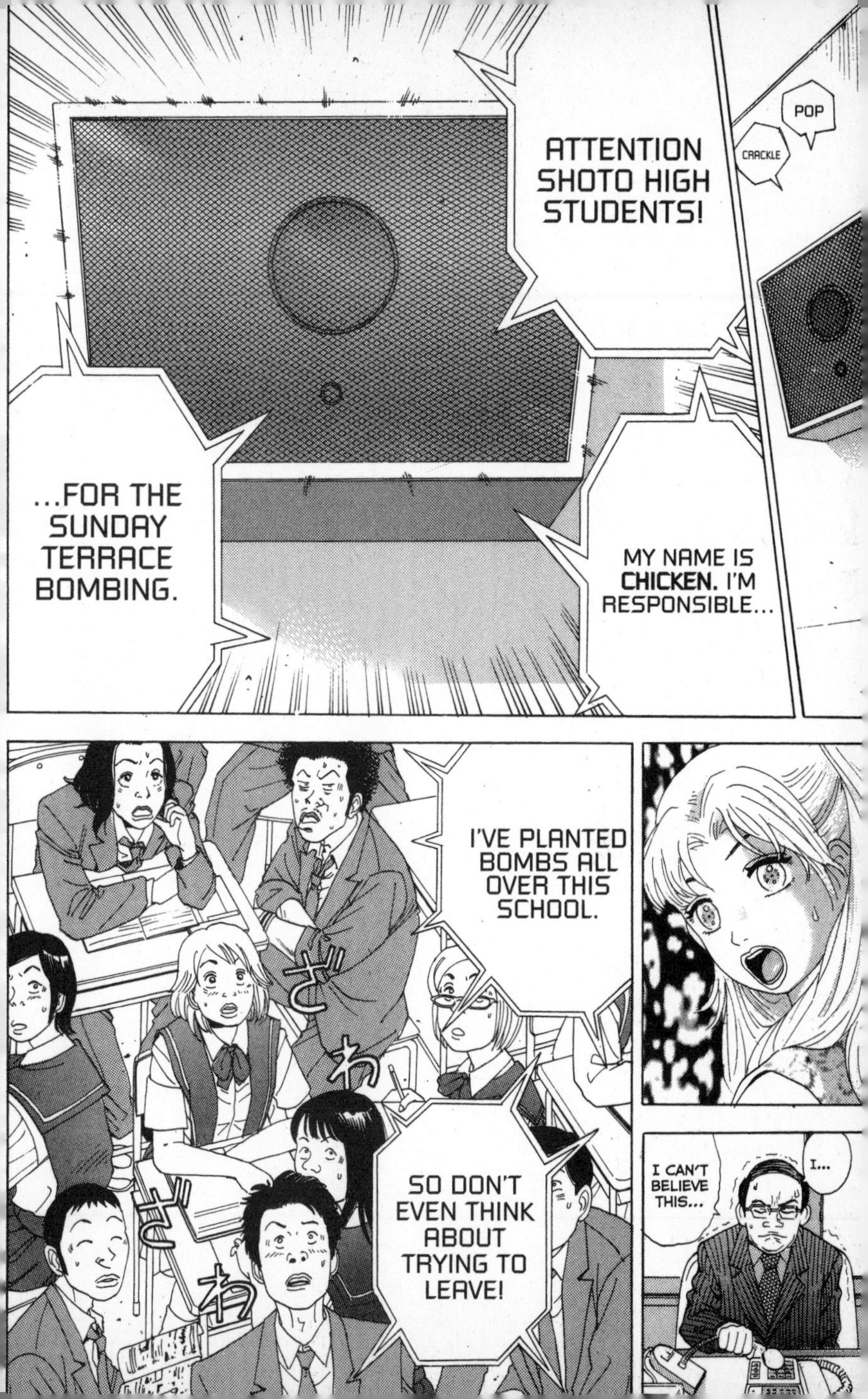
POP
CRACKLE
ATTENTION SHOTO HIGH STUDENTS!
MY NAME IS **CHICKEN.** I'M RESPONSIBLE...
...FOR THE SUNDAY TERRACE BOMBING.
I...
I CAN'T BELIEVE THIS...
I'VE PLANTED BOMBS ALL OVER THIS SCHOOL.
ざわ
ざわ
SO DON'T EVEN THINK ABOUT TRYING TO LEAVE!

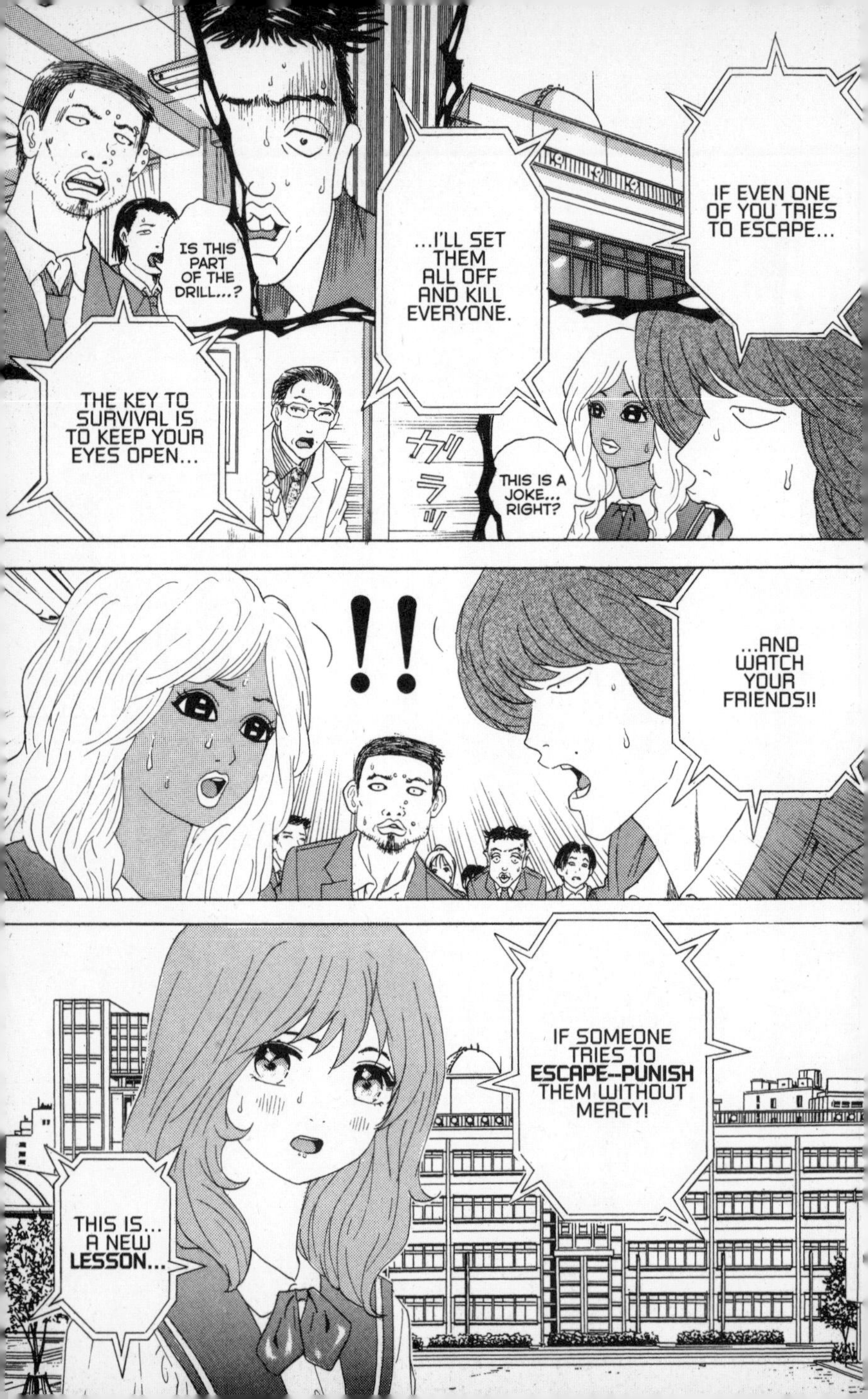
IF EVEN ONE OF YOU TRIES TO ESCAPE...
...I'LL SET THEM ALL OFF AND KILL EVERYONE.
IS THIS PART OF THE DRILL...?
ガラッ
THIS IS A JOKE... RIGHT?
THE KEY TO SURVIVAL IS TO KEEP YOUR EYES OPEN...
...AND WATCH YOUR FRIENDS!!
!!
IF SOMEONE TRIES TO **ESCAPE--PUNISH** THEM WITHOUT MERCY!
THIS IS... A NEW **LESSON**...

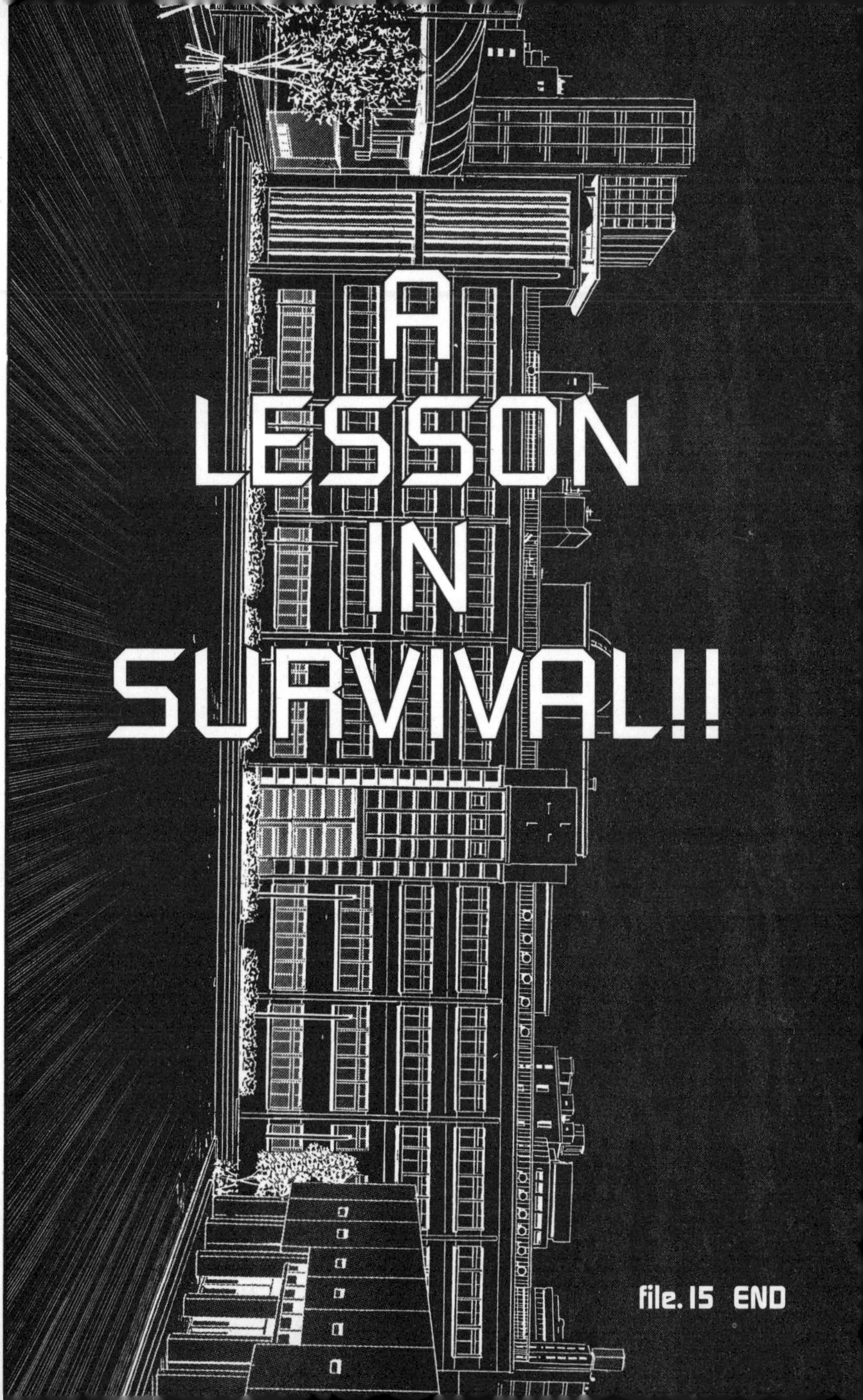
A LESSON IN SURVIVAL!!
file.15 END

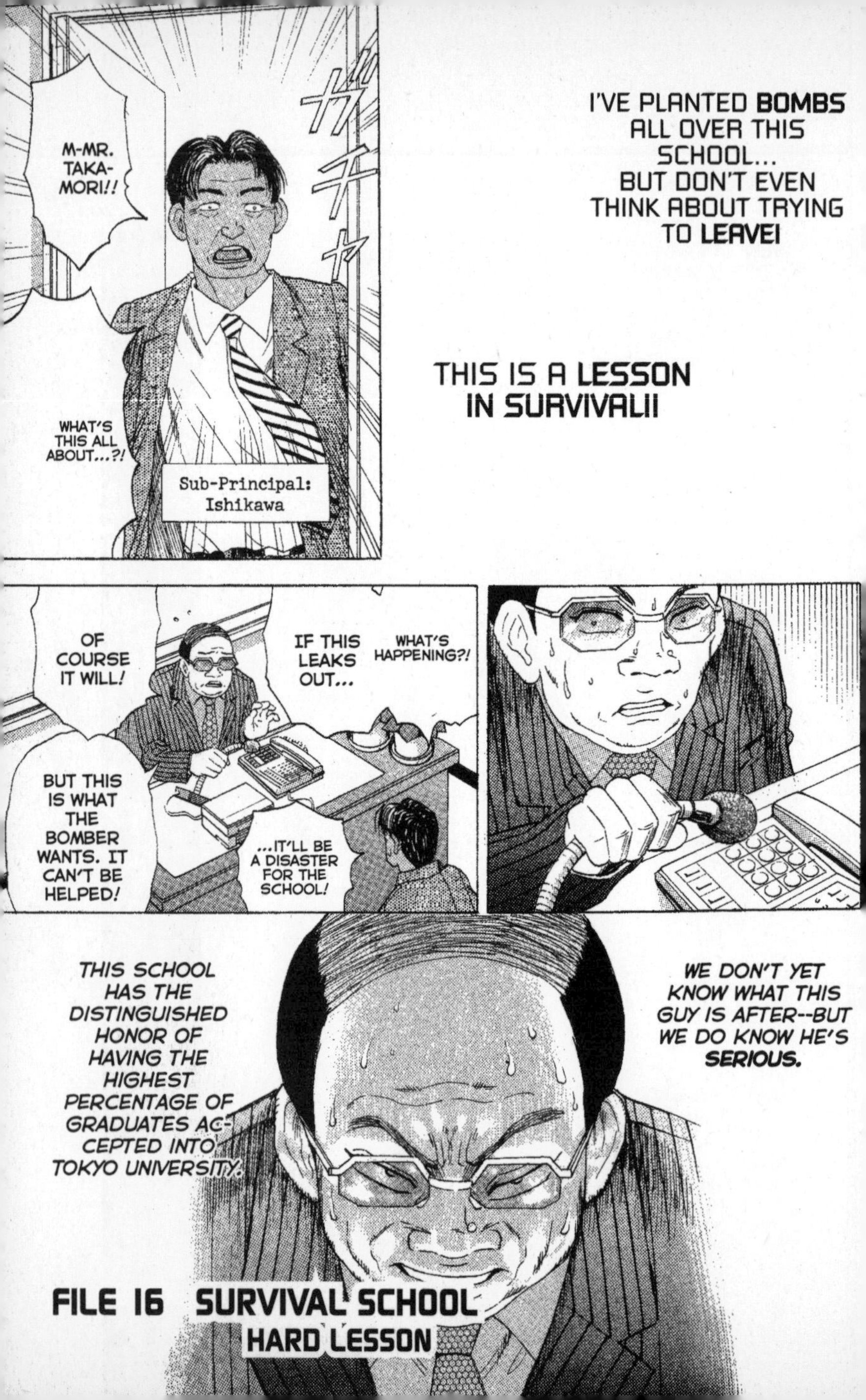

I'VE PLANTED BOMBS ALL OVER THIS SCHOOL... BUT DON'T EVEN THINK ABOUT TRYING TO LEAVE!
THIS IS A LESSON IN SURVIVAL!!
ガチャ
M-MR. TAKA-MORI!!
WHAT'S THIS ALL ABOUT...?!
Sub-Principal: Ishikawa
WHAT'S HAPPENING?!
IF THIS LEAKS OUT...
...IT'LL BE A DISASTER FOR THE SCHOOL!
OF COURSE IT WILL!
BUT THIS IS WHAT THE BOMBER WANTS. IT CAN'T BE HELPED!
WE DON'T YET KNOW WHAT THIS GUY IS AFTER--BUT WE DO KNOW HE'S SERIOUS.
THIS SCHOOL HAS THE DISTINGUISHED HONOR OF HAVING THE HIGHEST PERCENTAGE OF GRADUATES AC-CEPTED INTO TOKYO UNIVERSITY.
FILE 16 SURVIVAL SCHOOL
HARD LESSON

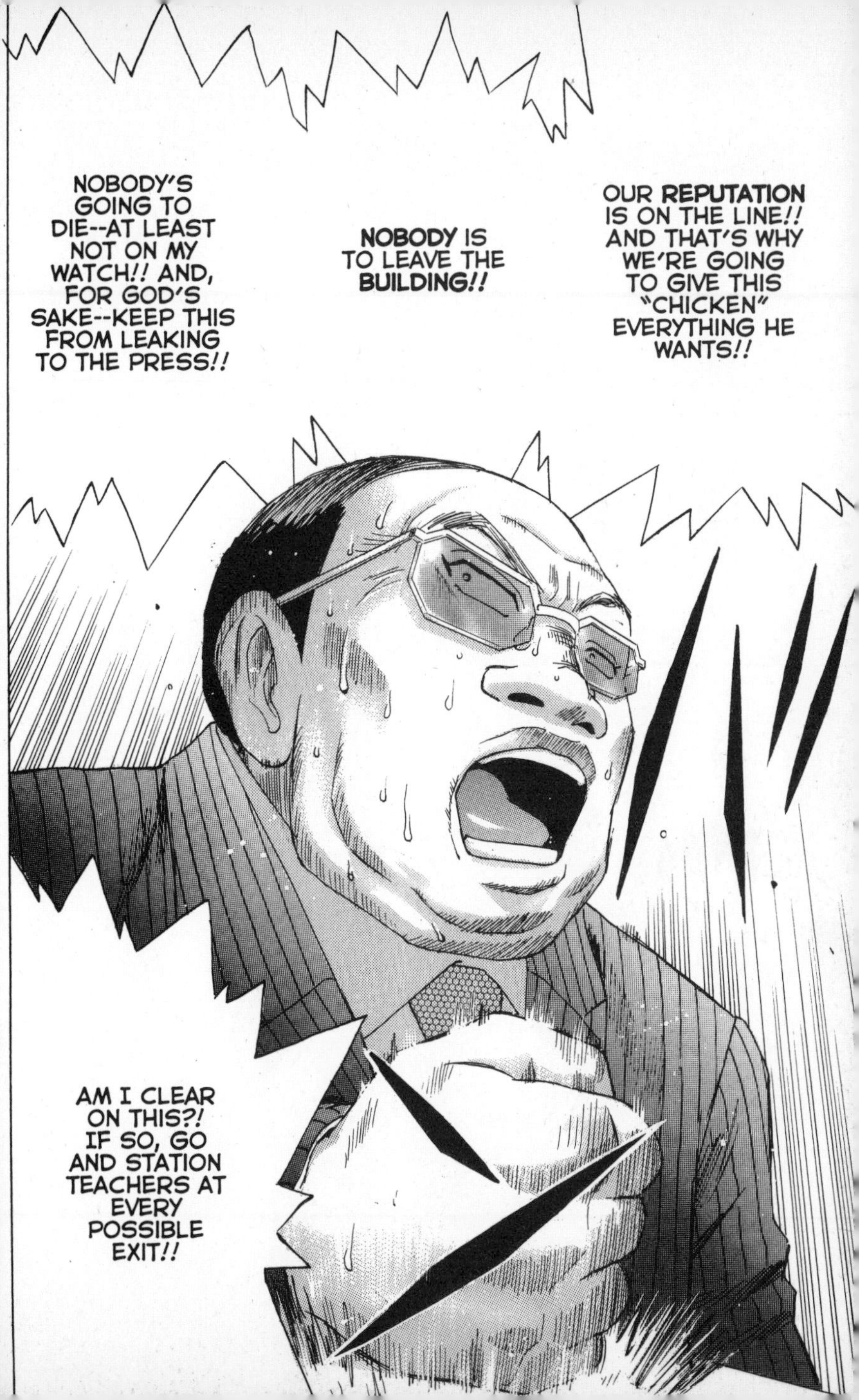
OUR **REPUTATION** IS ON THE LINE!! AND THAT'S WHY WE'RE GOING TO GIVE THIS "CHICKEN" EVERYTHING HE WANTS!!
NOBODY IS TO LEAVE THE **BUILDING!!**
NOBODY'S GOING TO DIE--AT LEAST NOT ON MY WATCH!! AND, FOR GOD'S SAKE--KEEP THIS FROM LEAKING TO THE PRESS!!
AM I CLEAR ON THIS?! IF SO, GO AND STATION TEACHERS AT EVERY POSSIBLE EXIT!!

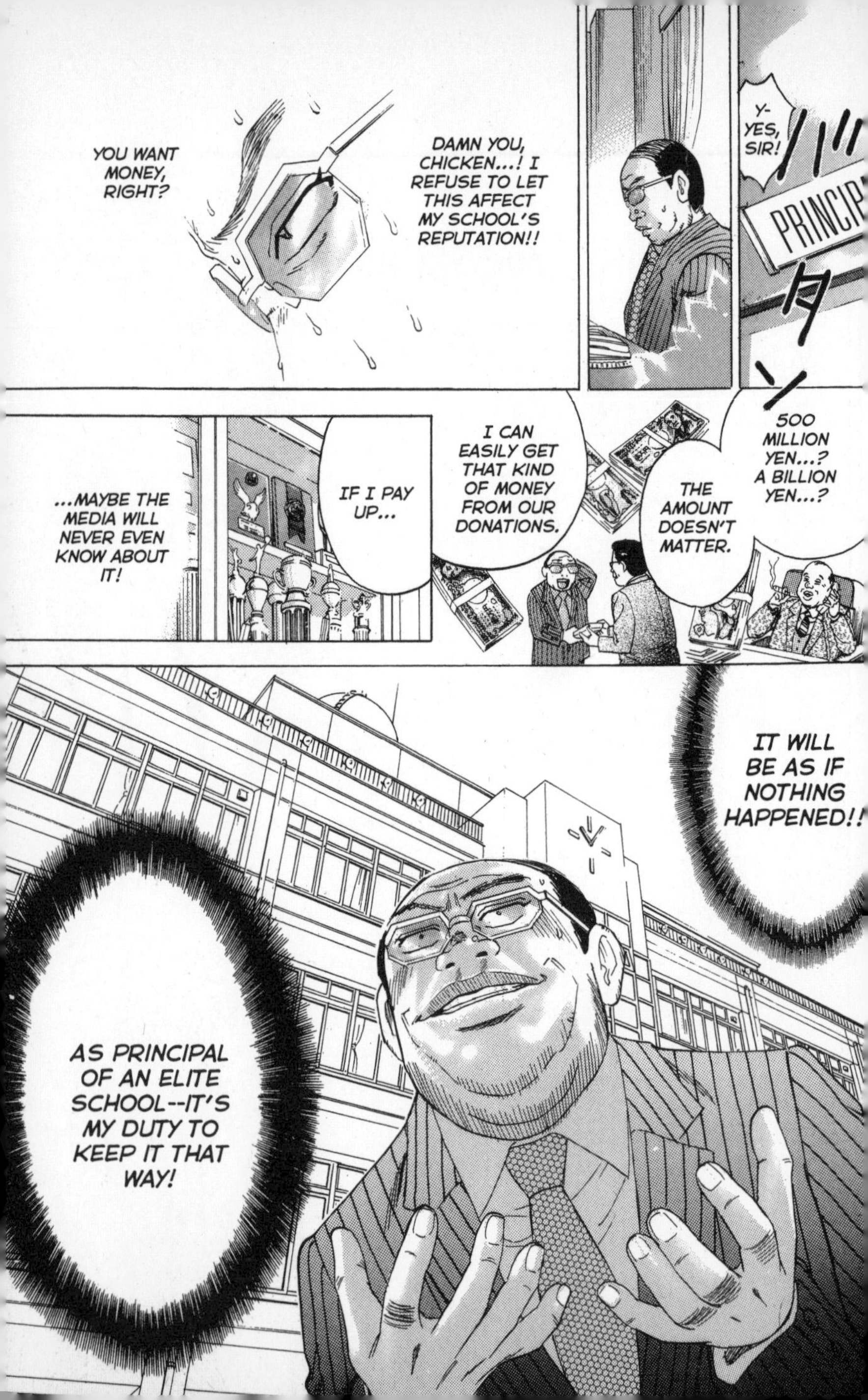
Y-YES, SIR!
PRINCIP
DAMN YOU, CHICKEN...! I REFUSE TO LET THIS AFFECT MY SCHOOL'S REPUTATION!!
YOU WANT MONEY, RIGHT?
500 MILLION YEN...? A BILLION YEN...?
THE AMOUNT DOESN'T MATTER.
I CAN EASILY GET THAT KIND OF MONEY FROM OUR DONATIONS.
IF I PAY UP...
...MAYBE THE MEDIA WILL NEVER EVEN KNOW ABOUT IT!
IT WILL BE AS IF NOTHING HAPPENED!!
AS PRINCIPAL OF AN ELITE SCHOOL--IT'S MY DUTY TO KEEP IT THAT WAY!

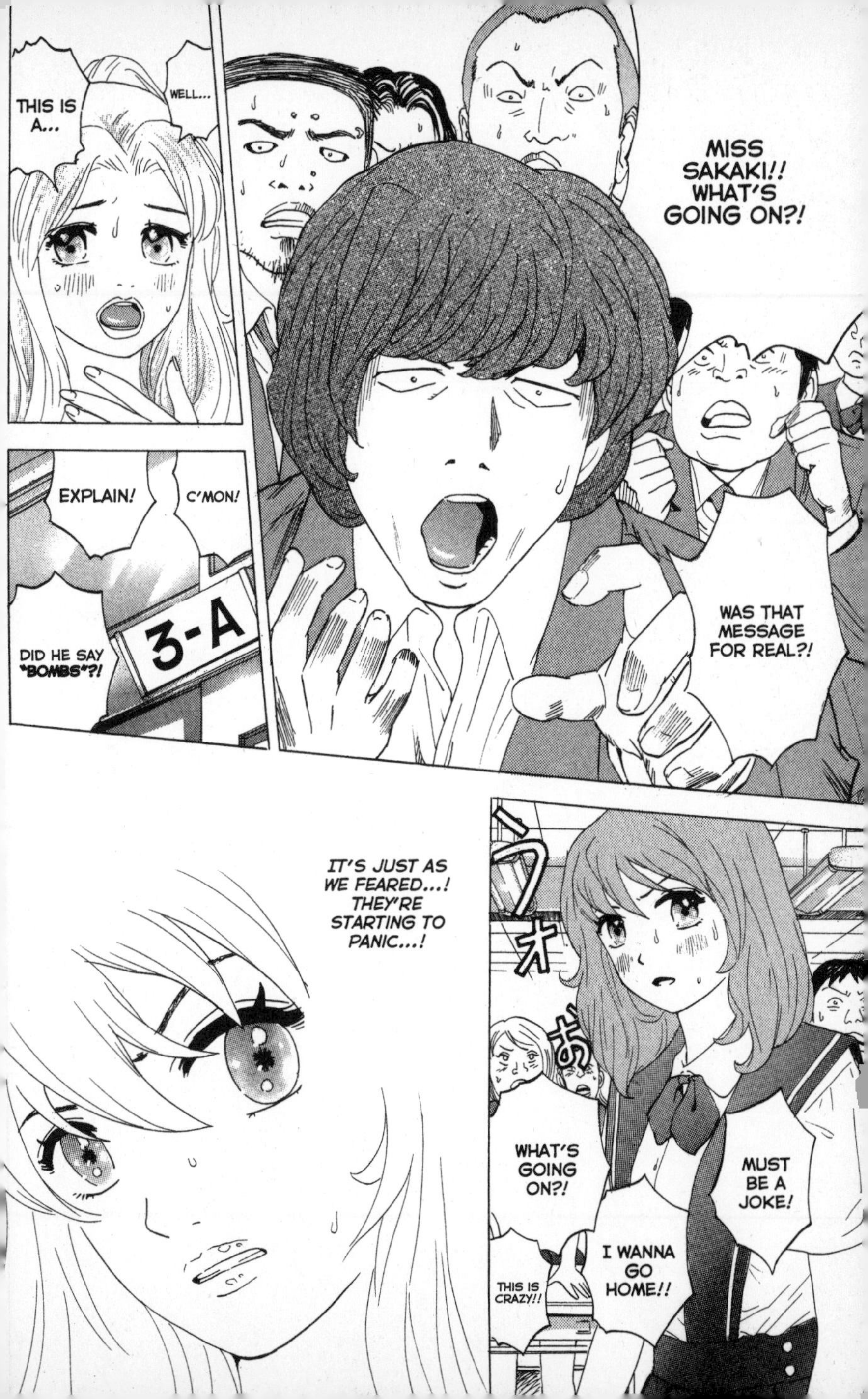
MISS SAKAKI!! WHAT'S GOING ON?!
WAS THAT MESSAGE FOR REAL?!
WELL...
THIS IS A...
C'MON!
EXPLAIN!
3-A
DID HE SAY "BOMBS"?!
MUST BE A JOKE!
WHAT'S GOING ON?!
I WANNA GO HOME!!
THIS IS CRAZY!!
IT'S JUST AS WE FEARED...! THEY'RE STARTING TO PANIC...!

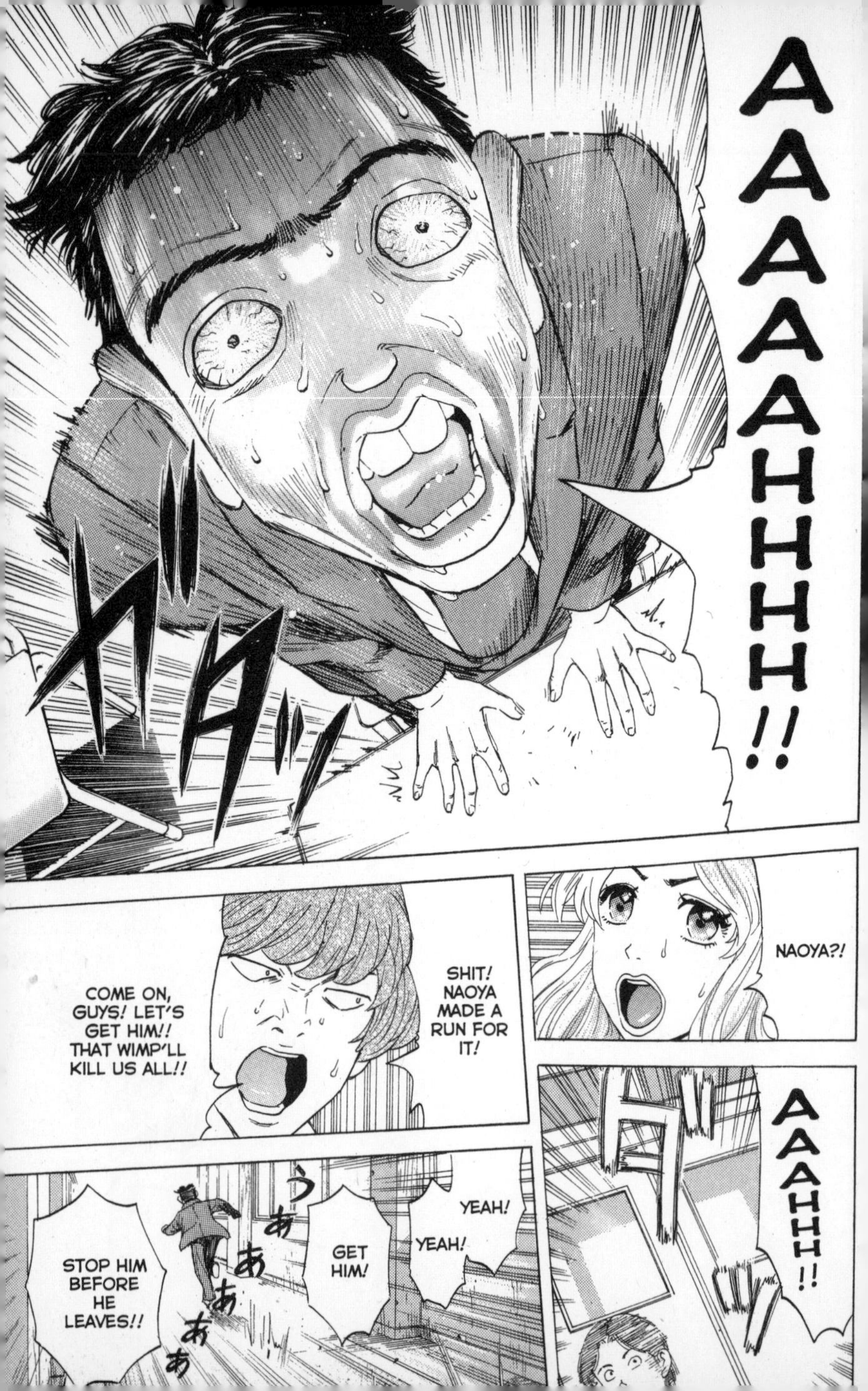
AAAAAAHHH!!
ガタッ
NAOYA?!
SHIT! NAOYA MADE A RUN FOR IT!
COME ON, GUYS! LET'S GET HIM!! THAT WIMP'LL KILL US ALL!!
AAAHHH!!
YEAH!
YEAH!
GET HIM!
うあああああ
STOP HIM BEFORE HE LEAVES!!

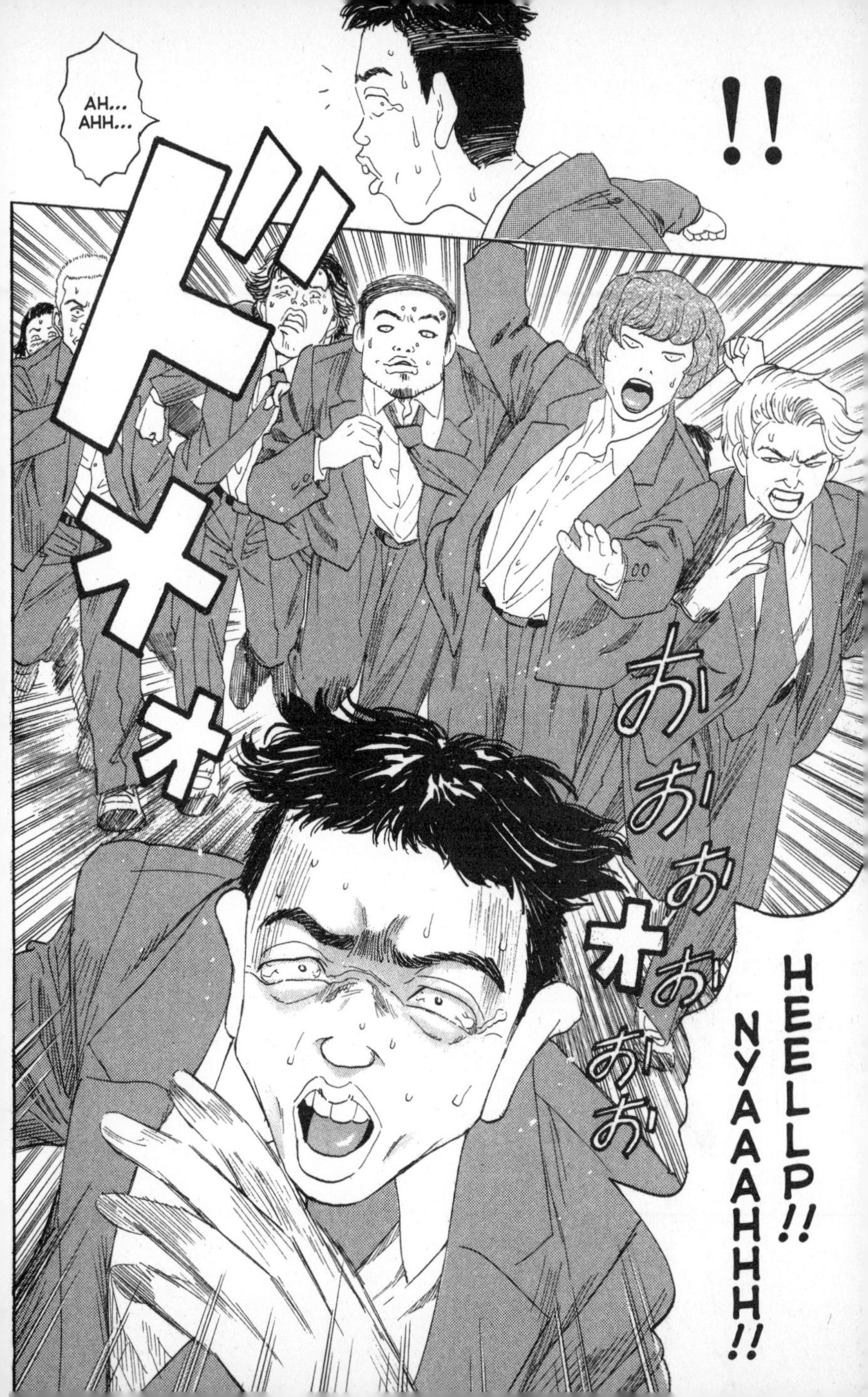
!!
AH... AHH...
ドドオオ
HEELLP!!
NYAAAHHH!!
おおおオおおお

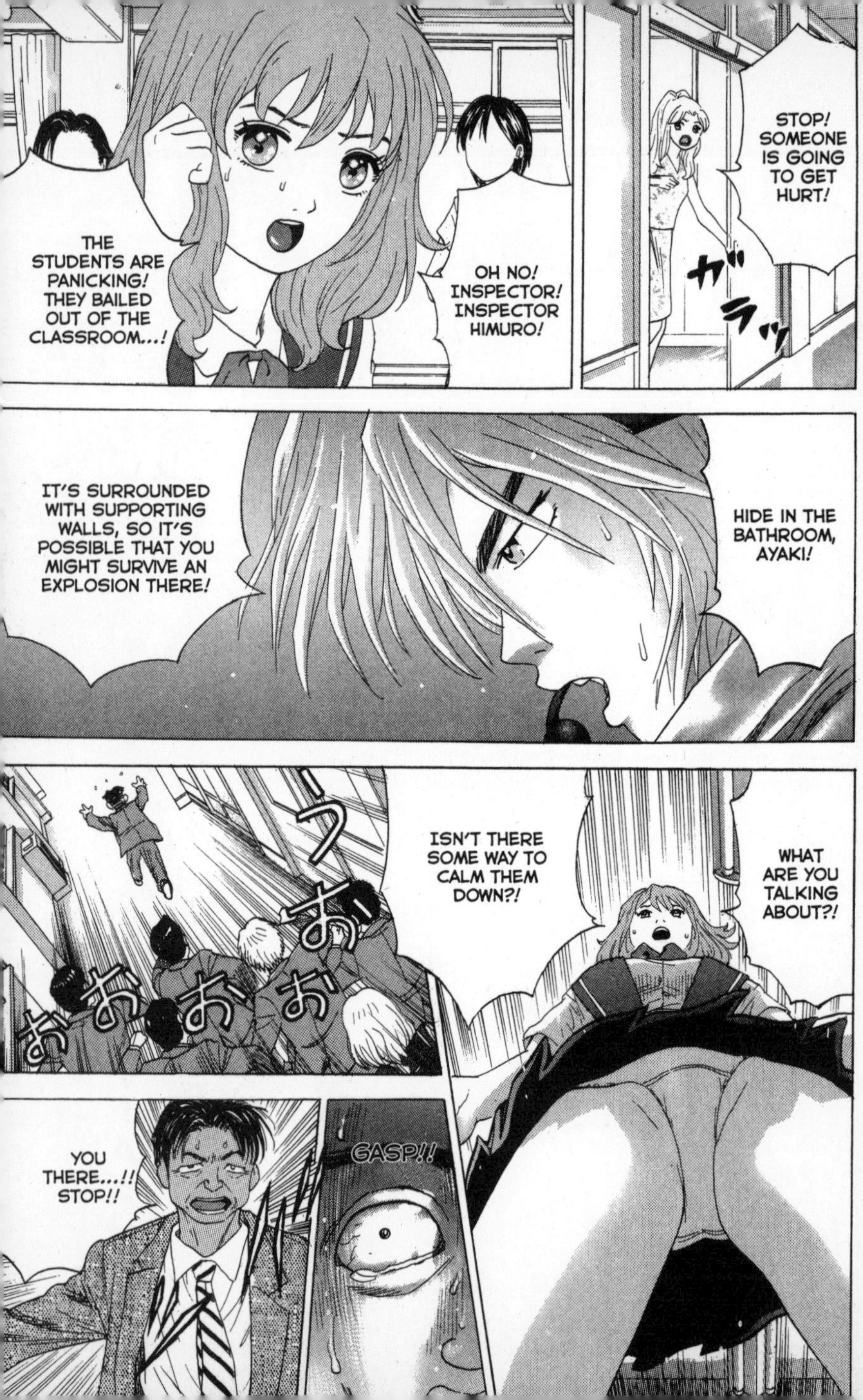

STOP! SOMEONE IS GOING TO GET HURT!
ガラッ
OH NO! INSPECTOR! INSPECTOR HIMURO!
THE STUDENTS ARE PANICKING! THEY BAILED OUT OF THE CLASSROOM...!
HIDE IN THE BATHROOM, AYAKI!
IT'S SURROUNDED WITH SUPPORTING WALLS, SO IT'S POSSIBLE THAT YOU MIGHT SURVIVE AN EXPLOSION THERE!
WHAT ARE YOU TALKING ABOUT?!
ISN'T THERE SOME WAY TO CALM THEM DOWN?!
おおおおおーっ
GASP!!
YOU THERE...!! STOP!!

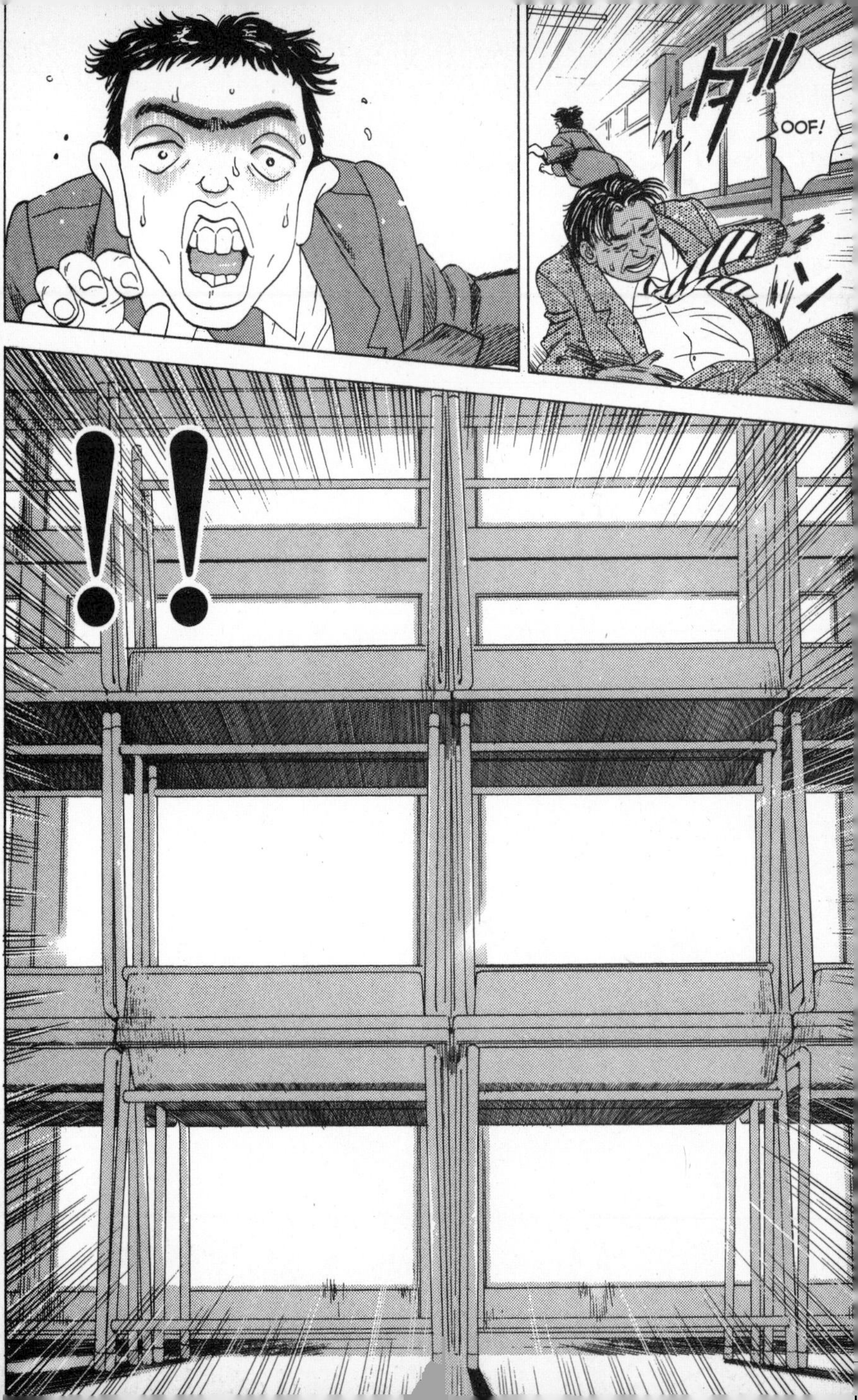
ダ
OOF!
ン
!!

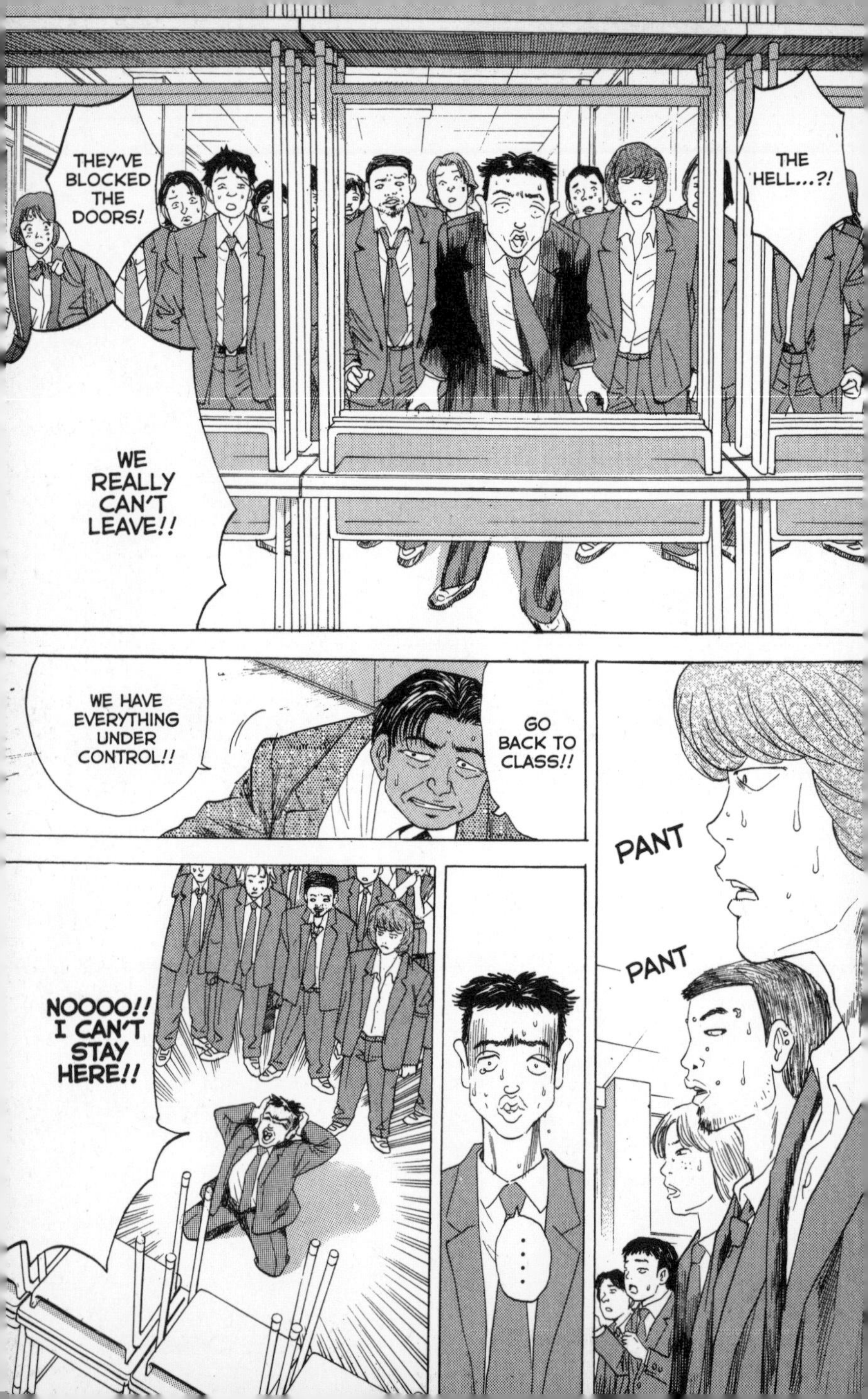
THE HELL...?!
THEY'VE BLOCKED THE DOORS!
WE REALLY CAN'T LEAVE!!
PANT
PANT
GO BACK TO CLASS!!
WE HAVE EVERYTHING UNDER CONTROL!!
.....
NOOOO!! I CAN'T STAY HERE!!

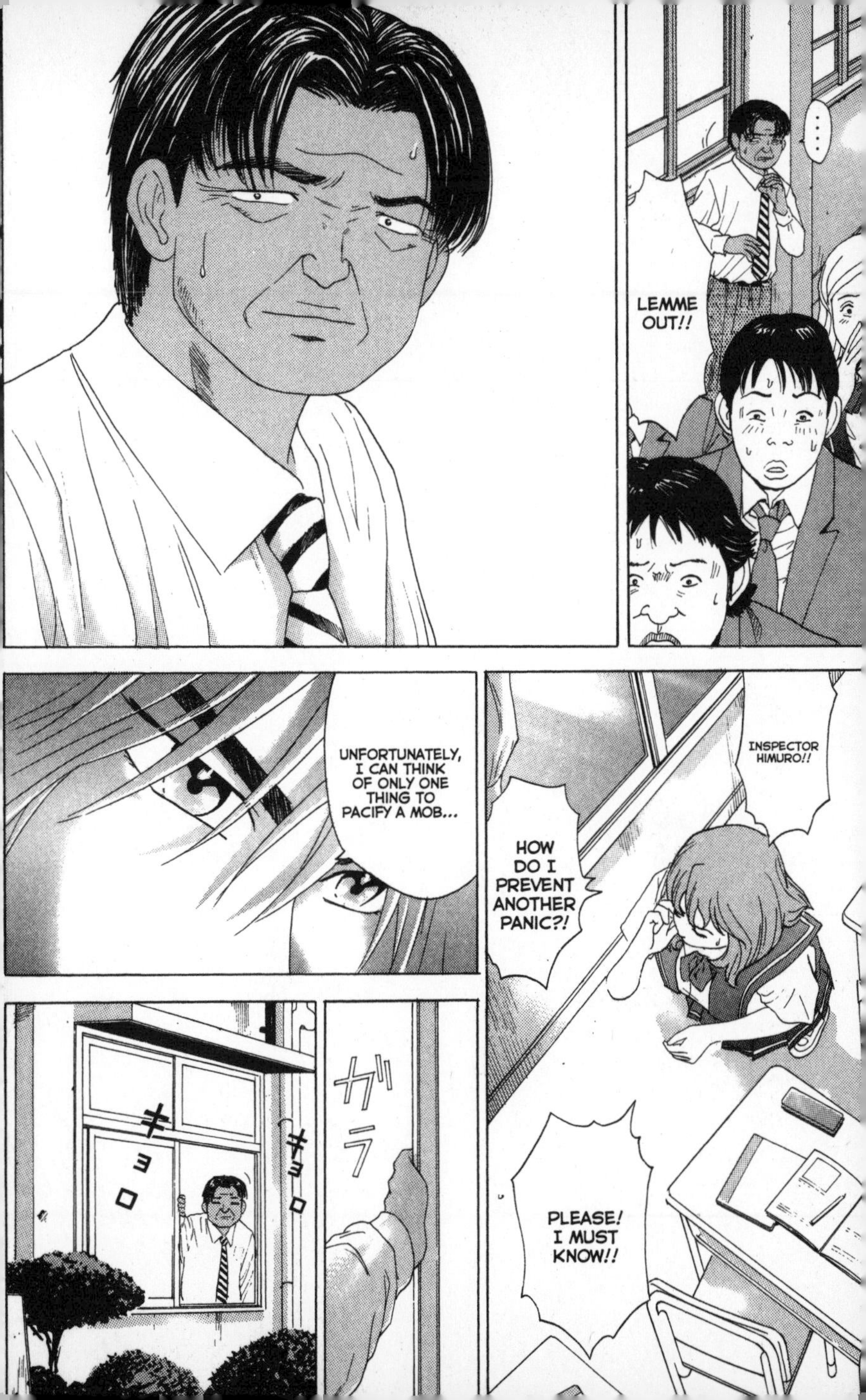
. . .
LEMME OUT!!
INSPECTOR HIMURO!!
HOW DO I PREVENT ANOTHER PANIC?!
PLEASE! I MUST KNOW!!
UNFORTUNATELY, I CAN THINK OF ONLY ONE THING TO PACIFY A MOB...
ガラ
キョロ
キョロ

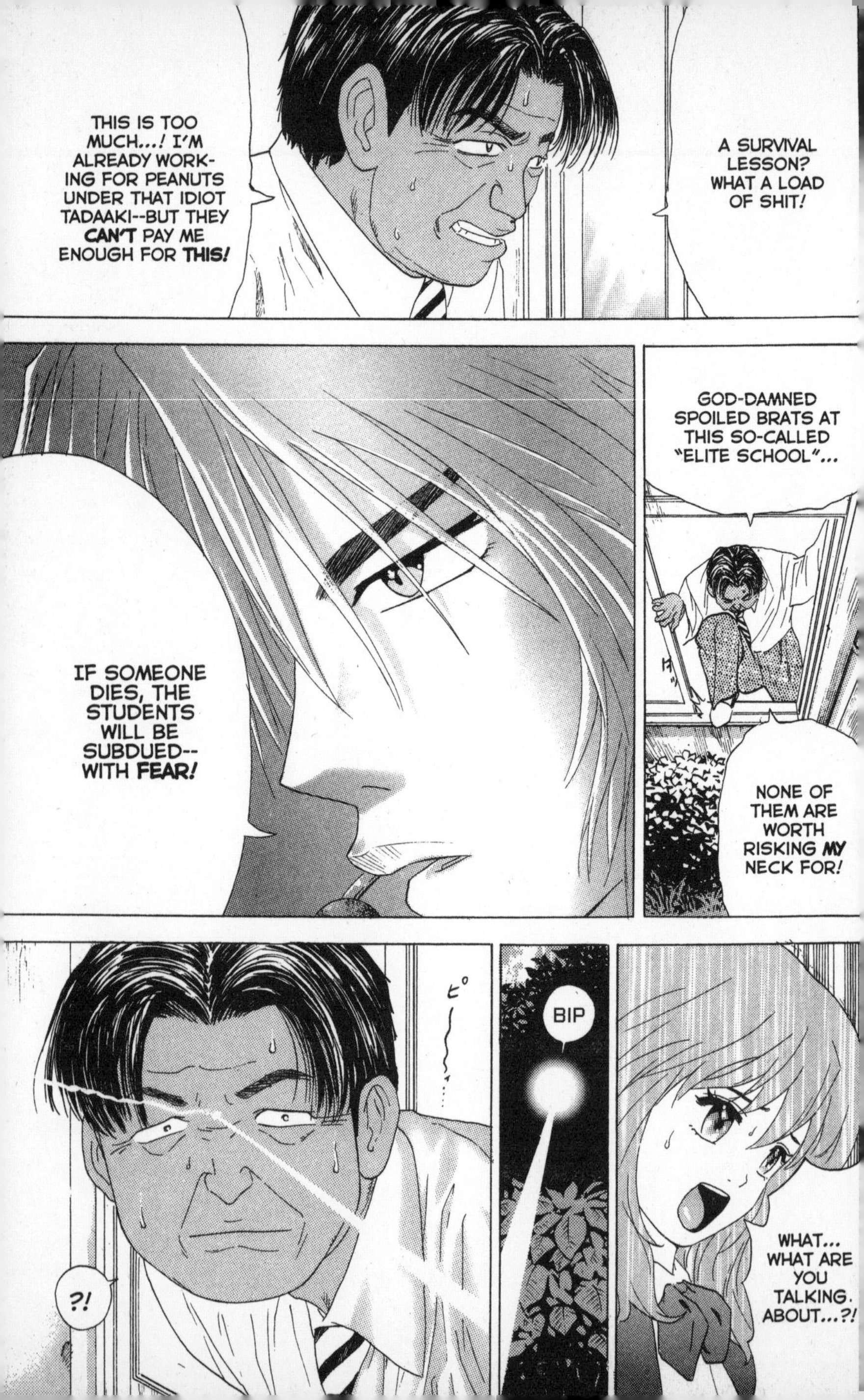
A SURVIVAL LESSON? WHAT A LOAD OF SHIT!
THIS IS TOO MUCH...! I'M ALREADY WORKING FOR PEANUTS UNDER THAT IDIOT TADAAKI--BUT THEY **CAN'T** PAY ME ENOUGH FOR **THIS!**
GOD-DAMNED SPOILED BRATS AT THIS SO-CALLED "ELITE SCHOOL"...
NONE OF THEM ARE WORTH RISKING **MY** NECK FOR!
IF SOMEONE DIES, THE STUDENTS WILL BE SUBDUED--WITH **FEAR!**
WHAT... WHAT ARE YOU TALKING. ABOUT...?!
BIP
?!

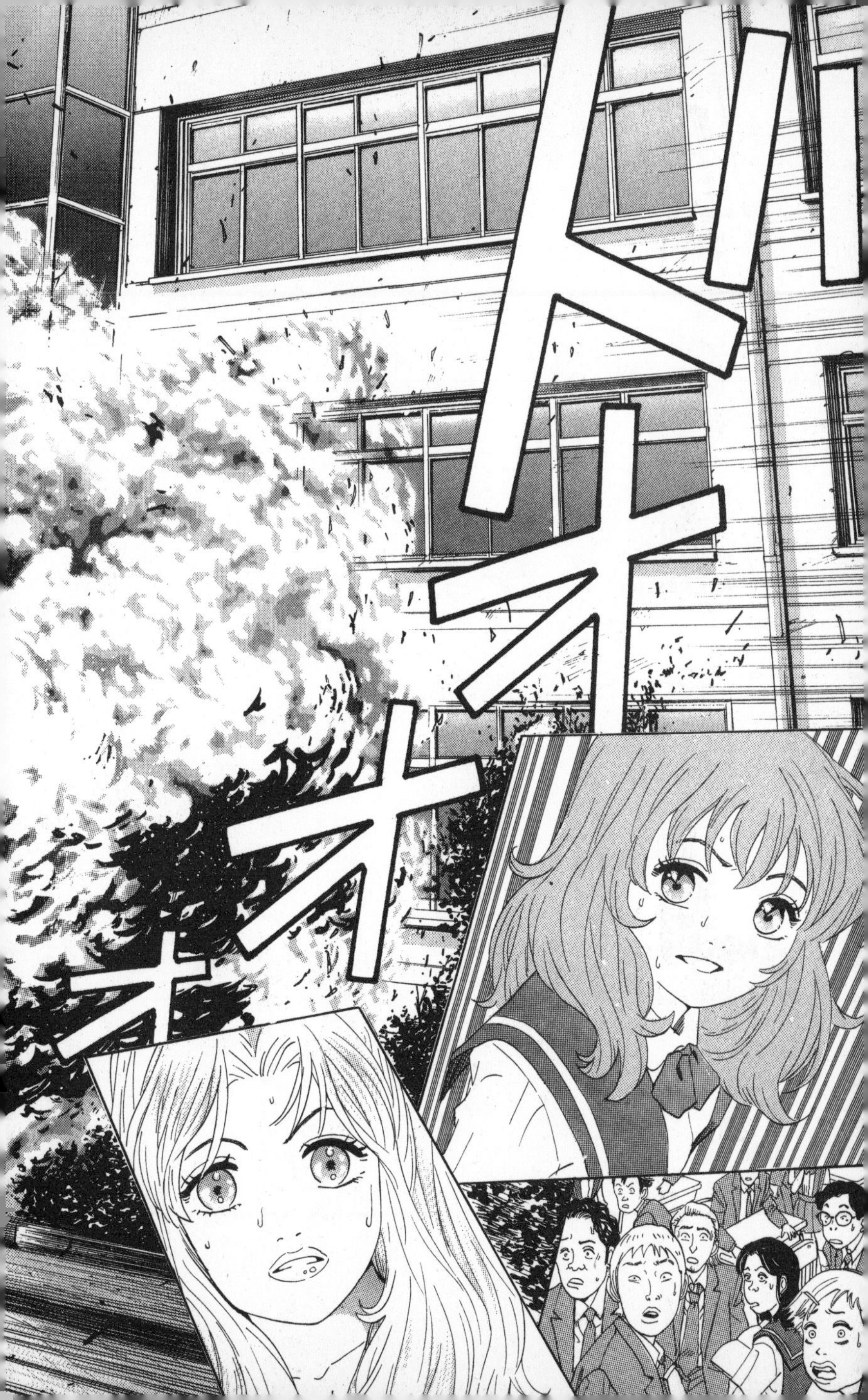
ドオオオ

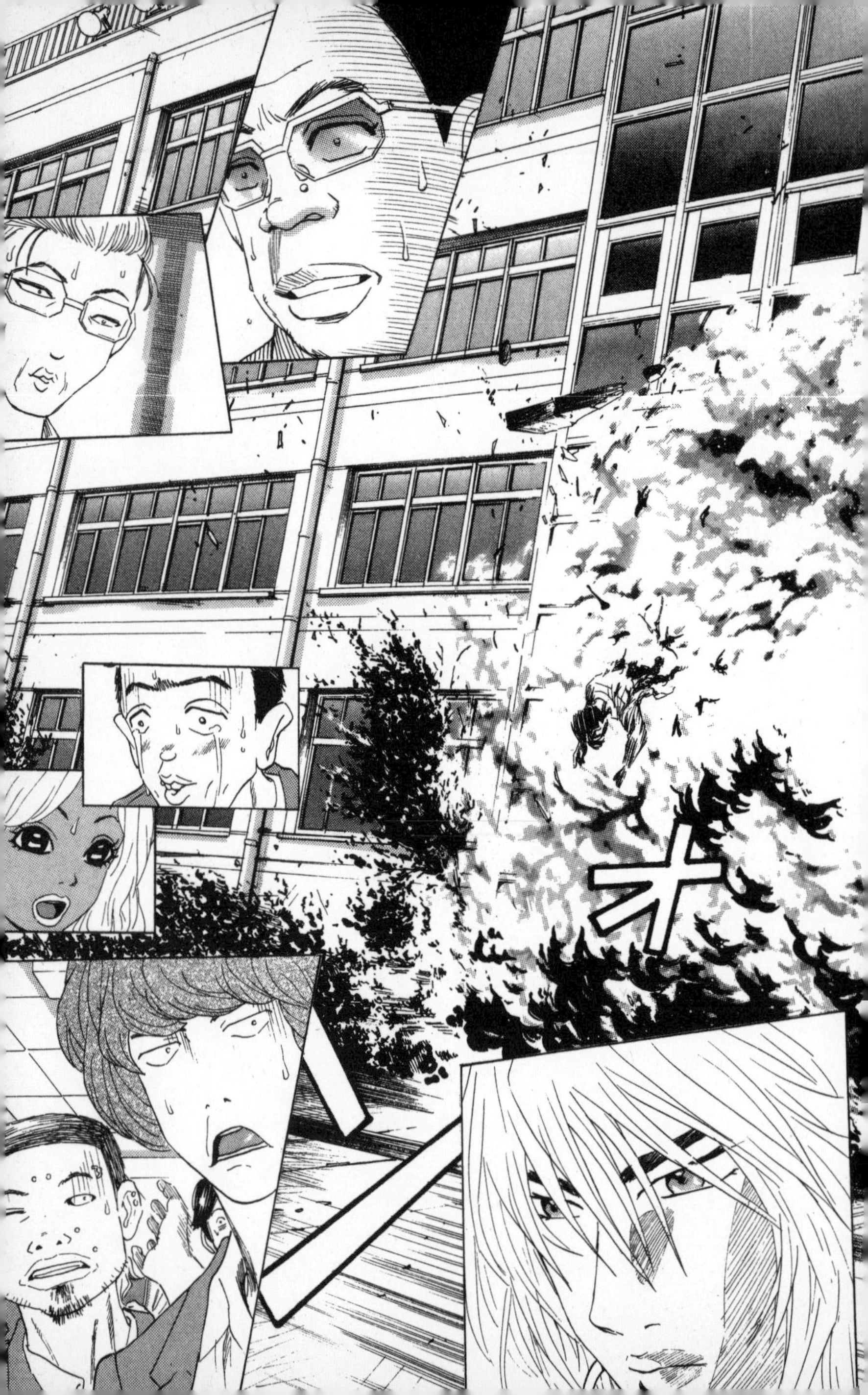
オ

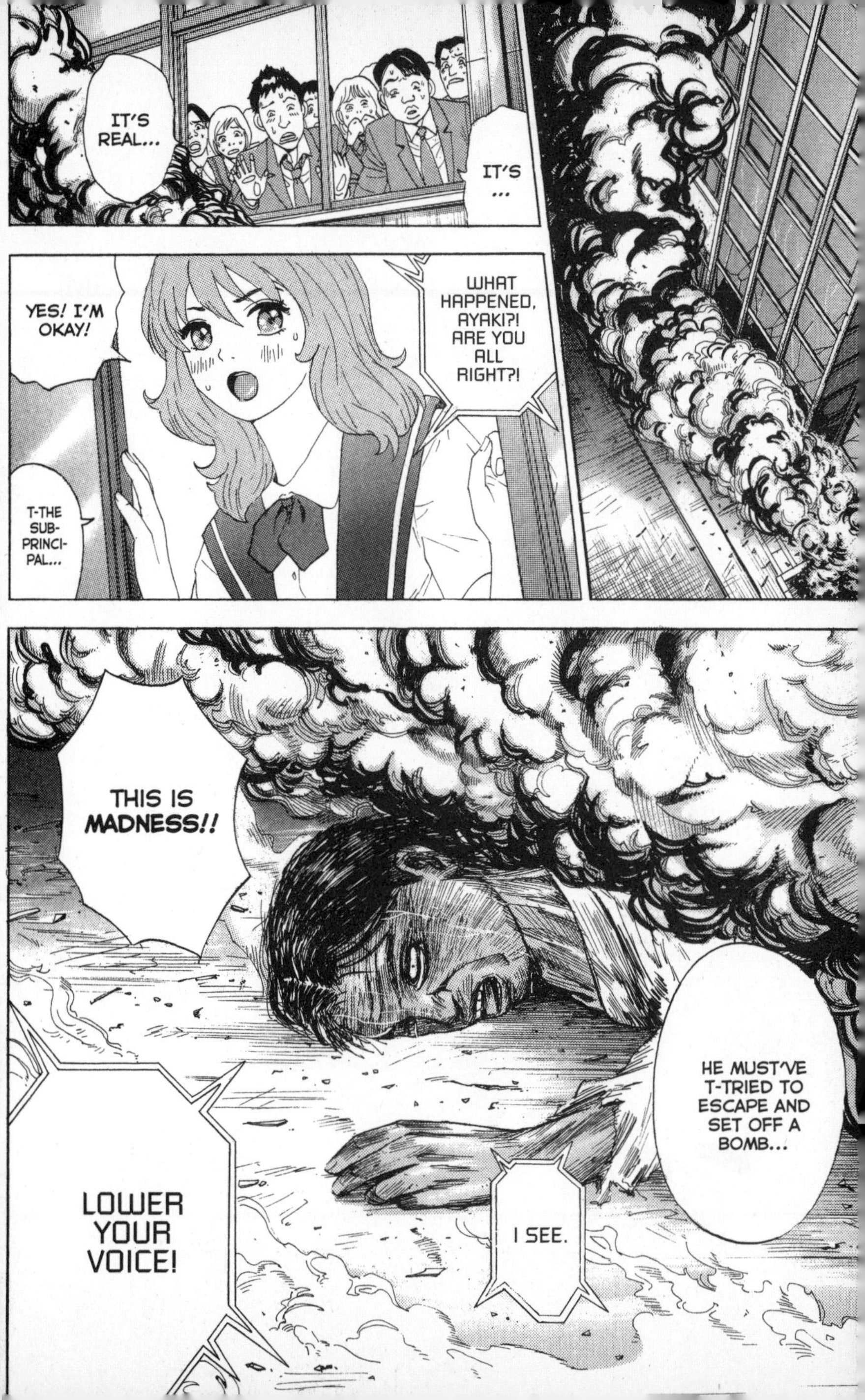
IT'S ...
IT'S REAL...
WHAT HAPPENED, AYAKI?! ARE YOU ALL RIGHT?!
YES! I'M OKAY!
T-THE SUB-PRINCI-PAL...
HE MUST'VE T-TRIED TO ESCAPE AND SET OFF A BOMB...
THIS IS MADNESS!!
I SEE.
LOWER YOUR VOICE!

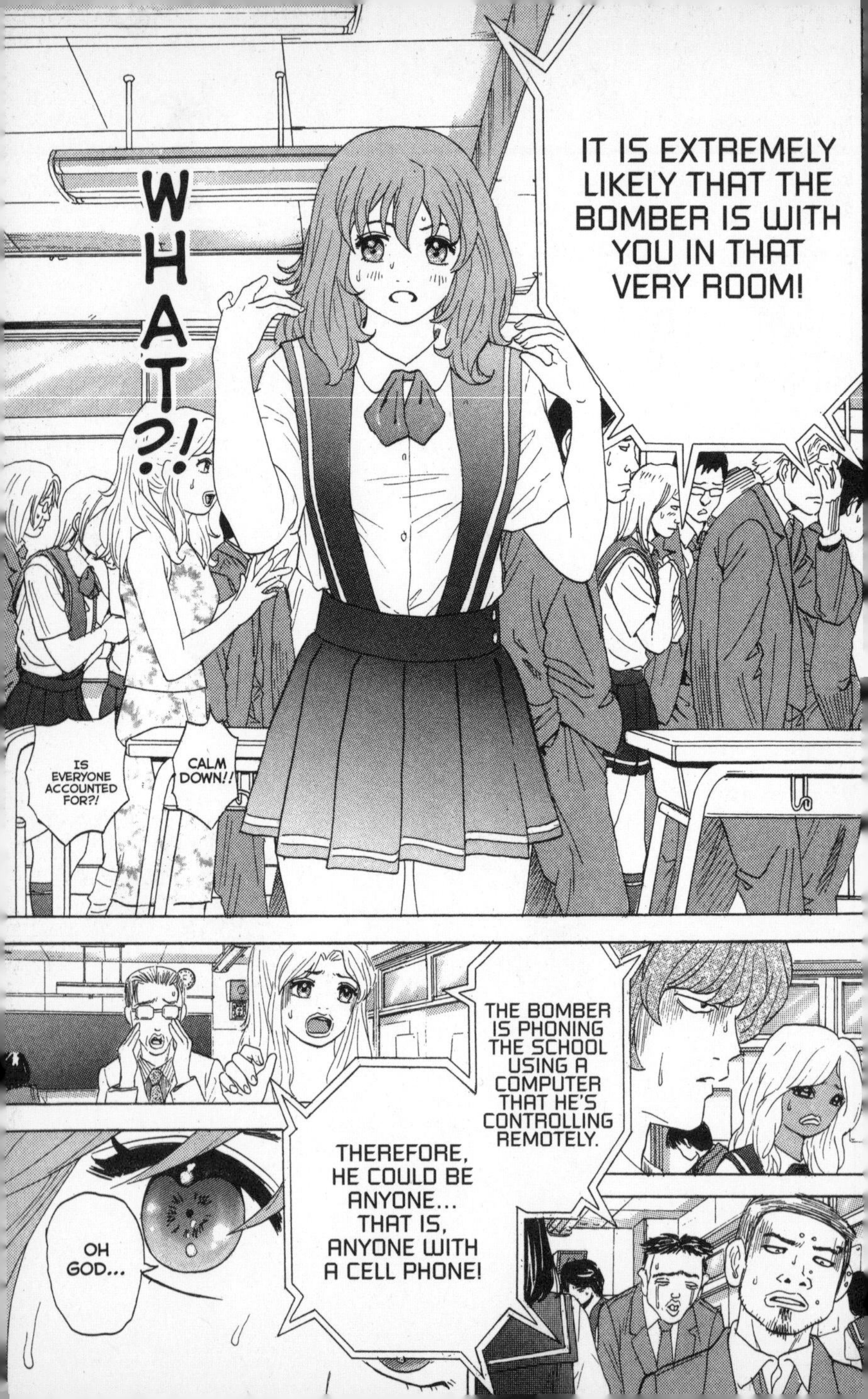
IT IS EXTREMELY LIKELY THAT THE BOMBER IS WITH YOU IN THAT VERY ROOM!
WHAT?!
CALM DOWN!!
IS EVERYONE ACCOUNTED FOR?!
THE BOMBER IS PHONING THE SCHOOL USING A COMPUTER THAT HE'S CONTROLLING REMOTELY.
THEREFORE, HE COULD BE ANYONE... THAT IS, ANYONE WITH A CELL PHONE!
OH GOD...

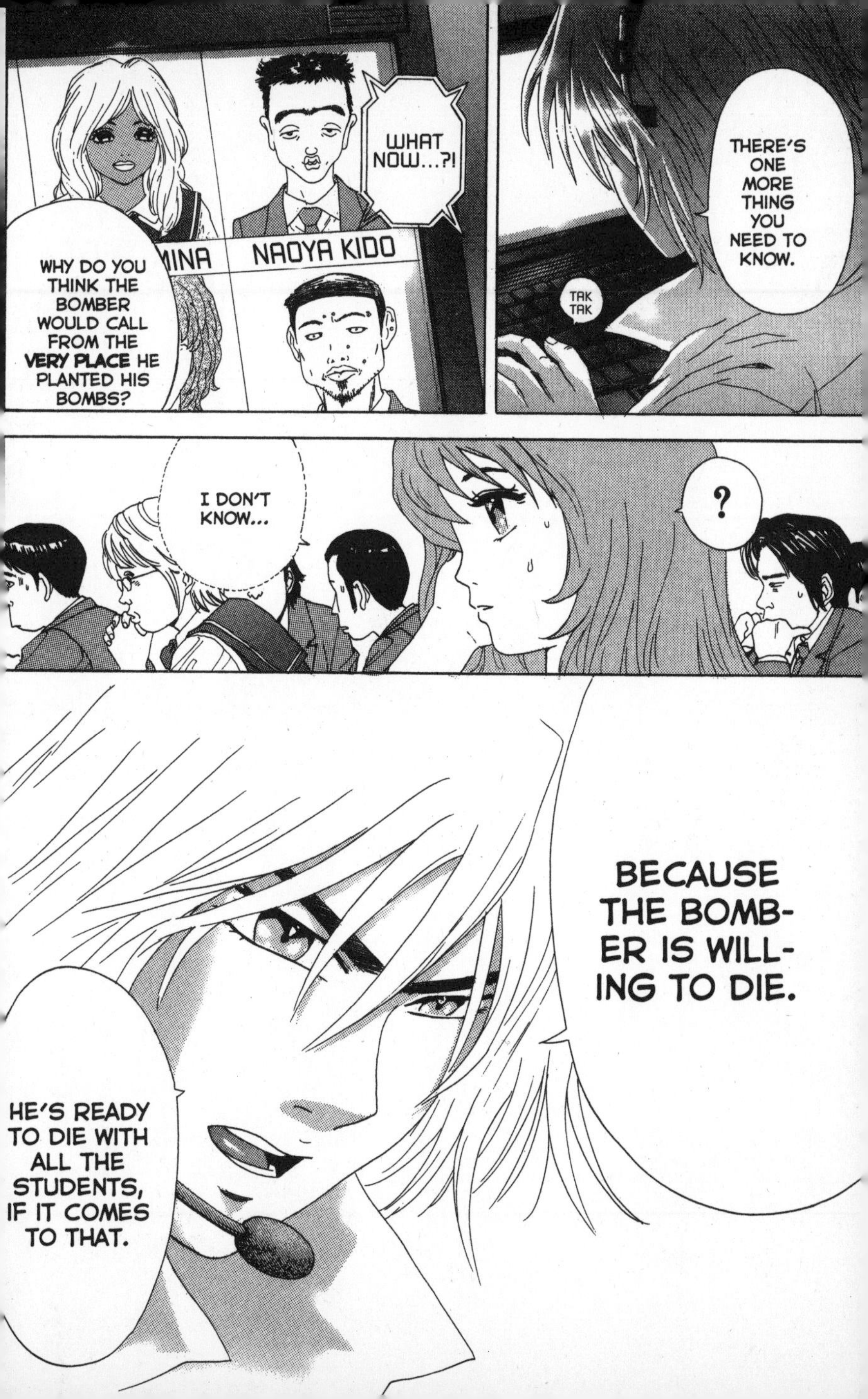
THERE'S ONE MORE THING YOU NEED TO KNOW.
TAK TAK
WHAT NOW...?!
NAOYA KIDO
WHY DO YOU THINK THE BOMBER WOULD CALL FROM THE **VERY PLACE** HE PLANTED HIS BOMBS?
?
I DON'T KNOW...
BECAUSE THE BOMB-ER IS WILL-ING TO DIE.
HE'S READY TO DIE WITH ALL THE STUDENTS, IF IT COMES TO THAT.

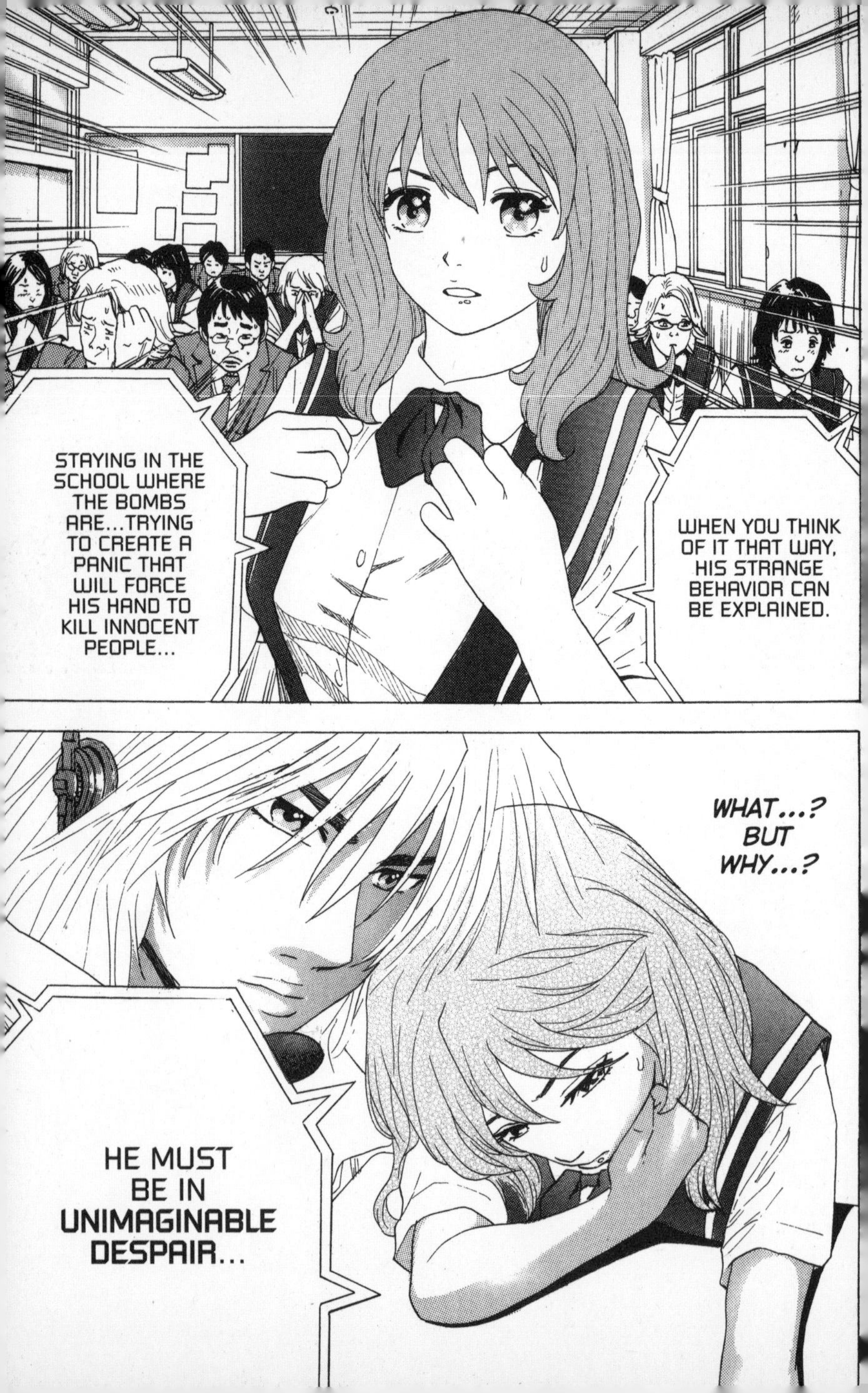
WHEN YOU THINK OF IT THAT WAY, HIS STRANGE BEHAVIOR CAN BE EXPLAINED.
STAYING IN THE SCHOOL WHERE THE BOMBS ARE...TRYING TO CREATE A PANIC THAT WILL FORCE HIS HAND TO KILL INNOCENT PEOPLE...
WHAT...? BUT WHY...?
HE MUST BE IN UNIMAGINABLE DESPAIR...

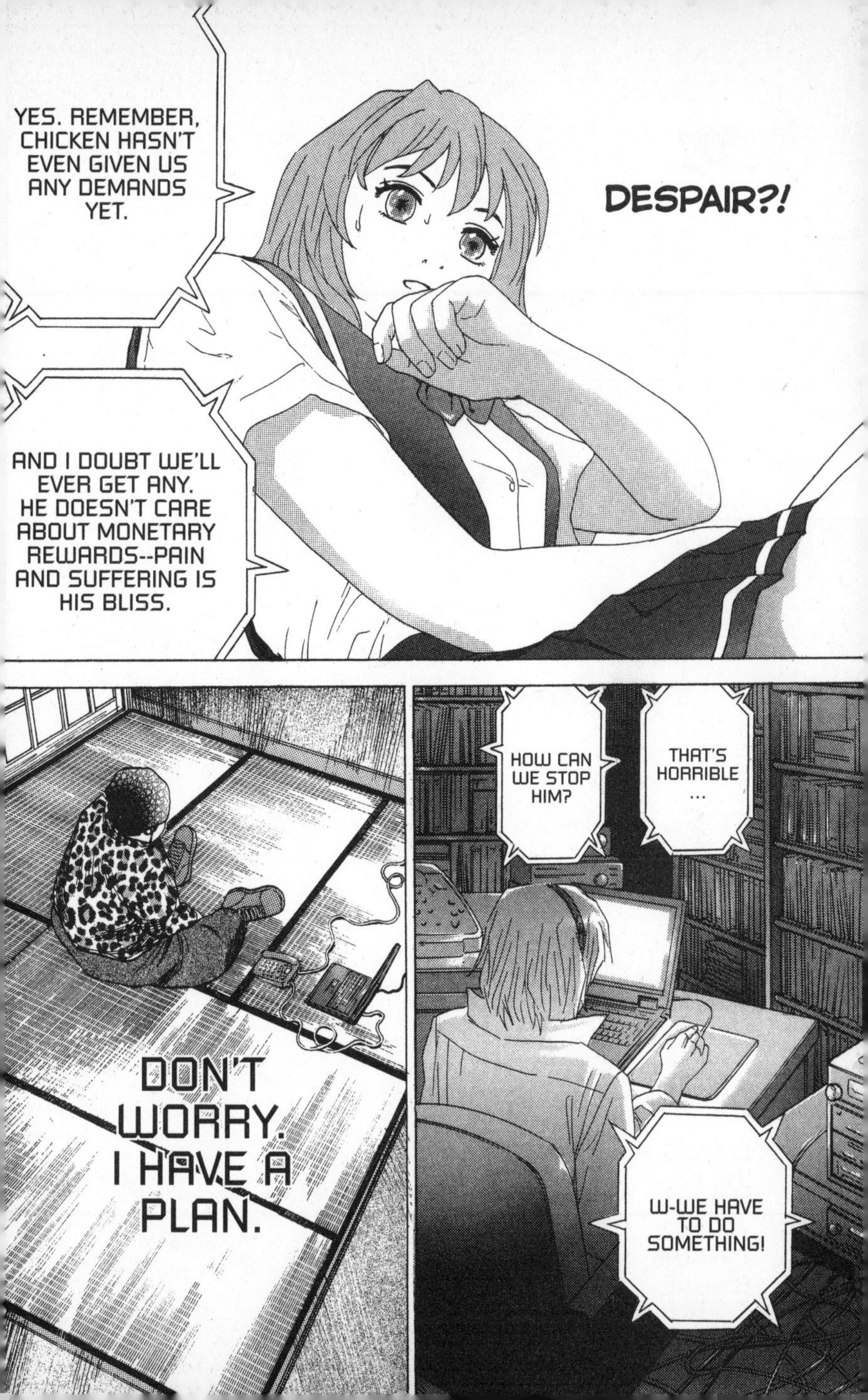
DESPAIR?!
YES. REMEMBER, CHICKEN HASN'T EVEN GIVEN US ANY DEMANDS YET.
AND I DOUBT WE'LL EVER GET ANY. HE DOESN'T CARE ABOUT MONETARY REWARDS--PAIN AND SUFFERING IS HIS BLISS.
THAT'S HORRIBLE ...
HOW CAN WE STOP HIM?
W-WE HAVE TO DO SOMETHING!
DON'T WORRY. I HAVE A PLAN.

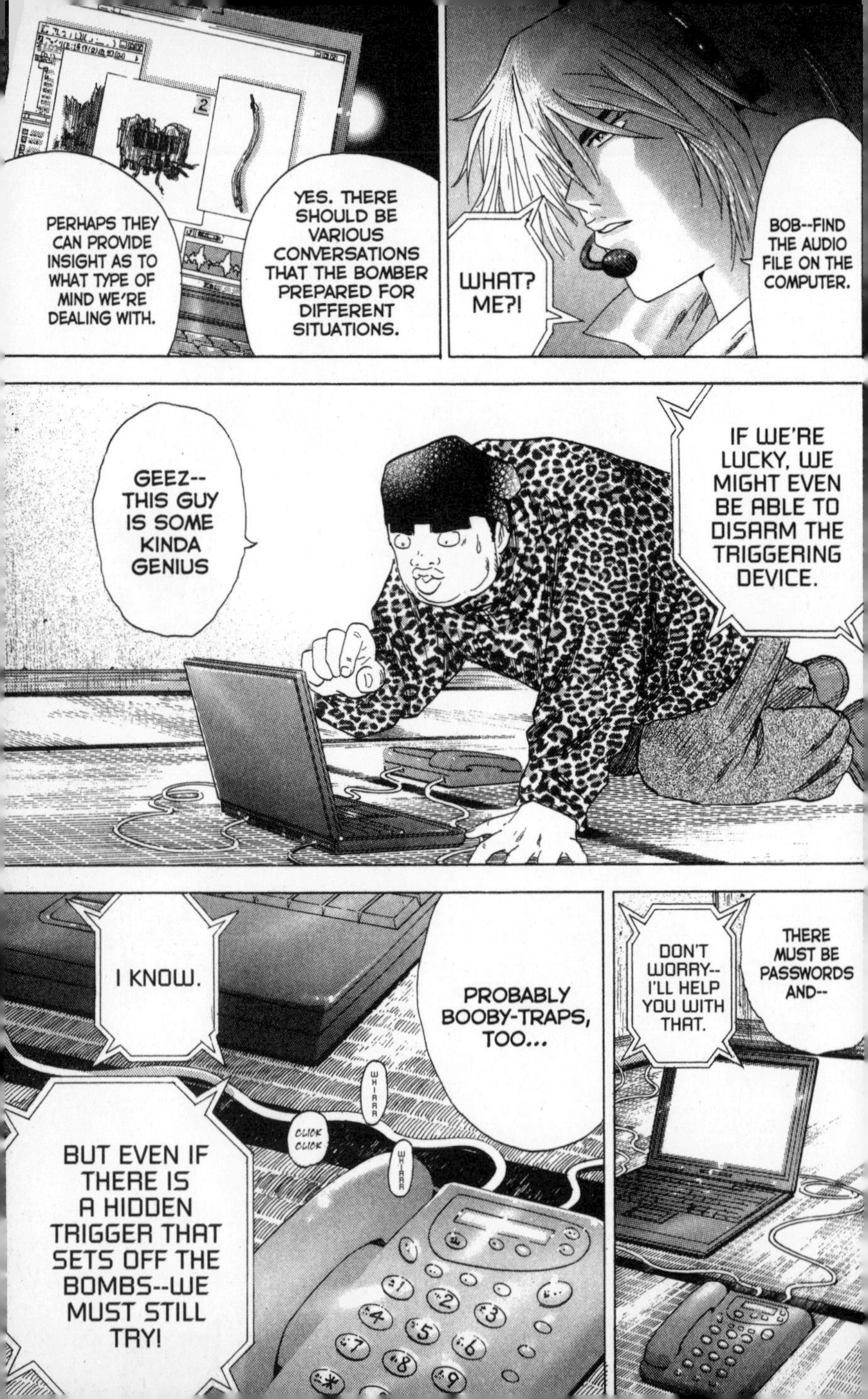
BOB--FIND THE AUDIO FILE ON THE COMPUTER.
WHAT? ME?!
YES. THERE SHOULD BE VARIOUS CONVERSATIONS THAT THE BOMBER PREPARED FOR DIFFERENT SITUATIONS.
PERHAPS THEY CAN PROVIDE INSIGHT AS TO WHAT TYPE OF MIND WE'RE DEALING WITH.
IF WE'RE LUCKY, WE MIGHT EVEN BE ABLE TO DISARM THE TRIGGERING DEVICE.
GEEZ-- THIS GUY IS SOME KINDA GENIUS
THERE MUST BE PASSWORDS AND--
DON'T WORRY-- I'LL HELP YOU WITH THAT.
PROBABLY BOOBY-TRAPS, TOO...
I KNOW.
WHIRRR
CLICK CLICK
WHIRRR
BUT EVEN IF THERE IS A HIDDEN TRIGGER THAT SETS OFF THE BOMBS--WE MUST STILL TRY!

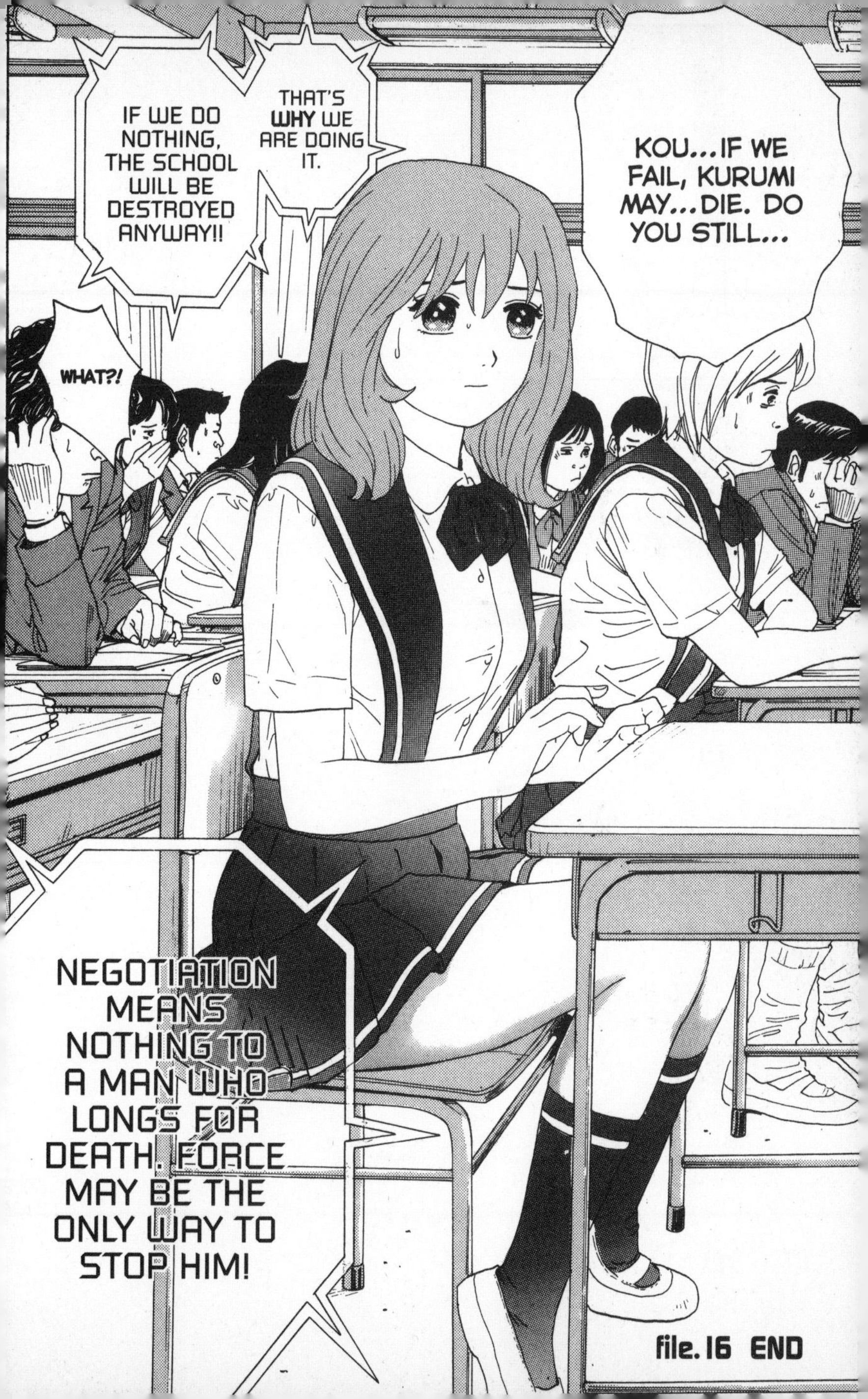
KOU...IF WE FAIL, KURUMI MAY...DIE. DO YOU STILL...
IF WE DO NOTHING, THE SCHOOL WILL BE DESTROYED ANYWAY!!
THAT'S WHY WE ARE DOING IT.
WHAT?!
NEGOTIATION MEANS NOTHING TO A MAN WHO LONGS FOR DEATH. FORCE MAY BE THE ONLY WAY TO STOP HIM!
file.16 END

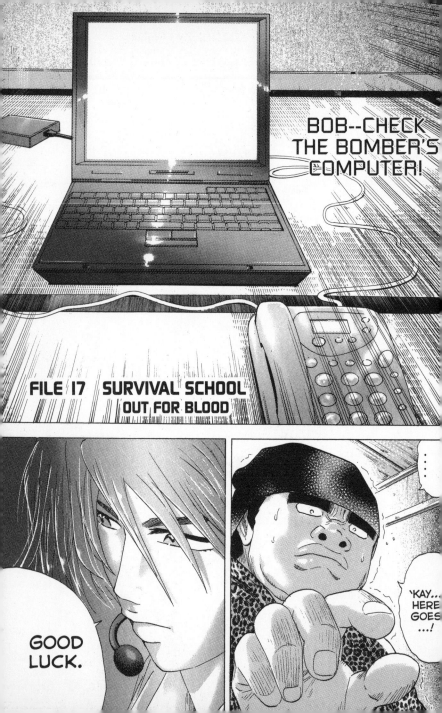

BOB--CHECK THE BOMBER'S COMPUTER!

FILE 17 SURVIVAL SCHOOL
OUT FOR BLOOD

GOOD LUCK.

'KAY... HERE GOES...!

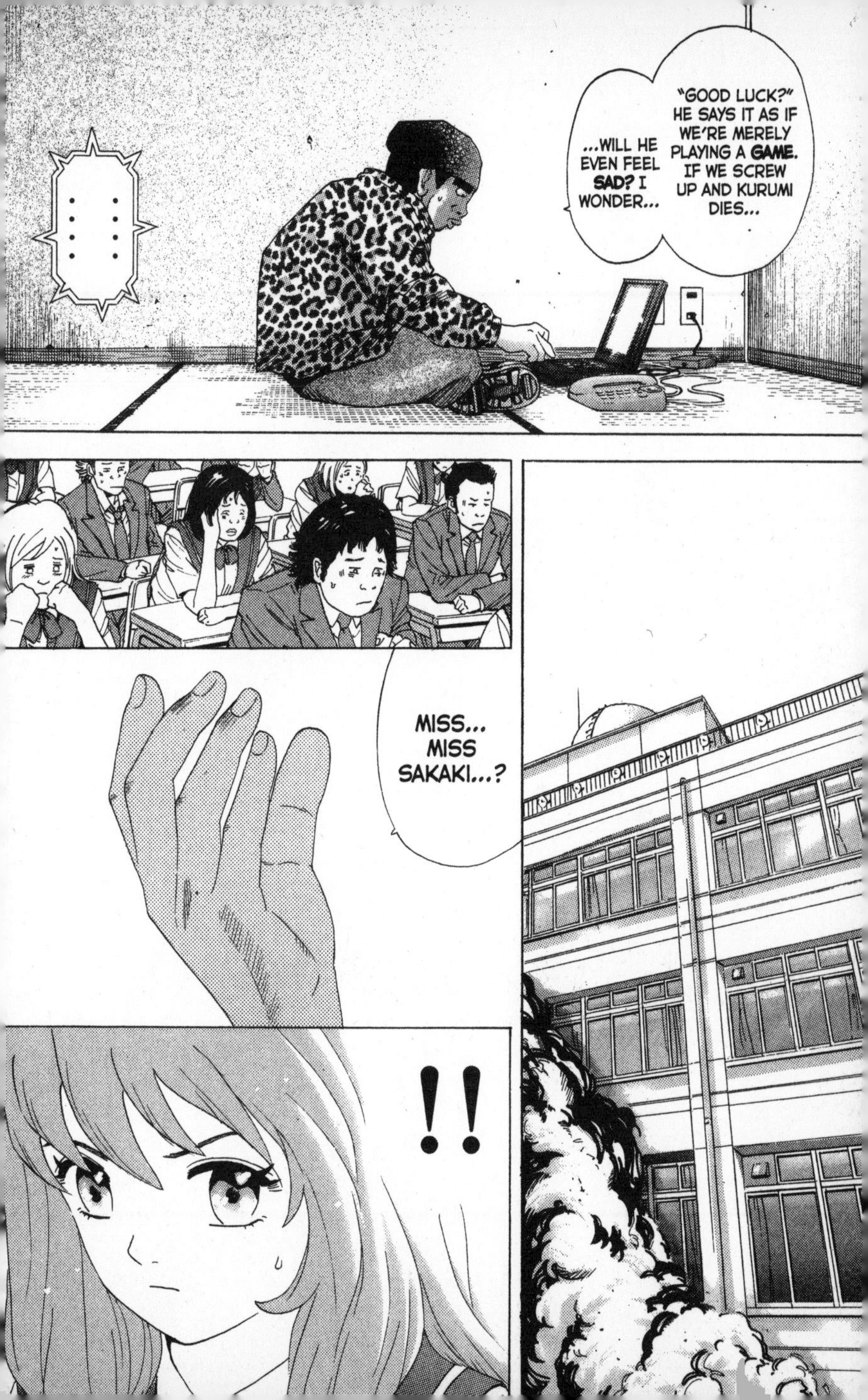
"GOOD LUCK?" HE SAYS IT AS IF WE'RE MERELY PLAYING A **GAME.** IF WE SCREW UP AND KURUMI DIES...
...WILL HE EVEN FEEL **SAD?** I WONDER...
......
MISS... MISS SAKAKI...?
!!

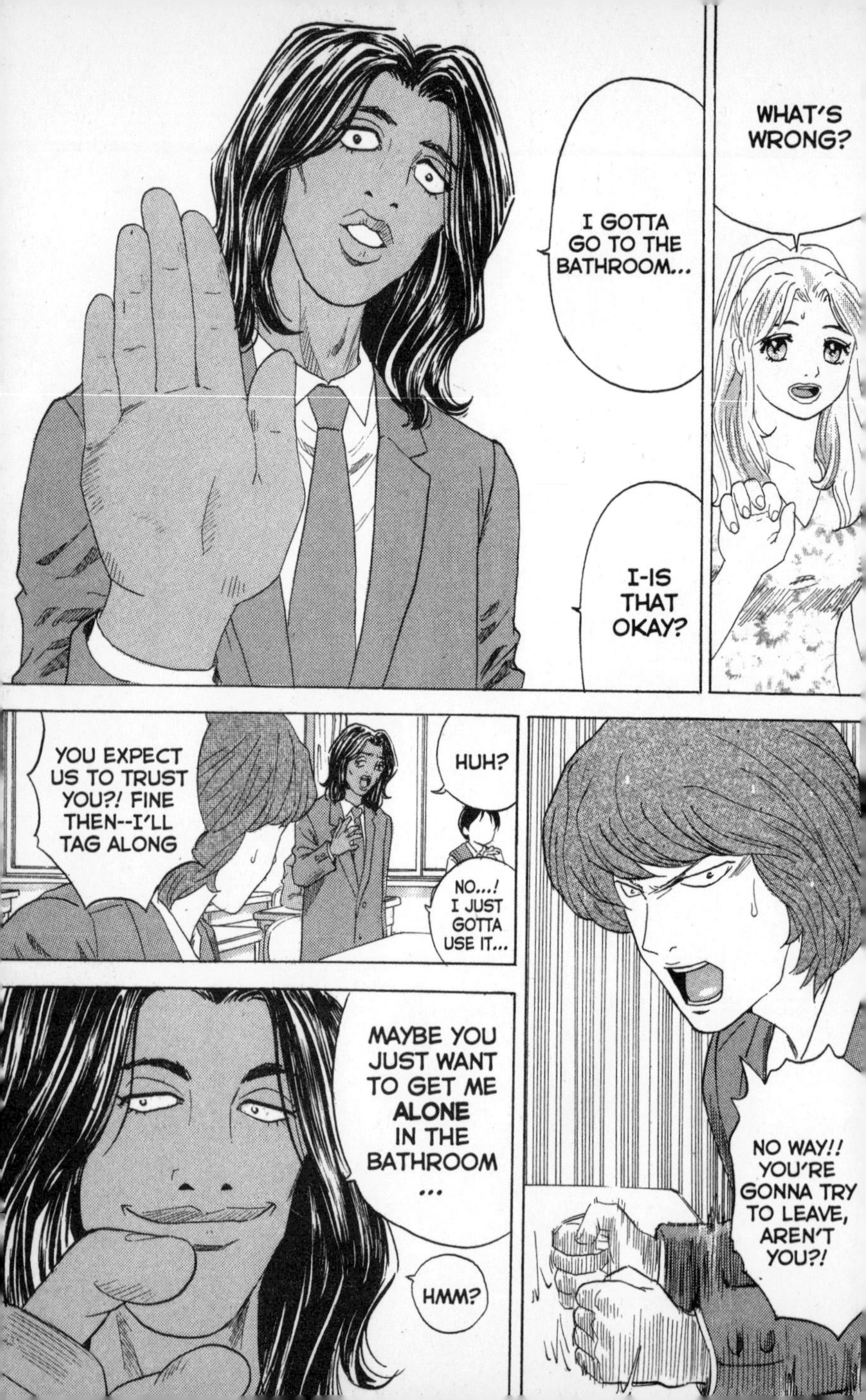
WHAT'S WRONG?
I GOTTA GO TO THE BATHROOM...
I-IS THAT OKAY?
NO WAY!! YOU'RE GONNA TRY TO LEAVE, AREN'T YOU?!
HUH?
NO...! I JUST GOTTA USE IT...
YOU EXPECT US TO TRUST YOU?! FINE THEN--I'LL TAG ALONG
MAYBE YOU JUST WANT TO GET ME ALONE IN THE BATHROOM ...
HMM?

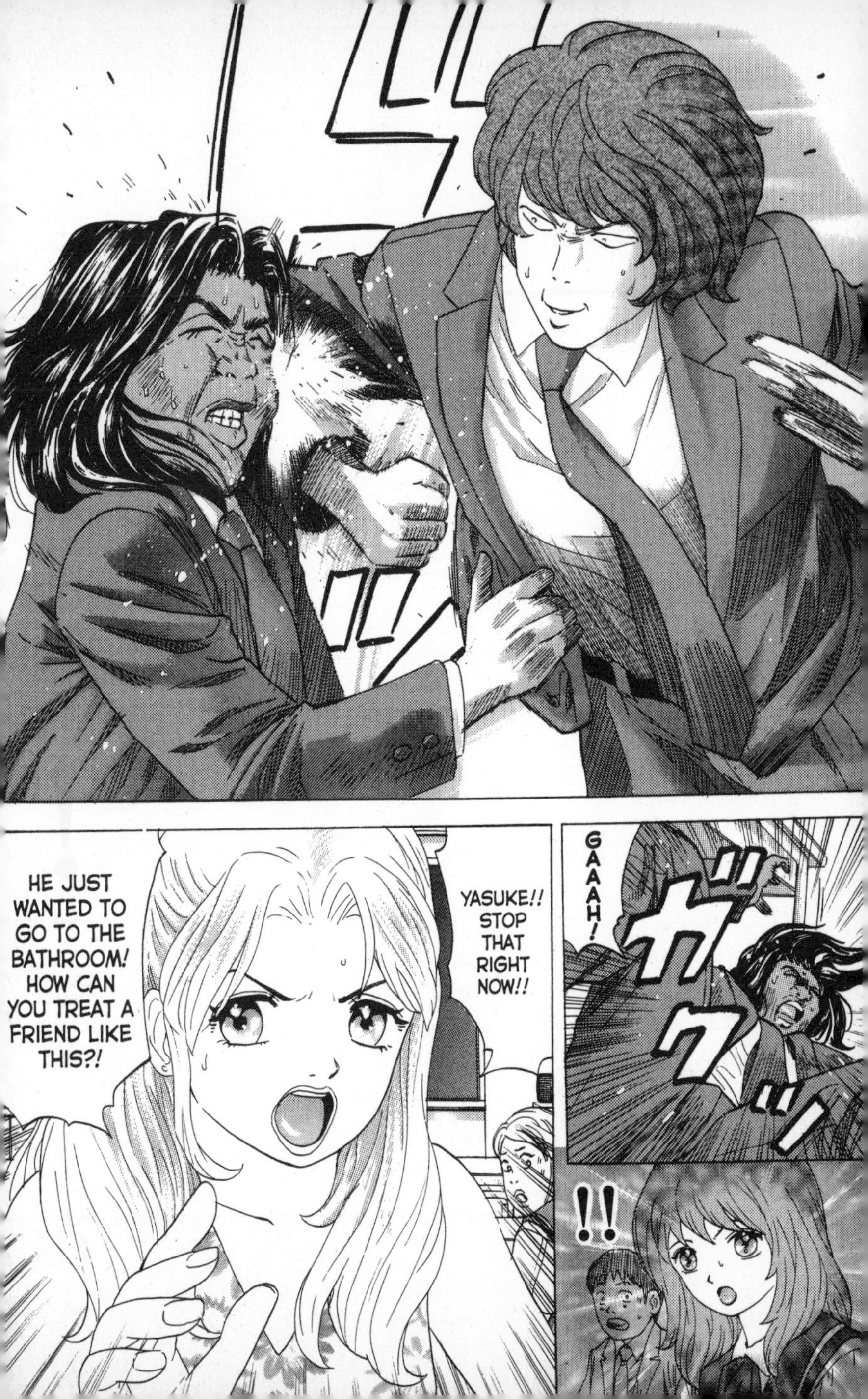
GAAAH!
ガクッ
!!
YASUKE!! STOP THAT RIGHT NOW!!
HE JUST WANTED TO GO TO THE BATHROOM! HOW CAN YOU TREAT A FRIEND LIKE THIS?!

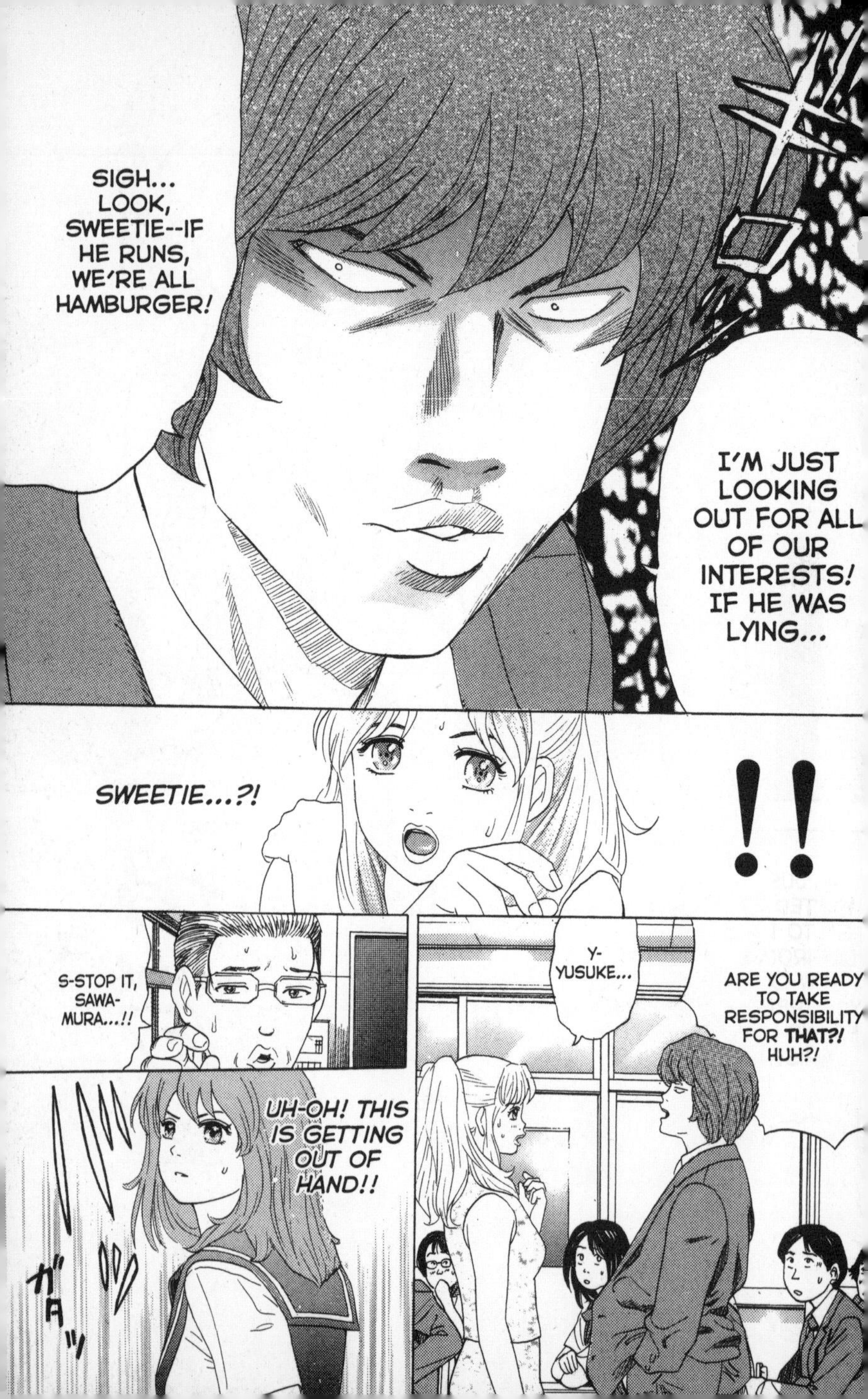
SIGH... LOOK, SWEETIE--IF HE RUNS, WE'RE ALL HAMBURGER!
I'M JUST LOOKING OUT FOR ALL OF OUR INTERESTS! IF HE WAS LYING...
!!
SWEETIE...?!
ARE YOU READY TO TAKE RESPONSIBILITY FOR THAT?! HUH?!
Y-YUSUKE...
S-STOP IT, SAWA-MURA...!!
UH-OH! THIS IS GETTING OUT OF HAND!!
ガタッ

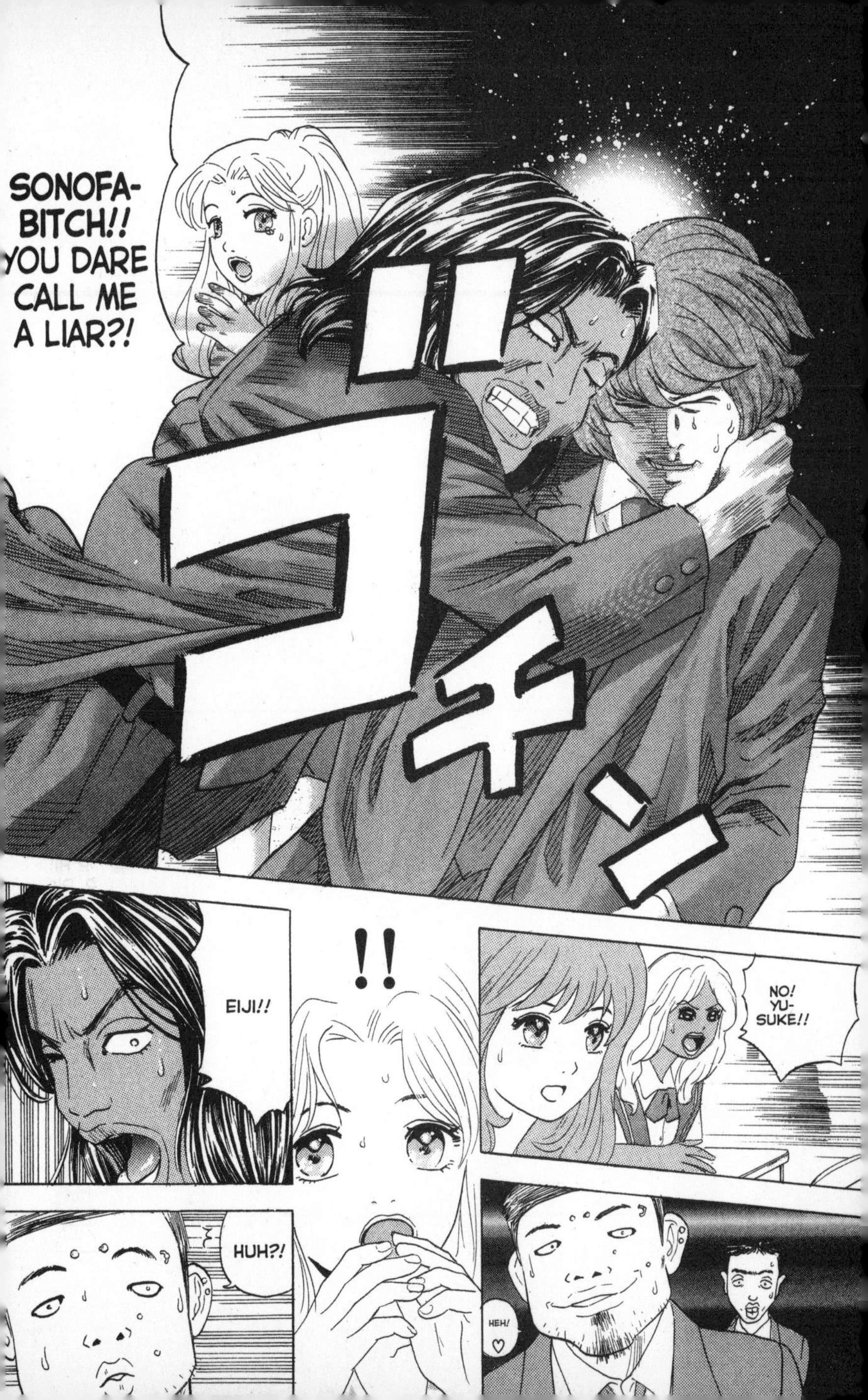
SONOFA-BITCH!! YOU DARE CALL ME A LIAR?!
ゴキッ
NO! YU-SUKE!!
!!
EIJI!!
HEH! ♡
HUH?!

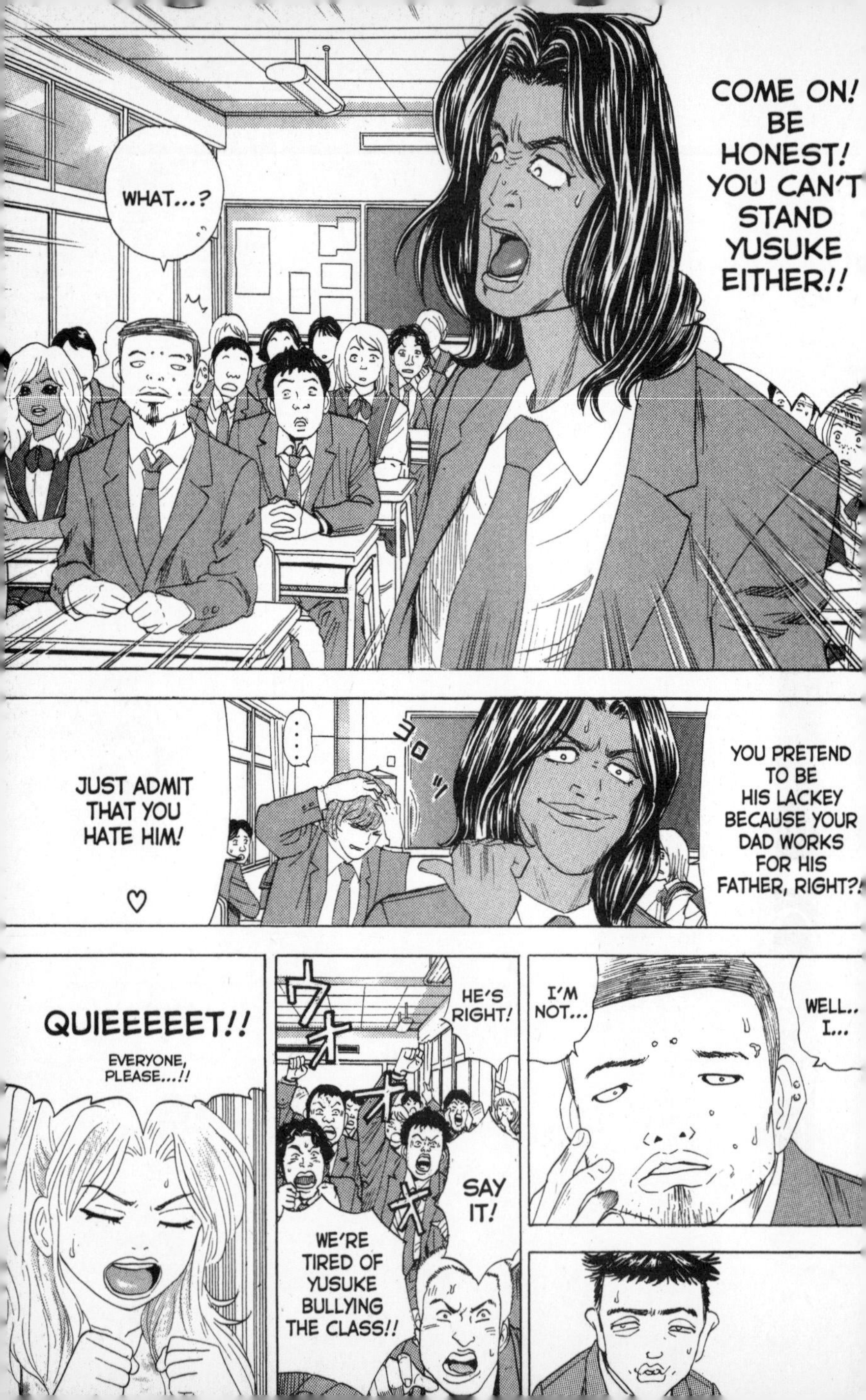
COME ON! BE HONEST! YOU CAN'T STAND YUSUKE EITHER!!
WHAT...?
YOU PRETEND TO BE HIS LACKEY BECAUSE YOUR DAD WORKS FOR HIS FATHER, RIGHT?!
...
JUST ADMIT THAT YOU HATE HIM! ♡
WELL.. I...
I'M NOT...
HE'S RIGHT!
SAY IT!
WE'RE TIRED OF YUSUKE BULLYING THE CLASS!!
QUIEEEEET!!
EVERYONE, PLEASE...!!

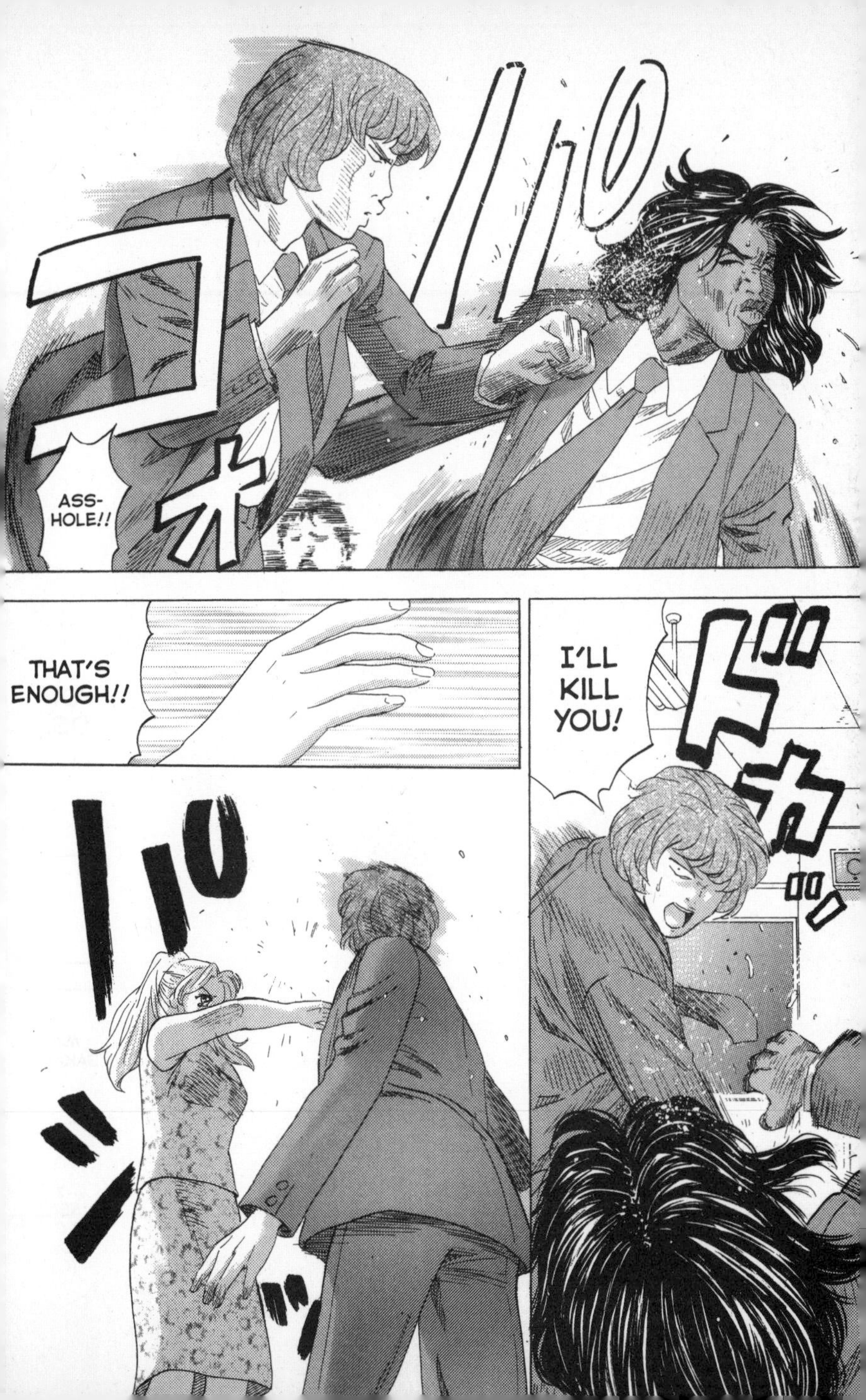
ASS-HOLE!!
I'LL KILL YOU!
THAT'S ENOUGH!!

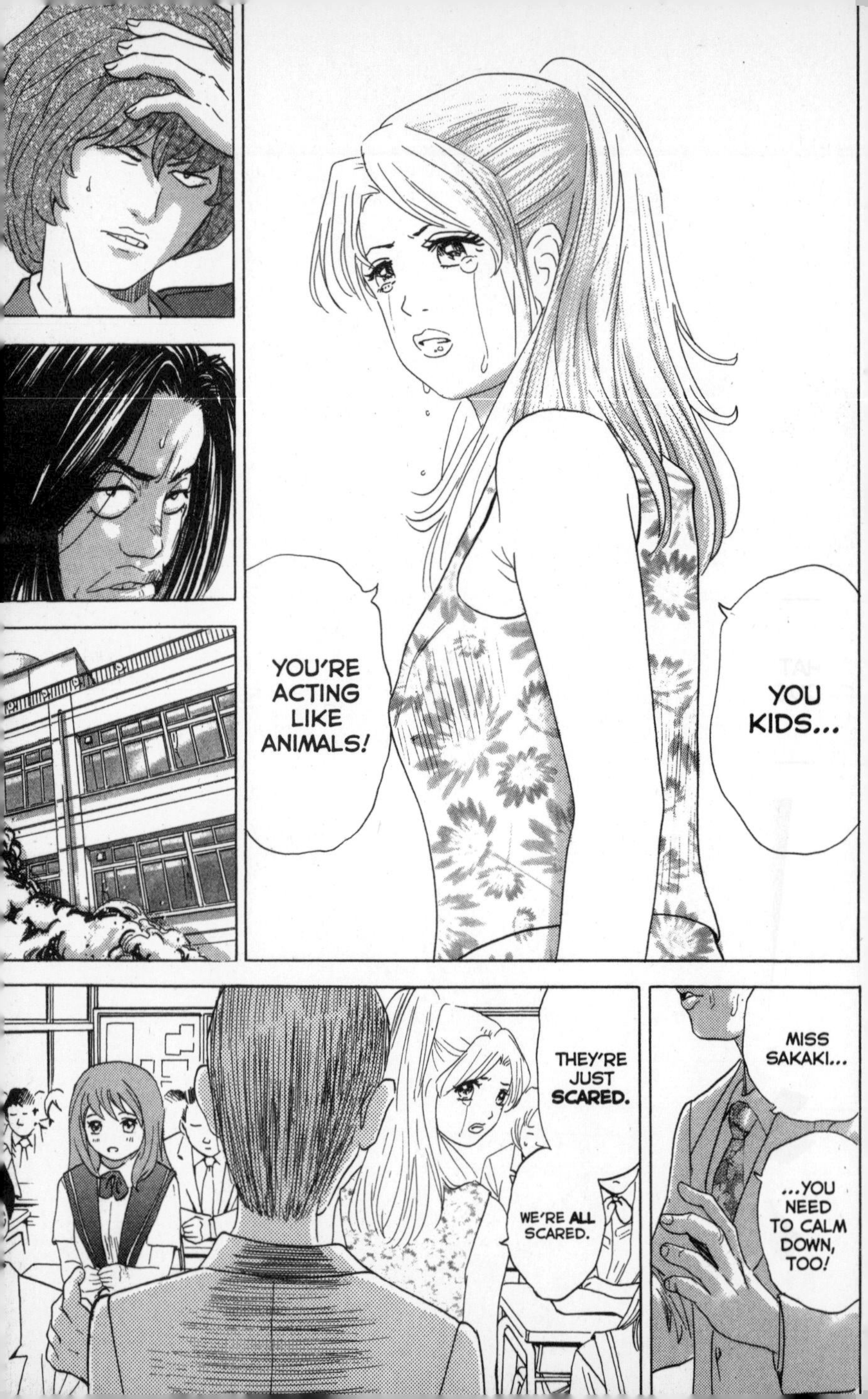
YOU KIDS...
YOU'RE ACTING LIKE ANIMALS!
MISS SAKAKI...
...YOU NEED TO CALM DOWN, TOO!
THEY'RE JUST SCARED.
WE'RE ALL SCARED.

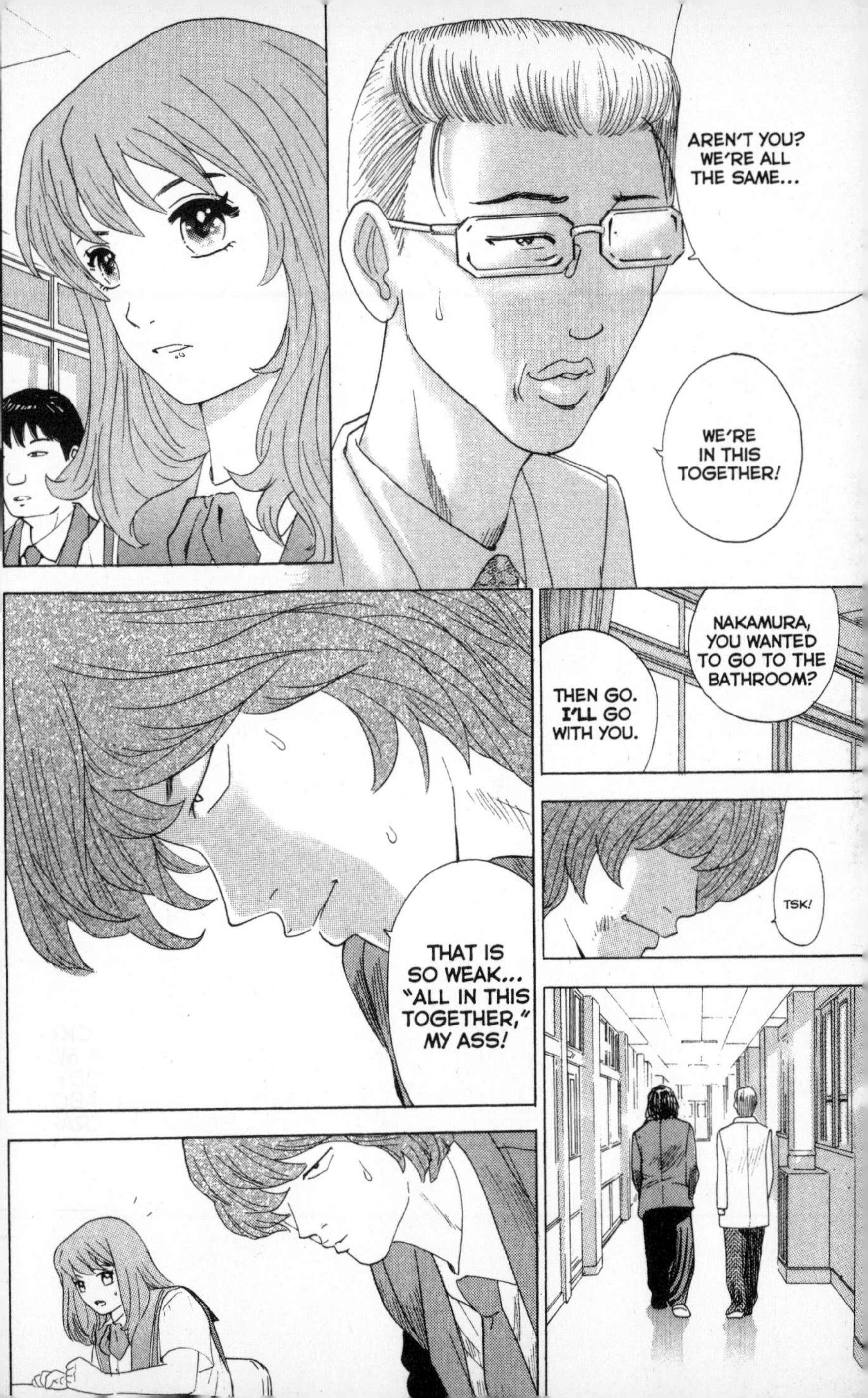
AREN'T YOU? WE'RE ALL THE SAME...
WE'RE IN THIS TOGETHER!
NAKAMURA, YOU WANTED TO GO TO THE BATHROOM?
THEN GO. **I'LL** GO WITH YOU.
TSK!
THAT IS SO WEAK... "ALL IN THIS TOGETHER," MY ASS!

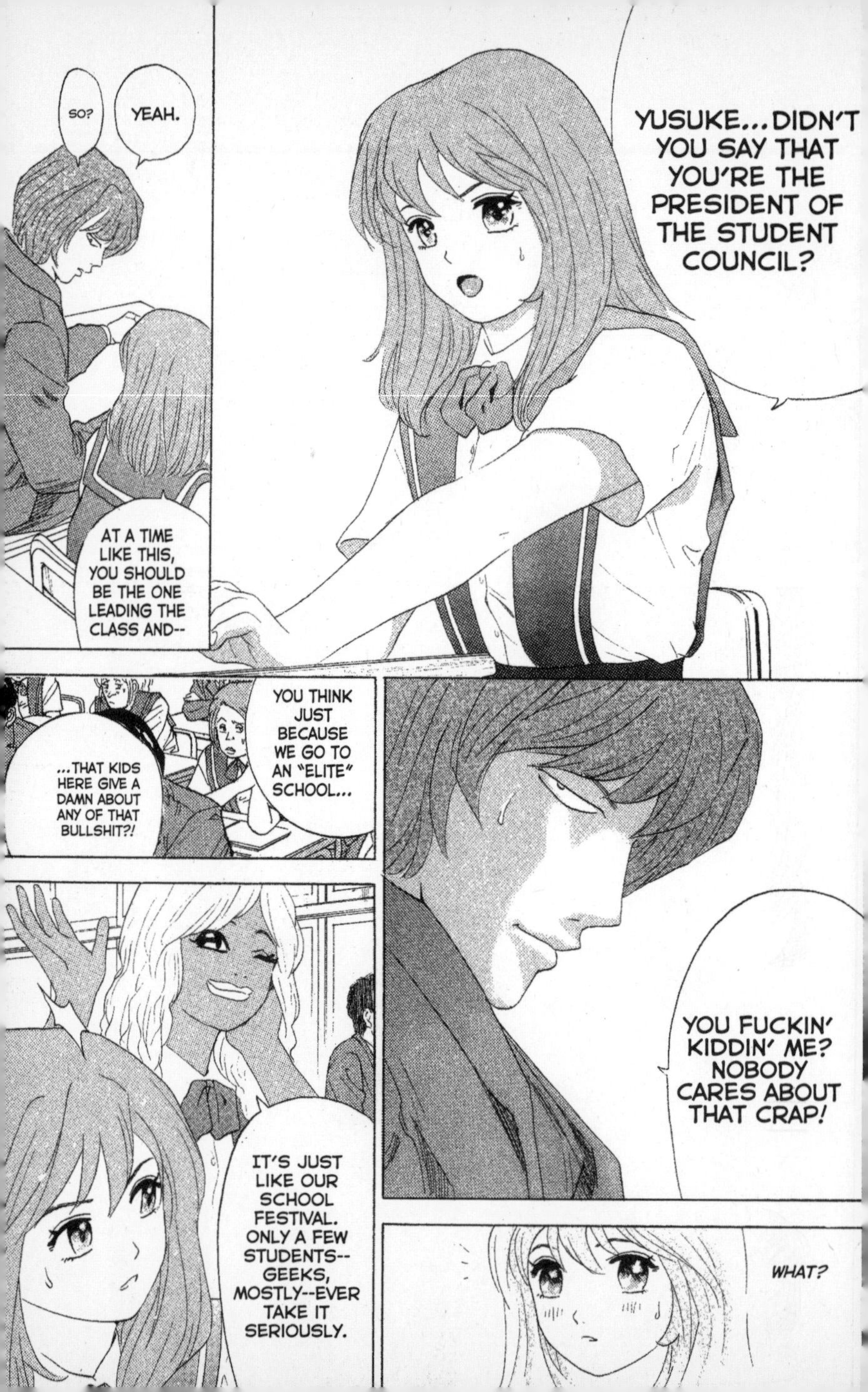
YUSUKE...DIDN'T YOU SAY THAT YOU'RE THE PRESIDENT OF THE STUDENT COUNCIL?
YEAH.
SO?
AT A TIME LIKE THIS, YOU SHOULD BE THE ONE LEADING THE CLASS AND--
YOU FUCKIN' KIDDIN' ME? NOBODY CARES ABOUT THAT CRAP!
YOU THINK JUST BECAUSE WE GO TO AN "ELITE" SCHOOL...
...THAT KIDS HERE GIVE A DAMN ABOUT ANY OF THAT BULLSHIT?!
IT'S JUST LIKE OUR SCHOOL FESTIVAL. ONLY A FEW STUDENTS--GEEKS, MOSTLY--EVER TAKE IT SERIOUSLY.
WHAT?

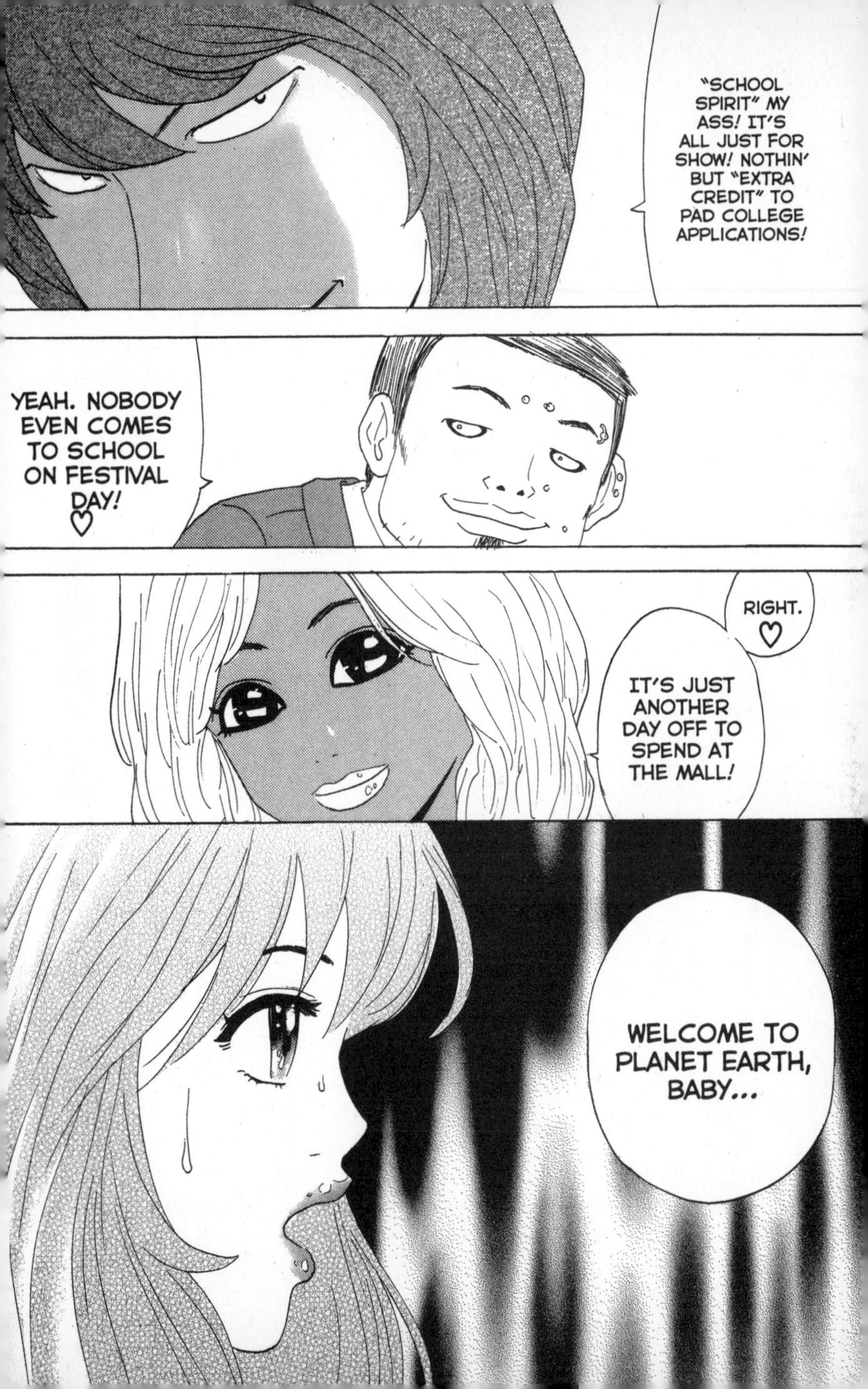
"SCHOOL SPIRIT" MY ASS! IT'S ALL JUST FOR SHOW! NOTHIN' BUT "EXTRA CREDIT" TO PAD COLLEGE APPLICATIONS!
YEAH. NOBODY EVEN COMES TO SCHOOL ON FESTIVAL DAY! ♡
RIGHT. ♡
IT'S JUST ANOTHER DAY OFF TO SPEND AT THE MALL!
WELCOME TO PLANET EARTH, BABY...

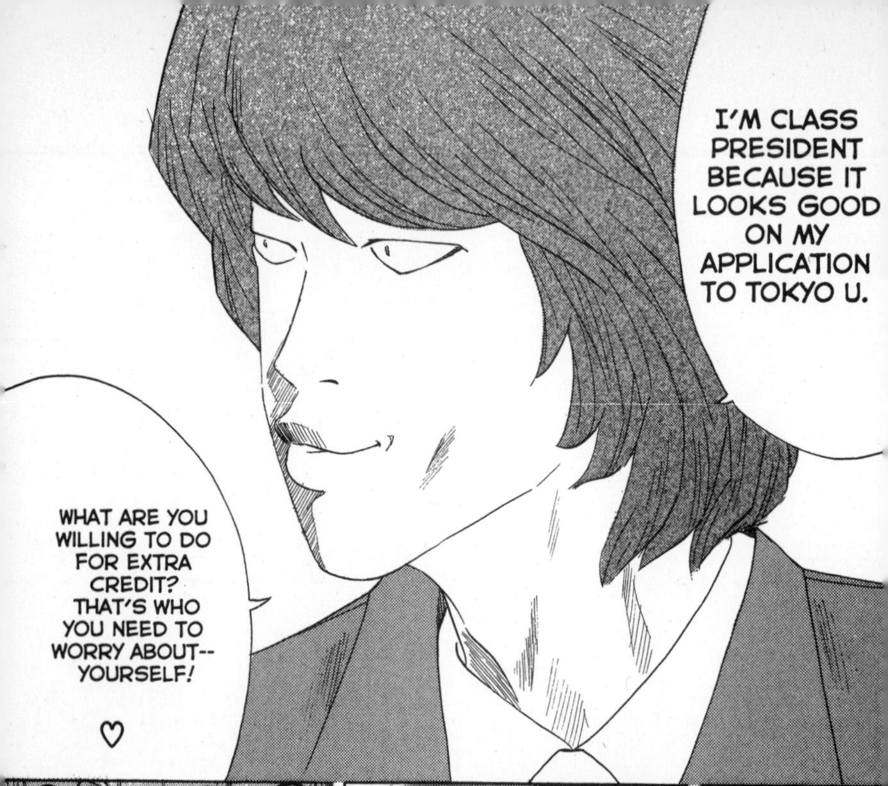
I'M CLASS PRESIDENT BECAUSE IT LOOKS GOOD ON MY APPLICATION TO TOKYO U.
WHAT ARE YOU WILLING TO DO FOR EXTRA CREDIT? THAT'S WHO YOU NEED TO WORRY ABOUT-- YOURSELF! ♡
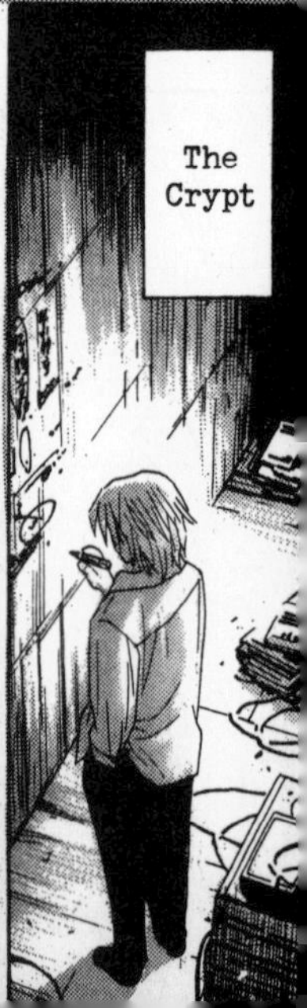
The Crypt
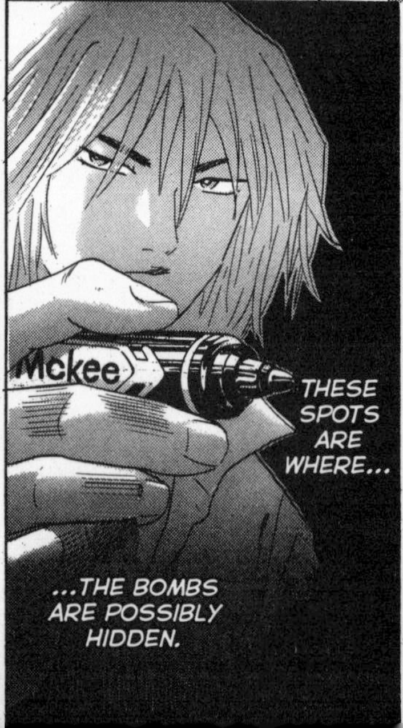
Mckee
THESE SPOTS ARE WHERE...
...THE BOMBS ARE POSSIBLY HIDDEN.
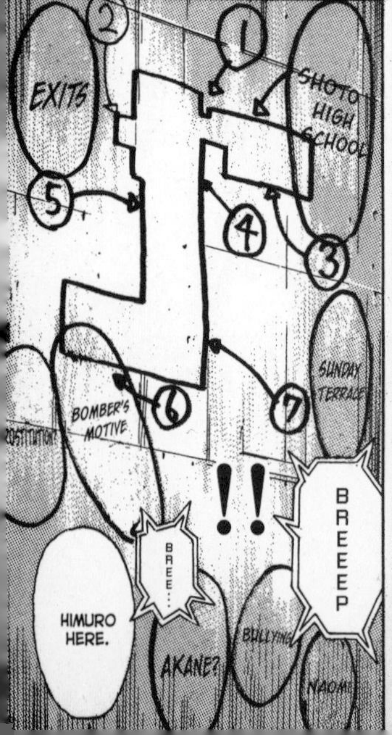
EXITS
SHOTO HIGH SCHOOL
SUNDAY TERRACE
BOMBER'S MOTIVE
!!
BREEEP
BREE...
HIMURO HERE.
AKANE?
BULLYING
NAOMI

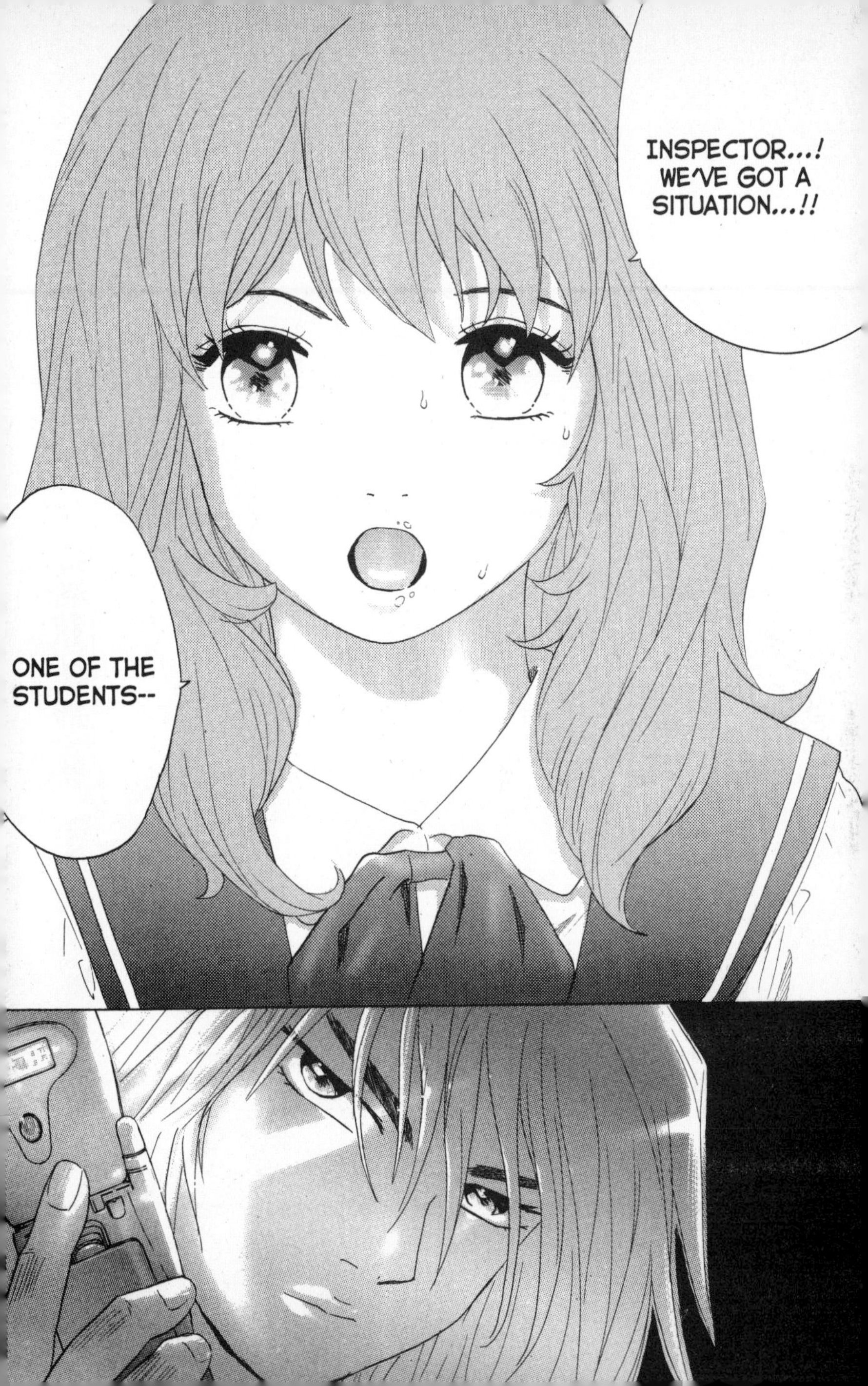
INSPECTOR...! WE'VE GOT A SITUATION...!!
ONE OF THE STUDENTS--

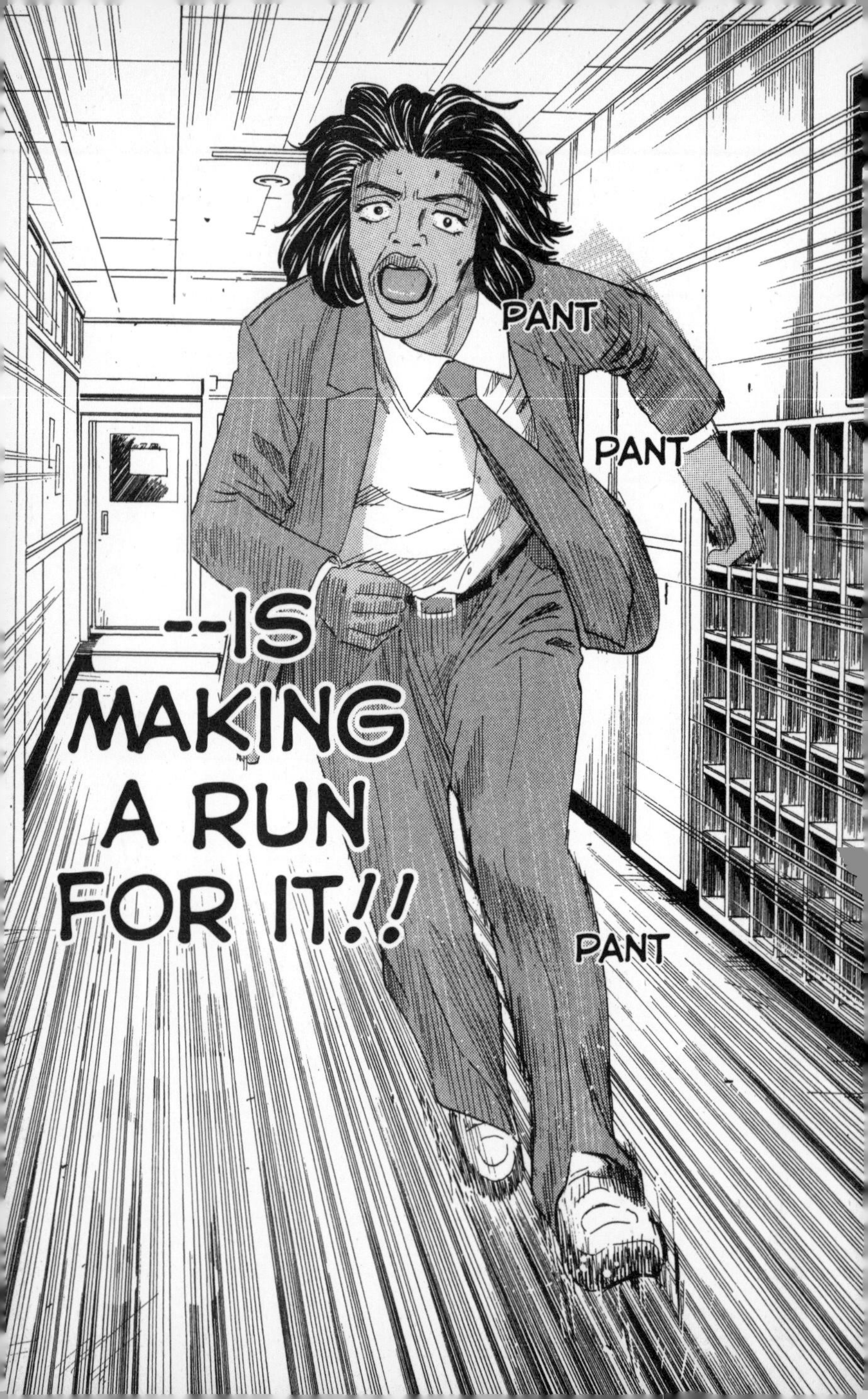
PANT
PANT
--IS MAKING A RUN FOR IT!!
PANT

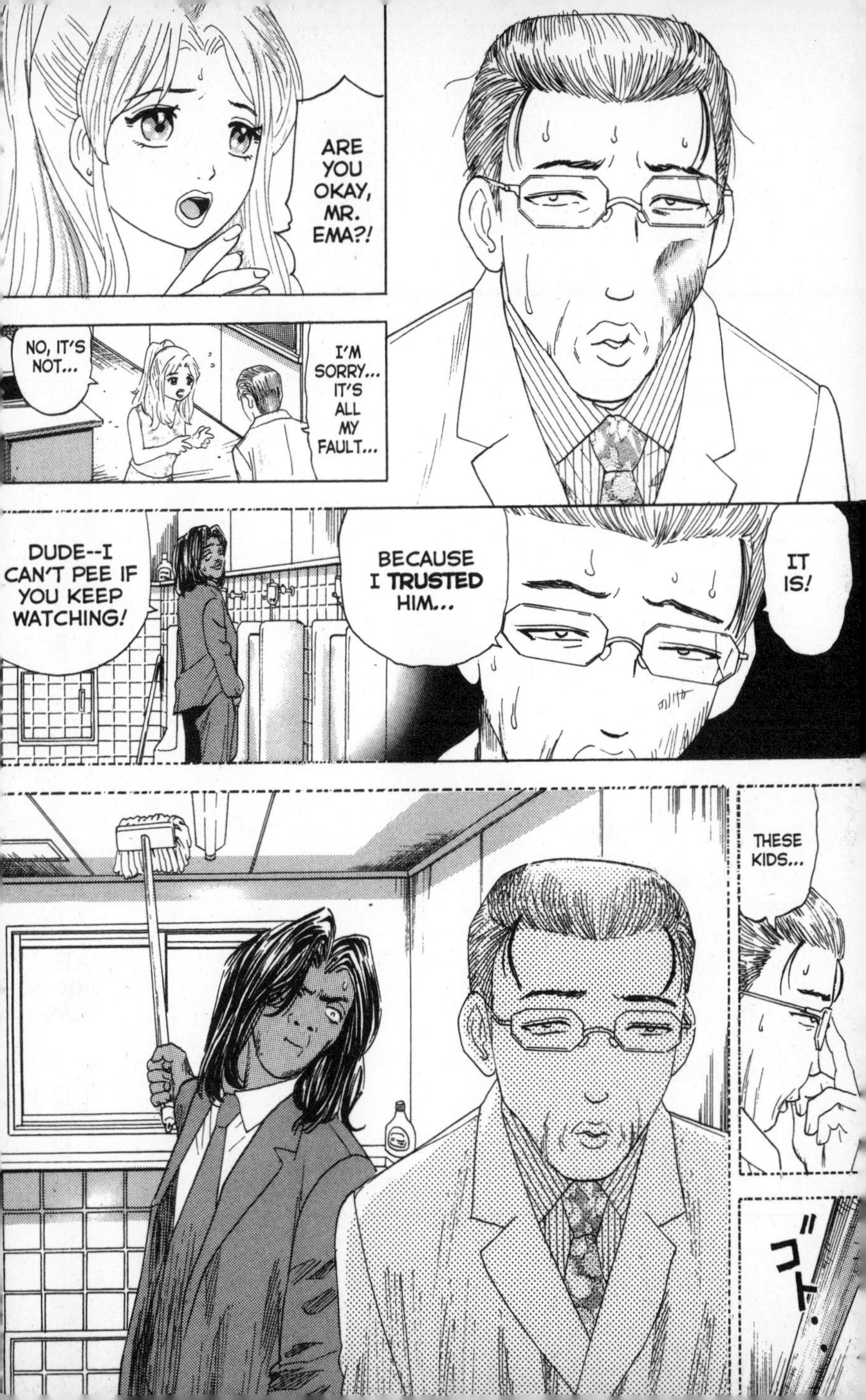
ARE YOU OKAY, MR. EMA?!
I'M SORRY... IT'S ALL MY FAULT...
NO, IT'S NOT...
IT IS!
BECAUSE I TRUSTED HIM...
DUDE--I CAN'T PEE IF YOU KEEP WATCHING!
THESE KIDS...
ゴト・・

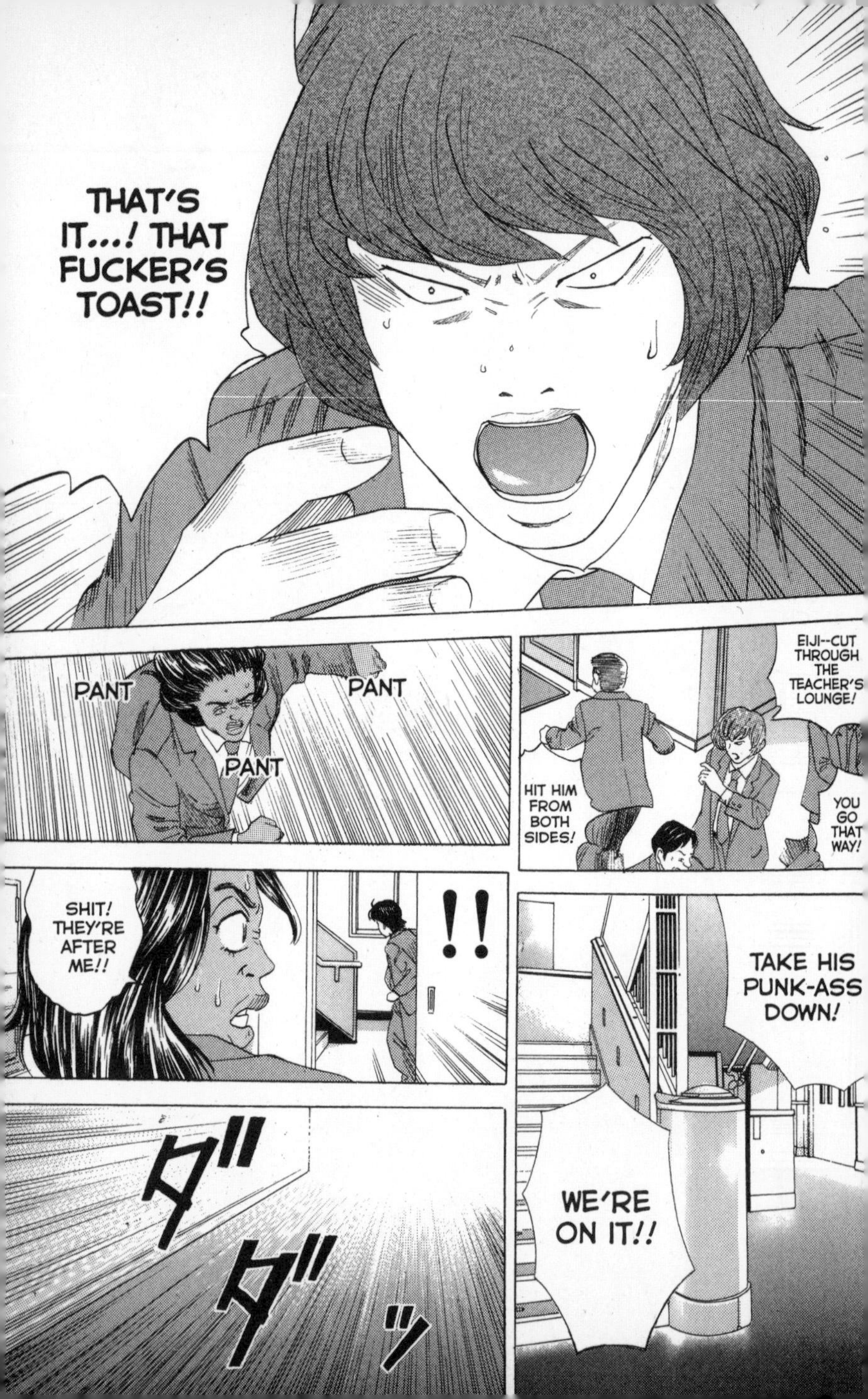
THAT'S IT...! THAT FUCKER'S TOAST!!
EIJI--CUT THROUGH THE TEACHER'S LOUNGE!
YOU GO THAT WAY!
HIT HIM FROM BOTH SIDES!
PANT
PANT
PANT
TAKE HIS PUNK-ASS DOWN!
WE'RE ON IT!!
!!
SHIT! THEY'RE AFTER ME!!
ダダッ

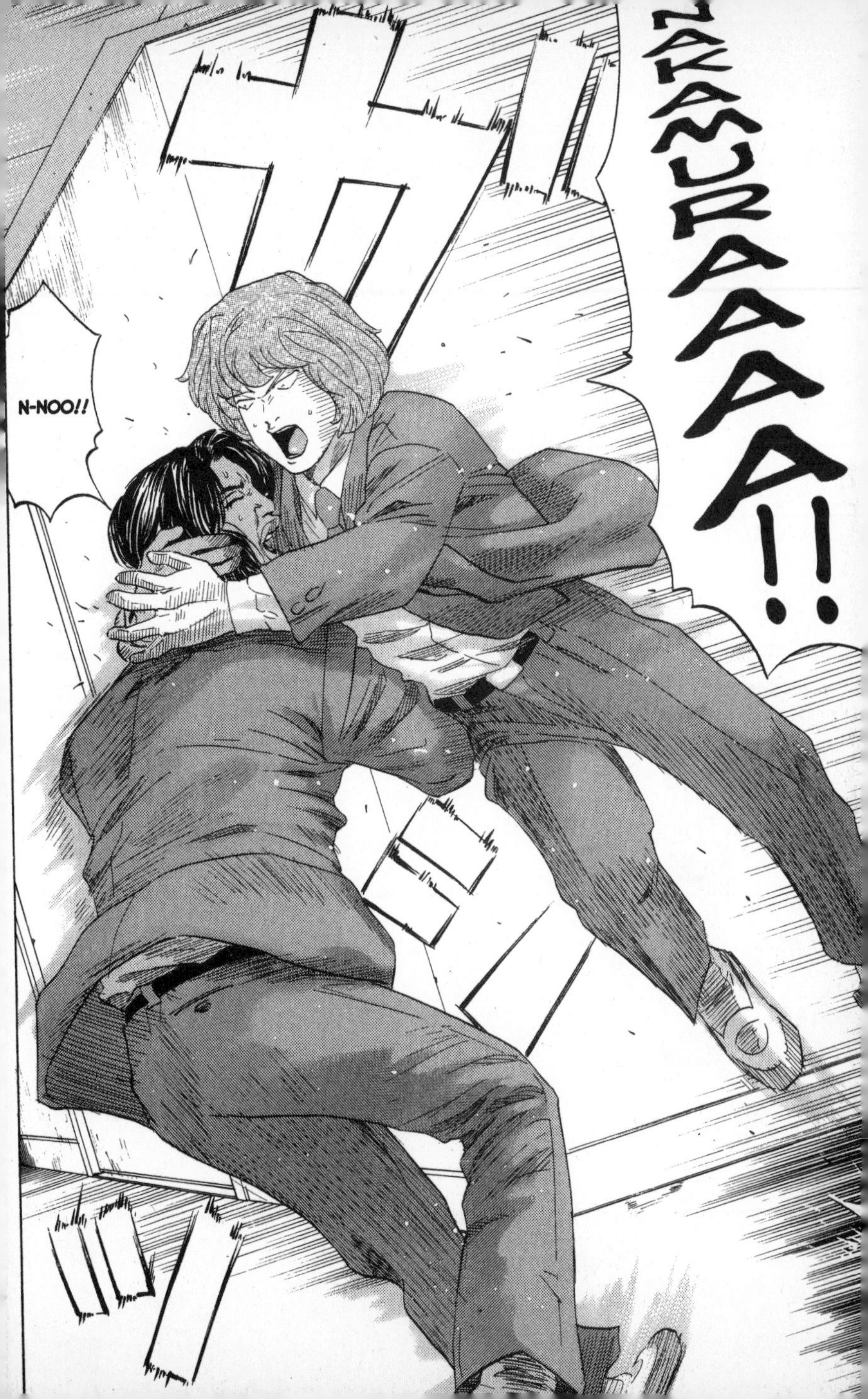
NAKAMURAAAAA!!
N-NOO!!

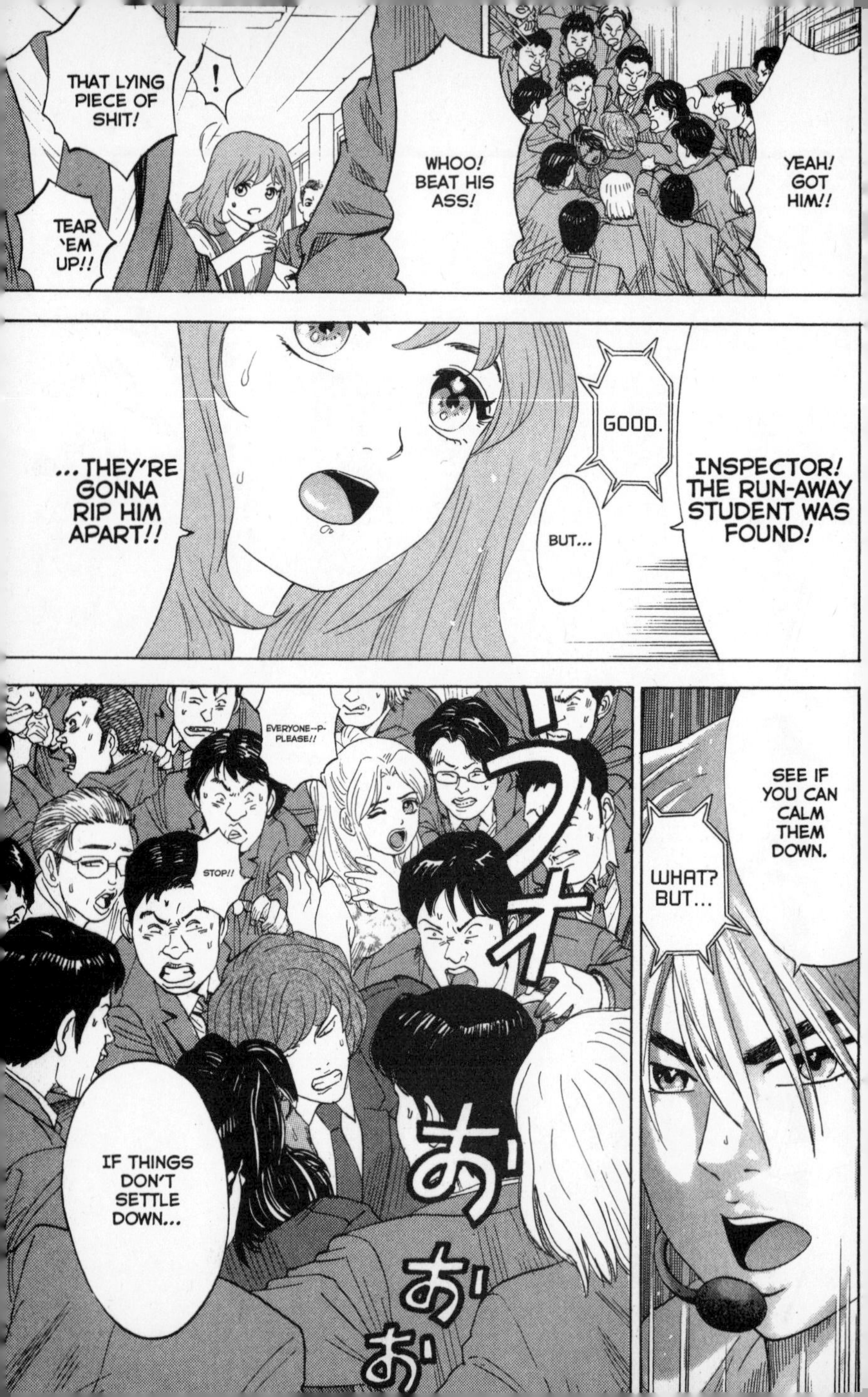
YEAH! GOT HIM!!
WHOO! BEAT HIS ASS!
!
THAT LYING PIECE OF SHIT!
TEAR 'EM UP!!
INSPECTOR! THE RUN-AWAY STUDENT WAS FOUND!
GOOD.
BUT...
...THEY'RE GONNA RIP HIM APART!!
SEE IF YOU CAN CALM THEM DOWN.
WHAT? BUT...
ウオ
EVERYONE--P-PLEASE!!
STOP!!
IF THINGS DON'T SETTLE DOWN...
あ゛あ゛お゛

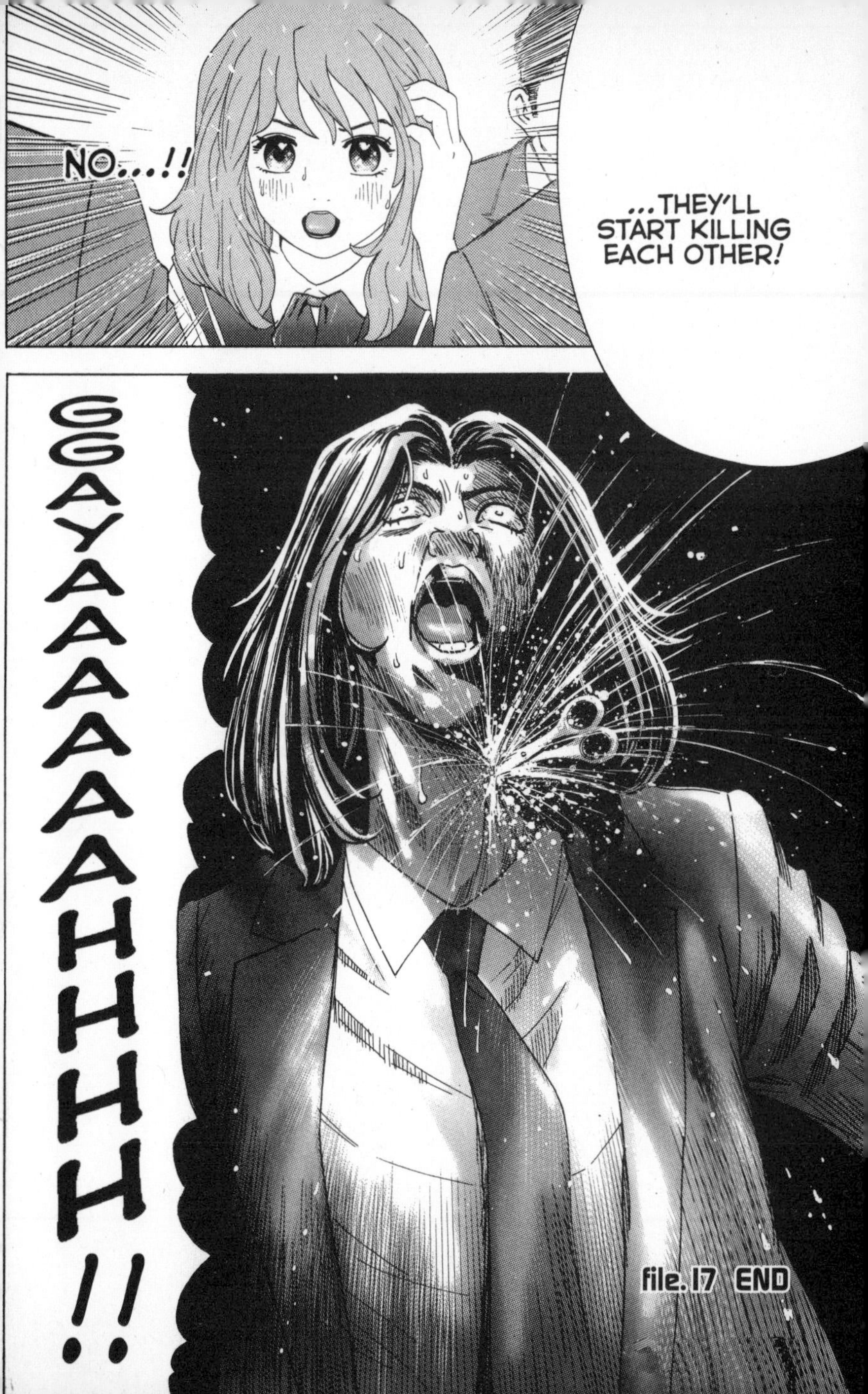
...THEY'LL START KILLING EACH OTHER!
NO...!!
GGAYAAAAAAHHHH!!
file. 17 END

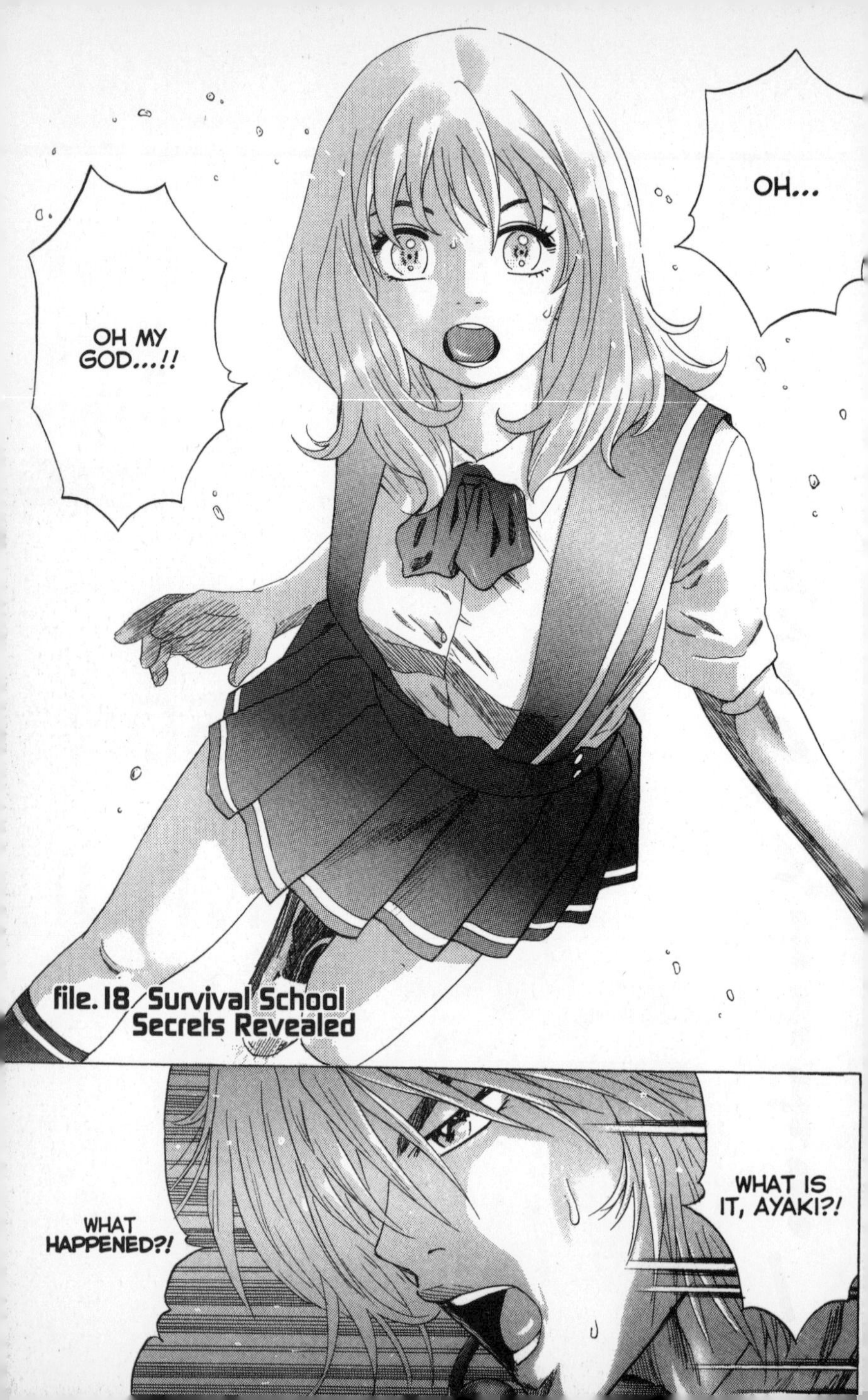
OH...
OH MY GOD...!!
file. 18 Survival School Secrets Revealed
WHAT IS IT, AYAKI?!
WHAT HAPPENED?!

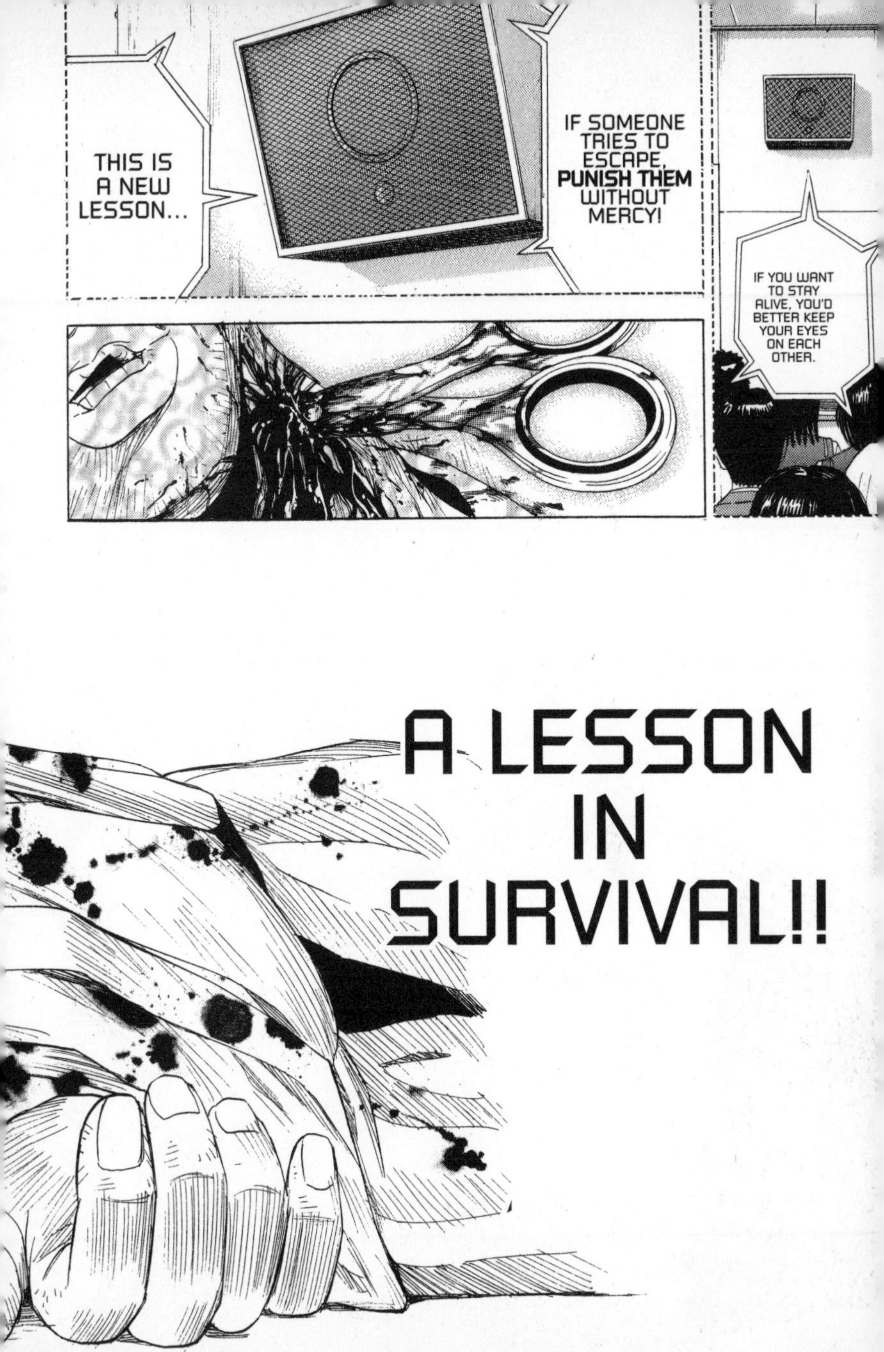
IF YOU WANT TO STAY ALIVE, YOU'D BETTER KEEP YOUR EYES ON EACH OTHER.
IF SOMEONE TRIES TO ESCAPE, **PUNISH THEM** WITHOUT MERCY!
THIS IS A NEW LESSON...
A LESSON IN SURVIVAL!!

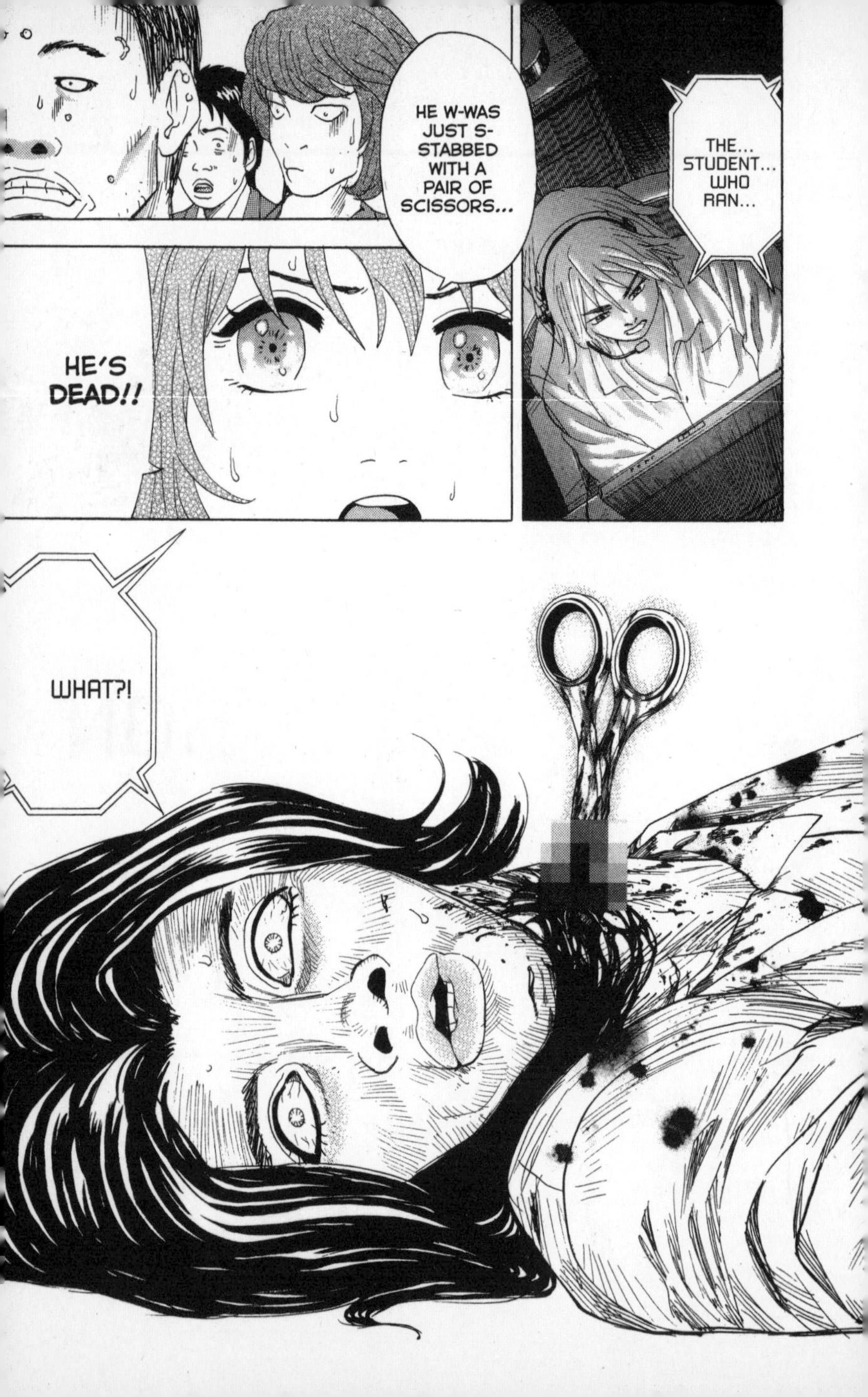
THE... STUDENT... WHO RAN...
HE W-WAS JUST S-STABBED WITH A PAIR OF SCISSORS...
HE'S DEAD!!
WHAT?!

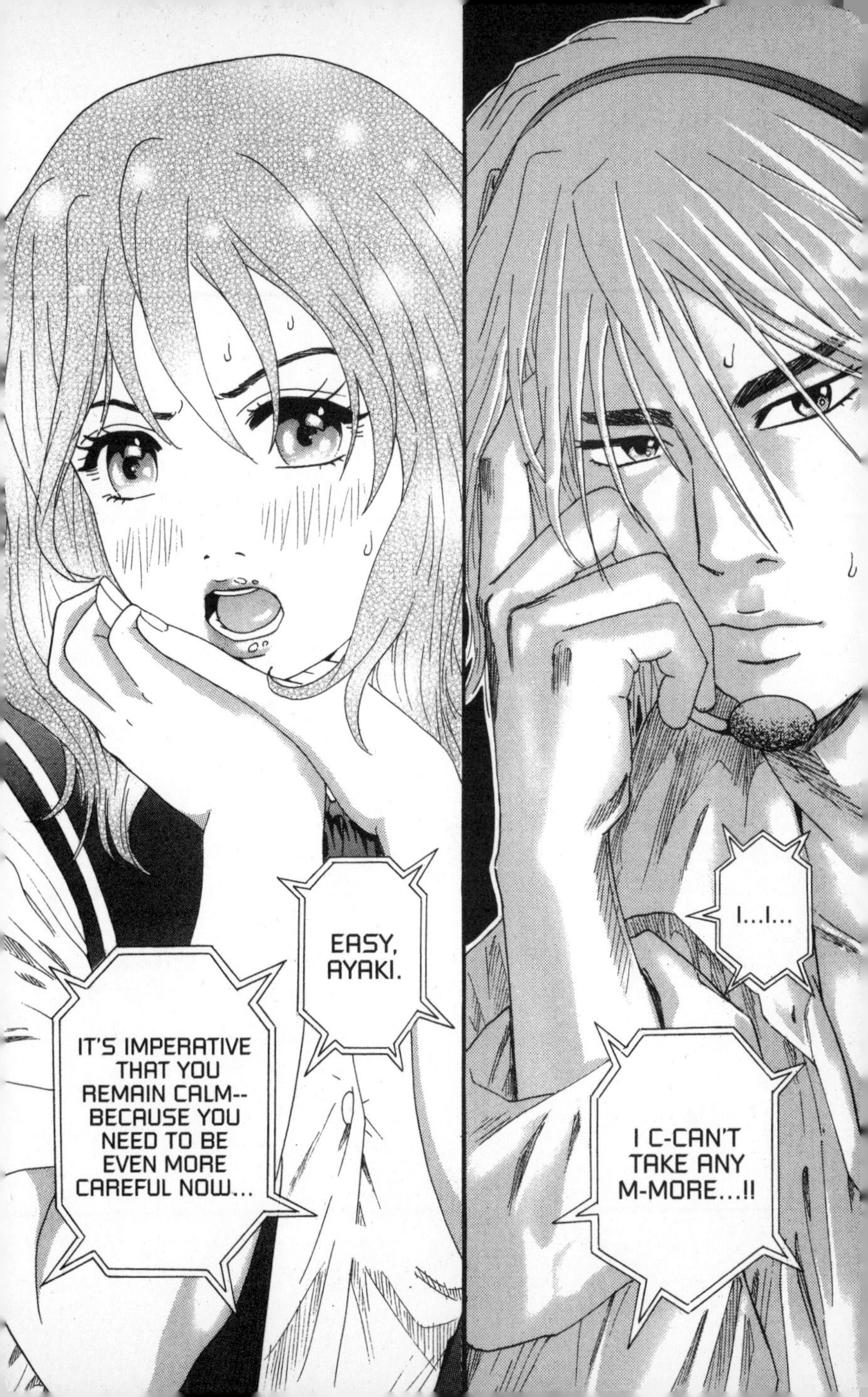
I...I...
I C-CAN'T TAKE ANY M-MORE...!!
EASY, AYAKI.
IT'S IMPERATIVE THAT YOU REMAIN CALM-- BECAUSE YOU NEED TO BE EVEN MORE CAREFUL NOW...

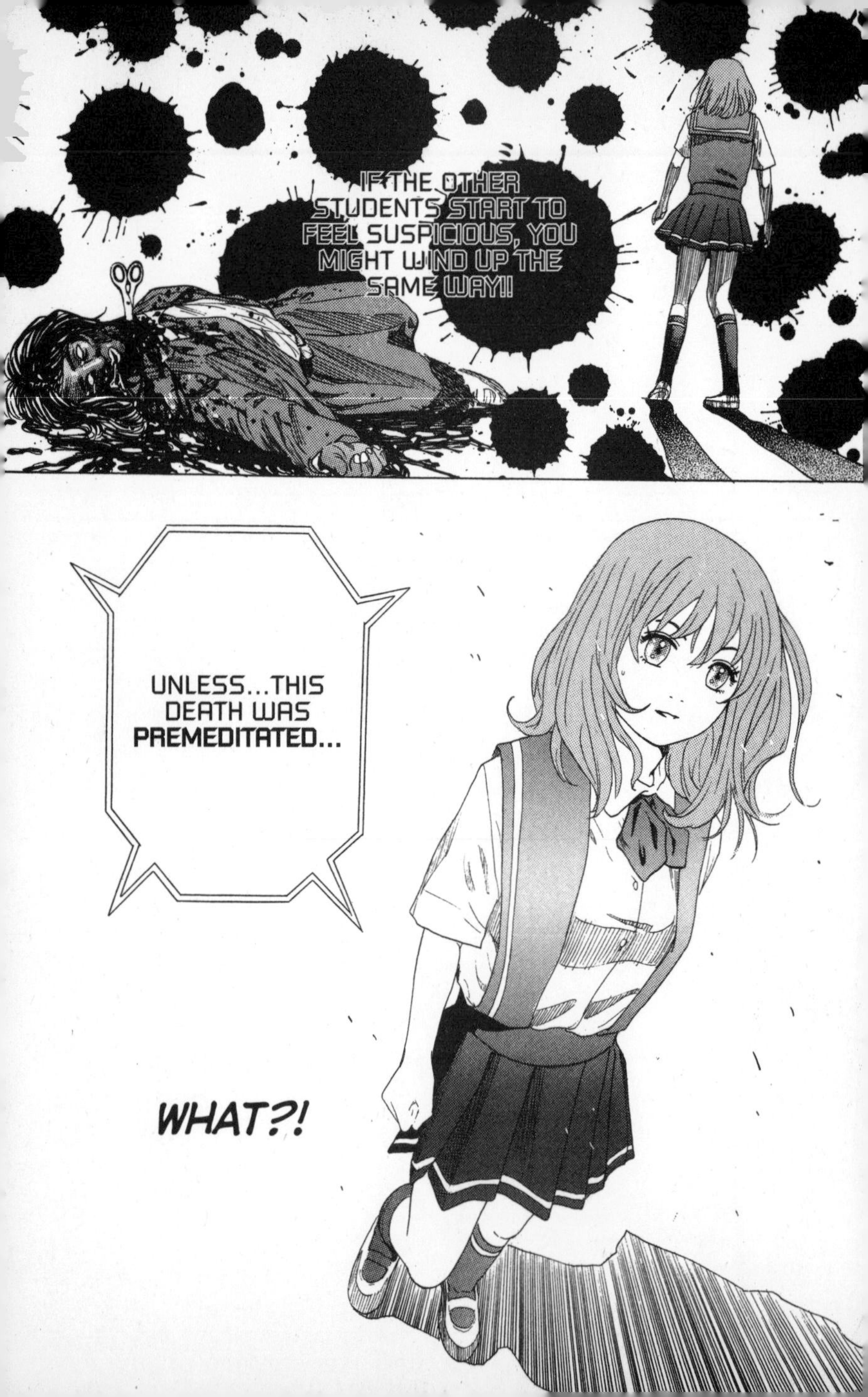
IF THE OTHER STUDENTS START TO FEEL SUSPICIOUS, YOU MIGHT WIND UP THE SAME WAY!!
UNLESS...THIS DEATH WAS PREMEDITATED...
WHAT?!

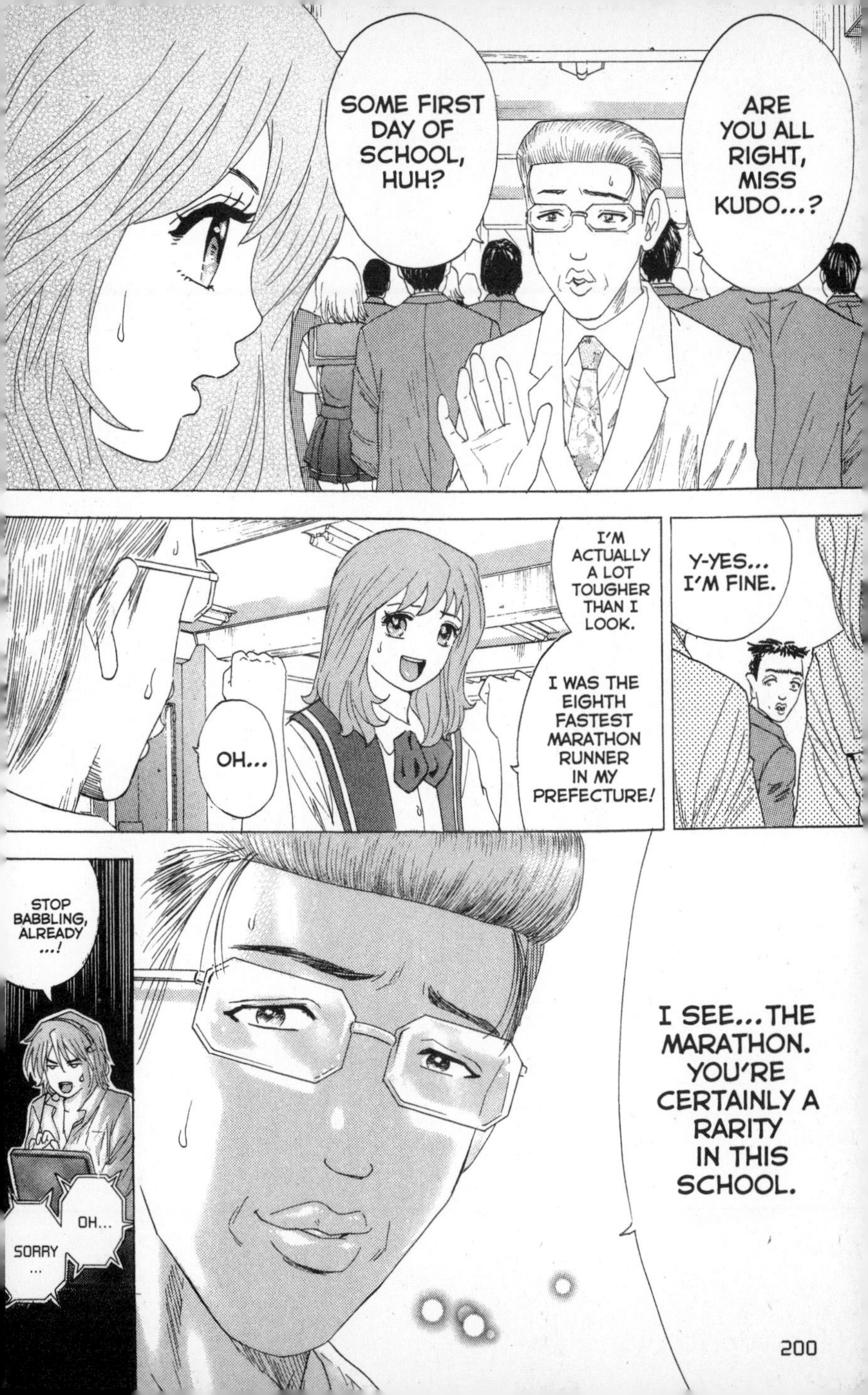
ARE YOU ALL RIGHT, MISS KUDO...?
SOME FIRST DAY OF SCHOOL, HUH?
Y-YES... I'M FINE.
I'M ACTUALLY A LOT TOUGHER THAN I LOOK.
I WAS THE EIGHTH FASTEST MARATHON RUNNER IN MY PREFECTURE!
OH...
I SEE...THE MARATHON. YOU'RE CERTAINLY A RARITY IN THIS SCHOOL.
STOP BABBLING, ALREADY...!
OH...
SORRY...

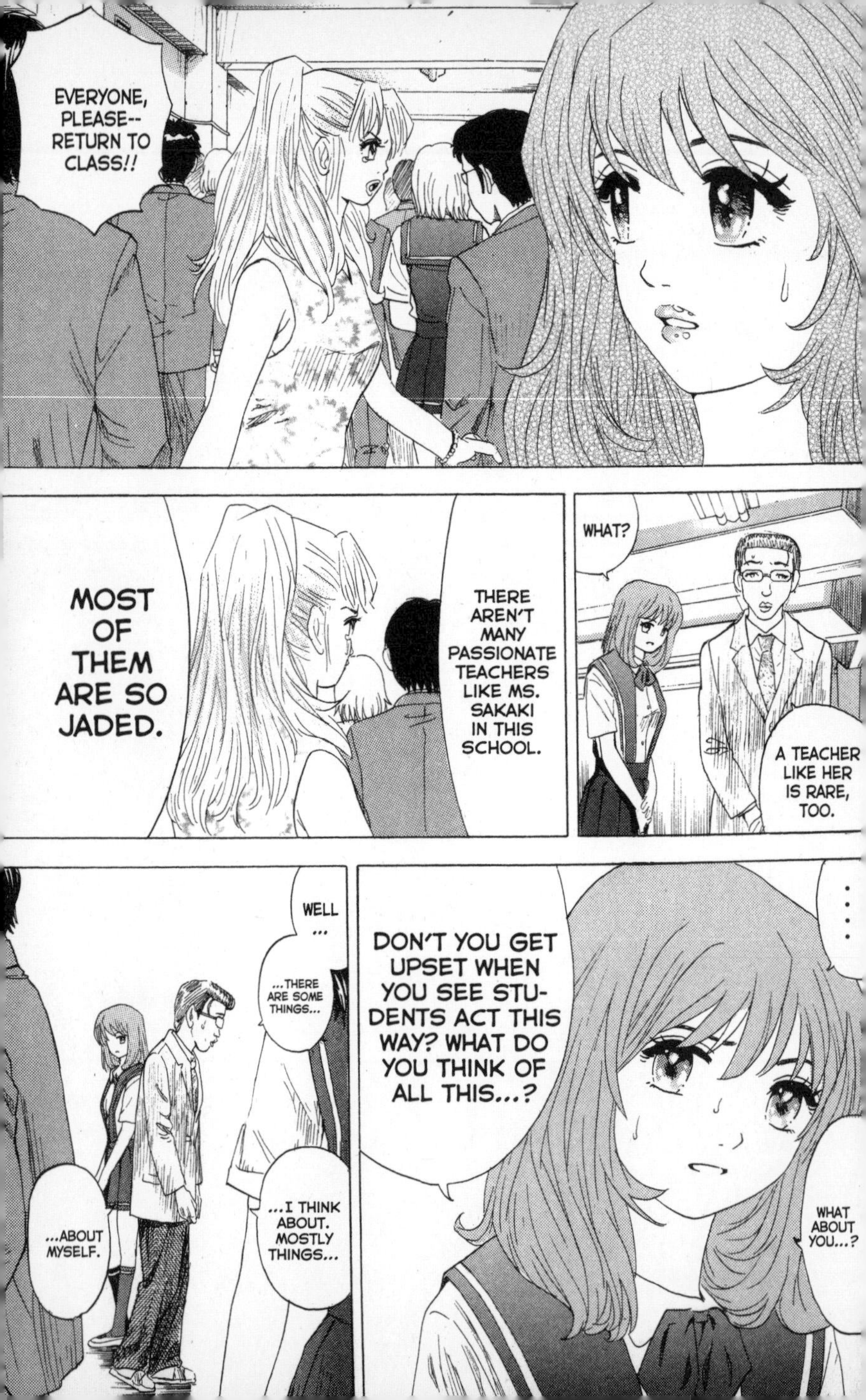
EVERYONE, PLEASE-- RETURN TO CLASS!!
WHAT?
A TEACHER LIKE HER IS RARE, TOO.
THERE AREN'T MANY PASSIONATE TEACHERS LIKE MS. SAKAKI IN THIS SCHOOL.
MOST OF THEM ARE SO JADED.
DON'T YOU GET UPSET WHEN YOU SEE STU-DENTS ACT THIS WAY? WHAT DO YOU THINK OF ALL THIS...?
....
WHAT ABOUT YOU...?
WELL ...
...THERE ARE SOME THINGS...
...I THINK ABOUT. MOSTLY THINGS...
...ABOUT MYSELF.

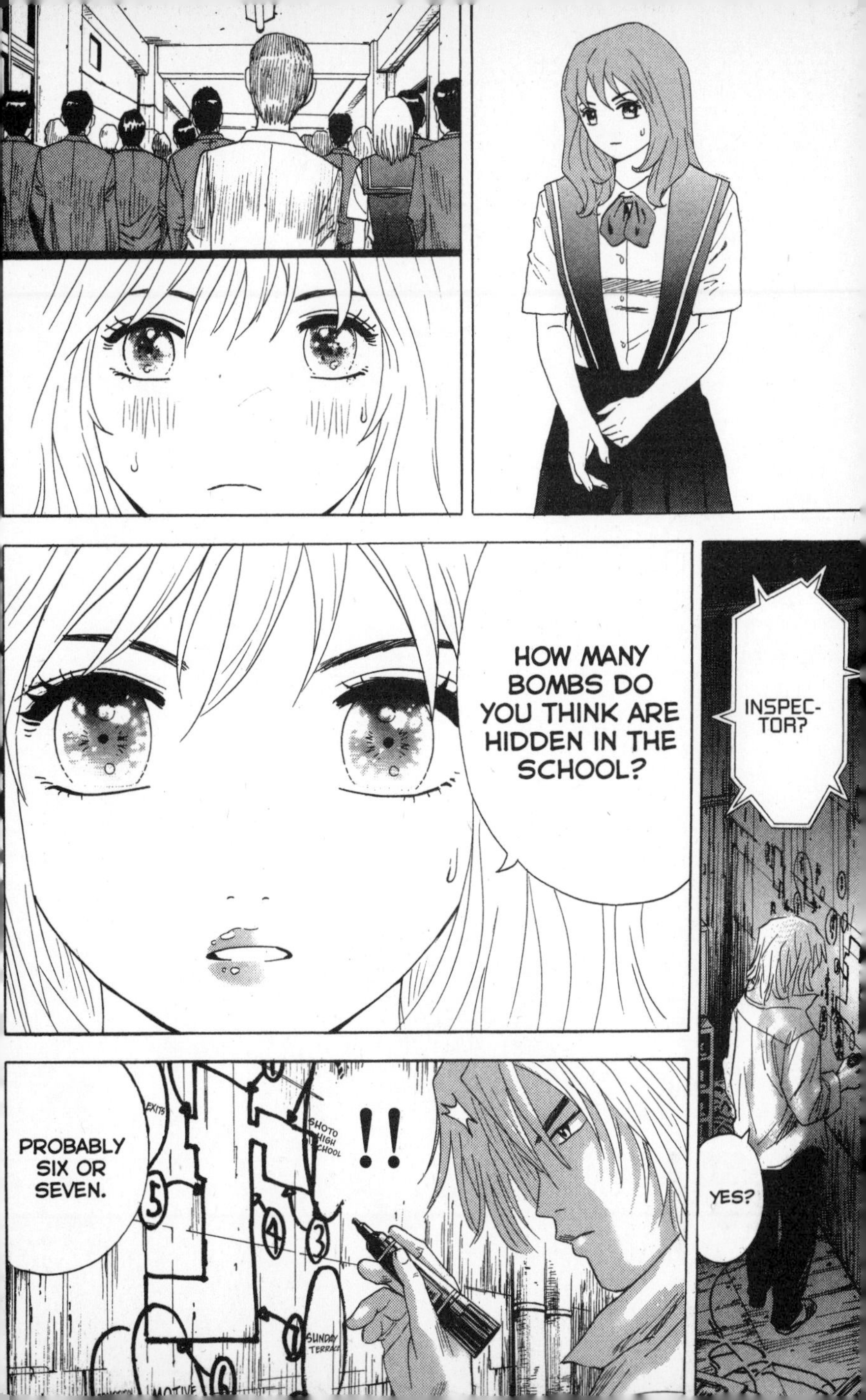
INSPEC-TOR?
YES?
HOW MANY BOMBS DO YOU THINK ARE HIDDEN IN THE SCHOOL?
!!
SHOTO HIGH SCHOOL
EXITS
SUNDAY TERRACE
MOTIVE
PROBABLY SIX OR SEVEN.

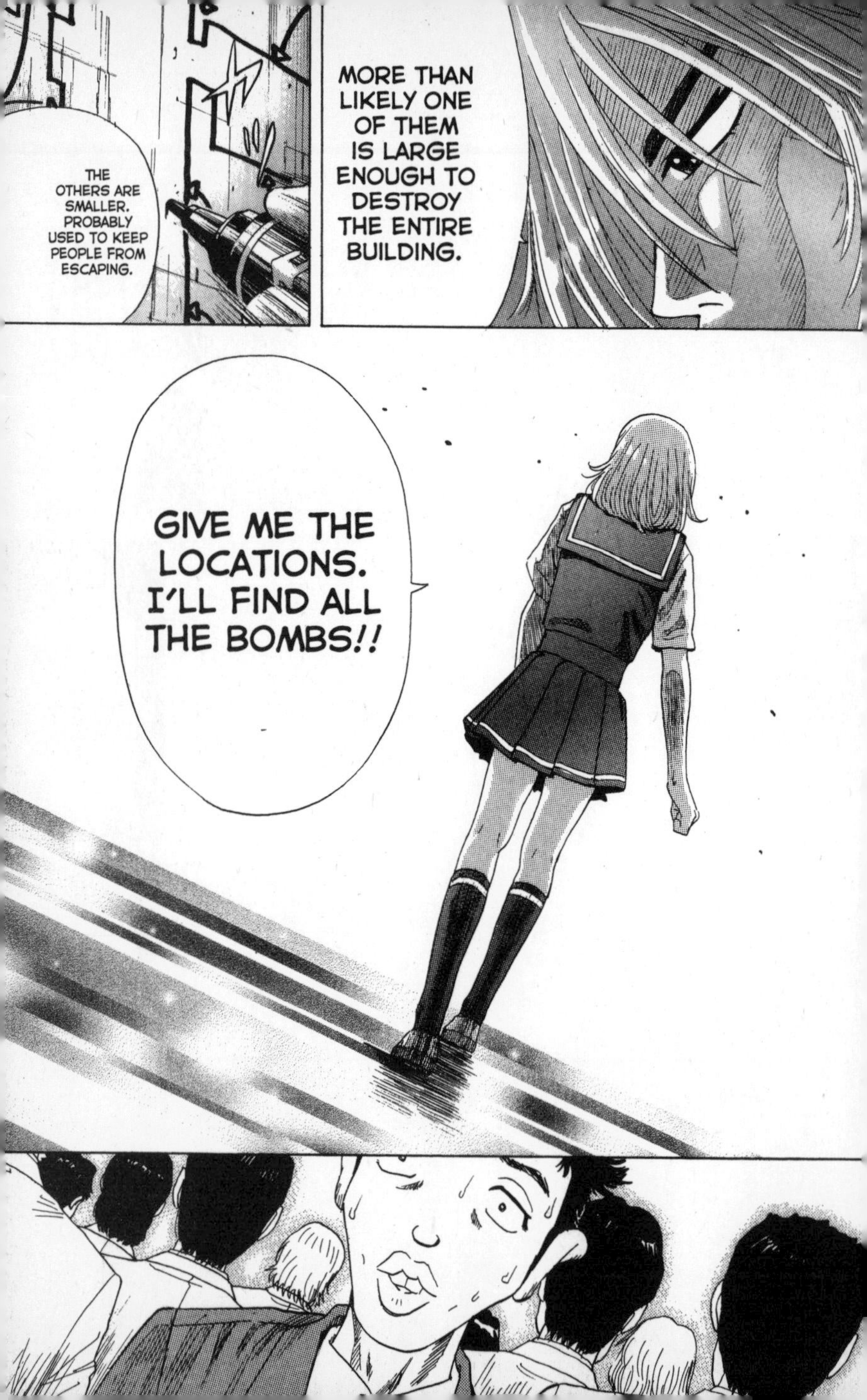
MORE THAN LIKELY ONE OF THEM IS LARGE ENOUGH TO DESTROY THE ENTIRE BUILDING.
THE OTHERS ARE SMALLER. PROBABLY USED TO KEEP PEOPLE FROM ESCAPING.
GIVE ME THE LOCATIONS. I'LL FIND ALL THE BOMBS!!

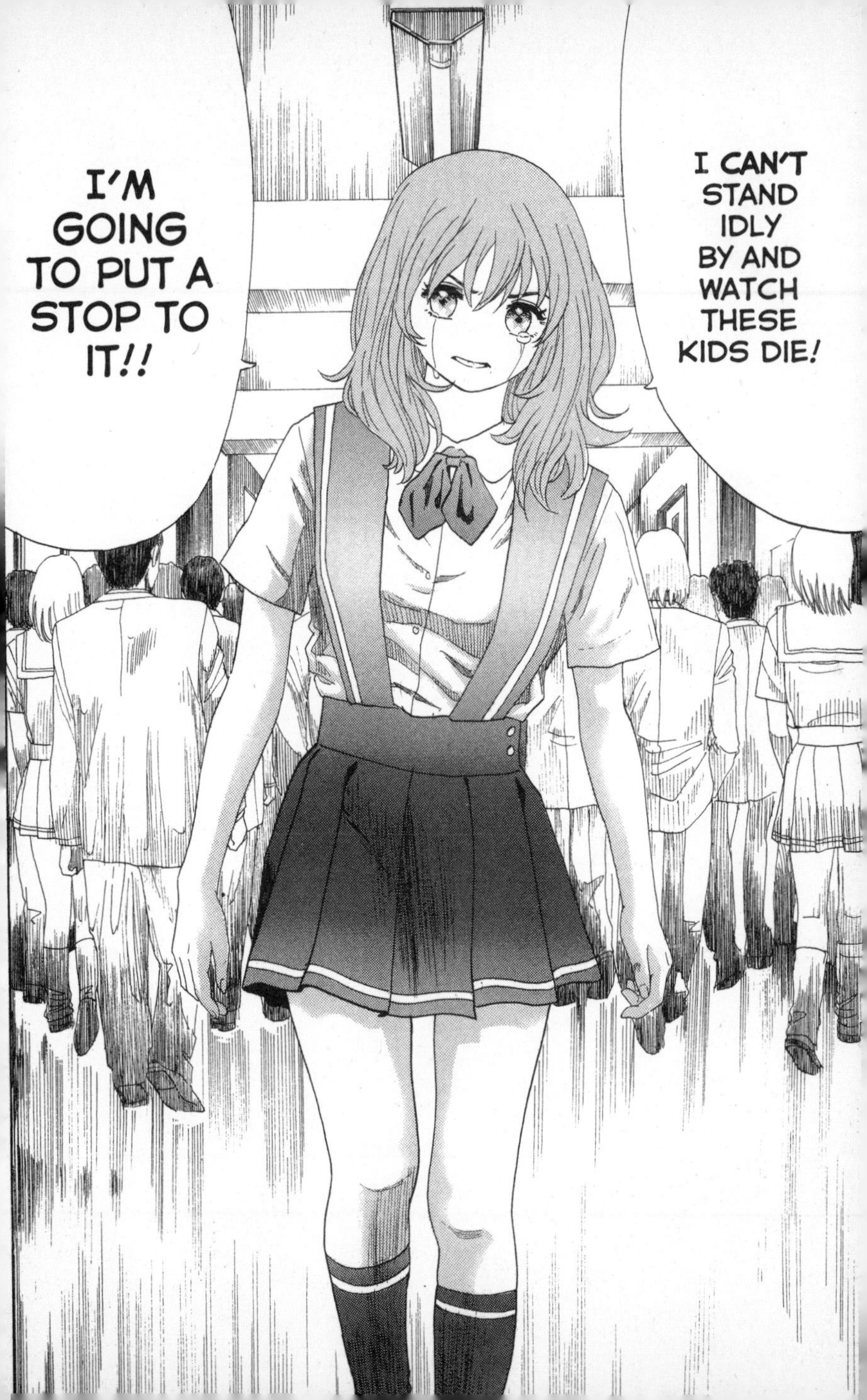
I CAN'T STAND IDLY BY AND WATCH THESE KIDS DIE!
I'M GOING TO PUT A STOP TO IT!!

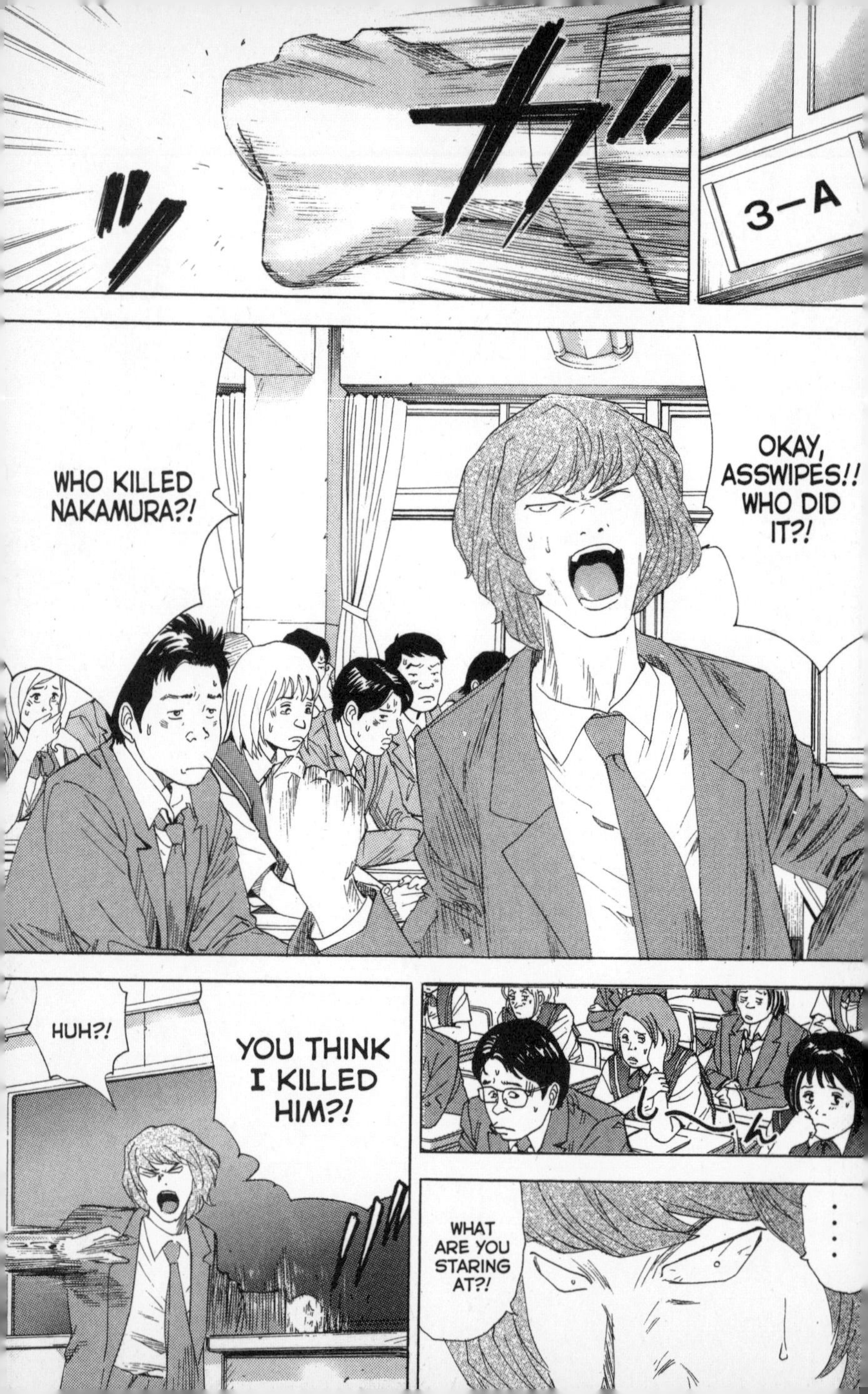
3—A
OKAY, ASSWIPES!! WHO DID IT?!
WHO KILLED NAKAMURA?!
し〜ん
....
WHAT ARE YOU STARING AT?!
YOU THINK I KILLED HIM?!
HUH?!

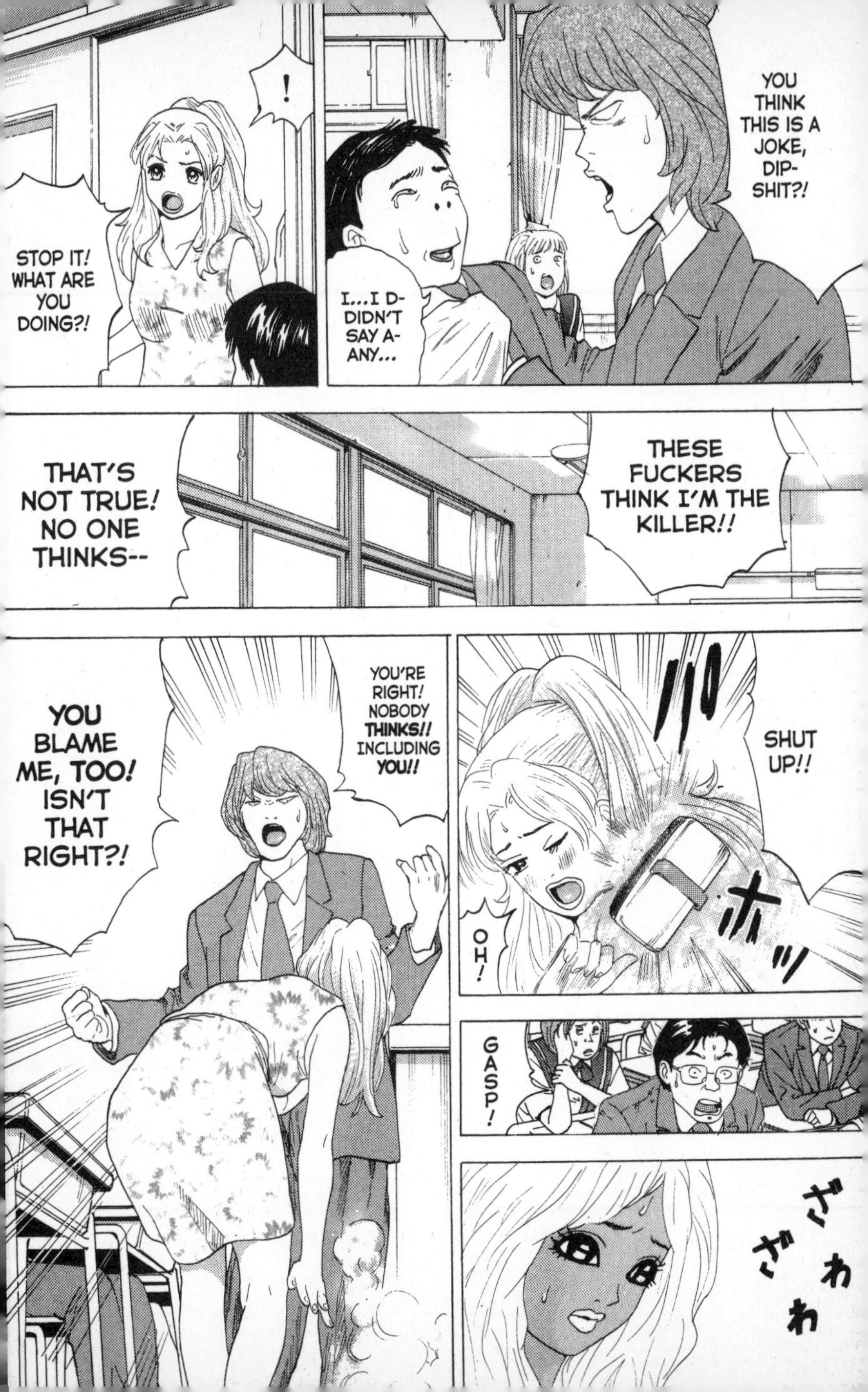

YOU THINK THIS IS A JOKE, DIP-SHIT?!
I...I D-DIDN'T SAY A-ANY...
!
STOP IT! WHAT ARE YOU DOING?!
THESE FUCKERS THINK I'M THE KILLER!!
THAT'S NOT TRUE! NO ONE THINKS--
SHUT UP!!
OH!
GASP!
ざわざわ
YOU'RE RIGHT! NOBODY **THINKS!!** INCLUDING **YOU!!**
YOU BLAME ME, TOO! ISN'T THAT RIGHT?!

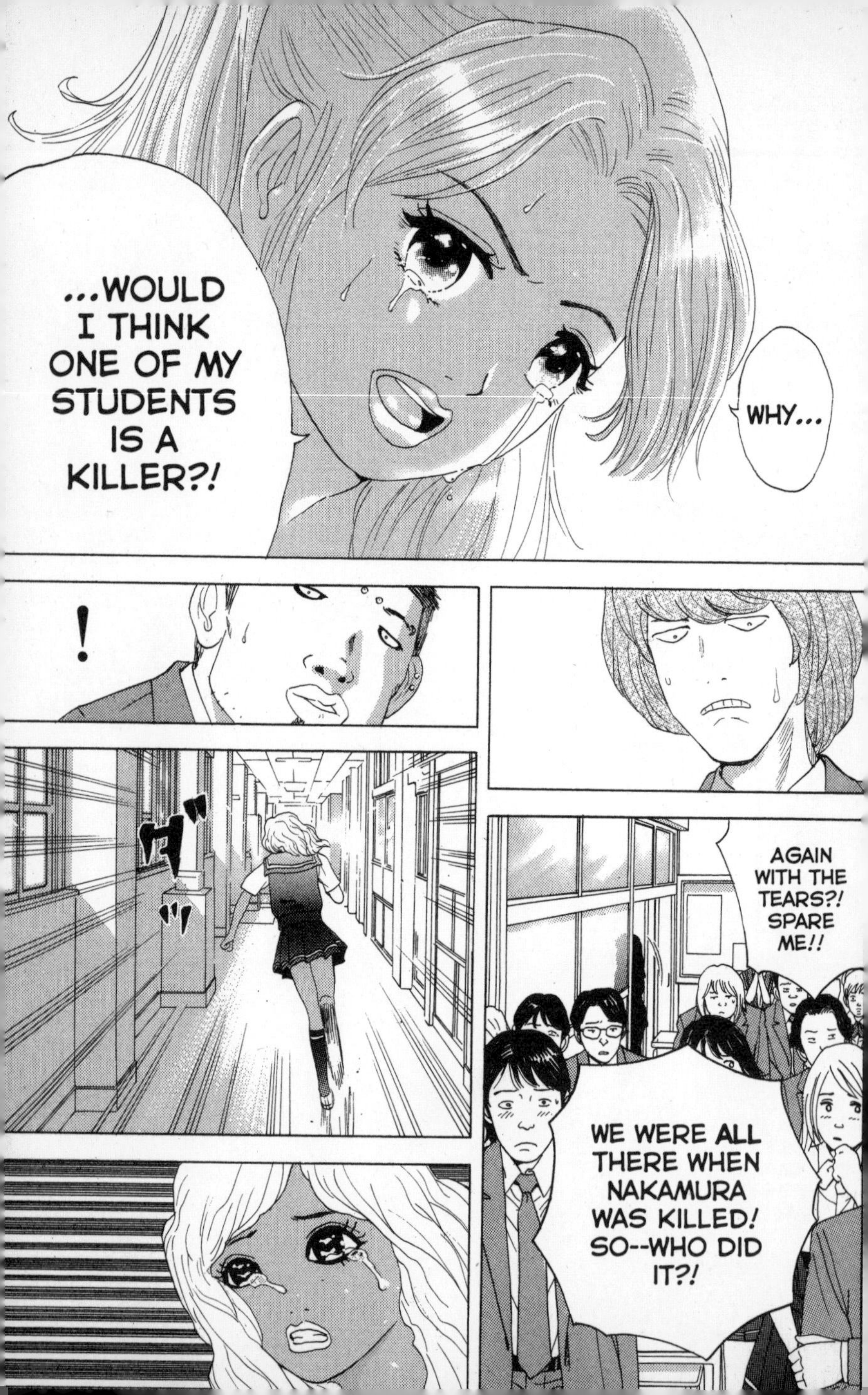
WHY...
...WOULD I THINK ONE OF MY STUDENTS IS A KILLER?!
!
AGAIN WITH THE TEARS?! SPARE ME!!
WE WERE ALL THERE WHEN NAKAMURA WAS KILLED! SO--WHO DID IT?!

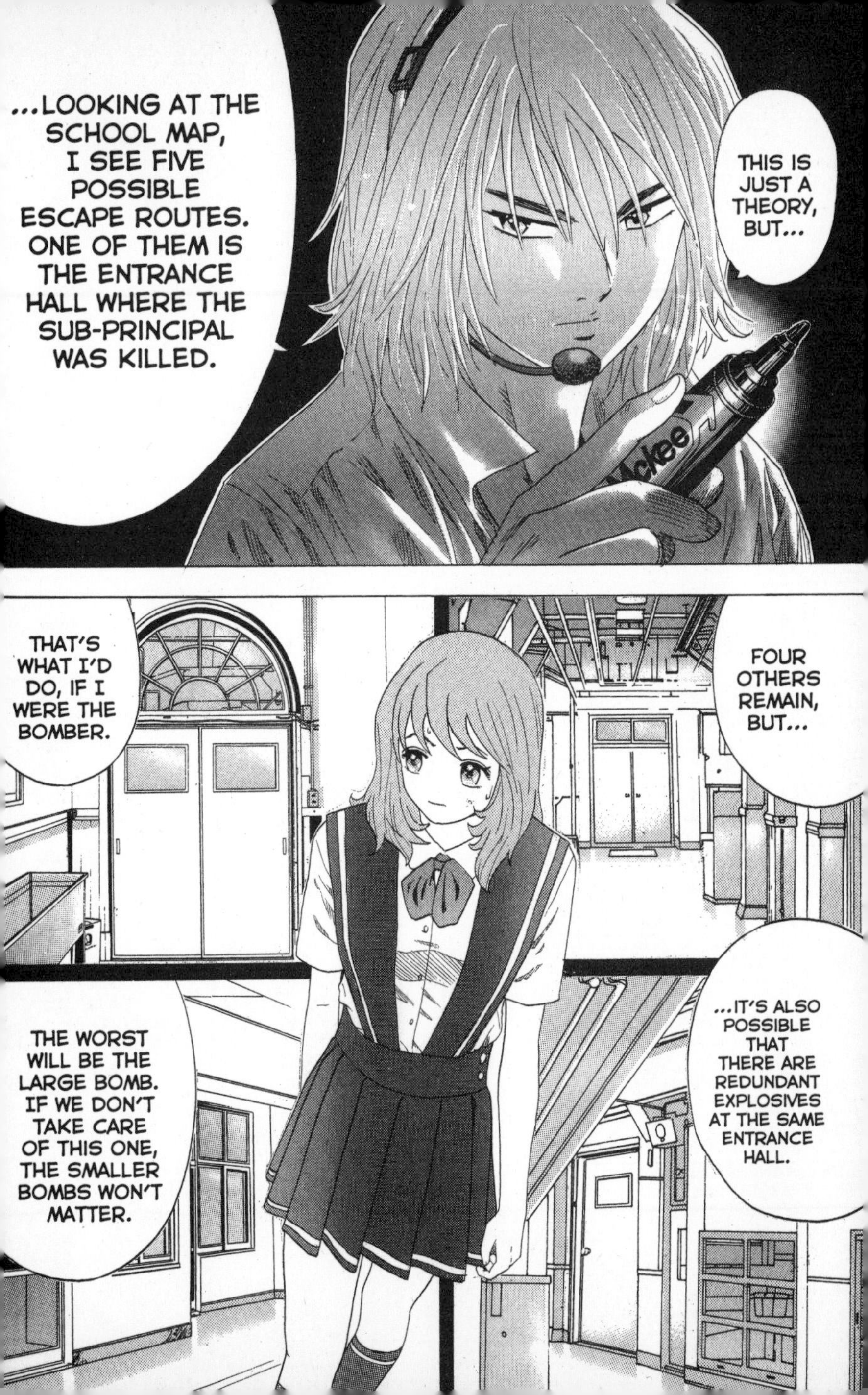
THIS IS JUST A THEORY, BUT...
...LOOKING AT THE SCHOOL MAP, I SEE FIVE POSSIBLE ESCAPE ROUTES. ONE OF THEM IS THE ENTRANCE HALL WHERE THE SUB-PRINCIPAL WAS KILLED.
FOUR OTHERS REMAIN, BUT...
THAT'S WHAT I'D DO, IF I WERE THE BOMBER.
...IT'S ALSO POSSIBLE THAT THERE ARE REDUNDANT EXPLOSIVES AT THE SAME ENTRANCE HALL.
THE WORST WILL BE THE LARGE BOMB. IF WE DON'T TAKE CARE OF THIS ONE, THE SMALLER BOMBS WON'T MATTER.

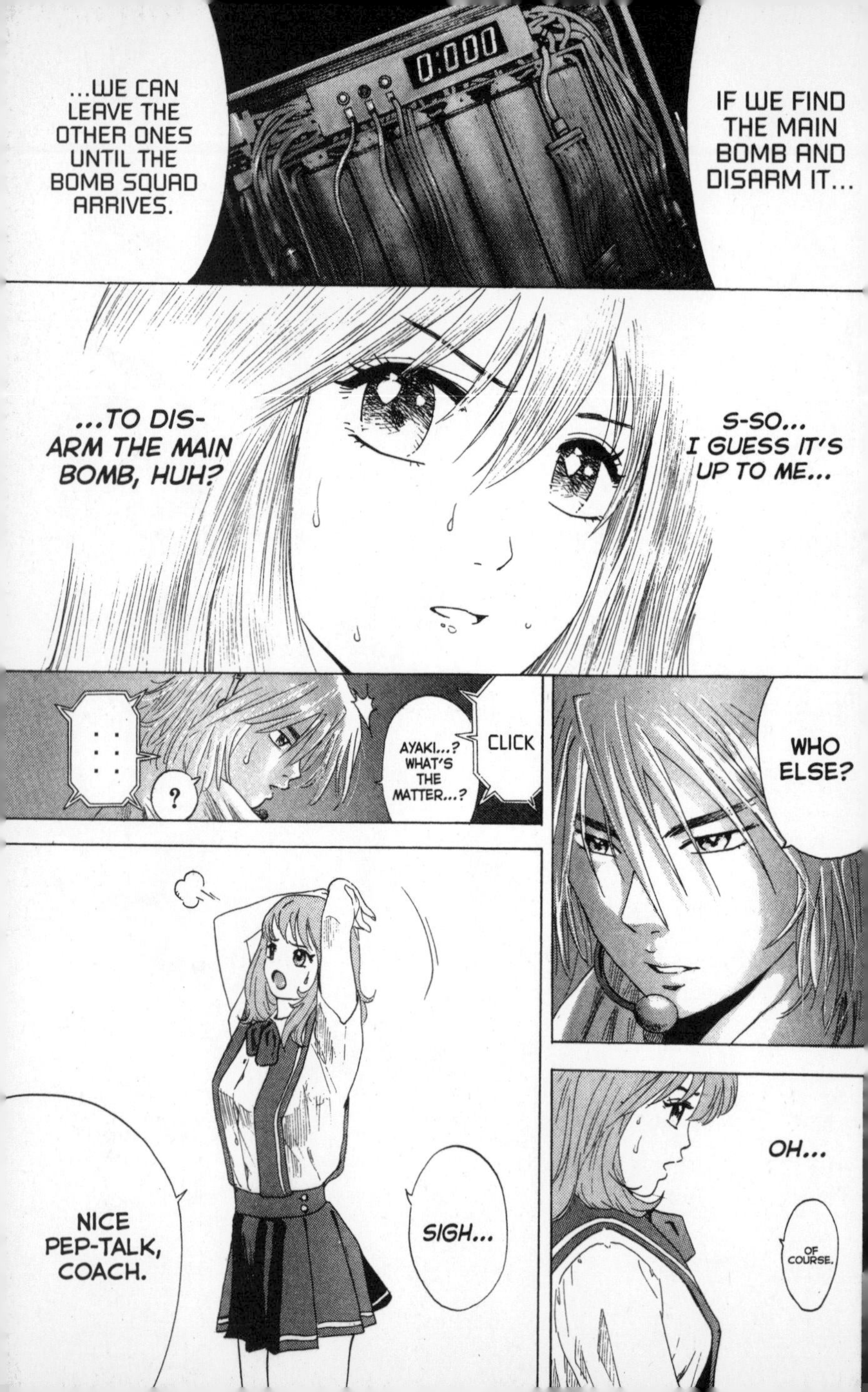
IF WE FIND THE MAIN BOMB AND DISARM IT...
...WE CAN LEAVE THE OTHER ONES UNTIL THE BOMB SQUAD ARRIVES.
S-SO... I GUESS IT'S UP TO ME...
...TO DIS-ARM THE MAIN BOMB, HUH?
WHO ELSE?
OH...
OF COURSE.
CLICK
AYAKI...? WHAT'S THE MATTER...?
...
?
SIGH...
NICE PEP-TALK, COACH.

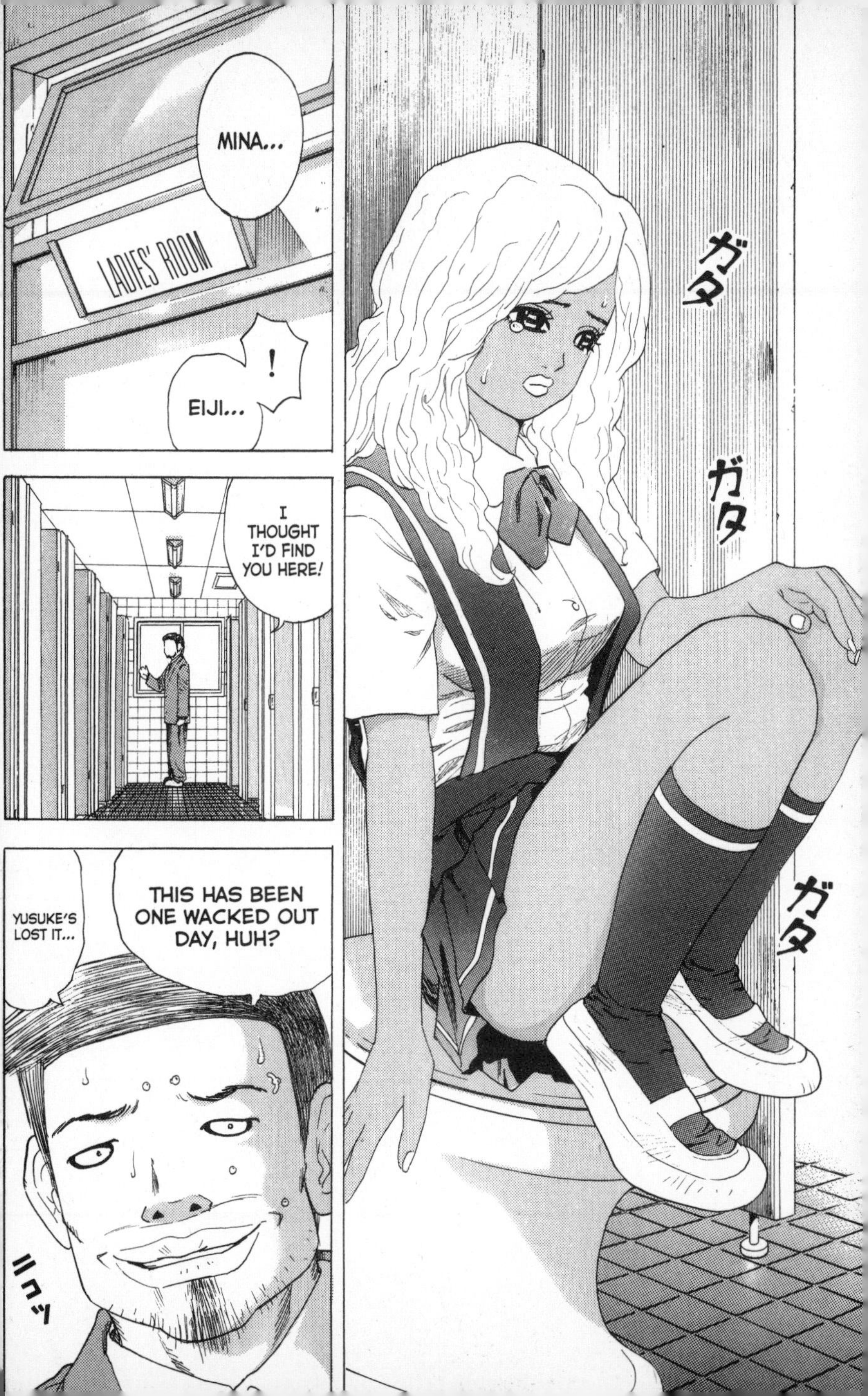
ガタ
ガタ
ガタ
MINA...
LADIES' ROOM
!
EIJI...
I THOUGHT I'D FIND YOU HERE!
THIS HAS BEEN ONE WACKED OUT DAY, HUH?
YUSUKE'S LOST IT...
ニコッ

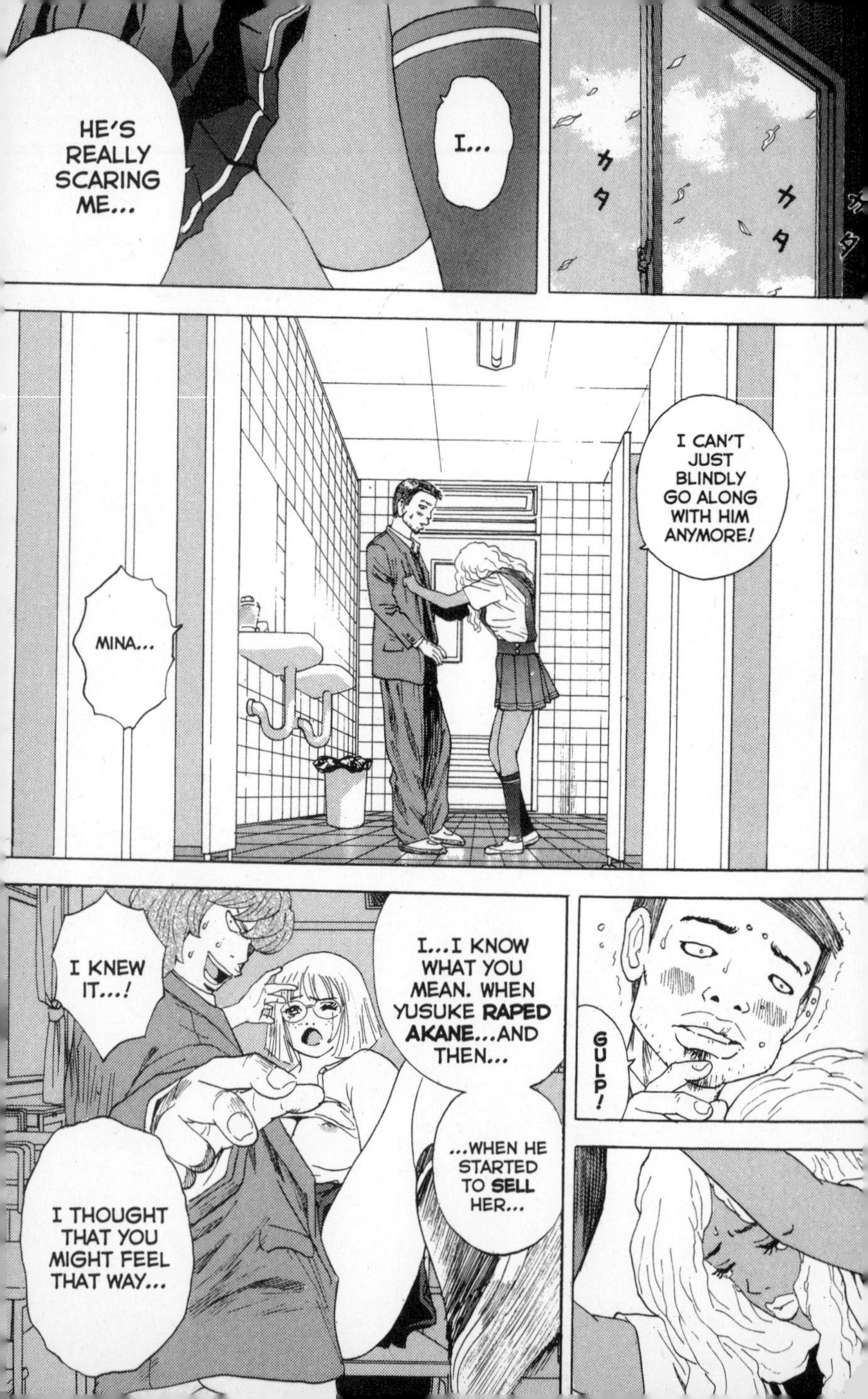
カタ
カタ
I...
HE'S REALLY SCARING ME...
I CAN'T JUST BLINDLY GO ALONG WITH HIM ANYMORE!
MINA...
GULP!
I...I KNOW WHAT YOU MEAN. WHEN YUSUKE RAPED AKANE...AND THEN...
...WHEN HE STARTED TO SELL HER...
I KNEW IT...!
I THOUGHT THAT YOU MIGHT FEEL THAT WAY...

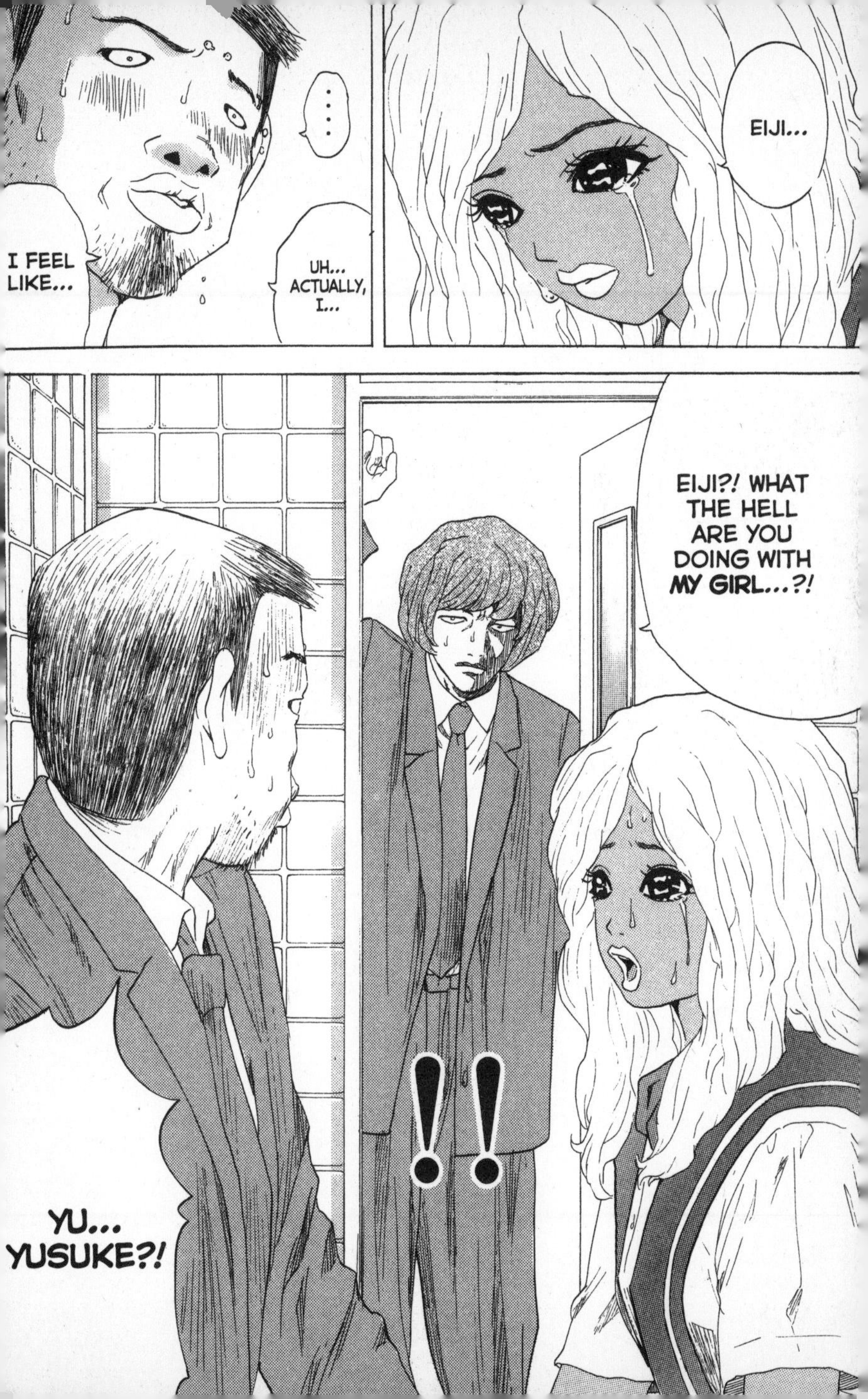
EIJI...
....
UH... ACTUALLY, I...
I FEEL LIKE...
EIJI?! WHAT THE HELL ARE YOU DOING WITH MY GIRL...?!
!!
YU... YUSUKE?!

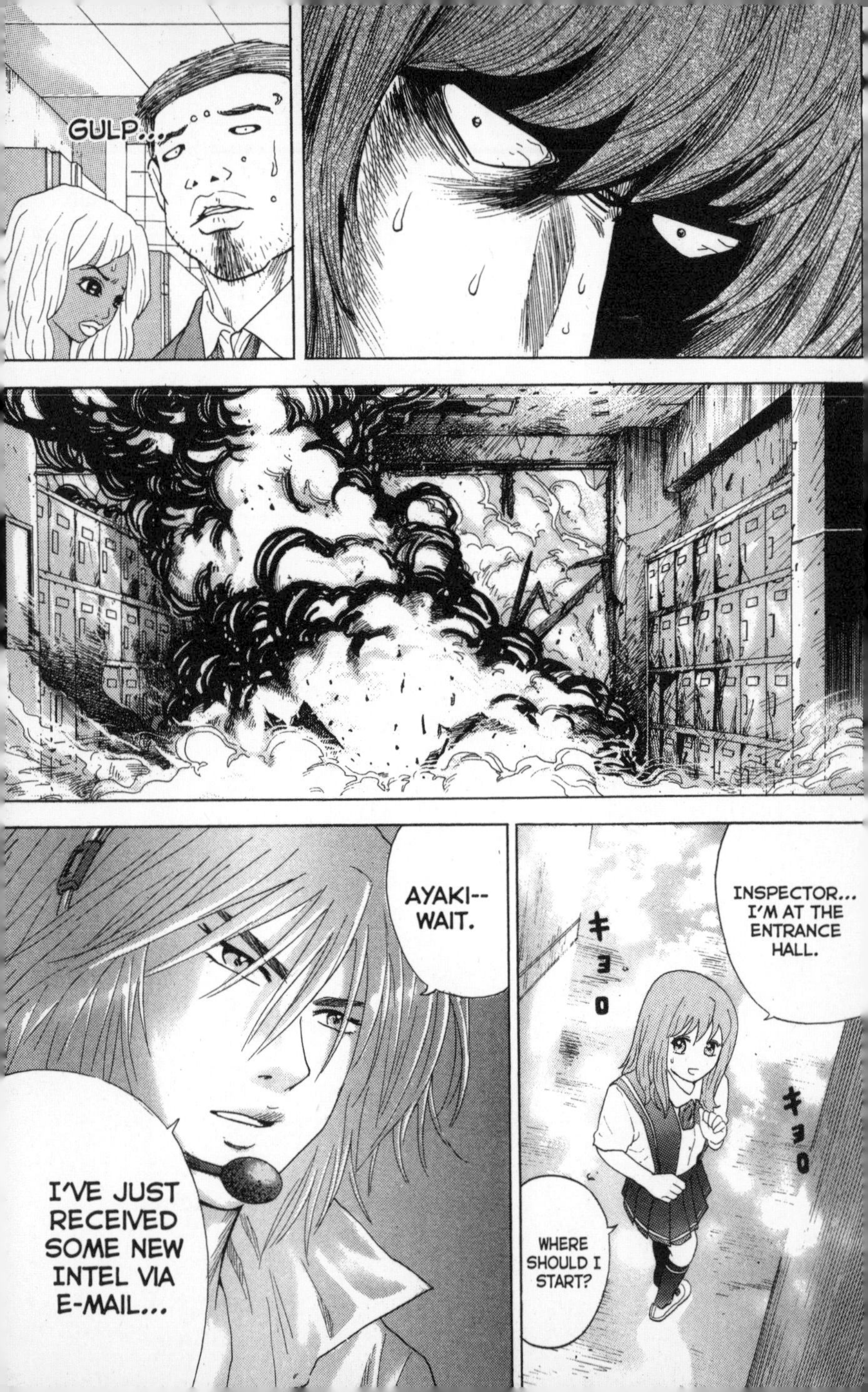
GULP...
INSPECTOR... I'M AT THE ENTRANCE HALL.
キョロ
キョロ
WHERE SHOULD I START?
AYAKI-- WAIT.
I'VE JUST RECEIVED SOME NEW INTEL VIA E-MAIL...

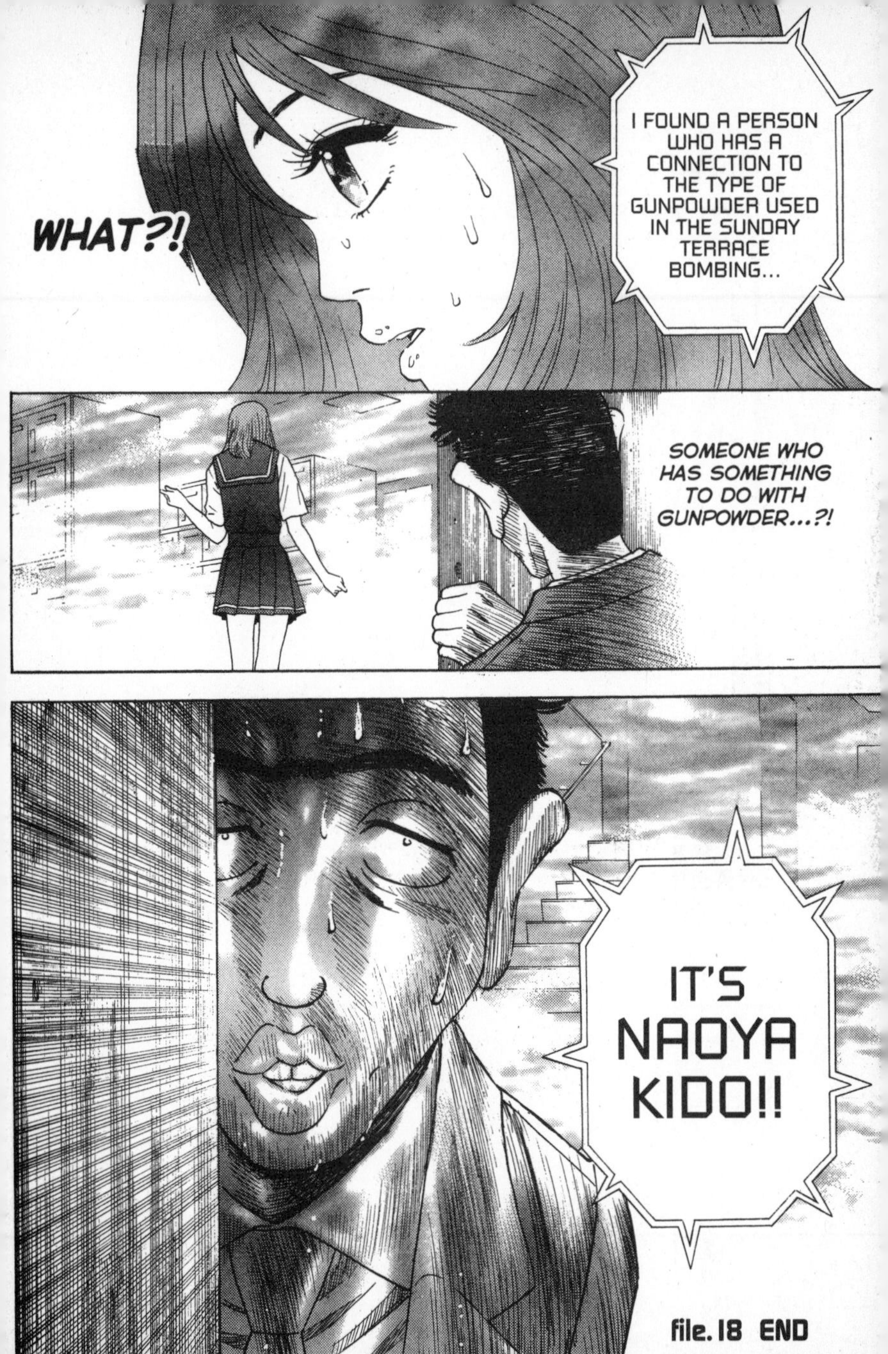
I FOUND A PERSON WHO HAS A CONNECTION TO THE TYPE OF GUNPOWDER USED IN THE SUNDAY TERRACE BOMBING...
WHAT?!
SOMEONE WHO HAS SOMETHING TO DO WITH GUNPOWDER...?!
IT'S NAOYA KIDO!!
file.18 END

FROM THE JOURNALS OF KOZABURO HIMURO:

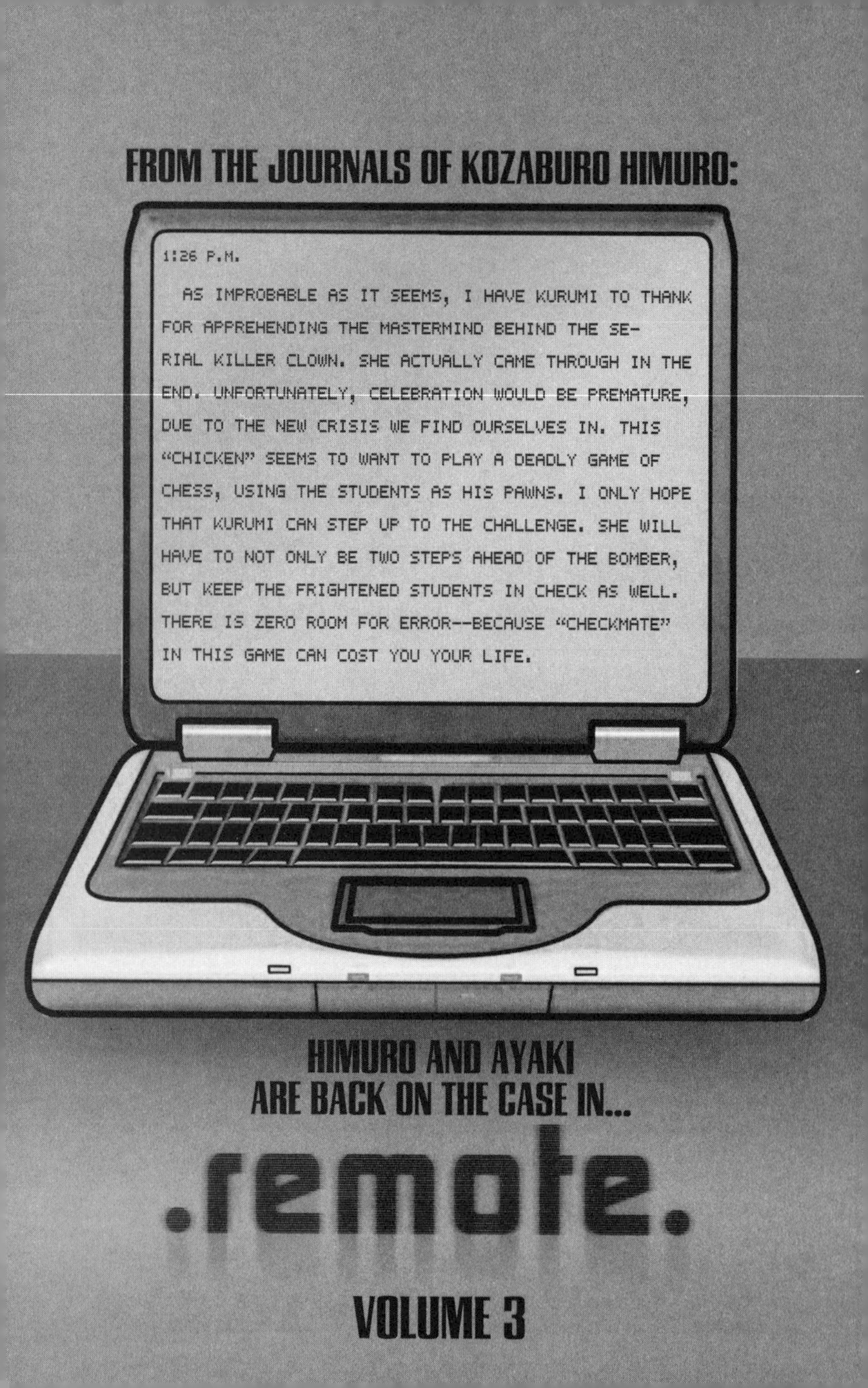
1:26 P.M.
AS IMPROBABLE AS IT SEEMS, I HAVE KURUMI TO THANK FOR APPREHENDING THE MASTERMIND BEHIND THE SERIAL KILLER CLOWN. SHE ACTUALLY CAME THROUGH IN THE END. UNFORTUNATELY, CELEBRATION WOULD BE PREMATURE, DUE TO THE NEW CRISIS WE FIND OURSELVES IN. THIS "CHICKEN" SEEMS TO WANT TO PLAY A DEADLY GAME OF CHESS, USING THE STUDENTS AS HIS PAWNS. I ONLY HOPE THAT KURUMI CAN STEP UP TO THE CHALLENGE. SHE WILL HAVE TO NOT ONLY BE TWO STEPS AHEAD OF THE BOMBER, BUT KEEP THE FRIGHTENED STUDENTS IN CHECK AS WELL. THERE IS ZERO ROOM FOR ERROR--BECAUSE "CHECKMATE" IN THIS GAME CAN COST YOU YOUR LIFE.

HIMURO AND AYAKI ARE BACK ON THE CASE IN...

.remote.

VOLUME 3

PRIEST

LAMENT of the LAMB

SHE CAN PROTECT HER BROTHER FROM THE WORLD.
CAN SHE PROTECT THE WORLD FROM HER BROTHER?

OT
OLDER TEEN
AGE 16+

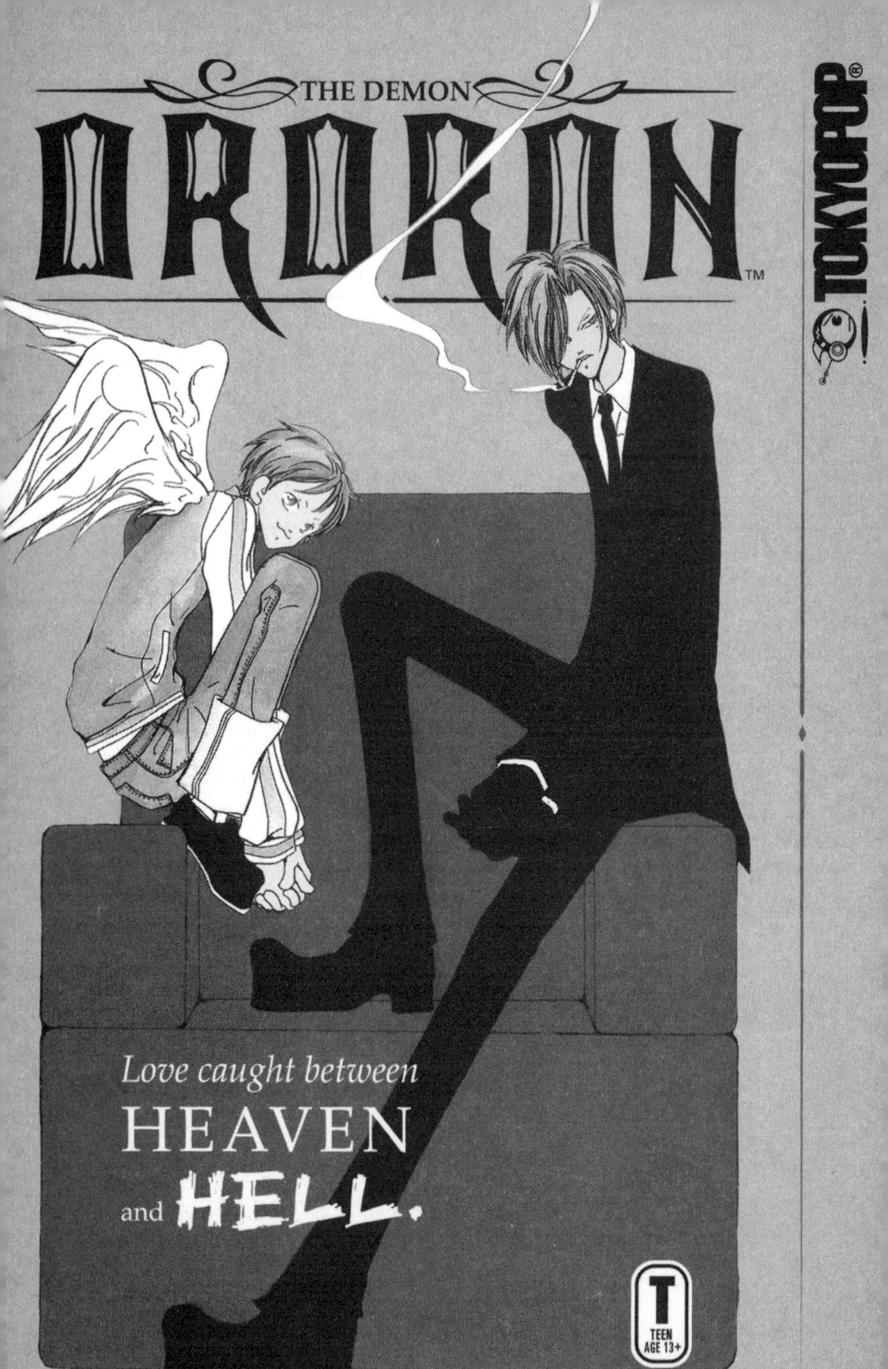
THE DEMON
ORORON™
TOKYOPOP®
Love caught between
HEAVEN
and HELL.
T
TEEN
AGE 13+

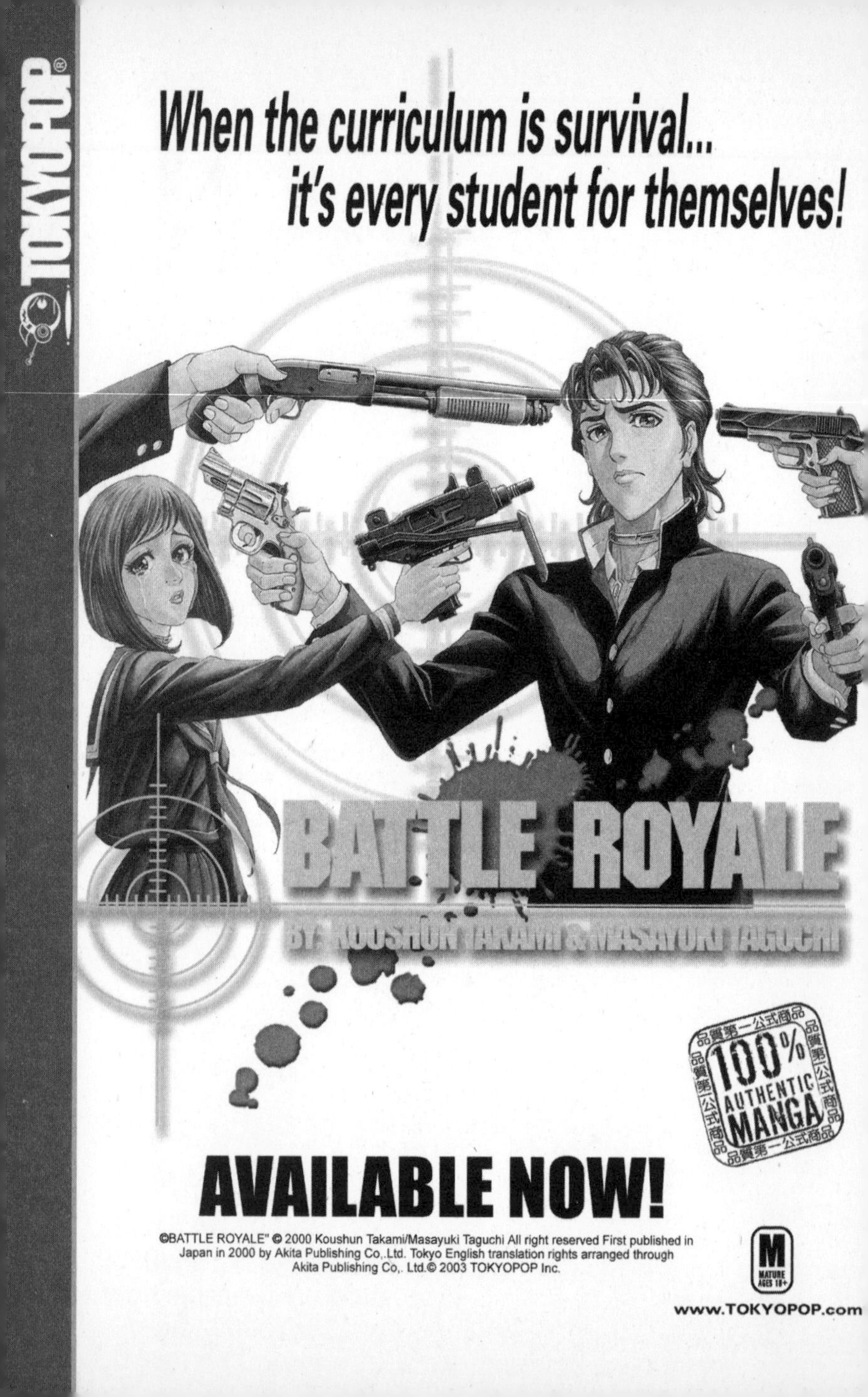
TOKYOPOP®
When the curriculum is survival...
it's every student for themselves!
BATTLE ROYALE
BY: KOUSHUN TAKAMI & MASAYUKI TAGUCHI
品質第一公式商品
100% AUTHENTIC MANGA
AVAILABLE NOW!
©BATTLE ROYALE" © 2000 Koushun Takami/Masayuki Taguchi All right reserved First published in Japan in 2000 by Akita Publishing Co,.Ltd. Tokyo English translation rights arranged through Akita Publishing Co,. Ltd.© 2003 TOKYOPOP Inc.
M MATURE AGES 18+
www.TOKYOPOP.com

ALSO AVAILABLE FROM TOKYOPOP®

**You want it? We got it!
A full range of TOKYOPOP
products are available now at:
www.TOKYOPOP.com/shop**

05.26.04T

ALSO AVAILABLE FROM TOKYOPOP

MANGA

.HACK//LEGEND OF THE TWILIGHT
@LARGE
ABENOBASHI: MAGICAL SHOPPING ARCADE
A.I. LOVE YOU
AI YORI AOSHI
ANGELIC LAYER
ARM OF KANNON
BABY BIRTH
BATTLE ROYALE
BATTLE VIXENS
BRAIN POWERED
BRIGADOON
B'TX
CANDIDATE FOR GODDESS, THE
CARDCAPTOR SAKURA
CARDCAPTOR SAKURA - MASTER OF THE CLOW
CHOBITS
CHRONICLES OF THE CURSED SWORD
CLAMP SCHOOL DETECTIVES
CLOVER
COMIC PARTY
CONFIDENTIAL CONFESSIONS
CORRECTOR YUI
COWBOY BEBOP
COWBOY BEBOP: SHOOTING STAR
CRAZY LOVE STORY
CRESCENT MOON
CROSS
CULDCEPT
CYBORG 009
D•N•ANGEL
DEMON DIARY
DEMON ORORON, THE
DEUS VITAE
DIABOLO
DIGIMON
DIGIMON TAMERS
DIGIMON ZERO TWO
DOLL
DRAGON HUNTER
DRAGON KNIGHTS
DRAGON VOICE
DREAM SAGA
DUKLYON: CLAMP SCHOOL DEFENDERS
EERIE QUEERIE!
ERICA SAKURAZAWA: COLLECTED WORKS
ET CETERA
ETERNITY
EVIL'S RETURN
FAERIES' LANDING
FAKE
FLCL
FLOWER OF THE DEEP SLEEP
FORBIDDEN DANCE
FRUITS BASKET
G GUNDAM

GATEKEEPERS
GETBACKERS
GIRL GOT GAME
GIRLS EDUCATIONAL CHARTER
GRAVITATION
GTO
GUNDAM BLUE DESTINY
GUNDAM SEED ASTRAY
GUNDAM WING
GUNDAM WING: BATTLEFIELD OF PACIFISTS
GUNDAM WING: ENDLESS WALTZ
GUNDAM WING: THE LAST OUTPOST (G-UNIT)
GUYS' GUIDE TO GIRLS
HANDS OFF!
HAPPY MANIA
HARLEM BEAT
HYPER RUNE
I.N.V.U.
IMMORTAL RAIN
INITIAL D
INSTANT TEEN: JUST ADD NUTS
ISLAND
JING: KING OF BANDITS
JING: KING OF BANDITS - TWILIGHT TALES
JULINE
KARE KANO
KILL ME, KISS ME
KINDAICHI CASE FILES, THE
KING OF HELL
KODOCHA: SANA'S STAGE
LAMENT OF THE LAMB
LEGAL DRUG
LEGEND OF CHUN HYANG, THE
LES BIJOUX
LOVE HINA
LUPIN III
LUPIN III: WORLD'S MOST WANTED
MAGIC KNIGHT RAYEARTH I
MAGIC KNIGHT RAYEARTH II
MAHOROMATIC: AUTOMATIC MAIDEN
MAN OF MANY FACES
MARMALADE BOY
MARS
MARS: HORSE WITH NO NAME
MINK
MIRACLE GIRLS
MIYUKI-CHAN IN WONDERLAND
MODEL
MOURYOU KIDEN
MY LOVE
NECK AND NECK
ONE
ONE I LOVE, THE
PARADISE KISS
PARASYTE
PASSION FRUIT
PEACH GIRL
PEACH GIRL: CHANGE OF HEART

05.26.04T

STOP!

This is the back of the book.
You wouldn't want to spoil a great ending!

This book is printed "manga-style," in the authentic Japanese right-to-left format. Since none of the artwork has been flipped or altered, readers get to experience the story just as the creator intended. You've been asking for it, so TOKYOPOP® delivered: authentic, hot-off-the-press, and far more fun!

DIRECTIONS

If this is your first time reading manga-style, here's a quick guide to help you understand how it works.

It's easy... just start in the top right panel and follow the numbers. Have fun, and look for more 100% authentic manga from TOKYOPOP®!